POVERTY, HEALTH AND DEVELOPMENT

Sujit Kumar Paul

Commonwealth

Poverty, Health and Development

Edition : 2027

ISBN : 978-81-311-0247-3

Published by :
COMMONWEALTH PUBLISHERS (P) LTD.
4831/24, Govind Lane,
Ansari Road, Darya Ganj,
New Delhi - 110002
Ph. : 23272541, 23242541
e-mail : commonwealthpublishers2016@gmail.com

Distributed by :
ARJUN PUBLISHING HOUSE
4831/24, Govind Lane,
Ansari Road, Darya Ganj,
New Delhi - 110002
Ph. : 23272541, 23242541
e-mail : arjunbooks2001@gmail.com

Laser Typesetting by :
Dimple Computers
Delhi

Printed at :
Milan Enterprises
Delhi

PREFACE

The volume is largely an outcome of a National Seminar on "Poverty, Health and Development" held at Palli Charcha Kendra, Visva-Bharati, Sriniketan, India in March 2007. Besides some of the selective articles of the Seminar, a good number of papers of the scholars have also been incorporated in this issue. This volume endeavours to put some of the crucial issues and perspectives relating to Poverty, Health and Development reflecting upon the initiatives of selected scholars. This volume has been organized thematically. Section – I contains papers on the theme : Poverty and Health. Section – II deals with the papers on the theme : Health and Development and Section - III discusses the theme : Gender and Health.

I express my deep sense of gratitude to Prof. Rajat Kanta Ray, Vice Chancellor, Visva-Bharati, for providing all the facilities and encouragement in the organization of the National Seminar on Poverty, Health and Development.

I would also like to express my gratitude and respect to Prof. Maitreyi Chaudhuri, Principal, Institute of Rural Reconstruction, Prof. Manas Ray, Head, Palli Charcha Kendra and Prof. Amit Hazra, Head, Rural Extension Centre, Visva-Bharati for their constant support and encouragement.

I also express my gratitude to all the contributors for their contribution to this volume.

I wish to express my appreciation to Commonwealth Publishers for publishing the volume.

Sujit Kumar Paul

Introduction

—Sujit Kumar Paul

"Health is the basis of Virtue (Dharma), Wealth (Artha), Desires (Karma), and Emancipation (Moksha)". The words of "Chakra Samhita" prove the necessity of good health for the human being. It is very familiar in present days that ill health is a symptom of social disequilibriam and thus development of health symbolize the all-round development of the human potential. According to the World Health Organization (WHO) health–"is not the mere absence of diseases but essentially conforms to the social, physical and mental well being", that leads to make the human being a 'complete man'. If we deeply concentrate on the concept of health provided by the World Health Organization, it is very clear to us that the concept of health is very much linked with every component of a human being through which the human being is able to fulfill the social as well as his personal goals. The definition given by WHO also indicates that health is an expression of total condition of human life *i.e.*–physical, genetic, chemical, environmental, cultural, economic, psychological, mental, intellectual and spiritual. The United Nation's declaration also established the health as the human's right through its statement–"*Everyone has the right to a standard of living adequate for health and well-being of himself and of his family, including food, clothing, housing and medical care and necessary social services, and the right to security in the event of unemployment, sickness, disability, widowhood, old age, or other lack of livelihood in circumstances beyond his control*" (UN General Assembly in December 10, 1948, article 25.1). Thus health would be considered a holistic approach, which is related to the quality of life of the human being and the quality of life is intimately related to the health and development.

But when we speak about development, we can see that the basic objective of any development programme is the eradication of poverty, which is the most responsible for depriving the human being in terms of economic, social, psychological and physical upliftment, among which there are some basic necessities like the health. Poverty markedly reduces the accessibility to health care services and makes people vulnerable to a majority of diseases. For various reasons the poor frequently fail to utilize properly even when free health care services provided by the government. The result is perpetual ill health and loss of labour days. Healthy labour force is an essential component for economic and social development of a country. It is, therefore, necessary to investigate properly the nature of health care services available to the poor and identify the causes that hinder them from proper utilization of such services.

Several kinds of research and development work carried out by the social reformists, scientists and other personalities reveal that the poverty, health and development are complementary and interwoven to each other. Rabindranath Tagore and Mahatma Gandhi, the two great souls of modern India, considered that eradication of poverty, developing the inner self and building up a good health to be the most important preconditions for sustainable national development.

The edited volume attempts to cover diverse aspects of studies by distinguished experts and researchers covering analytically the leading and diverse issues and experiences connected with poverty, health and development. Prof. Ravshanbek T. Dalimov in the article *From Poverty to Personal Growth and Healthy Development* discusses both personal and social aspects of poverty, together with means to change the status of poor which consist of charity, skills, training and entrepreneurship as well as social security benefits. Healthy development is provided in this case through health insurance systems.

Prof. G.C. De in his article *Perspective Planning to Prevent Perpetual Poverty* argues that in the present society improvement of any sort or part bring forth impoverishment of the other(s). Generation of new groups of poverty stricken people has been taking place and thus poverty is becoming a perpetual problem in the developing society. He opined that both the persisting and emergence of economically backward people require bringing to the forefront with suitable employment, engagement and earning from the regenerating resource base. Usually people of ill health and disabilities, weaker section and gender and resource poor suffer most from poverty or poverty like situation, causing susceptibility to a variety of diseases. In most cases they fail to avail of free medical services rather depend on traditional, non-scientific folk medicines, sorcery, quacks, herbal medicines, therapies, aurvedic, unani, homeopath and other forms of cures and rarely take the help of hospital, nursing homes, clinics and other costly treatments as they often perceive they are born to suffer and die. However, they remain as the source and store house of ailments. He suggested that special drives are required from different corners to educate and involve them on various development issues as the component of the society. Health care may be one of the issues. The arrangement of treatment may be made at zero or reduced cost considering the social impact of the patients. A comprehensive perspective planning and implementation of different untouched or less emphasised issues may be taken up through Panchayats or municipalities or authorities, boards etc in collaboration with NGOs, institutions, philanthropic societies etc. The local social institution must come forward with definite mission and vision in all round development activities of the society of the locality.

Prof. Debashis Das and Angshuman Ghosh discusses about the socio-economic specially the health condition of the rag pickers of Bolpur-Sriniketan Block of West Bengal in their article *Problems of Livelihood of Rag Pickers and Alternative Measures for Their Rehabilitation*. According to them the rag pickers are poor, ignorant, destitute, outcast, illiterate, and backward people of the society, work and reside in the midst of dirty environment.

They are engaged in various types of prohibited activities and suffer from serious health hazards. They suggested that it is the responsibility of the society to search for alternative measures to develop their economy and to rehabilate them.

Dr. Sujit Kumar Paul and Smt. Banasree Das relate poverty and poor health in their article *Poverty and Health in Jharkhand : Some Issues*. Poverty is a very important cause for poor health and the poor health has an impact on poverty. Due to low income or poverty, people are unable to access all kinds of health facilities. On the other hand due to poor health, people become unable to work hard and earn less money for their basic needs. They observed that there are lot of health related problems due to poverty and low income. Women are suffering from high maternal mortality rate, various degree of anemia. The children remain chronically malnourished. The rural people are suffering from various kinds of diseases and do not able to get the health facilities provided by the government.

Sudeshna Maitra in her paper *Is Socioeconomic Status Protective of Health? Some Evidence from Rural Udaipur* uses recent data of Rajasthan, India, to examine if socioeconomic status (SES) is protective to health. She defines the direct effect as the association between SES and self-reported health among respondents who have experienced the same symptoms in the last 30 days. The symptoms effect measures if SES is associated with a lower probability of experiencing the 'serious' symptoms, *viz*. symptoms that have an adverse impact on self-reported health. She finds that the protective effect of SES on health through the direct channel increases with the level of SES. However, the exact opposite pattern holds for symptoms effects. While increased SES lowers the probability of reporting serious conditions at low levels of SES, this protective effect fades out at higher levels of SES. The findings suggest that SES is not necessarily protective of health through the symptoms channel at all levels of SES.

Environmental pollution not only leads to deteriorating environmental conditions but also have adverse effects on the health of people and the eventual consequences on poverty . India is one of the most degraded environment countries in the world and it is paying heavy health and economic price for it. Pratap C. Mohanty and Sibabrata Das in their article *Poverty, Health and Environment Nexus: A Study of Community Forestry in India* reveals that rapid population growth plays an important role on environmental problems of the country, from deforestation to land degradation, air and water pollution to the spread of disease. The considerable magnitude of air and water pollution pulls up the number of people suffering from respiratory and water borne diseases and many a times leading to deaths and serious health hazards. Scarcity motivates the people more to participate in community forestry and participation improves the welfare of the people. The evidences and facts in the analysis suggest that the poor people are very much linked to common property resources (CPRs), thus the protection of natural resources is essential for reducing the extent of poverty and simultaneously regenerating the environment. The analysis also suggests that there is an urgent need to control population and environmental pollution in the country for better health at present and for future generation.

Forest resources can be conceived as the lifeblood of tribal economy. Evidently forestry can emerge as the real harbinger of rural prosperity and rural transformation. Joint Forest Management (JFM) tries to secure the ecological development of forest area and economic development of people of fringe area along with beneficiaries alleviating poverty and improving health condition. Arun Kumar Mandal in his paper *Poverty, Health and Tribal Development through Joint Forest Management : A Case Study of Tribal Village of Birbhum* highlights about the health status of tribal people and investigate the role of JFM for poverty alleviation and tribal development in the study area.

Poor countries, states and poor people suffer from a multiplicity of deprivations which translate into levels of ill health. Most obviously, they lack the financial resources to pay for health services, food, clean water, good sanitation, and the other key inputs to producing good health. It is not just lack of income that causes the high level of ill-health among poor people however, the health facilities serving them are often dilapidated, inaccessible, inadequately stocked with basic medicines, and run by poorly trained staff. Furthermore the poor are also disadvantaged by lack of knowledge about prevention and whereabouts of health care. The health and poverty situation in Orissa is very typical. Poverty and health condition is significantly worse in the Northern and Southern districts of the State. Thus, based on the secondary sources of data, Santosh Kumar Behera and Dr. K.C. Sahoo in their paper *Poverty and Health in Orissa : An Overview* attempt to analyze the scenario of poverty and health condition of the state of Orissa and recommended factors to eradicate poverty and improve the health status of the state.

Improvement in health is widely regarded as an important yardstick of the overall socio-economic development of any country. The relation between public health and development is very challenging in the sense that it is very much dualistic in nature. For economists, it is merely a measure of how society is doing well-being and for others it is a novel concept that focuses more towards social sustainability. However, proper emphases have been hardly given on the role and significance of public health in defining the meaning and scope of development. Negligence and failure with respect to health is more in developing societies due to several strategic or poorly conceived approaches to the socio-economic development. Generally, it is argued that the developing societies invested less in human capital formation in terms of spending on education and health. Furthermore, their priority for human capital formation was and still continues to be vague and questionable. However, with the majority of world's population will be living in cities by 2025, the situation needs to be revisited and it has been noticed that every city has its own strategies to maintain a healthy environment essential for urban sustainability. All futuristic cities want to be a healthy city and authorities at last had realized the significance. An attempt has been made by Ranabir Dey in his paper *Health and Development- Need for a Healthy City* demonstrates the major fault lines that need to be rectified within the health-development relationship, focusing attention on the concept of healthy cities.

Developing countries have a hard time getting their health situation improved. Constant reforms in health programs, international cooperation in the sector from USAID and other partners like World Health Organization did not achieve the improvement level as much as was expected. There are several issues to be discussed when talking about health and development in order to improve the situation in these countries. Arnold J.J. Hagens and Kathya Córdova Pozo in their paper *Quality of Governance as a Base for Health and Development* analyze different factors that affect health sector. The analysis is done on fragile countries in South America, with special focus in Bolivia. Results show that the lack of a good quality of governance impacts negatively on health, education and therefore on development.

In developing countries like India where a large section of people belong to BPL, there is an urgent need for improved of Health Care System (HCS). In a social life, health is of paramount importance as a national asset and basis of efficiency. On the other hand, health is a prerequisite for increasing productivity. It is directly related to fertility, mortality, life expectancy, education, per capita income etc. and indirectly related to reduction of exploitation. That is why, organized health care system is essential to achieve broader social goals. On the basis of that Dr. Manjari Sarkar (Basu) in her paper *Health Care System of Madhupur Subdivision, Jharkhand* discusses about the existing health care system and also the people's attitude towards better health of Jharkhand.

Health education is very much essential for the development of health of any nation. More research is needed to improve the ability of the professional health workers. Karen Wistoft in her paper *Research and Development in Health Education - Focused on Value Clarification Among Health Professionals* discusses about professional competence development and the qualification for value clarification not necessarily expressed through ethical rules but rather through fundamental views, reasoning, linguification and reflections. She also gives a methodological discussion about the developmental approach.

The research strategy is finally reflected into a systems-theoretical perspective. This article is basically concerned with the theme health education for the competence development of knowledge among health professionals.

Tribal concept of health is as varied as their culture. They have their own system of beliefs and practices concerning health, ill-health and treatment of diseases which they consider more functional than clinical. Their health concept is unique culture-bound constellations. To become healthy and disease free, generally the tribal maintain a three way relationship *viz.* man-man, man-nature and man–supernature. They perceive that diseases may caused by breach of taboos or by evil magical power of human agencies. Popular traditional tribal method of treatment involves magico-religious activities and application of herbal medicines. Due to regular contact with larger society, government's health alleviation programmes and commitment of "Health for All by 2000 A.D.", the tribal people are highly exposed to modern medical care and facilities. But they consider medical aid to be futile when disease is believed to be caused by supernatural agencies. In the paper *Socio-Cultural Dimensions of Tribal Health : A Challenging Domain of Social Workers in India,* Dr. Kakali Paul (Mitra) explores different aspects of health culture of the tribal people. An attempt has been made to know the tribal notions regarding health, ill-health and their way of treatment. An explicit study on their traditional belief system of health care and way of treatment is made which will make a comprehensive understanding about how the tribals are baffled between indigenous beliefs and practices and modern ideas of health care system. It gives a new dimension of health of the culture bound tribal people where an attempt has been made to suggest the role of social workers for the development of tribal health.

During the course of civilization it was realized gradually that the human beings are most valuable and precious resources of the society who will play a pivotal role in nation's development. The quality of a state depends upon the efficiency and quality of its human resources. Thus numerous kinds of efforts were taken into consideration for the overall development of human being, which include his physical, social, economic and psychological development. Frequent programmes on development of the above sector have been taken by the government and non-government organizations on the basis of "Right to Development". But it was realized that until and unless the people become spiritually developed the essence of development could not be achieved. Spirituality is nothing but the inherent quality or entity of the human being for knowing the self. It is one of the key ingredients for linking up physical activity of the human being with his thinking. Spiritual entity helps the human being to become self-less, self-dependent, self-confident, self-actualized, and self-powered, which will develop and enrich his inner beliefs as well as empowered him physically, socially, economically and psychologically to act as a sound development partner, who can be yoked to serve the society leading towards achieving the ultimate ambition of a civil society. Raja Ghosh in his paper *Spiritual Health : An Agent of Human Development* tries to highlight the inner force of the human being, which acts like catalytic agent for the overall development of them.

There is significant association between residential radon gas exposure and lung cancer. How exposures to colourless, tasteless and odourless radon gas cause environmental health problems worldwide is critically appraised using available literature by Manorama Bhattarai and Dr. Keshab Bhattarai in their paper *Radon Exposure in Homes and Environmental Health Problems: Causes and Solutions*. Harmful effects of indoor accumulation of radon and remediation efforts to minimise exposure hazards to human health are discussed along with a suggestion how can be awareness brought through better public health policies at national and international level to reduce this hazard.

The process of economic growth brings forth rapid industrialization and urbanization, which more often results in a race-to-bottom phenomenon as regards environmental deterioration. This phenomenon is apparent in low-income countries which experience a steady decline in the air quality as a result of increased industrial activity, congestion on streets, use of poorly maintained motor vehicles, etc. Poor air quality has a direct health impact on people, who also bear the economic burden related to it. It, therefore, becomes necessary to examine these impacts in urban settings in developing countries in order to come up with a policy rationale for implementing air quality programmes to ensure better quality of life to people. Mumbai, a crucial urban center, accounts for a population of close to 12 million and is known for attracting migrant population from all over the country. In recent years, it has witnessed a boom in construction activity, increasing vehicular traffic and congestion leading to high level of air pollution. Archana Patankar and Prof. Pushpa Trivedi in their paper *Assessing the Health Impacts of Air Pollution : A Case Study of Mumbai* use the cross-section data collected by the Environmental Pollution Research Centre (EPRC) at the King Edward Memorial (KEM) Hospital in Mumbai during December 2002 and March 2004. Logistic regression has been used to examine the association between air pollution and morbidity and a significant link has been established for a few respiratory symptoms and diseases. The results have further been used to develop the concentration-response coefficients that would help in estimating the economic costs of the health impacts of air pollution for the city.

Prof. Guru Prasad Chattopadhyay and Smt. Anupriya Chatterjee in their research paper *Environmental Impact on Health and Health Support Systems on the Tribal People of Kullu District, Himachal Pradesh* attempt to make an analytical study upon the significant aspects of health problems and the health support systems available in the district of Kullu, Himachal Pradesh particularly for the tribal people in this district. Existing situation of health of the people has been assessed holistically considering the major types of health problems. Special attention has been paid toward the degenerating health condition of the tribal communities. Identified health problems are leprosy, cataract and poor immunity power among the people living particularly below the poverty line and residing in the secluded pockets of Himachal Himalaya. The roles of regional hospitals, civil hospitals, public health centers, clinics, community health centers have been evaluated in this study.

Neeraj Kumar Thakur has made an anthropological study among the Kharwar tribes of Uttar Pradesh and discusses some issues on health in his paper *The Cultural and Industrial Context of Health : An Anthropological Study of the Kharwar Tribes of Uttar Pradesh.* According to him the normal health of tribal people cannot be said to be very bad but their condition become chronic after repeated infections. The tribes of this area face a great deal of hardship in medicinal treatment although they have their own traditional indigenous medicinal system, but most of them do not know the proper use of these medicines. The tribals suffer from many chronic diseases the most prevalent of them are air, water and noise pollution borne diseases. The main reason for this is the presence of several industries in the tribal regions of the district. Therefore the changing pattern of their life, contact and assimilation of various traits of others' culture are also causing health problems. Some occupational activities such as stone crushing and working in power plants are responsible for health hazards like tuberculosis, hearing defect and mental disturbances etc.

The Second National Family Health Survey (NFHS2) conducted during the year 1998-1999 furnished data on various health aspects of women and children for all states of India. Following a rigorous sampling procedure a large number of households were selected in each state. Ever married women and children below three years covered by the sample households were the units of study in the survey. The nutritional status of women and children was measured by using various anthropometric indicators. Prof. Maitreyi Chaudhuri in her paper *Nutritional Status of Women and Children in Three States of India* examines the nutritional status of women and children in Uttar Pradesh, West Bengal and Kerala. Uttar Pradesh is markedly having very low sex ratio, high infant mortality rate, low literacy rate and high fertility rate as compared to other two states. In respect of the above indicators of human development, Kerala occupies the highest position. She reveals the position of West Bengal in comparison to other two states in the field of nutrition of women and children. Analyzing the NFHS2 data an attempt has also been made by

Prof. Chaudhuri to find out the influence of various social, economic and health related factors on the nutritional status of women and children.

As discussed in the earlier paper, lack of sufficient nutrition leads to ill health and lack of access to modern health facilities leads to death at early age. These are common features among poor people especially among women living in rural areas. Heath is thus recognised as a significant indicator of the Gender Development Index. Gender discrimination in availing health facilities leads to poor health condition of women and are closely associated with the lower status of women in the society. Poor health conditions of women not only affect them but also affect the health of their children. Therefore, the health status of women should be an important concern of policy makers of a country. In India, several steps have been taken by the Central Government for improving the health status of women specially who are living below the poverty line. The policies and programmes which deserve special mention are National Nutrition Policy (1983), National Health Policy (1983), Integrated Child Development Scheme (ICDS), Development of Women and Children in Rural areas (DWCRA). Dr. Gopa Samanta in her paper *Poverty, Gender and Reproductive Health : A Case Study of Self-Help Groups in Burdwan District, West Bengal* highlights the health condition especially reproductive health of poor rural women in Burdwan district. These women are members of self-help groups under SGSY (Swarnajayanti Gram Swarojgar Yojana) and SHG (NABARD) programmes which have received much fanfare in the last ten years. According to the State agency, the women in rural areas organized under self-help groups are empowered and have good levels of awareness regarding health and nutrition. This paper tries to explore how this level of awareness has impacted on the reproductive health status of the members of SHGs. The indicators of reproductive health used in this study are age of marriage, age at the birth of first child, use of family planning measures, fertility rate, child mortality rate, rate of miscarriage and abortion, diseases and access to health facilities.

A reproductive health approach does not prevail anywhere

in the world. In India most women have to suffer from serious reproductive and sexual health problems. Mr. Rahul Bannerjee in his paper *Reproductive Health of Poor Urban Women in Indore* discusses the status of women's reproductive health in India. He also mentioned the status of women's reproductive health in the slums of Indore, Madhya Pradesh.The women living in slums have grossly excluded from the purview of qualified medical help and have to rely mostly on quacks. Thus it has been left to NGOs to deliver what little service they can provide to these poor women.

The Gender gap in access to health care is one of the most tangible evidences of genderisation in the society. The unequal gender relation in distribution of power, wealth etc. easily explains gender gap in health, but that is not all. As long as women's work is not valued at par with that of men's, women's life will remain less valuable, and incidences such as female infanticide and abandonment of girl child will continue. The unequal gender relation evident today around the globe, cutting across culture, religion and geographical territory simply points to us that the gender gap in health dates back to many centuries. In colonial Bengal attention was drawn towards the need for women's health care, especially the protection of reproductive health in the 19th century. Volumes were written about the dismal state of reproductive health and the starkly evident gender gap in health care. Women in low-income families have very poor access to health care even after 60 years of independence, but so do poor men, children and adolescents. Addressing the issue only in terms of gender gap will not solve the problem, unless the total health scenario changes. Narrowing of the gender gap in health among the middle and upper class clearly highlights the importance of availability and affordability of health care facilities. When we are talking about the gender gap in health, are we really talking in the classical sense of the term? Dr. Mausumi Manna in her article *The Changing Face of Gender Gap in Health* tries to explore it and suggests that the gap is no longer independent of all other background variables, which it was half a century back. Rather the gender gap in health is becoming increasingly depended upon the income gap and the rural-urban gap. The author refers to this phenomenon as the changing face of gender gap in health. The purpose of this article is to highlight this change and discuss its importance with respect to the women's question. Here she used the health experiences of women in West Bengal, owing to her familiarity with the region.

Recent works suggests that the process of economic restructuring is related to the increasing presence of women in informal sector of work done at home or in intermediary work spaces like subcontractor's home. Such emerging forms of informal employment have implications on women's overall time allocation behaviour. The broad objective of B. Vaithegi in her paper *Time Allocation, Overlapping Activities and Work Intensity : Implications for Well Being of Women Workers* is to examine the quantitative dimensions of time use of women workers in the formal and informal segments (subcontract) of export-oriented leather footwear industry in Pondicherry. She also documents about the perception of their health. The primary data used in the study suggests that nature of employment (formal and informal) make substantial difference in time allocation behaviour of women workers. Informal subcontract women workers spend more time for domestic and market work than formal factory workers. The nature of employment and domestic responsibilities resulted in lengthening of working time for women workers. Thus nature of employment plays a major role in pattern of work organization. A high work burden leading to lengthening of working time and work intensity has been associated with negative implications for well being of the worker.

It is estimated that 1600 women die world-wide each day as a result of problems during the pregnancy or child birth. A large portion of the deaths is preventable and so far there is little progress to reach the Millennium Development Goals (MDGs). Traditional public health policies of governments and international donor agencies are input oriented. Experience has shown that financing inputs do not necessarily result in the improvement of health outcomes. Output Based Aid (OBA) is a way of allocating public resources, which could eliminate some of the constraints for achieving MGDs. The Output based voucher concept envisages financing agreed outputs, rather than pre-defined inputs, by selling vouchers to the beneficiaries at subsidized price. Evidence shows that in India the majority of health care (out patients) is provided by the private sector and funded by out-of-pocket payments. However, voucher approach have the full potential to increase use of services by target populations, engage the private providers, increase competition, and improve quality of service of the providers. On the other hand voucher system could be a good entry point for mainstreaming private providers, integrating private medical practitioners into the health care system and use their potential for improved health care. Biswajit Panda, David Griffith, Hengjin Dong and Abdul Rahim in their paper *OBA Voucher Approach in Health : Promoting Safe Motherhood through Participation of Private Medical Practitioners in West Bengal* discuss the public health importance to maternal health in West Bengal, India. OBA voucher schemes have many effects which have the potential to improve access and quality of health in specific areas. The authors studied the impact of OBA voucher programme in this paper. They also tried to bring in the issue of cross cutting experience of voucher schemes in health and also lessons learnt from voucher programme across the countries. According to them taking the full advantage of the voucher approach may require a change in mind set to look beyond the traditional boundaries for better access, equity and quality.

Contents

List of Contributors

Abdul Rahim
Deputy Team Leader
TAST managed by Option & IPE
Kolkata
India

Angshuman Ghosh
Research scholar
Department of Geography
Visva-Bharati University
Santiniketan – 731235
Birbhum, West Bengal
India

Anupriya Chatterjee
Junior Research Fellow (UGC)
Department of Geography
Visva-Bharati
Santiniketan – 731235
Birbhum, West Bengal
India

Archana Patankar
Research Scholar
Department of Humanities and Social Sciences
Indian Institute of Technology (IIT), Bombay
Mumbai
India

Arnold J.J. Hagens
South Group
Edif. Alba II
Av. Heroínas O-165 Piso 2B
Cochabamba – Bolivia

Arun Kumar Mandal
Research Scholar
Palli Charcha Kendra
Visva Bharati
Sriniketan – 731236
Birbhum, West Bengal
India

Banasree Das
Research Scholar
Deptt. of Social Studies and Rural Development
Palli Charcha Kendra
Visva-Bharati
Sriniketan – 731236
Birbhum, West Bengal
India

Biswajit Panda
MScIH
Department of Tropical Hygiene and Public Health
Heidelberg University
INF 324, 69120, Heidelberg
Germany.

B. Vaithegi
Research Officer
Tata Institute of Social Sciences
Mumbai
India

David Griffith
Consultant (Kfw-German Development Bank)
Department of Tropical Hygiene and Public Health
Heidelberg University, INF 324, 69120, Heidelberg
Germany.

Dr. Debashis Das
Professor of Geography
Department of Geography
Visva-Bharati University
Santiniketan – 731235
Birbhum, West Bengal
India

Dr. G. C. De
Professor
Palli Siksha Bhavana (Institute of Agriculture)
Visva-Bharati
Sriniketan-731236
Birbhum, West Bengal
India

Dr. Gopa Samanta
Lecturer
Department of Geography
The University of Burdwan
Burdwan – 713104
West Bengal
India

Dr. Guru Prasad Chattopadhyay
Professor
Department of Geography
Visva-Bharati
Santiniketan – 731235
Birbhum, West Bengal
India

Hengjin Dong
Senior Lecturer in Health Financing and Health Economics
Department of Tropical Hygiene and Public Health
Heidelberg University
INF 324, 69120, Heidelberg
Germany.

Dr. Kakali Paul (Mitra)
Executive Director
Society for Research Extension and Development of Knowledge
Bolpur Trisulapatty
Bolpur – 731204
Birbhum, West Bengal
India

Karen Wistoft
M.Ed., Project Manager, Ph.D. student
Research Programme for Environmental and Health Education
Danish University of Education
Department of Curriculum Research
Tuborgvej 164, DK-2400 Copenhagen NV

Kathya Córdova Pozo,
South Group
Edif. Alba II
Av. Heroínas O-165 Piso 2B
Cochabamba – Bolivia

Dr. K.C. Sahoo
Vinaya Bhavan
Visva-Bharati University
Santiniketan – 731235
Birbhum, West Bengal
India

Dr. Keshab Bhattarai
Lecturer in Economics
Business School
University of Hull
HU6 7RX, UK.

Dr. Maitreyi Chaudhuri
Professor
Deptt. of Social Studies and Rural Development
Palli Charcha Kendra
Visva-Bharati
Sriniketan – 731236
Birbhum, West Bengal
India

Dr. Manjari Sarkar (Basu)
Lecturer
Dept. of Geography
Kandra R.K.K. Mahavidyalaya
Burdwan, West Bengal
India

Manorama Bhattarai
4th year Medical Student
University of Aberdeen
Scotland

Mausumi Manna
Department of Economics
Scottish Church College
Kolkata, West Bengal
India

Neeraj Kumar Thakur
Guest Lecturer and Research Scholar
Department of Anthropology
University of Allahabad
Allahabad
India

Pratap C. Mohanty
Doctoral Fellow
Centre for Economic Studies and Planning (CESP)
Jawaharlal Nehru University (JNU)
New Delhi, India

Pushpa Trivedi
Professor of Economics
Department of Humanities and Social Sciences
Indian Institute of Technology (IIT), Bombay
Mumbai
India

Rahul Banerjee
74, Krishnodayanagar
Indore
Madhya Pradesh – 452001
India

Raja Ghosh
Senior Technical Assistant
Rural Extension Centre,
Visva-Bharati
Sriniketan-731236
Birbhum, West Bengal
India

Ranabir Dey
M.Phil. (Planning and Development)
Institute-Indian Institute of Technology, Bombay
Postal Address-H-7 Room-247
IIT Bombay
Powai, Mumbai-400076
India

Ravshanbek T. Dalimov
Assistant Professor
Business Administration Unit
Economics Department
National University of Uzbekistan
Suite 506, 1 Universitetskaya Street
Tashkent, Uzbekistan 100174

Santosh Kumar Behera
Research Scholar
Vinaya Bhavan
Visva-Bharati University
Santiniketan – 731235
Birbhum, West Bengal
India

Sibabrata Das
Doctoral Fellow
Centre for the Study of Regional Development (CSRD)
Jawaharlal Nehru University (JNU)
New Delhi
India

Sudeshna Maitra
Department of Economics
York University
1038 Vari Hall
4700 Keele Street
Toronto, ON M3J 1P3

Dr. Sujit Kumar Paul
Sr. Lecturer in Rural Development
Deptt. of Social Studies and Rural Development
Palli Charcha Kendra
Visva-Bharati
Sriniketan – 731236
Birbhum, West Bengal
India

Section—I
Poverty and Health

1

From Poverty to Personal Growth and Healthy Development

—Ravshanbek T. Dalimov

1. Introduction

When a person grows up and enters adult life than there come two options : to be poor and unhappy, or to become solvent and stay comfortable with challenges of the surrounding world. Happiness in this regard may be defined as a realization of a man's wishes in practice. The life itself seems to be as almost never-ending chain of events from poor through live development to rich; for some it is successful, for a few—it is not.

Person's wealth and ability to address his main needs depends on his personal striving to financial success as well as participation of governments assisting members of societies to have means of social security as well as possibly equal chances to prosper in business. It also depends on healthiness of adult persons which assumes their ability to accept and process information as well as to obtain funds and food to feed themselves and their successors. When any of these mighties are lost, a person becomes incapable of doing things and starts needing assistance: social, mercy or charity ones.

By definition, none of governments claim poverty as a main purpose; quite oppositely, people's welfare, increase of welfare and growth are staying among fundamental tasks of the modern societies. Nevertheless, we may witness in many parts of the world as well as sometimes in our neighbourhood signs of poverty.

So the world and people living in it will always, now and in the future, confront a puzzle : how, having little resources, to provide everyone a wealth, enough to overcome poverty, or better to stay solvent. The article is an overview of methods and ways to do it.

2. Poverty : Main Features

Poverty is a comparative phenomenon since usually, if we can't afford to have something, and someone can, we tend to think that we are less solvent or even poor, while forgetting that we may own a house, car and many other things we became already accustomed with and don't notice them anymore. But actually, poverty is a state when a man has only means to stay alive, and to reach those means he has to either earn a living by work or receive a charity. Since poor man cannot buy things which would otherwise change his life to better, poverty is considered by most people as humiliating state of existence, with no or a few means to change the *status-quo*.

Poverty with no outside assistance can expand itself, and it does not make anything good for society. Indeed, when you look to filled-in shelves of supermarkets, and ask manufacturers : "Do they want their goods purchased?"—you are going to get quite certain positive answer. And the cycle of producing something for the others to consume requires people to have financial means to do it, and does not want in principle anyone to be poor.

When we purchase goods, we are financing production plants, providing salary and wages to employees at the same time, dividends to stocks and bonds etc. Consumers also enable plants pay back interest and loans thus providing financial system to work as clocks, as well as giving options for modernizing factories' technological capacities. Imagine what would happen with all of these things if there would be a society consisting mainly of poor people. It is why poverty and economic development of societies contradict each other, although a fear of becoming a poor is among basic reasons of personal economic development.

Poverty is something which is annually met by hundred of millions of people: it is youth after finishing high school or universities. Each of them proceeds according to their skills and education to find a job, then to settle an issue of "no poverty", and then to start a new independent life. And since this process is essential as life, together with the means to go about poverty repeated every year by millions of the people, then we may discuss some recipes how to do it, with an aim to follow best accumulated experience.

Poverty is a state of human's life quite hard to leave, making people usually weak and irresistible to external influence. Financial abyss is probably the deepest among those which humans meet in this world. It is due to the point that whenever one wants to leave it, there needed incredible efforts, and often simple luck. At some point when poor people are absorbing revolutional ideas, foundation of societies easily quakes to become the society of equals—poor workers, and history has seen many of such examples in the past led by recent unsuccessful Soviet experience.

People who are in poverty belong to following several types :

1. they are permanently ill handicapped persons;
2. they are healthy, but do not have financial means at this current phase of their life; or
3. they are healthy, but not well educated or treated persons.

Poor live in their niche of the society and either don't know how to work, what to do to earn a living, or they just don't want to do it, since social security system in many developed countries is good enough to provide feasible financial aid in this case. Handicapped people need a charity by any and all means, along with a medical treatment of them if their society makes it possible.

Persons of the second group spend sometimes all their life to become solvent. For instance, parents, who are going to educate their children, start it actually before the wedding when a groom waits when his wage would become sufficient to pay for mortgage and other expenses necessary to have a happy family.

There are a few ways to manage poverty depending on how crucial are going to be changes we want.

1. First is usually assistance to those who are in class of the society who work for rich. In this case we cannot change their status, and being realistic, we don't want to do it. One of the reasons for that is a clear understanding that everyone cannot be rich, and someone has to work in factories anyway; in other words, always there has to be someone who should work for someone, and we can't change this.

Unless a person is poor and healthy, he is only under the moral stress of his own financial inconsistency. But if he is also sick or ill, no one can help him much. Here comes the time for charity, which mainly aims helping people not to die. Charity, in respect of poor, supposes satisfaction of their main needs generally balancing those who are trying to survive, and thus is an aid of the first order for those who can't for some reason help themselves.

Charity is also provided for those who do not have enough financial means but ready to have personal development and further to work. If society's level of welfare is high enough, volume on charity spending is large enough. Means to provide charity are different types of foundations, promoted by support of governments establishing specific tax shelters.

Charity stops when there comes ability of a person to work and help himself/herself. When I lived in the US back in 1990 staying in gorgeous Seattle as a student for almost a year I noticed that US citizens help foreigners to quickly get accustomed to their habits, language, city etc. As long as I stated that I just came into the city and ask for directions, many were eager to help me. But as soon as I was ready to compete with other members of the society, say, for jobs or best wages, doors open to me, were getting closed. I became equal, and no more charity seemed fair enough for local people. The same thing is with poverty evolution.

It is usually a mistake to assume that charity can change the status of poverty. Charity can hardly do this, so compassion is to have a limit, as well as any other emotion humans feel towards each other. Person must have a chance to change his/her own life himself. This is his/her freedom of choice, action and true happiness to create himself/herself everyone is born with. It is important to note that it is not a feature of only entrepreneurs to create things and their own. If someone wants to become, for instance, a doctor and becomes it, than a man thoroughly approaches his purpose, developing his self inner ego. And that is what life is all about.

There is no doubt that in personal development as in anything else there is the presence of Providence' hand which pushes each of us ahead during our lifetime. But to think that all positive, what a human is up to in life, will appear by itself, is also wrong. Money, happiness, success come through real hard working, education and striving to different aims—all quite similar to process when a new baby is born.

Once before when I was in business during 1991-2000, I noticed an old lady staying on the street near the door of our firm. Her hand was begging for some, and she was wearing wide thick glasses. I thought this was just a poor lady, but wanted to keep a style of a firm and somehow try to help. We invited her to office, asked for proof if she was ill: indeed, she was incapable of working, 70 years old, and needed around US$ 300 a month for medicine.

We did not bargain and proposed her a deal now one may say as too optimistic or idealistic: she doesn't beg, especially near our office, and gets those 300 dollars by visiting our office twice a month. She agreed, and this continued only 2 months. Our staff pointed out once that she was begging again, on our street, quite close to us. Why? There was no point for begging, money was more than enough for medicine. In many years later I realized that was her personal karma which did not allow an old lady to stop doing this.

2. The other option is if you want poor people to "exit" their current phase of life and change it radically. Ways are a few, and one can implement them in case there is an effort on both the side of poor applicants, capable and willing to change their existing status, and on the side of sponsors who are taking the risk of spending the time, funds and efforts, with no guarantee for success in the end. One has to provide *skills training* depending specifically on a person's abilities; then newly skilled labour has to get employment whose monthly salary shall be higher than an aid for unemployed.

More sophisticated mean to help poor in this case is to provide them ability to succeed in business. Certainly, not everyone is born for business while many want to be rich. It is probably right to mark here that being rich is not always something greedy. Being rich, as rich men say, is being free, not only from a pain of poverty, but freedom to create, to live in happiness.

Each of us attempts to improve our own life; this is built into us from our birth and is an instinct of survival. Thus, personal striving to become rich, natural in its essence, shall not be suppressed if to look at it from a view point to provide healthy and happy style of life and welfare in a family. At the same time, most people barely thought of the fact that religions were never reluctant to this very basics—personal striving to welfare. There is no such thing in Writings, but it is naturally essential and was meant at its foundation. Religion has only requested that personal issues were not to be over Divine, and that is why preference was for altruistic approach—enforced by overwhelming presence of greediness of a profit-oriented people.

Entrepreneurial approach is available to those who feel they have strength to start a new business and who would risk their existing assets, if any, for unwarranted reward somewhere in the future.

Business basically is a thing which does need assets. They can be used as collateral to obtain a loan, then to conduct a business and to obtain a profit, and finally to have more assets.

Assets in collateral insure the risk of not paying back, and that is one of the main principles of capitalistic society. So in this case one may see that there is a cycle when rich are going to become richer, with no chances for poor to change their style of living.

The thing with the poor is that one doesn't have assets and wants to make business at the same time; we expect that a man seeking a loan would be having skills and idea necessary for specific business and now consider only financial aspect of it. Solution is to find means when some other people or entities would be willing to provide that required asset.

To be true, there are not too many options in this respect one can look for in the neighborhood! People : wealthier relatives, close friends may be willing to share your risk, but in case of business failure you risk to loose them all together. Is it worth—is up to you. Venture capitalists would be willing to participate in business, but they have so many proposals that very few get lucky to start business with them, especially if you have nothing to invest except your own idea.

Finally, in case there is promising worked-out business plan, and if you are in the United States, one can look for loans from Small Business Administration which can back up a business idea when getting a loan. But this is too has done in exceptional cases, because usually one cannot approach SBA directly since it is served by US banks taking care of end customers. And banks, when you request an SBA's financing, require regular banking procedures including collateral. It may sound ironic but anyone who wants to earn a fortune really needs to be fortunate for these very reasons. I can remind you a tough Turkish saying : "If you don't have, than no one has". That is about situation that it is quite difficult to obtain a loan if you don't possess anything.

With all difficulties existing in business for start-ups, it is commonly known that annually around 80% of new companies starting a new business will fail. And after that takes place, there has to be something which will preserve people from falling down to poverty in such a case.

3. This is *public and private social security programmes*. With comprehension that it is unrealistic to change life for huge masses of poor population, the task of managing poor goes to the point where powers of societies try to establish such rules that wealth is distributed in a way to provide most of its members the means available to flourish rather than no option but to be poor. That kind of strong thoughts created back in early decades of the 20th century pension schemes both funded by governments (PAYG systems) and by the people themselves (fully funded schemes). Taken together with the stock markets, this type of financial structure created flourishing capitalistic society since 1930s up to now.

PAYG (Pay-As-You-Go) system of pension benefits is set up under the principle when pensions of retired people are funded by working population. There are different standards of the benefits depending on average salary earned during the last 40 working years; it covers sometimes 10 or 20 years period. International Labour Organization requires to have at least 40% average salary to be replaced in pension benefits. The EU has set probably the highest requirement of this kind—65% replacement ratio.

During 1930s when the US social security system was setting up, relation of workers to retired pensioners was 40 to 1. That means that the share of salaries workers would pay for pensions schemes was not much. Currently there are nearly 3 workers for one pensioner, with the ratio further falling down in the near future. That creates a problem, since workers cannot give substantial part of their salary to fund pensions provided by governments within social security programmes. In general, social security of PAYG systems look like a "basin" where one can never fill it out: whatever is poured into the system, then redistributed as pension benefits in just a few days.

This issue of increasing dependency ratio (relation of pensioners towards workers, see Table 1) has forced the UN back in 2002 to announce the 21st century as a century of the so called "ageing" problem. Means to resolve it are through a change to fully or partially *funded schemes*, both in public and private sector. That means that a worker will start saving for himself funds to be consumed after retirement by paying a little of his wage to special accounts—what was previously spent in PAYG systems.

Such mandatory obligation is done under stately regulated so-called second pillar of state pension systems, while "*quasi-mandatory*" system is applied as concession of corporations with trade unions to do it on behalf of companies-employers.

No-one knows yet how the pension reform is going to develop in up-coming 5 to 45 years. Sure thing is that industrial countries—members of OECD will have this issue on their agenda very soon–since 2012, when pension schemes are projected to have negative balance. In PRC and many other rapidly developing Asian states the crisis is projected for period of 2040-2050. In due course OECD member states quite soon will be forced to open doors for immigrants and foreigners to enter their Labour markets, while many of Asian states still have the time necessary to make major changes and move to funded schemes.

Dependency Ratio in OECD Member States in 1960-2030

Country G7	*1960*	*1990*	*2000*	*210*	*2020*	*2030*
Canada	13.0	16.7	18.2	20.4	28.4	39.1
France	18.8	20.8	23.6	24.6	32.3	39.1
Germany	16.0	21.7	23.8	30.3	35.4	49.2
Japan	9.5	17.1	24.3	33.0	43.0	44.5
Italy	13.3	21.6	26.5	31.2	37.5	48.3
UK	17.9	24.0	24.4	25.8	31.2	38.7
USA	15.4	19.1	19.0	20.4	27.6	36.8
The rest of the countries						
Australia	13.9	16.0	16.7	18.6	25.1	33.0
Austria	18.6	22.4	23.3	27.7	32.6	44.0
Belgium	18.5	22.4	25.1	25.6	31.9	41.1
Greece	12.3	21.2	25.5	28.8	33.3	40.9
Denmark	16.5	22.7	21.6	24.9	31.7	37.7
Finland	11.7	19.7	21.5	24.3	34.7	41.1
Ireland	18.6	187.4	16.7	18.0	21.7	25.3

(Contd. . .)

(Contd. . .)

Island	14.1	16.6	17.3	18.1	24.1	32.1
Luxembourg	15.9	19.9	21.9	25.9	33.2	44.2
Mexico	-	6.4	7.0	8.0	10.4	14.8
Netherlands	14.7	19.1	20.8	24.2	33.9	45.1
New Zealand	-	16.7	17.1	18.9	24.6	30.5
Norway	17.3	25.2	23.9	24.0	31.2	38.7
Portugal	12.7	19.5	20.9	22.0	25.3	33.5
Singapore		-	10	-		30
Spain	12.7	19.8	23.5	25.9	30.7	41.0
Sweden	17.8	27.6	26.9	29.1	35.6	39.4
Switzerland	15.5	22.0	23.6	29.4	37.8	48.6
Turkey	6.7	7.1	8.9	9.4	11.7	16.2

Sources : Retirement income systems : the reform process across OECD countries. David W. Kalisch and Tetsuya Aman, Social Policy Division, OECD conference "Pension Systems in Crisis" held at Harvard Institute for International Development—World Bank Institute, June 14-25, 1999, Cambridge, Massachusetts, USA, p. 47, data on Singapore – according to annual report of Central Provident Fund Board Annual Report 2000 (Singapore), www.cpf.gov.sg

3. Health Issues

Our discussion still misses quite important part of personal development, which is health and means to stay healthy. Healthy society in its true meaning has both physically healthy people able to work, educate, save and to take care of their children and retired persons. We are going to consider a care of physical health in the society.

Poverty usually accompanies handicapped persons, except in developed countries sufficiently spending to settle the issue, which here was recognized both socially and on government's level. But states in many other parts of the world just cannot afford to do it on the same level.

As an obligation fixed in treaties of International Labour Organization, first medical aid is provided by governments free of charge, with its expenses paid by workers in the same way as PAYG system during the time when workers obtain their salaries. For example, in the US a spending on PAYG and first aid totals to 15.3% of the payroll where 12.4% are paid to PAYG system, and 2.9% for medical aid. While many of states may say that they have the same relative numbers in per cents, their absolute figures may be much less compared to the US.

Spending on health works well in case if there is systematic approach to the issue—through health insurance. The longer is a period of systematic change when such system is adopted by society, the larger are accumulated savings considered together with people's habit to save for health, and the better is a health system in the state. When health insurance savings do not match the needs of health industry, governments should assist it by pouring necessary funds into the system. And it also depends on capacities of national economies if they can do it.

Probably, among the best examples are health systems of Israel, US and member states in "older" part of the EU (which, obviously, excludes its new member states). Among major health systems change one may recall a US experience during Clinton administration.

Health systems with no health insurance can either provide a little or no serious medical assistance to people when needed, and enforce patients to travel abroad to places where such sophisticated means exist. Unfortunately, very few can afford to pay right away for medical services in such cases since patients are treated as foreigners and do not obtain the same privileges compared to locals who have a hold of health insurance policies and are not requested a lump sum for specific treatment. For instance, medical services are mainly free for citizens of Israel, whereas any foreigner pays just for medical treatment itself beginning from 15-20K US dollars.

Hence, poor countries with little values of GDP per capita and having no health insurance system, exclude substantial part of Labour force from ability for recreation through medical treatment. In turn, this decreases number of a Labour force, and in a longer term harms a growth of national GDP.

Among states which started to move towards health insurance system are transition economies, where currently it is treated as quite expensive way of health spending compared to what was in these states before their economies became market oriented. Under planned economy, health spending was sufficient as long as a state economy continued to prosper : health spending was a part of a state budget. In comparatively new market economies of these countries the health insurance savings are not substantial yet, as well as wages. So actually needed financial spending on health is either skipped, or barely funded by governments depending on indicators of country's national growth.

For example, Russia's experience which recently (2006-2007) announced national programme to re-equip its state health system, is among few exceptions when a government tries to establish sound health system with quite large on-going "oil revenues" funding. But even after the end of this reform, hopefully successful, there should be a change towards market oriented health insurance system which establishes health branch as independent and self-motivated part of a market economy. It is important for the reason that in such a case the health system will not be jeopardized by economical downturns, and in 20 to 40 years will move step-by-step to private self-sustained health system.

Once again, we may see another kind of a closed cycle : healthy worker is needed to keep economy grow; in turn, economies with low GDP per capita cannot afford to have sufficient spending on health. In order to exit from such dependency situation is to set up a health insurance system which usually requires several decades to become nationally efficient.

As for the poor people living in poor countries the only way to take care of their own and children is to be in business, or to start voluntary savings specified for healthcare.

4. Conclusion

In the article we discussed main methods of dealing with poverty : They depend on ability and willingness of persons how radically they want to change their poor life. Methods are charity, skills training and entrepreneurship as well as benefits of social security systems. The problem has personal side of the issue as well as it depends on capabilities of the society and its main values which set up then how less harmful is a poverty in the society.

Health issues of poor people need to be settled by structural changes of governments to create health insurance, first as addition to stately provided medical aid, then by state subsidies to health system of the state as well as creation of tax shelters and promotions to develop private health system.

REFERENCES

Old Age Pension Schemes, OECD 1977, Paris, France, 206 p.

Progress Report to the ECOFIN Council on the Impact of Ageing Populations on Public Pension Systems. November 2000, Economic Pension Policy Committee, 55 p.

The 2001 OASDI Trustees Report. Office of the Chief Actuary (USA), 164 p.

The Future Evolution of Social Protection from a Long-Term Point of View: Safe and Sustainable Pensions. Communication of Commission to the European Council, to the European Parliament and to the Economic and Social Committee. Brussels, 11.10.2000 COM (2000) 622 final, 20 p.

Opening Speech of the UN Secretary General in the World Assembly on Ageing in Madrid, Spain, April, 2002.

2

Perspective Planning to Prevent Perpetual Poverty and to Pursue Progress of the People Especially on Health Care

G. C. De

1. Introduction

Poverty is a socio-economic condition of the people under distress situation in which their basic needs like food, clothing, shelter, healthcare, education and recreation are not properly met with in a civilized society. Currently the rural folks having monthly consumption of Rs. 211.30 and the urban folks it is of Rs. 454.11 are considered below the poverty line though the amounts are very meagre to sustain. Poverty may grab a family, a community or a geographical area. Family being the smallest social unit it suffers most when its basic needs especially earnings are in scarcity over a period of time. However, there may be disowned or rejected persons away from the family under any stress or distress, *e.g.* lepers, victims of AIDS, insane etc. Within a family the weakest member or the gender having less access to earning opportunity or scope to contribute, suffers the most. There are options for equal sharing of the suffering by all the members of the family, by the neighbouring families, borrowing from others without being trapped in the debt, receiving assistance from individuals, groups or institutions for the time being to overcome the difficult situation of the concerned families. The repeated disaster may lead to some families in distress and compel to live on and bequeath the poverty. Increase in dependable members in a non-affordable family may lead to dire consequences. There may be shifts of poverty stricken families from one to the other owing to various reasons within or beyond the control of man.

2. Dynamism of Poverty in an Ever-changing Society

A society is dynamic in various fronts. There are ups and downs but the overall trend is progressing. There are shifts of poverty stricken families, communities and areas especially in inhospitable locations and from one to the others. Thus there are new poverty victims though some of the affected ones overcome the situation over time and intensity. Therefore, poverty remains as a perpetual problem in a developing society.

3. Social Development and Generation of Poverty Victims

Social developments are of various types and forms over time and space. For bringing about any improvement there is requirement of a strong base that must bear the burden, rear and steer the same to widen the scope of further development in future. Improvement in some fronts or locations at a particular time may bring impoverishment in other fronts and locations. Prosperity in a part may bring forth poverty in other part and so a new generation of poverty victims come in to being. Repetition of the same process results a perpetual problem in a developing society. Natural disasters, the curses on the society, may convert the people of prosperity to pauperism and a new set of have-nots is providing additional burden to the society and in some extensive cases even social development is at stake. Faulty social policies and their perpetuation over decades or generations are causing a serious set back among the non-beneficiaries. The system of reservation over decades for a sect without the consideration of economic position is seriously depriving the non-reserved community.

4. Causes of Poverty

In depth studies help understand the causes and that may be anthropogenic or natural. The anthropogenic causes may be individual, societal or socio-political and the natural causes may be direct or indirect. An individual may be diseased, disable and disowned and live on alms, life saving support or in homes of rehabilitation. An individual may be an addict of drugs, intoxicants, extravagant or egoistic and thus faces poor pecuniary position in a short span of time. An individual may be compelled to spend more for treatment or other genuine purposes even by borrowing, mortgaging or leasing out properties and bears the consequences later on. There are social factors of generation of poverty. Both in tribal community and settled society a considerable number of people are to move to other areas in search of employment and earning on a seasonal, periodic or semi-permanent and even permanent basis. Some people are to roam distant areas for a considerable period in a year. In such cases more than one establishment are to be maintained and thus a greater part of their income spends and very often they suffer from miserable financial crunch. During off and lean seasons of employment in agriculture; closure, suspension of work, retrenchment of employees etc. may put the working force in disarray and compel to face the consequences of stoppage of assured income. In modern days also, in private sector 'hire and fire' form of employment transform some people under the grip the poverty. In some specific clan or community there are social or religious restrictions of savings as it was in *Santhals* and *Vaisnavites* who would live on their daily earnings. A considerable part of the communities of remote areas live on collection or gathering from forest, inland water bodies, marines etc. They may be fuel wood collectors, fishermen, collectors of honey, mushroom, fruits, roots, fibres etc. Usually they do not have the habit or knowledge of savings and whatever they collect or earn in a day spend but when they fail to gather they starve. Periodic starvation is a regular occurrence in their lives. Some daily wage earners or earners of daily work including potters, rickshaw pullers, cart pullers, artisans, helpers in masonry work can not save or do not have the mentality to save rather have the tendency to enjoy from whatever a little earning they obtain from hard labour and to put some morsel to the hungry members of their family. Very often they are compelled to be indifferent from hungriness of their near and dear ones and consume alcohol to be inebriated and also to get relief from fatigue or to enjoy pleasure. A portion or the entire amount of earning is spent on the way to home that is turned into den of discord and scarcity. There are other social factors like dacoity, snatching, extortion, grabbing, seizure, litigation, refusal to properties even home sites etc that turn the victims penniless. Spending beyond the capacity for wedding, last rites of family members, social commitments, paying taxes, rents, fees etc put the people under poverty over time. In different work sites like construction, transport, water supply and drainage, electricity generation and supply, mining, running machineries in industries, exposure to poisonous gas, chemicals, heat, sound etc. there are regular occurrence of accidents leading to disability and even death rendering disaster of individuals or the surviving family members and dependents and very often plunge them under poverty. The socio-political causes of poverty may be from eviction, forced displacement, income ceiling, fixing ceiling price for produces, forcible collection of payments in cash or kind, irrespective of hazards or failure with a little or no concession. Releasing loans at exorbitant rate of interest or fixing time for repayment when market runs with distress sale are the other causes. Very poor or no opening up of employment or earning for the ever growing population and demand rather shrinkage or polarization of employment leads to increase of unemployed and non or less earning people convert to below subsistence level. Distress employment discourages self-development or skill and thus encourages poverty like situation of families or communities. No delineation of human resources based on capabilities makes the persons misfit and incapable in production system. Politicalization including regimentation, group or party formation for enjoying rights without bearing responsibilities put the employer in distress. Polarization of power, property and pelf leads greater majority of settled and civilized society to suffer and very often the victims fall under the grip of poverty. Unethical and illogical socio-political situation some times cause unrest, rivalry, fight and even homicide that create poverty, loss of peace and happiness. Natural disasters like flood, drought, tremor, landslide, subsidence, fire, thunder strike, gale etc directly and suddenly convert the people in to have-nots. Extensive damage or failure of crops, epidemic in crop plants and animals, closure of industry or business enterprises may lead to disaster in indirect way.

5. Impact of Poverty on the Society

The victims of poverty always occupy certain per centage of the population and may spread over the rural and urban areas of the country. The number is usually more in remote and inhospitable areas where the sources of assured income is less however people of these areas very often contended with whatever they get to meet their need ignoring the greed and thus they never consider them as under the grip of poverty. Being the structural component of the populous society even one per cent is enough to bring down the mean economic level of the society as a whole. In this era of globalisation such a weaker section make the human kind weaker and poorer. The victims not only suffer themselves from hunger, malnutrition, under-nutrition, poor sanitation, healthcare, education and so on but also seriously affect the population above the poverty line especially those who are on the fence line and the new generation under poverty. Even the members of the economically solid class are to depend on such have-nots for their daily life and family scores. Physically weak, diseased especially with contagious, infectious and communicable diseases and pollution-affected persons may act as the source of dissemination of diseases among healthy and wealthy persons. Poor sanitation and environment surrounding the poverty victims may be the heeding, breeding and hiding sites of carriers and vectors of pathogens that may spread over to areas and people of higher economic class. Most of the victims of poverty are also exposed to different sources of pollution like water, wind, gas, soil, chemical, nuclear, sound, food, flora and fauna and suffer most as they have very little or no prevention and protection measure to afford. On the other hand they also act as the source of pollution owing to ignorance or negligence or not having any way out. Most of them are compelled to perform Labourious, tedious, risk-prone, hazardous jobs and succumb to many diseases and disabilities. In many cases they fail to avail modern medical facilities and services rather depend on traditional, non-scientific folk medicines, sorcery, quacks, herbal medicines, therapeutic, *ayurvedic, unani,* homeopath, worshipping, sacrificing, ethno-magical and other forms of cures of low or no cost and rarely take the help of hospitals, nursing homes, clinics and other costly treatments as they often perceive they are born to suffer and die. However, in most cases they remain as the source and storehouse of germs of ailments. In pursuit of employment and earning some people under poverty compel to leave their families including parents in home and require regular, periodic, seasonal or permanent movement to other areas where they become the victims of many sorts including sex related troubles, exploitation, abuse, rape etc. Very often they become despair and desperate that lead them to commit the act of desperateness, destruction, addiction, terrorism and in extreme suicide and homicide. All these in one way or other affect the society, its culture and tradition.

6. Impact of Poverty on Health Care and Development

It is a dream desire to completely eradicate poverty from a society. Intensity, duration and spread of poverty have serious consequences on various developmental steps including human health, environmental health, financial health and so on. Nutritious and healthy food keeps away many diseases, as the stomach is the seat of many ailments. Similarly sanitation and cleanliness prevent people to be sick. Use of fresh potable water, clean and free air, fertile soil, human friendly flora and fauna, pollution-free working place, clean dress and domestic sites help maintain sound health and mind. Poverty seriously affects victims and beyond and even at lethal proportion in epidemic, endemic and pandemic forms. Financial weakness creates weakness in structural and functional abilities as the spending on non-food essential items are far more than the expenditure on food in a civilized society. So called weaker section of the society bears maximum number of dependable members at least at certain stages and that aggravate the situation of poverty and thus health care. People of poor health and mind and of low financial power cannot think of development as when the stomach remains hungry, mind is directed to fill it first at any cost. Most of the development endeavours go waste as the major share is used to fill the stomach and quench the thirst of desire to the plinth level as more funds is spent on earth filling in a ditch before the construction of a building. Still then the load bearing capacity will be lower than the site with firm base. The poverty stricken people absorb most of the efforts of development. Therefore, a slow but steady, prolonged but ceaseless endeavour is required to reduce the scenario of poverty and development.

7. Measures to Mitigate both Persistent and Emerging Victims of Poverty

Family-wise a thorough data base of the economically backward individuals and families is to be prepared by the local body like *panchayat*, municipality, authority, board etc. in collaboration and coordination with NGOs, institutions, philanthropic societies etc for technical and material support. Identification of the victims of poverty is the primary objective. On an annual basis review of the data for addition or deletion as per requirement is to be made. For mitigation of poverty prioritisation is required to provide employment and earning on the basis of manual and mental labour as well as skills on local resource utilization and development. Special comprehensive drives from different corners are to make to provide food, clothes, shelters, medicines etc. on emergent basis and education, scopes of earning, training to motivate in savings as well as involving them in various development issues as the component of the society. They are required to be taught to improve them as the human resource. For this they will enjoy the services they deserve and rights they are entitled to and at the same time they will feel their dignity and respect in the society. Health care may be one of the issues in which arrangement of primary health care may be made available at the nearest primary health centre at zero or reduced cost. Awareness programme must be ensured about nutrition, use of clean drinking water, health and hygiene, common disinfection, immunization etc from pre-natal stage. There must have the arrangement for reporting of out break of diseases for undertaking adequate measures in time to check further spread of the same over time, space and number. Disables, destitute and handicapped should be protected under the support and service systems in the folds of self-help groups, cooperatives etc. It is better to create revolving fund and regenerating source of income of the incumbents. They are to be included under the shares and savings. For the purpose noble mission and vision are essential and that will develop required fund, infrastructure, manpower etc. exploring different sources already existing and also by creating new sources at initial stage. The local social institution should come forward to help themselves and the community as a whole. For this we, the HUMAN should prove that we bear Heart, Understanding, Mind, Avenues and Nerves and that are to be utilized for the needy persons residing surrounding us. It is better to follow to act locally considering the social demand and expectations.

3

Problems of Livelihood of Rag Pickers and Alternative Measures for Their Rehabilitation

—Debashis Das
—Angshuman Ghosh

1. Introduction

The rag pickers are poor, have not, ignorant, destitute, untouchable, illiterate, and backward people of the society, work and reside in the midst of dirty environment, but put their level best effort to make it clean where the inhabitants reside. They are engaged in antisocial and prohibited activities and suffer from serious health hazards.

Therefore, the moral duty of the scientists and reformers to search for their rehabilitation. In this respect they have studied the nature of livelihood of rag pickers and suggested measures for their rehabilitation.

(a) The scientists explained their demographic characteristics which include their number, distribution, age structure, sex ratio, migration, size of the family, religion, language and alike aspects. Most of them observed that the rag pickers are more or less children and female. Their families migrated from different backward regions to the urban centers and have larger size if family residing in a small hut (Focus 1992, IMWED 1986, Ghosh 1988, Venkateshwaran 1994, Disha

1996, Bhattacharya and Sen 1997, Hunt and Haysman 1994, Furedy and Alamgyr 1992, Srivastava 2006.)

There are many researchers who studied the contribution of rag pickers to keep the environment clean and to the solid wastes management activities. They observed about how they collect, sort, wash, carry and sell the wastes which vary from place to place, and have become a traing ground for a new class of entrepreneurs and innovators (Focus 1992, Paul Hamlyn Foundation 1993, Agarwal 1998, Sheshu 2002, Sharma *et.al.* 1994, Chandra, Department of local self government 2005, Shah 2003, Shaner 2004, World Bank Report 2004, Mitra 2006, Stephanie 2006).

In this solid wastes management network apart from rag pickers there are others who contribute significantly to keep the environment clean. They are itinerant traders, municipalities, panchayats, local level dealers and alike. The functional relationships and linkages between rag pickers and others determine the livelihood of rag pickers which are observed by many scientists. (Beukering 1996, Furedy and Alamgyr 1992, Bose and Blore 1993, Mukherjee and Sen 1998, EEF 1995)

The quality of life of rag pickers shows their deep routed poverty within which they are engrossed into and they thrive. They always spend struggle life which compel them to be under and mal nutrition, thus are suffered from many diseases. They lead their lives in the midst of polluted environment and do not find any leisure time to take rest, because in other times they have to search for other legal or illegal activities to earn their bread. (Bose and Blore 1993, EEF 1995, Disha 1996, Focus 1992, Bhattacharyya and Sen 1997, Deb 1998, Kamat 2006, Vasantha *et.al.* 2004, Sheshu 2002, Sharma 1994, Da Silva *et.al.* 2006, Senthalir 2003, Stephanie 2006).

Therefore, The activities of rag pickers are essential to keep the environment clean, unpolluted and to save the soul of inhabitants and to provide comfort to the inhabitants it is necessary to develop their economy and to rehabilitate them, economically and socially through various governmental and non governmental measures. Most of the scientists have shown different ways of their rehabilitation measures and programmes (Focus 1992, Mukherji 1994, EEF 1995, Bhattacharya and Sen 1997, Mishra 1998, Doen 1996, Van Beukering 1997, Paul Hamlyn Foundation, London, 1993, High Commission of India London (2006), Sheshu 2006, Ram Kumar *et.al*. 2002, Department of local self Government 2005, Shah 2003, Shaner 2004, Rhodes 1874, Senthalir 2003, Adukia 2005.

(b) Objectives of the Study. The present study possesses following objectives :

(i) To find out the demographic and socio-economic characteristics of the rag pickers.

(ii) To illustrate the nature of their contribution to solid wastes disposal.

(iii) To discuss their functional relationships with others who are also involved in the same occupation.

(iv) To describe their quality of life.

(v) To uncover the problems which are associated with their livelihood and to suggest the alternative measures to develop their economy and to suggest the rehabilitation programmes of the rag pickers.

(c) Analytical Procedure. There are 57 numbers of rag pickers interviewed and different data about their socio-economic and demographic characteristics, occupation and survival including their problems are collected. The data are processed statistically and simple tables are prepared. The absolute relationships between them are computed by correlation coefficients which are also shown in the table form.

(d) The Study Area. Bolpur is a small town located at the centre of Bolpur-Sriniketan Block, southern part of Birbhum district, western part of West Bengal and eastern part of India. It is located at the Rarh natural region of West Bengal, within Ajoy-Mayurakshy interriverine tract and most of her populations are engaged in poverty induced tertiary sector. It is about 35 km. far from the district headquarter—Suri.

2. Socio-economic and Demographic Characteristics of Rag Pickers

(a) Distribution of Castes. In Bolpur town 57 numbers of rag pickers are interviewed. It is observed that out of them the numerical strength of scheduled castes and Muslim population is larger. Although a few people belong to high and middle castes Hindu, scheduled tribes and Christian communities who are engaged themselves in rag picking activities. (table 1)

Table 1 : Distribution of Castes

Name of the Castes	*No.*	%
High castes Hindu	2	3.51
Middle Castes Hindu	2	3.51
Scheduled Castes	25	43.86
Scheduled Tribes	2	3.51
Muslim	25	43.86
Christian	1	1.75

(b) Distribution of Sex. The numerical strength of male category of rag pickers is quite larger than the female, which indicates that the females are not interested in this unsafe activity, who prefer to engage themselves in other activities, like maid servant, collection of twigs and branches and cow dung. (Table 2).

Table 2 : Distribution of Sex

Distribution of Sex	*No.*	%
Male	62	87.33
Female	9	12.67
Total	71	100.00

(c) Distribution of Age. The age distribution of rag pickers indicates that large numbers of them are children and number of youth category is smaller than them. But relatively older category of rag pickers is relatively smaller in numerical strength. This indicates that children an adolescent category of people are largely engaged in this occupation (Table 3)

Table 3 : Distribution of Age

Range of Age	*No.*	%
7–15	27	38.57
15–30	18	25.71
30–40	18	25.71
40–55	7	10.00

Distribution of Children, Adult Men and Adult Women

Range of Children	*No.*	%
1–2	10	27.03
2–3	14	37.84
3–4	8	21.62
4–5	5	13.51
Range of Adult Men	*No.*	%
1-3	31	79.49
3-4	3	7.69
4-5	5	12.82
Range of Adult Women	*No*	%
1	15	34.10
2	20	45.45
3	9	20.45

(d) Distribution of Educational Status. The distribution of education all status of the rag pickers reveals that most of them are illiterate; however a few have studied up to primary level. Very few of them have studied up to middle school level. It indicates that poverty compels them to search for their earning instead of getting education in the school.

Table 4 : Distribution of Educational Status

Item	*No.*	%
Illiterate	42	60.00
I–IV	19	27.14
V–VI	6	8.57
Can sign only	3	4.29

(e) Distribution of Occupation. As far as distribution of occupation is concerned some rag pickers are engaged also in cultivation and as daily Labour. The study indicates that most of them are mainly rag collector; however, few of them work as daily Labour and also in cultivation. However, 38% of the persons are engaged in rag picking activities as subsidiary occupation where as 62% are engaged in cultivation as secondary occupation.

Table 5 : Distribution of Main and Subsidiary Occupations

Name of Main Occupation	*No.*	%
Rag picking	64	87.67
Cultivation	4	5.48
Daily Labour	5	6.85
Name of subsidiary occupation	*No.*	%
Rag picking	11	38.00
Cultivation	18	62.00

(f) Distribution of Land Holdings. Very few rag pickers (12.67%) have the ownership of landholding however; all of them are marginal farmers. As for example, 88% of them are owner of 0.02 to 0.03 acres of land where as 11% own 0.5 to 0.6 acre of land, indicating their deep routed poverty.

Table 6 : Distribution of Land Holdings

Range in Acre	*No.*	%
.0165–.033	8	88.89
.0495–.066	1	11.11

(g) Distribution of Income Per Month. The rag pickers earn very small amount of money per month which ranges between Rs. 100 and Rs. 1200 only. Among them 23% earn the smallest amount of income where as roughly 2% earn relatively larger amount of income indicating acute poverty under which they thrive.

Table 7 : Distribution of Income Per Month

Income in Rs.	*No.*	*%*
100–200	14	23.33
200–300	5	8.33
300–400	9	15.00
400–500	7	11.67
500–600	8	13.33
600–700	8	13.33
700–800	6	10.00
800–1000	2	3.33
1000–1200	1	1.67

(h) Distribution of Family Members. Size of the family shows that relatively smaller number of families has larger size and *vise-versa*. Same fact also holds good in case of male and female members separately in the family. Their sizes are inversely proportional to the number of families (Table 8).

The distribution of family members of the rag pickers indicates that there are relatively larger numbers of families where only 1 to 3 persons dwell. On the other hand as low as 14% of the families where 4 to 5 member of children reside. As far as adult man is concern in 79% of the families 1 to 3 adult man reside and 45% of the families only 3 adult women dwell. (Table 8)

Table 8 : Distribution of Family Members

Male Members	*No.*	*%*
1–2	20	28.17
2–4	32	45.07
4–6	10	14.08
6–8	9	12.68
Female Members	*No.*	*%*
1–2	29	42.03
2–4	30	43.48
4–6	6	8.70
6–8	4	5.80

Total Members	*No.*	*%*
1–4	14	20.00
4–6	26	37.14
6–8	13	18.57
8–10	10	14.28
10–12	7	10.00

(i) Origin Place of Rag Pickers Migrants. These rag pickers come to Bolpur town to carry out their rag picking activities mostly from nearby villages and from within the township. However, some rag pickers have come from Bihar and Jharkhand states and Nalhati, Muraroi, Illambazar, Panrui, Labpur, etc. P.S. and Burdhaman district etc. areas. However large chunk of them have come here from surrounding areas mainly (Table 9).

Table 9 : Place of Origin of Migration

Name of Origin Place	*No.*	*%*
Makrampur	3	4.69
Surul	1	1.56
Jadavpur	1	1.56
Saltor	1	1.56
Kedangal	1	1.56
Ballabhpur	1	1.56
Dangapara	1	1.56
Kendradangal	2	3.12
Kankalitola	1	1.56
Bhubandanga	7	10.94
Laldaha	1	1.56
Raipur	2	3.12
Labpur	3	4.69
Panrui	2	3.12
Nalhati	1	1.56
Miraroi	1	1.56
Illambazar	3	4.69
Jharkhand/Bihar	4	6.25

(j) Distribution of Distances of Origin Place of Rag Pickers Migrants. The above mentioned analysis is further supported by the distance factor of rag pickers' origin places. More than half of the total rag pickers come from within the distance between 1 and 3 km. and slightly less than one eighth of them come from distance in between 30 km. and 60 km. However, less than 5% of the rag pickers have come from Bihar and Jharkhand states (Table 10).

Table 10 : Distribution of Distances of Origin Places in km

Distances in km.	*No.*	%
1–3	37	52.86
3–7	7	10.00
7–11	5	7.14
11–13	1	1.43
13–15	4	5.71
15–20	1	1.43
20–25	3	4.28
25–30	4	5.71
30–60	5	7.14
530	3	4.28

(k) Distribution of Religion. These rag pickers believe either in Hinduism or Islam or Cristianism of the study area Persons believing in Hindu religion are larger (Table 11).

Table 11 : Distribution of People Believing in Religions

Name of Religion	*No.*	%
Hindu	42	59.16
Muslim	28	39.44
Christian	1	1.40

3. Contribution of Rag Pickers to Solid Wastes Disposal

(a) Distribution of Items Collected. Rag pickers mainly collect plastic, paper, glass, metal, battery, clothing, iron pieces, tin, leather, coal and other materials from surrounding areas of the settlements. Present study indicates that the plastic, paper,

glass, metal and battery items are collected in relatively larger amount than other types of wastes (Table 12).

Table 12 : Distribution of Items Collected

Items	*No.*	%
Plastic	69	15.16
Paper	66	14.50
Glass	66	14.50
Metal	59	12.97
Battery	47	10.33
Clothing	24	5.27
Iron	28	6.15
Tin	33	7.25
Leather	32	7.03
Coal	17	3.74
Others	14	3.10

The above mentioned wastes materials are collected from dust bins, roadside, outside houses, industries and alike areas which are located at eight wards. The further indicates that considerable amount of wastes are collected from the dust bins and rest sources rank next to it. (Table 13).

Table 13 : Name of Collection Places

Name of collection places	*No.*	%
Bhubandanga	21	17.65
Hattola	18	15.13
Beside Railway Station	1	0.84
Professor Colony	5	4.20
Jambuni	16	13.44
Ramkrishna Road	8	6.72
Kachari Pukur	9	7.56
Mistripara	10	8.40
Gurupalli	24	20.17
7 Palli	3	2.52
Rail Colony	4	3.36

Table 14 : Distribution of Source of Collection

Source of collection	*No.*	*%*
Dust bin	20	40.00
Road side	10	20.00
Outside houses	10	20.00
Outside industries	10	20.00

(b) Sorting Places of Rag pickers. After the collection of the rag items are sorted out by them and then they sell to the local level receivers. In this respect more than 50% of rag pickers sort out their items on the area in between 1 and 2 katha (60 katha = 1 acre), where as 40% do their same job on below half katha and 6% of them work in between 2 and 4 katha for this purpose (Table 15).

Table 15 : Distribution of Sorting Places of Rag in Katha (60 katha=1 acre)

Range in Katha	*No.*	*%*
0–.5	25	40.32
1–2	33	53.23
2–4	4	6.45

(c) Sale of Items. After sorting out rags these are sold to different local level receivers within Bolpur town. Normally they collect rags through out morning and after 12 o'clock in the noon they start selling their commodities. Here two local receivers stalls purchase considerable amount of rags from the pickers, followed by others (Table 16).

Table 16: Items Sold to Whom by Numbers of Rag Pickers

Name of Local Receiver	*No.*	*%*
Jagadish Roy	3	6.25
Oriya	6	12.50
Bachalal Gupta	9	18.75
Sriram Routh	9	18.75
Ambia Mallick	7	14.58
Local receiver	9	18.75
Itinerant trader	5	10.42

(d) Amount and Prices of Items. Although several solid waste items are sold to the local level receivers but relatively larger amount of glass, tin, plastic, etc. items are brought by individual for selling. On the other hand if total amount of wastes are taken into consideration, then glass, metal, plastic, etc. items are sold all together by the rag pickers. But at the same time although larger amount of glass materials are sold, with the price only 1 Re/kg. On the other hand metal and battery products are sold by relatively higher prices like Rs. 4-5/kg. (Table 17).

Table 17 : Amount Collected and Prices Per Unit of Rag Items

Name of Item	*Amount Collected Per Day in kg*	*Selling Price in Rupees per kilo gram*
Glass	10–11	1
Tin	5–7	3
Metal	4–5	5
Battery	2–3	5
Plastic	5–6	4
Paper	3–6	1
Others	5–6	-

(e) Distribution of Number of Years of Occupations. There are 20% of the rag pickers engaged in this job in between 2 or 4 years, 23% are engaged in between 10 and 16 years where as

Table 18 : Distribution of Numbers of Years of Rag Pickers are in This Occupation

Range of Years	*No.*	*%*
1–2	11	13.75
2–4	16	20.00
4–6	2	2.50
6–8	13	16.25
8–10	13	16.25
10–16	18	22.50
16–20	7	8.75

16% each of rag pickers are engaged either in between 6 and 8 years or in between 8 and 10 years (Table 18).

(f) Working hours in a day. The rag pickers normally work in between 2 and 12 hours but largest numbers collect their wastes in between 6 and 8 hours. Where as roughly one third of them work in a day in between 4 and 6 hours. Besides, relatively smaller proportion of rag pickers works in between 2 and 8 and 10 and 12 hours in a day (Table 19).

Table 19 : Distribution of Working Hours of Rag Pickers

Range of Hours	*No.*	%
2–4	4	5.63
4–6	23	32.39
6–8	25	35.21
8–10	15	21.13
10–12	4	5.63

(g) Working Day in a Month. These rag pickers work in between 5 and 30/31 days in a month. Most of them work in between 25 and 30 days where as one fifth or slightly less than that rag pickers work in between either 20 or 25 days or 15 and 20 days in a month. However, very small number of them works in between 5 and 15 days in a month because in other days they are engaged in other activities (Table 20).

Table 20 : Distribution of Working Days in a Month

Range of Days	*No.*	%
5–10	6	8.45
10–15	5	7.04
15–20	13	18.31
20–25	14	19.72
25–30	33	46.48

(h) Working Months in a Year. The rag pickers work in between 4 and 12 months in a year. Slightly less than half of them work in between 6 and 8 months, less than one third work in between 8 and 10 months, where as relatively small number

of rag pickers work either almost through out the year or in very few months of the year (Table 21).

Table 21 : Distribution of Working Months in a Year

Range of Months	*No.*	%
4–6	3	6.25
6–8	20	41.67
8–10	15	31.25
10–12	10	20.83

(i) Time of Collection. The rag pickers collect this waste either in between 10 a.m. and 1 p.m. or in between early morning that is from 6 a.m. till 3 p.m. However, as high as 63% of them work in between 10 a.m. and 1 p.m. (Table 22).

Table 22 : Distribution of Time of Collection

Time of Collection	*No.*	%
10 a.m.–1 p.m.	29	63.04
6 a.m.–3 p.m.	17	36.96

(j) Damaged Items after Sorting. The waste materials often are broken damaged. These are damaged either during collecting time or during transport or dumping of them. The study further indicates that less than half of the rag pickers damage their waste materials during collection. Slightly larger than one third of them damage their materials during transportation time and rest (one fourth) damage during the time of dumping (Table 23).

Table 23 : Materials Damaged During

Materials Damaged During	*No.*	%
During collection	24	40.68
During transport	21	35.59
During dumping	14	23.73

(k) Sale Value of Items. The rag pickers after collection and sorting of materials sell their wastes to the local level receivers. Generally, they collect glass, tin, metal, paper, plastic, battery,

and alike materials. The study further shows that the metal wastes have relatively higher sale prices than others and glass, battery materials have very small amount of waste price (Table 24).

Table 24 : Distribution of Sale Value of Materials and Nature of Fluctuation

Materials	*Sale price per kg.*	*Fluctuated price per kg.*
Glass	50 paise–1 Re	50 paise
Tin	80 paise–1 Re	20 paise
Metal	Rs. 3–Rs. 5	Rs. 2
Paper	Rs.4–Rs. 4.50	50 paise
Plastic	Rs. 2–Rs. 6	Rs. 4
Battery	50 paise–Re 1	50 paise

(l) Distribution of Peak and Lean Months/seasons. These rag pickers work to a large extent during winter, spring, and autumn seasons because during this time neither scorching sun nor rain obstructs their activities. However, they cannot work under the scorching sun during summer or under the rainfall during rainy season. Therefore, they normally work hard for a longer time all of nine months except April, May and June which which are the lean months. It is also found from the survey that during summer and rainy seasons most of them may be engaged in harvesting, land preparation and sowing activities of crops. (Table 25).

Table 25 : Distribution of Peak and Lean Months and Seasons

Peak months	Jan., Feb., Mar., July, Aug., Sept., Oct., Nov., Dec.
Lean months	April, May, June
Peak seasons	Autumn, winter, spring
Lean seasons	Summer, rainy

4. Functional Relationships between Rag Pickers and others in This Activity

These rag pickers interact functionally with the itinerant waste traders, staffs of municipal conservancy service and with local level receivers. The study shows that largest number of rag pickers have good relation with the local level receivers followed by itinerant waste traders and municipality (Table 26).

Table 26 : Functional and Economic Relationships between Rag Pickers and others in this field Relationship with Itinerant Traders

Good	58	87.88
Bad	8	12.12
Relationship with workers of municipal conservancy service		
Good	49	81.67
Bad	11	18.33
Relationship with local receivers		
Good	54	90.00
Bad	6	10.00

(a) Receiving Loan, Interest, or any other Benefits. These rag pickers are very much poor. They belong to the poorest of the poor category of people. Therefore, to maintain their daily life what ever income they earn seems to be inadequate. Therefore, they have no other alternative but to borrow loan from the itinerant waste traders and local level receivers. They are deprived of getting loan from the bank because they are unable to repay back, but this loan will be deducted from their earning which they get from the itinerant waste traders and local level receivers (Table 27)

Table 27 : Distribution of Loan Giving Sources

Item	*No.*	%
Loan from Bank	0	0
Interest	0	0
Loan from itinerant traders	19	100.00
Loan from local receivers	-	-

(b) Nature of Movement. These rag pickers either move alone for collection of wastes or move with their family members and with friends. Generally some of them prefer to move with their family members (Table 28).

Table 28 : Rag Pickers Moving with Whom

Himself	15	27.78
With family members	27	50.00
With friends	12	22.22

5. Quality of Life

(a) Distribution of Diseases which Attack them. The rag pickers dwell in the dirty slums. They collect dirty materials therefore they have to spend each and every second within the dirty environment. This causes several diseases and makes them weak. They do not have strong resistant power and do not have adequate money to undergo medical treatment. All these are responsible for the deep rooted diseases. There are 13 different types of diseases found among the rag pickers. Large proportion of rag pickers suffer from fever followed by skin problem, cold and cough and stomach problems. Relatively smaller numbers are affected by rest types of diseases. It may be believed that the females are also manhandled or, abortion or molestation are their regular happenings. However, the female rag pickers do not confess all these events (Table 29).

Table 29 : Distribution of Diseases

Name of Diseases	*No.*	*%*
Dog bites	18	7.11
Rat bites	2	0.79
Jaundice	15	5.93
Stomach problem	32	12.65
Skin problem	35	13.83
Cut injuries	16	6.32
Fever with infections	37	14.62
Cold and cough	34	13.44
Burning	4	1.58
Mal nutrition	25	9.88
Diarrhea	12	4.74
Pin prick	4	1.58
Eye problem	19	7.51

(b) Residence Place. The abovementioned rag pickers mostly reside in different slums of the urban area because the urban areas are the main sources of waste materials. Besides, the distances between their residence and the working place are smaller than those who reside in the villages (table 30).

Table 30 : Distribution of Place of Residence of Rag Pickers

Item	*No.*	%
Slum of town	41	57.75
Village	30	42.25

(c) Distribution of Facilities and Amenities. As far as distribution of facilities and amenities are concerned it is found that 37% of them get clean drinking water. Only 17% have drainage facilities around their household, 13% have cooking facilities, where as 11%, 10% and 9% of the rag pickers have ventilation, toilet and electricity facilities. All these facts indicate the poor condition which is associated with their daily livelihood of each rag picker (Table 31).

Table 31 : Distribution of Facilities which Rag Pickers Enjoy

Item	*No.*	%
Drinking water	49	37.12
Electricity	13	3.85
Drain	23	17.42
Lavatory/toilet	14	10.61
Cooking place	18	13.64
Ventilation	15	11.36

Although slightly more than one third of the rag pickers get relatively cleaner drinking water, among them about 67% get it from either tube well or tap, where as rest get the same from either pond or well (Table 32).

Table 32 : Distribution of Source of Drinking Water

Item	*No.*	%
Tube well/tap	33	67.35
Pond/well	16	32.65

(d) Sorting and Washing Place of Rag Pickers. After collection of the wastes these are needed to be washed and sorted out before they are disposed off to the local level receivers. The most precarious condition is that only 38% of the rag pickers get washing facility. However 61% are benefited by sorting facility (Table 33)

Table 33 : Distribution of Washing and Sorting Places of Wastes

Item	*No.*	%
Washing places of wastes	26	38.24
Sorting places of wastes	42	61.76

(e) Suspected as Thief. Rag picking activities is very difficult because they will have to move around different corners of the vacant places around which settlements are found and where wastes are thrown out. While dong so, they may enter the courtyard of the household. Under such a situation they may be suspected as thief. Often they steal the clothing or shoes or utensils which are kept outside by the residents. However, the study shows that as large as 87% of the total rag pickers said that they are not suspected as thief (Table 34).

Table 34 : Whether Suspected as Thief

Item	*No.*	%
Yes	6	12.24
No	43	87.76

(f) Welfare Arrangements. It is astonishing fact that although the rag pickers keep themselves busy to clean the environment, in spite of this fact they are not at all benefited by any means of welfare activities made by either municipality, N.G.O's and any other organization (Table 35).

Table 35 : Welfare Activity Made by Organizations

Item	*No.*	*%*
Municipality	Nil	Nil
N.G.O.	Nil	Nil
Other organization	Nil	Nil

The above mentioned statements about the rag pickers prove that although they are keeping themselves busy to provide comfort to the people of the society in various ways with little social infrastructural and economic benefits. In spite of this fact they can not expect love or mercy from the people of the society at all. More over they are often bitten by them without proving them as thief.

6. Sythesised Observations

The most striking feature is that the aged rag pickers are either illiterate or have very low educational status, but earn considerable amount of monthly income from their standpoint. Besides most of these rag pickers holding larger amount of land ownership, so that they are also engaged in agricultural activities specially during rainy season (Table 36).

The study further speaks that the rag pickers belonging to relatively higher cast Hindu population are engaged in different subsidiary occupations and own larger amount of land, earn considerable amount of monthly income. Besides the aged rag pickers with relatively higher educational status are engaged in different subsidiary occupations, they also own larger amount of land.

The relatively aged rag pickers who earn larger amount of monthly income have come to Bolpur town from longer distances. Besides another fact to be noted here is that among them who own considerable amount of land ownership and earn substantial amount of monthly income within themselves are engaged in this occupation for longer period of time (Table 37).

Table 36 : Interrelationships between Socio-economic Characteristics of Rag Pickers

	Caste	*Age*	*Educational Status*	*Subsidiary Occupation*	*Land Holding*	*Monthly Income*	*Family Member*
Caste	1.00	–.03	.03	–.12	–.25	.13	–.26
Age	–.03	1.00	–.44**	.07	.17	.51**	–.14
Educational Status	.03	–.44**	1.00	.12	–.06	–.02	.06
SubsidiaryOccupation	-.12	.07	.12	1.00	.43**	.25	.27
Land-holding	–.25	.17	–.06	.43**	1.00	.12	.25
Monthly income	.13	.51**	–.02	.25	.12	1.00	–.05
Family member	–.26	–.14	.06	.27	.25	–.05	1.00

Table 37 : Interrelationships between Socio-economic Characteristics and Migration, Sorting Place, and Years of Occupation Distance of Origin

Place	*Sorting Place*	*Years in this Occupation*	
Caste	.15	–.17	–.16
Age	.33*	.18	.84**
Educational status	.19	–.17	–.39**
Subsidiary occupation	.24	–.28*	.26
Land holding	.19	.03	.38**
Monthly income	.29*	–.25	.31*
Family member	–.08	–.13	.03
Distance of origin place	1.00	–.01	.24
Sorting place	–.01	1.00	.20
Years in this occupation	.24	.20	1.00

The above mentioned rag pickers who earn larger amount of monthly income work for longer period of time, days, month and year. But those who have relatively higher educational status work in this occupation for relatively smaller period of time, hours, days, month and year (table 38).

The study indicates that the rag pickers collect paper, plastic, glass, battery, leather, cloth materials to a large extent. They are mostly aged, own relatively lager amount of land and prefer to collect metal wastes, where as the rag pickers who earn considerable amount of monthly income prefer to collect waste paper largely (table 39).

The aged rag pickers who own larger amount of land ownership sell waste paper and plastics in higher prices, but among them who earn considerable amount of monthly income sell metal items in higher price (table 40).

The aged rag pickers, having lager amount of land ownership and earn considerable amount of monthly income enjoy better quality of life, because they manage to get facilities and amenities like electricity, drains, toilets, cooking places,

Table 38 : Interrelationships between Socio-economic Factors and Working Time of Rag Pickers

	Working Hours	*Working Days*	*Working Months*
Caste	–.10	–.19	.18
Age	.29**	.42**	.25
Educational status	–.31*	–.38**	–.16
Subsidiary occupation	–.01	–.02	.01
Land holding	.10	.16	.03
Monthly income	.19	.31*	.52**
Family member	.25	–.04	.12
Working hours	1.00	.29*	.32*
Working days	.29*	1.00	.05
Working months	.32*	.05	1.00

Table 40 : Interrelationships between Socio-economic Characteristics and Average Amount of Wastes Per day in kg of Rag Pickers

	Paper	*Plastic*	*Glass*	*Metal*	*Others*
Caste	.09	.02	–.07	–.26	–.07
Age	.32*	.002	.53**	.26	–.93**
Educational status	–.32*	–.18	–.39**	–.23	.27
Subsidiary occupation	–.09	–.26	–.04	.13	–.23
Land holding	.10	–.13	.26	.75**	–.009
Monthly income	–.45**	–.03	.16	.10	–.46**
Family member	–.02	.05	.02	.09	.001
Paper	1.00	.47**	.35*	.12	–.29*
Plastic	.47**	1.00	–.25	–.13	–.03
Glass	.35*	.25	1.00	.52**	–.07
Metal	.12	.13	.52**	1.00	–.20
Others	–.29*	–.03	–.27	–.20	1.00

ventilation etc. Set against this these rag pickers are engaged in different secondary occupations also earn larger amount of monthly income enjoy electricity, drains, toilet, facilities (table 41).

Table 39 : Interrelationships between Socio-economic Characteristics and Quality of Life of Rag Pickers

Ventilation	*Drinking Water No. of Rooms*		*Electricity*		*Drains*	*Toilet*	*Cooking Place*
Caste	.32*	–.14	–.13	.17	.04	.19	.03
Age	.05	.41**	.02	.20	.30*	–.17	–.02
Educational							
Status	.08	–.09	.14	.24	–.06	.30*	.02
Subsidiary							
Occupation	–.08	.10	.08	.36**.05	.12	.03	.11
Land holding	–.11	.28*	–.07	.98**	.21	–.13	–.10
Monthly income	.25	.45**	.16	–.08	–.06	–.28*	–.05
Family member	–.13	–.17	.04	.22	–.02	–.03	.005
Drinking water	1.00	–.12	–.23	.32*	–.11	–.05	.03
Electricity	–.12	1.00	.35*	.44**	.39**	–.39**	–.13
Drains	–.23	.35*	1.00	1.00	.21	.12	–.12
Toilet	.22	.32*	.44**	.22	.22	.03	.04
Cooking place	–.11	.39**	.21	.03	1.00	–.08	.05
Ventilation	–.05	–.34*	.12	.04	–.08	1.00	.08
No. of rooms	.03	–.13	–.12		.05	.08	1.00

Table 41 : Interrelationships between Socio-economic Characteristics and Sale Price of Wastes of Rag Pickers

	Paper	*Plastic*	*Glass*	*Metal*
Caste	–.19	–.42**	.007	.23
Age	.32*	.17	.15	.97**
Educational status	–.25	–.22	–.21	.03
Subsidiary occupation	.07	.04	–.27*	.13
Land holding	.27	.28*	–.25	–.05
Monthly income	.42**	–.21	–.17	.61**
Family member	.24	.12	–.18	–.32*
Paper	1.00	.39**	.03	.12
Plastic	.39**	1.00	–.06	–.32*
Glass	.03	–.06	1.00	–.03
Metal	.12	–.32*	–.03	1.00

7. Problems of Rag Pickers

Total number of rag pickers increases considerably which reduces per capita availability of wastes materials, which compels them to search for wastes over wider area by spending long time. The children and the females become tired by putting more Labour but getting less food.

The children work for half a day and their earnings become considerable parts of family's income, which indicates deep rooted poverty of rag pickers.

Since the materials are not separated at source, the physical quality of the recovered recycle able materials goes down. During collection, transport and dumping, many items are damaged. Therefore, the sale values of materials from the dumping ground are generally low.

Working conditions for the wastes pickers and in the dumping ground are very unhygienic. Dogs, cats, rats and some cows, which use the open vats as sources of food, always surround the pickers. Here kitchen wastes are easily available for the animals. The dumping areas are always a good breeding ground for mosquitoes, especially during the rainy season.

Diseases borne by mosquitoes affect the pickers. All the pickers work barefooted and with hands without gloves. This is a very dangerous practice, particularly where the waste heaps are of a mixed nature. The amount of toxic wastes in such places is very high. The habit of washing themselves immediately after the work is over amongst the waste pickers.

The waste pickers collect marketable items. The estimating total value of revenue is very difficult, partly because the trade is a part of the black economy that means income is not disclosed to the tax authority and the criminal elements operate protection rackets.

There seems to exist no direct relation between the private households and the rag pickers. But they are somewhat indirectly connected. Also between the pickers and the itinerant traders buying recycle able waste from house visits, there seems to exist no direct relation.

The rag pickers do not know enough about the prices and possible profit rates of the dealers and especially of the wholesalers. They have to accept the prices offered by the brokers without dispute. In such situations, the children are particularly handicaped.

Rag pickers do not operate as an organization, such as co-operative. A big problem seems to be the constant influx of new Labour force into the picking business. The rag pickers complained of declining returns because of steady increase in the number of new comers. The volume of useful waste for the pickers is not growing at the same rate as immigrants. This competitive situation enables the dealers to push down the prices.

An insufficient return for the rag pickers, notwithstanding the disadvantage faced by child workers. Their total amount of earned daily or monthly income places them in the class of poor people. The income varies between the seasons. To pick up wastes in the monsoon season is tough job and result is hardly worthy of the Labour spent. Paper becomes wet and not saleable. All items are dirty.

The large majority of rag pickers is either living in slums, village, or in squatter settlements. These residences are less than acceptable quality. There is lack of water, electricity supply, and drainage. The quarters are more than overpopulated. So that the living space is very restricted. Lack of toilet facilities, cooking space, and bad ventilation are the other discouraging factors.

Large number of rag pickers suffers from dog bites, rat bites, jaundice, diarrhoea, skin problems, cut injuries, fever, cold and cough etc. are the typical illness for the waste pickers related to their working conditions. These may be referred as poverty oriented diseases.

The rag pickers can be called as poorest of the poor followed by the beggars. They are unhappy with this occupation. They have low income status and treated as outcasts. They are the garbage of the society. They are often considered as thieves in the upper income group residential areas. Hence they are hesitant to collect marketable items directly from the residential quarters. On the streets and market places conflicts occur mainly with the traders or with the stuff of the municipal conservancy service.

The rag pickers do not have their own premise for sorting and washing the materials, they use the public places. They use pavements, street, parks, green spaces, leads to a conflict of perception. The rag pickers are blamed for the filth. The activities related to sorting and washing of wastes contribute towards bad hygienic situations within crowded town. Thus the useful role of rag pickers is lost sight of.

The operated areas are dirty, offensive, and filthy.

Rag pickers are poor, illiterate and face the menace of malnutrition and suffer from severe diseases. They are often engaged by middlemen and are exploited economically by them. They are addicted to tobacco, alcohol and drugs. They have free sex with street walkers and hence become victims of aids.

The rag pickers are the soft target of those involved of child trafficking. The police exploit the rag pickers for they find it easy to register petty cases of theft etc. falsely. The health hazards faced by them are very acute. Most of them suffer from seasonal fever, malaria, and other skin ailments, T.B. due to very bad hygiene. The children became easy victims of all bad habits and become real criminal due to misuse may die at an early age for they are unaware of any health problems they face due to other profession . They do not know the means to save or use money properly they earn by rag picking.

The conditions are pathetic as the women struggle for offensive smells and smoke generated from mounds of garbage. The garbage catches fire due to heat generated by metal in the garbage and other rag pickers try to melt plastic and iron objects. The atmosphere becomes unbearly hot. During the rains of the monsoons the garbage becomes terrific. Then hurt their hands while handling kitchen garbage mixed with glass pieces, sharp metal and even razor blades in other occupational hazards.

Rag picking is the most hazardous, debasing and worst form of Labour. They are afraid of every one and do not trust any one outside their profession. They work from dawn to dusk. They have to cover long distances with their weights lack of means of transportation is the big problem. They no time for education, recreation, and game. They visit hotels in the night to collect left over food for them and families. Some of them work as casual Labour in the day and rag picking in the evening, which is risky because they may be caught by police and are kept in the lock up. They are faced with verbal and sexual abuse. The basic reason for entering to this job is extreme poverty coupled with lack of resources, education and knowledge. They also work as beggar and pros. There is always a chance to be caught red handed and are beaten up for steeling wastes from hospitals, which can be sold at higher prices. The most common illness are ear, throat, infection, spinal pain, rashes, skin related problems, fever, headache and cough. Majority of the sexual abusers are policemen, shopkeepers, chowkidars, old man and co-workers. People believe them as dirty person, they hate to socialize them. They feel inferity complex with fear, alienation and revenge.

The rag pickers reported higher prevalence for most awkward postures and ergonomic exposures, occupational hazards etc. The prevalence of low back pain, lower and upper extremity pain musculoskeletal pain are important diseases. The rag pickers are orphans or abandoned by parents. Gradually they take the drugs, drinking, smoking or fall to pimps and sex worker who exploit them. Most of them are affected by the sexually transmitted diseases.

The rag pickers face range of hazards and problems in the hostile physical and social environments where they survive. Burried by garbage, run over by garbage trucks, or bulldozers, subject ot smoke and flames while shifting to burning debris- all constitute risk associated with this work. The degree of vulnerability depends on age and physical ability.

8. Rehabilitation and Dvelopment of Economy of Rag Pickers

The above mentioned problems are to be tackled by means of rehabilitation programmes. As for example in some places the programmes for children rag pickers include non-formal education with meals at the educational centers, health check up, legal advice for the parents etc. are included.

An attempt should be made to intervene in to the waste trade to arrange for better working conditions and higher income for the child waste pickers.

Under the supervision of government and non government organization the children waste pickers will collect mainly marketable items, separated beforehand by the households and commercial houses. Then they will be helped to arrange proper storage and sale of recovered items. The waste pickers will get the profit.

An attempt should be made to have social advantages with the improved recovery of wastes. Increased underemployment among rag pickers can be balanced by the growing need for Labour in the expanding waste trade network and recycling industries. Another social gain is that they do not have to perform unhealthy work, which has low status. The NGO and the policy makers should extend their views to the well being and functioning of rag pickers.

Our government should collect taxes on the pretext of rehabilitation of rag pickers. In some places they get identity cards from the municipal corporation, set up co-operatives, intervene their difficulties with police and authorities and link them with government development schemes.

The se rag pickers should be provided formal employment, recognition and better condition to work in and those live in colonies need more cleanliness.

They should be trained to produce handbags by using recycled plastic. These plastics are scavenged from the rubbish heaps and sold to the cottage industries where such bags are produced. Some sympathetic social workers should help them with good guidance and protection.

The women rag pickers are to be organized and women associations should be made and then they should be trained to undertake environmental activities. They should be redesignated as neighbourhood sisters collect garbage, segregate them. These are then made compost. By making it they get steady income above minimum wage. They get dignity and self respect.

The rag pickers need periodic in service orientation programmes for health care personnel and they should be suggested some acceptable and affordable alternative measures for disposal of hospital wastes.

In Chennai 10,000 rag pickers in a year produce total value added about Rs. 6 crore, but the cost incurred by state and public through a rag picker is nil. By considering this vast help they should be properly, scientifically rehabilitated.

The arrangements may be made to provide group insurance cover. The rag pickers have formed a cooperative with its own depot where the members can market their recyclables direct eliminating intermediaries. The rag pickers may pool their savings to create self-help groups to have loans from different loan giving institution for self help group. Arrangement may be made for rag pickers and their children to have health care and service medical camps may be organized for pre and post natal care and planed parenthood.

They should be integrated with the mainstream of the society by providing them access to the houses, shops, and establishments. They should be successfully organized to the level of door step waste collectors by giving them proper training and accreditation.

Arrangement may be made to open a new school, hospital, rehabilitation centre, compulsory education system with some monetary help to these poor families and complete ban on waste collection by the children, let us hope for welfare state and civilized society.

The Nightingale institute for health and environment of USA provided eleven recommendations for their rehabilitation *(a)* clearly define their problem, *(b)* Focus on segregation, *(c)* Institute a sharp management system, *(d)* keep focus on reduction, *(e)* ensure rag pickers safety through education, training and proper personal protective equipment, *(f)* provide secure collection and transportation, *(g)* requires plans and policies, *(h)* investment in training and equipment for reprocessing of supplies, *(i)* investment in environmentally sound and cost effective medical waste treatment and disposal technologies, *(j)* develop an infrastructure for the safe disposal and recycling for hazardous materials and *(k)* develop an infrastructure for safe disposal of municipal solid waste.

There is a branch of French Government for relieving the necessities of rag pickers. According to the law the poor man had the right to demand charity of the states. The law is to allow the government discrenery power in dispensing charity. Under the present system prudence in combined with humanity.

All rag pickers in a particular locality should be brought together by the municipal authority's assigned areas of rehabilitation. They could also be given the task of picking up segregated wastes from house holds for which they could be paid fixed monthly amount by residents. The rag pickers could also be trained to do compositing and a certain amount from proceeds of the sale allotted to them.

Rag pickers get employment to produce vermicompost which is inexpensive. The rag pickers are connected with waste reduction to the income generation, public-private partnerships, entrepreneurships, and increased status. The activities of rag pickers clearly indicate an unnoticed an unacknowledged subsidy by the rag pickers to the government. Their activities are beneficial to the waste producer households and the civic agencies. It also benefits the compositing units by saving them from sorting out sizeable portions of the recyclables.

In some places rag pickers' education and development scheme were started with the aim of rehabilitation to the orphaned rag pickers. It is the home for the abandoned children and an institute to bring awareness to the rag pickers about their health, education etc. These rag pickers are either orphans or abandoned by parents or hail from poor families.

9. Conclusion

The poor rag pickers work with the dirty wastes to clean the environment so that the people can reside in unpolluted society.

The aged rag pickers are mostly illiterate, though earn relatively larger amount of monthly income, because some of them own land and cultivate their land. Besides, they who belong to relatively higher caste Hindu group are engaged in various low paid subsidiary occupations.

These aged rag pickers have come from longer distances and are engaged in this occupation for longer period of time. They also work over larger span of hours in a day, days in a month and months in a year.

They who are aged mostly collect paper, plastic, glass, battery, leather, cloth etc. variety of wastes. The rag pickers who own land prefer to collect metal and who earn considerable amount of monthly income collect paper, wastes largely.

The same aged rag pickers who own land and earn larger amount of monthly income sell income, metal and plastic wastes in higher prices.

The above aged rag pickers with land ownership and earning larger amount of monthly income manage to enjoy better quality of life as they are facilitated by electricity, drains, toilets, cooking places, ventilation etc. facilities, where as other suffer from worse quality of life.

The rag pickers do not have fixed income, so that the amount of food they get each day may vary, which makes them under and mal nourished. They work with nasty odourful wastes which cause their severe health hazards. They are considered as untouchables and the ladies are often used to meet the sex hunger of males. They search and eat food from the same dumping ground from where cattle, dog, cat, pig, rat etc. animals get their food.

Therefore, the clubs, government and non-government organizations should attempt to rehabilitate them and to develop their economy by providing education, proper employment nutrias food, health check up, legal advice, better working environment and alike aspects.

REFERENCES

Bhattacharyya. M. and Sen. N. (1991) : "A socio-economic study on the rag picker children in Calcutta", prepared foe Tiljala Society for Human and Educational Development, Calcutta

Bose. A., and Blore, I (1993) : "The economics of solid wastes management in Calcutta", Nagarlok-Urban affairs quarterly, Centre for Urban Studies, IIPA, Vol. 25, No. 2, p 32.

Direct initiative for social and health action (Disha) (1996) : "A rapid assessment survey of the health and environmental impacts of solid wastes recycling", Calcutta.

Ekta Ecological Foundation (EEF) (1995) : " Solid wastes disposal and public participation in the city of Calcutta", Study Report Calcutta.

Forum of communities united in service (Focus) (1992) : "Historical background of rag picking in Calcutta and socio-economic analysis of solid wastes management in Calcutta", Research paper, Calcutta (unpublished).

Furedy, Ch. and Alamgir M. (1992) : Case study 1–"Street pickers in Calcutta slums", Environment and Urbanization, Vol. 4, No. 2, Oct. 1992.

Ghosh, A.K. (1988) : "Urban ecology–A case study of Calcutta," Institute of local government and urban studies, Government of West Bengal–ILGUS (ed.), Calcutta.

Hunt. C. (1994) : "Child waste pickers in India, the occupation and its health risk", Environment and Urbanization, Vol. 4, No. 2, October, London, pp. 111-118.

Huysman. M. (1994) : "Waste picking as a survival strategy for women in Indian cities", Environment and Urbanization, Vol. 4, No. 2, October , London pp 155-174.

Mukherji, S. (1994) : "Marginal population in Calcutta and their future", Calcutta (unpublished).

Venkateswaran, S. (1994) : "The wealth of waste–waste pickers", Solid wastes and urban development, Friedrich Ebert Stiftung, F.R. Germany.

4

Poverty and Health in Jharkhand : Some Issues

—*Sujit Kumar Paul, Banasree Das*

1. Introduction

Social services are important component of public sector outlays on account of their role in human resource development and in raising the quality of life of the deprived sections of society. The most important factors, which lead to human resource development, are health, education, nutrition, sanitation, hygiene, and social welfare, improved socio economic opportunity with regard to under privileged sections of society. In developing countries like India a large segment of the population is poor and is unable to buy the services at market prices.

Health is of paramount importance as a national asset and basis to sustain as well as stimulate optimum levels of efficiency. Health is a prerequisite for increasing productivity. Health and nutrition do affect employment, productivity, wages and substantially so among the poorest of the poor. It has a significant impact on income levels as well. Mass poverty is one of the major problems in India. Poverty is more deep rooted covering several interlocked aspects such as under employment, low income, illiteracy and proneness to diseases.

Poverty and health is a very closely related word. Poverty is a very important cause for poor health and the poor health has an impact on poverty. Due to low income or poverty, people are unable to access all kind of health facilities which is require. On the other hand due to poor health, people become unable to work hard and earn money for their basic needs.

On the above background, the objectives of the study are to find out the relationship between the health and poverty, the causes of those two factors and present status of the study area.

2. Study Area

Jharkhand has a population of 26.90 million, consisting of 13.86 million males and 13.04 million females. The sex ratio is 941 females to 1000 males. The population consists of 28% tribals, 12% Scheduled Castes and 60% others. There are 274 persons for each square kilometer of land. However, the population density varies considerably from as low as 148 per square kilometer in Gumla district to as high as 1167 per square kilometer in Dhanbad district. Around 10% of the population is Bengali speaking and 70% speak various dialects of Hindi.

The santhal pargana division in Jharkhand is the north-eastern fringe of the Vindyan Plateau, comprising six districts Dumka, Sahebganj, Pakur, Deogharh, Jamtara and Godda. The Jamtara district of Santhal Pargana is one of the backward districts in Jharkhand. This district is selected keeping in view the predominance of tribal population. The study is undertaken in the 43 villages of 4 panchayats of the Jamtara District. In this area the total population is 12817 from the 2197 households. The male and female population of this area is 6492 and 6325 respectively. The children up to 5 years of age are 2556. Out of 12817 population scheduled caste is 1941, Muslim is 1976, General caste is 495, others is 247 and the tribal are dominated with population of 8158. The study area is tribal dominated and interior area. The population is very much scattered. The villages are covered by forest and surrounded by the rivers.

3. Background of the Study

Duladih, Supaidih, Saharpura, Dakhinbhal panchayats of Jamtara District of Jharkhand State are taken as the study area.

The villages are very interior and tribal dominated. Other castes are very nominal. Muslim and Scheduled caste people are staying in separate hamlets. Caste consciousness is very high in the study area. The higher caste people keep distance from the lower caste people. Some general caste people are engaged in business. The literacy rate is very low. The male literacy rate is near about 30 per cent. Female literacy rate is less than 15 per cent. Only 3 ladies are graduate from the entire study are. The age of marriage among the girls is less than 18 years, which is the common cause of health problem. Divorce is very prominent in the tribal society in this area. After the child birth the parents are get separated and the child become helpless and had to depend on their grandmother or grandfather or sometime other relatives. All kinds of development facilities are minimal. Agriculture is the main source of income. Near about 90% families have less than 2 ha. of land. Land is largely unproductive due to undulating and unfertile and also erratic nature of rainfall. The per centage of BPL families is 72%. Due to poor agricultural facilities the income level is very low. Farmers often have to take cash or kind loan from the local moneylenders who trap them with their heavy rate of interest. Beside the agriculture, collection of forest product is an important addition to their income. Generally tribal people collect various kinds of forests product like fire wood, honey, leaf etc. but at the present time huge deforestation creating problem on collecting these kinds of the products, which also influencing their economy. Most important thing of this area is heavy alcoholic intake, which is the main cause of both the poor health and poverty.

The study area is very much tribal dominated but cultivation is the main and common occupation. Most of the people are engaged in cultivation but near about 90 per cent of the people do not have enough land for cultivation. Some people are engaging in other kinds of occupation like rickshaw pulling, animal rearing, fishing, vegetable vendering etc. Some upper caste people are engaged in various kinds of business in the nearest district town Jamtara. Apart from the cultivation most of the people work as a casual labourer in the nearest market as a secondary engagement. Sometime they migrate to the outside of their state as a casual labourer.

The income is lesser than the expenditure. The people of the study area spend their money in food, cloth, transport, medicine, education, entertainment and others (festivals, alcohol etc.). At the time of study, PRA was used for data collection. Through the PRA the local participants informed that their other mode of expenditure is higher than all kind of expenditure. If they earn rupees 100 at the end of the day they spent 60-70 rupees in alcohol and other addiction. And the rest 30 rupees used for food and other necessaries. Tribal and scheduled caste male and female both are alcoholic but the Muslims and general caste people also take alcohol but women keep distance from alcohol. They don't have any savings practice though the Self Help Group (SHG) formation project is running by government as well as non-government organizations. But due to irregular saving practices the SHGs are not sustaining. Due to lack of savings at the time of need they have to take loan from the local moneylender with high rate of interest. Some times the rate of interest goes up to the 180-200 per cent. After taking loan they could not release themselves from the trap of moneylender and their maximum part of the income goes for repayment of loan.

As per the World Food Programme and MS Swaminathan Foundation the food insecurity issue in Jharkhand can be classified as follows :

Food availability	Extreme problem
Food Access	High problem
Food Insecurity	Extreme problem
Food absorption and utilization	Extreme problem
Environmental sustainability	Moderate problem

(*Source* : Health and development challenges, VHAI).

This is also the common feature in the study area. Poor health and the poverty both are correlated in the study area. 72% of people are BPL. Their average annual income is 12000.

Due to low income and large family size most of the people are unable to take enough nutritious food in their daily diet.

There are lots of causes identified for poverty. Some causes of poverty are vital which are given below :

1. Lack of enough cultivable land for agriculture.
2. Large family size.
3. Huge loan from local moneylender with high rate of interest.
4. Large portion of the income spent on addiction like alcohol, *gutka* etc.
5. Unavailability of government facilities.
6. Lack of higher technology for good production from the agriculture.
7. Very low literacy rate.
8. Belief in superstitions.
9. Suffering from various kinds of diseases, which decrease the workability.
10. Lack of saving practices.
11. Oftenly cheated by the sly businessman.

3. Problems of Health

The health status of the study area is very poor. The main cause of poor health is high level of morbidity and mortality, resulting from extensive malnutrition emanating out of lack of adequate nutrients in their daily food intake. Prolonged iron deficiency leads to anemia. Anemia is the most common cause of maternal deaths accounting to a fifth of all maternal deaths. Severe anemia accounts for 20.3% of maternal deaths. The risk of dying due to hemorrhage and infection is five to ten times greater in anemic woman as compared to non-anemic women. Anemia among women also causes infant deaths by contributing to intra uterine growth retardation, low birth weight and ultimate natal mortality. From the following table we can imagine the anemic condition of the area.

Prevalence of Anemia in Jharkhand

	General Population	*ST Population*
Mild	44.3%	43.9%
Moderate	28.6%	38.6%
Severe	1.8%	3.1%

Source : NFHS 2

Further, they have belief in magical practices by the Ojha for cure of any aliment. They like to go to the Ojha at first then only to the doctor. Though there is a huge source of medicinal plants but they don't have that kind of technology for utilizing those plants and most of the time they do not use those plants properly which become sometime harmful. The health status of women and children is very poor among the tribals. The governmental health services is inadequate rather nonfunctional in the study area. The main problems are lack of proper diagnostic, preventive and curative measures in the area. In certain areas of Jharkhand, poverty and consequent malnutrition have given rise to diseases like tuberculosis (TB). In fact, TB has assumed epidemic proportions in certain areas of the state. The study area is also facing this problem. The prevalence of asthma, tuberculosis, and malaria is much higher in rural areas. Near about 30 per cent suffered from malaria in a year, and 6 per cent suffered from various degree of jaundice during the year. The people of the study area are suffering from various kinds of diseases. Through the PRA we found the various diseases among the people of the area. These are – Anemia, Diarrhoea, Descentry, Malaria, Tuberculosis, Night Blindness, Typhoid, Leprosy, Various kinds of worm infections, Kala-azar, Jaundice, Flue, Various types of skin disease, Filaria, Liver enlargement, Viral infection etc.

Some health problems of the area pointed through this study is given below :

(1) The health status of women is very poor in the study area due to negligence against the women folk. A comprehensive list of task performed by the women.

The women perform 80% of the agricultural work or wage labourer activities with 100% of household work.

(2) Maternal Mortality rate is 400/100000. Nearly 82 per cent delivery takes place at home by local Daimaa. Due to the poor government health facilities and lack of awareness about the delivery system among the women as well as the men, the untrained birth attendant takes responsibility of delivery. At the time of delivery they do not follow the proper hygienic methods.

(3) About 72.9% mothers are suffering from various degrees of Anemia. At the time of pregnancy and after childbirth the mother does not receive nutritious food. Some time they are unable to take and some time they just ignore the problems of anemia due to lack of awareness.

(4) Infant Mortality Rate is about 70 per 1000 live birth. Due to unsafe birth practice the IMR is higher in this area. Untrained Dai takes the responsibility of birth. Some time they uses unhygienic method at the time of birth, like they some times uses the spit at the time of child separation from the mothers body, they also use the bamboo stick for cutting the umbilical artery etc.

(5) Mal nutrition is a major problem of this area. About 49% of children in the age group of 3-35 months are chronically malnourished. Due to large family size and low income of the family the food intake are insufficient for the children. The children are not getting any nutritious food for their health.

(6) Only 8% of the children are fully immunized. Superstition and lack of awareness among the people of the study area is a major cause for poor immunization. The parents are unwilling to immunize their children. They think that this immunization is the major cause of the various kinds of diseases.

(7) Water-borne diseases are very common in this area. Nearly 80% people of the area suffer from the water borne diseases, which are largely attributed to unsafe

drinking water. The villages are suffering from the various kinds of water born diseases like diarrhoea, jaundice etc. there is no safe drinking water in the villages. The tube wells are also not running properly. Some time water is highly contaminated with fluoride.

4. Causes of Health Problem

There are various causes of health problems in the study area. Through PRA, we have identified numerous problems for their poor health, which is given below :

(1) Belief in superstition and traditional healers—The local people initially depend on Ojhas but when the situation become critical, they go to nearer health centres for medical treatment.

(2) Lack of awareness among the people on health preventive measures—They do not know about the health care system and totally ignore their health condition.

(3) Lack of safe drinking water—Most of the time they drink pond-water, and also use this water for cooking and household activities which is highly contaminated and a major cause of various kinds of diseases like diarrhoea, descentry etc.

(4) Poor nutritional intake by children and women—Due to poor economy most of the time women has to sacrifice their food. At the time of pregnancy they get insufficient food so the result is malnourished childbirth.

(5) Consumption of liquor in abundance – Almost 95 per cent population of this study consumes liquor. One side of this becomes a reason of poverty and family problem and another side it creates health hazards.

(6) Poor access of health facilities—The villages of the study area are very scattered and small in size so the average distance of Sub Health center from a village is 5-6 km. Not only that the condition of the Sub Health Centres is very poor.

(7) Unsafe delivery practices—Most of the time the local people prefer to deliver their child with the help of Dai Maa. Maximum dai maas are untrained. So after delivery, mother and child both suffer from various kinds of health problems.

(8) Unable to get costly medical services—Due to low income and poor economy most of the time the local people become unable to receive costly medicine for their health.

5. Poverty and Health

Poverty and poor health are creating problems for the development on the rural people in the study area. Poverty in its various forms represents a barrier to communication and access to services, as well as a major health risk and people living in poverty are vulnerable to the consequences of disasters and conflicts. Absolute poverty is a condition characterized by severe deprivation of basic human needs including food, safe drinking water, sanitation, health, shelter and education. Poverty and health not only depend on income but also on access to social services. Due to poverty, the people are unable to get proper health services. That is why, they again and again suffer from various kinds of diseases and their health becomes poorer and poorer.

A schematic representation is given below to understand the poverty and healthcare :

There is only one Block Primary Health Center, 6 Sub centers and 24 Integrated Child Development Centers for giving health assistance to the villagers of 43 villages. The women being anemic and in the absence of proper food and nutrition a large part of the work force lacks effectiveness. Child mortality rate is very high. Ill health is responsible for premature deaths and low level of life expectancy. Various kinds of diseases are also responsible for poor health.

Most of the children are malnourished due to unavailability of nutritious food. At the time of pregnancy most of the women had to perform hard work for their livelihood. They don't take

Attribute	*Community and Family oriented constrains to self care*	*Problem*	*Consequences*
Kowledge	Low Literacy and low knowledge of caring practices among the poor, particularly women	Low accessibility of technical information	Low demand for key services
Empowerment	Household allocation unfavourable to women and children and poor	No control over the socially powerful providers	Low decision making power of poor particularly women
Affordability	Low affordability of safe drinking water, food and other basic needs especially health care	Low affordability of basic needs due to poor health and poverty	Suffer in various problems
Availability of human resources	Community leaders and political leaders and influential persons resist change	Poor-rich region, rural-urban region imbalance in quaified human resources	Poor quality service delivery
Governance	Capture of services by the richer group people	Lack of transparency in financing of health facilities and government programme	Poor programme, automatically depend on other for development

any rest or nutritious food. As a result, most of them suffer from chronic anemia. Due to untrained birth practices neonatal death rate is very high in this area. Women are not aware of pre-natal and postnatal care. Moreover the non-availability of Government health services in the villages compounds the problem. Men too, on the other, hand are illiterate and ignorant as their women folk are. The heavy alcohol intake makes the problem more acute. Due to poverty men migrate to nearby cities for work. When they come back, they bring with them not only some money, but also some infections, which are transferred, to the innocent women at home. Most of the families are in the hard grip of local moneylender (mahajans). Sometime moneylender takes the crop from the field as his interest. The work opportunity is very low in this area for both men and women. Majority of the rural people are found in vast rural and urban un-organized sector as landless workers and petty sharecroppers in the agriculture sector and as contractual wage-labourers in mining and construction sectors and also as domestic help. As per 2001 Census, only 37.64 per cent people are workers (main and marginal) and the rest *i.e.*

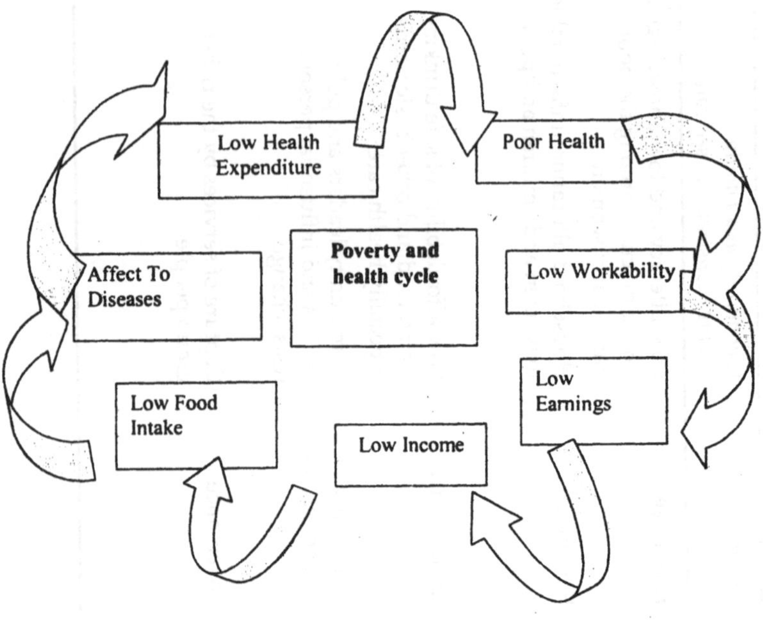

62.36 per cent are non-workers in the state. The situation of the study area is almost the same. The condition of the female workforce is also not satisfactory. As per the available data only 31.7% of the women have been employed in any form in past 12 months. More than 90% of this employment has been in the unorganized sector mainly comprising of Agriculture and daily wages. Women get comparatively low wages than the men folk. Thus poverty is adding to the existing health woes of the people in the study area. In a way it can be said that poverty and poor health are complementing each other making more and more people vulnerable.

A poverty and health cycle has been represented below for batter understanding the relationship between poverty and health.

6. Conclusion

It is said that health is wealth. But in the study area health and wealth, both are eluding the rural people. Poverty and health is very closely related to each other. Poverty is a vital cause for poor health and the poor heath has an impact on poverty. Due to poor health the people are unable to work hard, which is very necessary for earning the money, on the other hand, due to low income the people cannot afford their minimal medical expenditure. Poverty and lower level of literacy particularly among the women has led to alarming health status of women and children. Infant and mother mortality is very high in this area. Inspite of the work taken up by Government and NGOs the problem still remain and the people are unable to come out from this situation. While the government has made some effective efforts to develop the health care infrastructure but it lacks adequate positive interests from both political and administrative levels. A comprehensive perspective planning and implementation of different issues related to health and poverty may be taken up through appropriate authorities in collaboration with NGOs, institutions etc. Required fund, infrastructure, manpower may be made available on priority basis from State, National or any other possible sources. The local social institutions must come forward with definite mission and vision in all round development activities of the locality. To eradicate the poverty and establish a healthy society everybody needs to play his or her respective roles.

REFERENCES

Health and Nutritional Services : *World Development Report*, 2004

Human Development Report of Jharkhand, 2001.

Kamalakannan, K. (2006) : Rural Industrialisation and Poverty Alleviation; *Kurukshetra*–A Journal on Rural Development (May, 2006), Vol. 54, No. 7.

Kaptan, Sanjay S. & Pimpale, Vinita (2005) : Medical Tourism; *Yojana*, July 2005, Vol- 49.

Ojha, Rabindra Nath (2006) : National Rural Health Mission; *Kurukshetra*, A Journal on Rural Development (June, 2006), Vol. 54, No. 8.

Paul, Sujit Kumar & Paul, Kakali (2006) : Health Care System among the Tribals–The Shifting Paradigm through Self Help Group. *Health for the Millions*, Vol. 32 No. 2, July-August 2006.

Verma K.K., 1992 : Health Care and Family Welfare, Mittal Publications, New Delhi, 110059 (India).

5

Is Socioeconomic Status Protective of Health? Some Evidence from Rural Udaipur

—*Sudeshna Maitra*

1. Introduction

The link between socioeconomic status (SES) and health outcomes and the mechanisms that drive the relationship have important implications for health policy. Hence the nature of the health-SES relationship has received substantial attention in the economic literature. There is a large literature documenting the protective effect of socioeconomic status on health outcomes, also known as the (positive) health-SES 'gradient' (Adler (1994), Smith (1999)). This is backed by evidence that the effect can work in both directions – the effect of SES on health (Case-(2004), Lleras-Muney (2005)) and that of health on SES (Thomas (2003)). At the same time, there is also evidence of people with high SES reporting worse health outcomes (Chen and Murray (1992), Sen (2002)).

The multidimensionality of health makes it a challenge to find an appropriate measure of overall health. The studies mentioned above use different health outcomes to study the health-SES relationship–*e.g.* mortality rates (Lleras-Muney (2005)), iron deficiency (Thomas (2003)) – many of which may fail to provide a complete picture of the overall health of a living respondent. Several studies (Smith (1999)) use 'self-reported health status' (SRHS) as an indicator of overall health. This is an integer – typically, on a scale of 1 to 10, with higher numbers denoting better health—which each respondent is asked to report to describe her overall condition of health. Self-reported health status has been found to be highly predictive of health outcomes such as subsequent morbidity and mortality (Strauss and Thomas (1998)), and is increasingly being used as a measure of overall health.

Banerjee, Deaton and Duflo (2004a, b) use data from a recent survey conducted in rural Udaipur, Rajasthan, to find that respondents report surprisingly optimistic figures of self-reported health status (compared with reports from developed countries) for individuals who are not only among the poorest of the poor but are also far from enjoying good health as indicated by certain health measurements (*e.g.* BMI, peak flow meter readings of lung capacity etc.). While the finding is puzzling, this anomaly could be the result of many factors including environmental factors–such as a different perception of what 'good' health ought to comprise–that vary across different countries and societies. It is therefore meaningful to examine the relationship between SES and health *within* the respondents of the survey. Since the respondents belong to the same environment they are more likely to share a common perception or awareness of health.

In this paper, I examine if socioeconomic status (SES) – measured by per capita monthly non-health household expenditure–is protective of health among the respondents of the Banerjee–Deaton-Duflo survey conducted in Udaipur. Specifically, I use respondents' reports of experiencing various symptoms–*e.g.* colds, night sweats and diarrhoea–to estimate if increased SES is associated with a lower probability of reporting the more 'serious' conditions, defined as symptoms that have a more adverse effect on self-reported health. I call this effect the *symptoms effect* since it operates through the probability of reporting symptoms. I define the *direct effect* as the association of SES and health (measured by self-reported health status) after controlling for the symptoms. The direct effect may be interpreted as the relationship between SES and health among individuals who experience the same symptoms. Some factors that could drive the direct effect are access to better health care or better nutritional status and personal behaviours (such as better disease management) of individuals with higher SES. Banerjee, Deaton and Duflo report a positive relationship between SES and self-reported health status in the sample. This paper presents a more structured approach for estimating the relationship between health and SES by individually estimating the direct component and the symptoms-driven components of the SES-health relationship.[1]

I find two contradictory patterns in the relationship between health and SES depending on whether the channel of operation is direct or symptoms-driven. I find that the protective effect of SES on health through the direct channel increases with the level of SES. However, the exact opposite pattern holds for the symptoms effect. While increased SES is associated with a lower probability of reporting serious conditions at low levels of SES (*i.e.* the symptoms effect is positive) this effect decreases in magnitude at higher levels of SES. At the 75th per centile the symptoms effect becomes negative indicating that higher SES increases the probability of reporting the more serious conditions. Hence, the symptoms-driven effect of SES on health becomes less protective at higher levels of SES. However, all estimates are small and fail to be statistically significant.

The rest of the paper is organized as follows. In the next section, I provide a brief account of the data I use, along with a summary of variables relevant to this analysis. In Section III, I

---

1. Note that the mechanisms that drive the associations between SES and health could operate from SES to health (*e.g.* if higher SES enables access to better healthcare) as well as from health to SES (*e.g.* if better health leads to less days absent from work and hence more income). The 'protective effect of SES on health' could, therefore, be indicative of causal links in both directions (SES to health *and* health to SES).

outline the econometric model that I shall estimate, describing how the coefficients may be interpreted as direct and symptoms effects. Section IV reports and interprets the results I obtain and Section V summarizes and concludes the paper.

2. Data

The data was collected in 2002-03 from 100 hamlets in Udaipur district in Rajasthan, India. The sample is stratified by access to road, and hamlets within each stratum are selected randomly, with the probability of selection being proportional to the population of the hamlet. There are four components of the data – a village survey describing each village's physical infrastructure; a facility survey describing all public facilities serving the sample villages; a weekly visit to all public facilities checking for absenteeism of health care providers; and a household and individual survey of 5759 individuals in 1024 households.[2] I have used data on adults from the individual survey. The sample size is 2515 adults.

Summary statistics of variables are listed in Table A. A close look at the SES and health variables suggests that on average respondents appear to be doing well in health outcomes despite their poverty. For example, per capita monthly non-health expenditure is not very high in the sample; it ranges from Rs. 74 to Rs. 5522 with a mean of Rs. 419[3]. However, when respondents are asked to describe their own health using a number between 1 and 10 (with higher numbers denoting better health) the mean number reported is 6. This mean value of self-reported health status is comparable to those found for respondents from developed countries (Banerjee, Deaton and Duflo (2004a, b)). This apparently anomalous finding provides the motivation to further explore the relationship between

---

2. See Banerjee, Deaton; Duflo (2004a, b) for further details of the design of the survey.

3. Per capita *aggregate* monthly expenditure includes health expenditure, which is likely to be higher in households with sicker respondents. Per capita monthly *non-health* expenditure is therefore used as a measure of SES.

Table A : Summary Statistics of Variables

Variable	*Obs.*	*Mean*	*Std. Dev.*	*Min.*	*Max.*
1	2	3	4	5	6
Self-reported health status	2077	5.953	2.199	1	10
Indicator for 'Female'	2515	0.546	0.498	0	1
Age	2515	36.330	15.687	14	90
Education Dummies :					
Illiterate	2515	0.740	0.439	0	1
Literate, but unschooled	2515	0.008	0.089	0	1
Max. Completed Class: 1-10	2515	0.229	0.420	0	1
Max. Completed Class: 11-12	2515	0.010	0.099	0	1
Graduate or above/ Diploma	2515	0.013	0.112	0	1
Per capita monthly expenditure (non-health)	2514	418.64	309.56	74.00	5522.29
SES: Log per capita monthly expenditure (non-health)	2514	5.87	0.54	4.30	8.62
Squared SES: Squared log per capita monthly expenditure (non-health)	2514	34.79	6.53	18.52	74.24
Symptom Dummies					
Cold	2515	0.330	0.470	0	1
Dry cough	2515	0.199	0.399	0	1
Productive cough	2515	0.109	0.312	0	1
Blood in cough	2515	0.012	0.107	0	1
Blood in spit	2515	0.009	.095	0	1
Fever	2515	0.322	0.468	0	1
Diarrhoea	2515	0.157	0.364	0	1
Bodyache	2515	0.418	0.493	0	1
Fatigue	2515	0.229	0.420	0	1
Vision problems	2515	0.138	0.345	0	1
Headache	2515	0.420	0.494	0	1
Backache	2515	0.328	0.470	0	1
Vomit	2515	0.092	0.289	0	1

1	2	3	4	5	6
Worms	2515	0.031	0.172	0	1
Breathlessness	2515	0.074	0.262	0	1
Upper abdominal pain	2515	0.231	0.422	0	1
Lower abdominal pain	2515	0.122	0.327	0	1
Genital ulcers	2515	0.014	0.116	0	1
Painful urination	2515	0.096	0.295	0	1
Swollen ankless	2515	0.015	0.120	0	1
Hearing problems	2515	0.035	0.184	0	1
Skin problems	2515	0.033	0.178	0	1
Chest pain	2515	0.111	0.314	0	1
Memory loss	2515	0.015	0.120	0	1
Paralysis	2515	0.006	0.080	0	1
Night sweats	2515	0.029	0.168	0	1
Weight loss	2515	0.112	0.315	0	1
Other' problems	2515	0.073	0.260	0	1
Menstrual problems (Women only)	1374	0.060	0.238	0	1
White discharge (Women only)	1374	0.084	0.274	0	1
Total number of symptoms experienced	2515	3.838	3.729	0	22

socioeconomic status (SES)—as measured by log per capita non-health expenditure–and health outcomes, in this sample.

Respondents are asked about 30 different symptoms – such as cold, wet cough, dry cough, blood in cough, fever–and whether they have experienced these symptoms in the last 30 days. The total number of symptoms experienced in the last 30 days could serve as an alternative indicator of health. This indicator ranges between 0 and 22 in the sample with a mean of approximately 4, indicating that respondents in the survey do well on average even by this alternative health measure. Note that the symptoms are all easily identifiable conditions that respondents can observe on their own without the help of medical practitioners. Hence there is no reason to expect an under-reporting of symptoms based on lack of health knowledge or poor access to health care, both of which could be associated with low SES.

Figures A(i) and A(ii) present the predicted values of health outcomes from locally weighted regressions (Lowess plots) of health on log per capita non-health expenditures (SES). Some very interesting patterns emerge from these figures. Figure A(i) shows a positive relationship between SRHS and SES. However, the relationship between the total number of experienced symptoms and SES is clearly U-shaped in the region where most observations lie (Figure A(ii)). This suggests that at low levels of SES, an increase in SES leads to a decrease in the number of symptoms experienced. However, at high levels of SES the pattern is reversed, i.e. an increase in SES leads to an increase in the total number of symptoms.

The U-shaped pattern in Figure A (ii) is puzzling as it suggests that at high levels of SES, it ceases to be protective of health and could even be associated with a worsening of health. However, the U-shaped pattern could still be consistent with SES being protective of health if the symptoms that are reported by wealthier respondents are less 'serious' than the ones reported by poorer agents. I define the 'seriousness' of a condition by the (negative) effect it has on self-reported health. The objective of this paper is to estimate if SES has a protective effect on health by lowering the probability of experiencing the more serious conditions, as defined above. The model that formally captures this idea is described in the next section.

3. The Model

This section outlines the econometric model I use to estimate the effect of SES on SRHS via the reporting of symptoms.

Consider the following model :

$$y = \alpha + \beta_1 X + \beta_2 X^2 + \beta_3^1 D_1 + \ldots + \beta_3^n D_n + \beta_4 Z + \varepsilon \qquad \ldots (1)$$

Figure A(i): Self-Reported Health Status (1-10) and SES

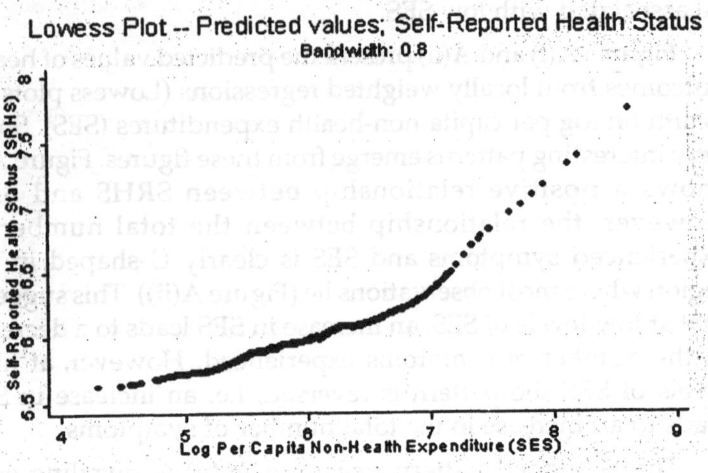

Figure A(ii): Total Number of Symptoms (out of 30) and SES

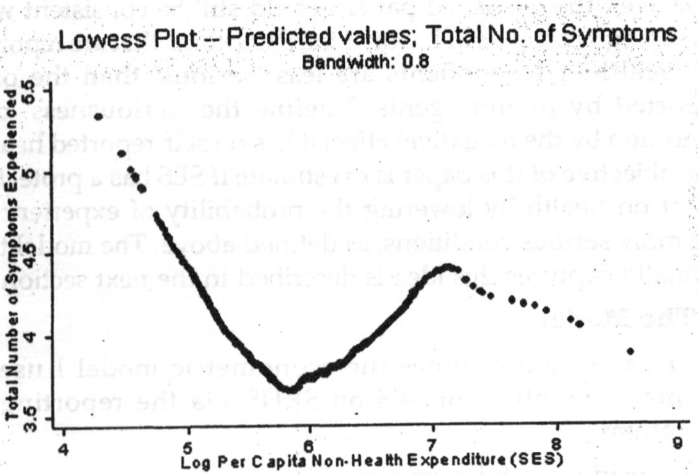

$$P(D_i = 1) = \gamma^i + \delta_1^i X + \delta_2^i X^2 + \delta_3^i Z + v_i \quad i = 1,\ldots, n \qquad \ldots (2)$$

where,

y: measure of overall health (self-reported health status)

X: SES (measured by log per capita monthly non-health expenditure)

D_i: indicator variable for symptom i, $i = 1,\ldots, n$

Z: controls for age, gender and education

I use self-reported health status as a measure of overall health (y) and log per capita monthly non-health expenditure as a measure of SES (X). The reason for using per capita *non-health* expenditure (instead of per capita aggregate expenditure) as a measure of SES is that health expenditure is likely to be higher in households with sicker respondents; hence including health expenditure in a measure of SES could drive the positive association between SES and health. I include a second-order SES term in both equations (1) and (2) to allow for non-linearities such as those present in Figures A *(i)* and A *(ii)*.

SES is said to be protective of health if higher SES is associated with better health. The association between SES and health can operate through two channels.

The first channel works through the association between SES and health after controlling for the presence of symptoms. I shall call this channel the *direct effect*. The direct effect may be interpreted as the relationship between SES and health among individuals who experience the same symptoms. Some factors that could drive the direct effect are access to better health care or the better nutritional status and personal behaviours (such as better disease management or less risky health behaviour such as smoking or drinking) of individuals with higher SES.

The second channel measures the relationship between SES and health via its impact on the probability of experiencing each symptom D_i. I shall call this effect the *symptom effect* of SES on health via the symptom D_i. The symptom effect via D_i incorporates the adverse effect on health of experiencing D_i as well as the impact of increased SES in reducing the probability of reporting D_i. The *total symptoms effect*—which is the sum of symptom effects for all symptoms—measures if higher SES is likely to reduce the probability of experiencing more 'serious' symptoms, viz. the symptoms that have an *adverse effect* on health. The total symptoms effect is the main focus of this paper as it enables us to determine if SES is protective of health at high levels of SES, despite the U-shaped relationship between SES and symptoms reported in Figure A(ii).

In the model represented by (1) and (2), the direct and symptom effects can be derived as follows. Using the Law of Iterated Expectations on (1) we obtain, for each symptom D_i,

$$E(y/X,Z,D_{-i}) = P(D_i = 1/X,Z)E(y/X,Z,D_{-i},D_i = 1) + P(D_i = 0/X,Z)E(y/X,Z,D_{-i},D_i = 0)$$

where $D_{-i} = (D_1,\ldots, D_{i-1}, D_{i+1},\ldots D_n)$

Then,

$$\frac{\partial E(y/X,Z,D_{-i})}{\partial X} = P(D_i = 1/X,Z)\frac{\partial E(y/X,Z,D_{-i},D_i = 1)}{\partial X}] + E(y/X,Z,D_{-i},D_i = 1)\frac{\partial P(D_i = 1/X,Z)}{\partial X} \quad \ldots (3)$$

$$+P(D_i = 0/X,Z)\frac{\partial E(y/X,Z,D_{-i},D_i = 0)}{\partial X} + E(y/X,Z,D_{-i},D_i = 0)\frac{\partial P(D_i = 0/X,Z)}{\partial X}$$

Let DE^i_X and SE^i_X denote the direct and symptoms effects of SES on health via D_i. Then (3) can be broken down into the direct and symptom effects as follows.

$$DE_X^i = P(D_i = 1/X, Z_1)\frac{\partial E(y/X, Z, D_{-i}, D_i = 1)}{\partial X}$$
$$+P(D_i = 0/X, Z_1)\frac{\partial E(y/X, Z, D_{-i}, D_i = 0)}{\partial X}$$

The direct effect measures the effect of SES on health among individuals who experience the same symptoms.

The symptom effect via D_i can be written as

$$SE_X^i = \frac{\partial P(D_i = 1/X, Z_1)}{\partial X}E(y/X, Z, D_{-i}, D_i = 1)$$
$$+\frac{\partial P(D_i = 0/X, Z_1)}{\partial X}E(y/X, Z, D_{-i}, D_i = 0)$$

Clearly, $\frac{\partial E(y/X, Z, D_{-i})}{\partial X} = SE_X^i + DE_X^i$

Since $P(D_i = 1/X, Z_1) + P(D_i = 0/X, Z_1) = 1$, we have, from (4) and (5),

$$DE_X^i = P(D_i = 1/X, Z_1)\left[\frac{\partial E(y/X, Z, D_{-i}, D_i = 1)}{\partial X} - \frac{\partial E(y/X, Z, D_{-i}, D_i = 0)}{\partial X}\right]$$
$$+\frac{\partial E(y/X, Z, D_{-i}, D_i = 0)}{\partial X} \quad \ldots (6)$$

$$SE_X^i = \frac{\partial P(D = 1/X, Z_1)}{\partial X}[E(y/X, Z, D = 1)$$
$$-E(y/X, Z, D = 0)] \quad \ldots (7)$$

Notice, from (7), that the symptom effect via D_i is the product of two terms. The first term is the change in the probability of reporting D_i due to increased SES. The second term is the impact of experiencing symptom D_i on expected overall health. For a symptom with an adverse impact on health on average, the second term is negative. In order to be protective of good health, higher SES would have to be associated with a lower probability of reporting such a symptom—that is, the first term would also have to be negative. Hence the product of the two terms–the symptom effect $SE^i{}_X$ —would be expected to be positive in sign, if SES is to have a protective effect on health via symptom D_i.

Applying equations (6) and (7) to the model represented by equations (1) and (2), we obtain,

$$DE^i_X = DE_X = \beta_1 + 2\beta_2 X \quad \text{... (8)}$$

$$IE^i_X = (\delta^i_1 + 2\delta^i_2 X)\beta^i_3 \quad \text{... (9)}$$

Further, by repeated use of the Law of Iterated Expectations on (2), it is possible to show that

$$\frac{\partial E(y/X,Z)}{\partial X} = \beta_1 + 2\beta_2 X + [\sum_{i=1}^{n} (\delta^i_1 + 2\delta^i_2 X)\beta^i_3] \quad \text{... (10)}$$

The bracketed term in equation (10) represents the *total symptoms effect* of SES on health for all the symptoms taken together. It is the sum of the individual symptom effect for each symptom D_i. A positive total symptoms effect will demonstrate that SES protects health by lowering the probability of experiencing symptoms that have an adverse effect on health. The component $(\hat{a}_1 + \hat{a}_2 X)$ in equation (10) represents the effect of SES on health among individuals who experience the same symptoms, *viz*. the direct effect.

The estimation strategy will be to run regressions (1) and (2) and estimate the direct and symptoms effects of SES on health, as derived in (8), (9) and (10). The next section reports the results obtained from this exercise.

4. Results

Table 1 reports the coefficients of interest from equation (1). The estimates of $\hat{a}_1$ and $\hat{a}_2$ – which define the direct effect – are both significant, the former negative and the latter positive in magnitude. This indicates that for individuals experiencing the same symptoms, an increase in SES at low levels of the same leads to a decline in self-reported health, whereas an increase in SES at high levels of the same leads to an improvement in self-reported health. The pattern seems to suggest that perception of health could be important in determining the level of self-reported health.[4] For instance, consistent with the observed relationship would be a situation in which an increase in income initially acts to increase the apprehension of ill health (due to an increased awareness of the implications of disease and due to higher expectations regarding health) lowering SRHS, but subsequently works to generate a perception of better health due to a greater ability to access better healthcare. The significance of the estimates of $\hat{a}_1$ and $\hat{a}_2$ points to the importance of future research on the effects of SES on health perception.

Table 1 also reports estimates of the coefficients $\hat{a}^i_3$ on the symptom dummies in equation (1). Of the thirty symptoms considered[5], twenty six are negatively associated with self-reported health. For ten of these twenty six symptoms the association with self-reported health (SRHS) is significant at the 5% level or less. These symptoms are (in decreasing order of magnitude of the coefficient) paralysis, fatigue, productive cough, dry cough, breathlessness, weight loss, 'other' symptoms, headache, fever and upper abdominal pain. Fatigue, weight loss and headaches (reported by 23%, 11% and 42% of the sample respectively[6]) indicate generally low nutrition status and poor overall health. This is confirmed by widespread iron deficiency and low Body Mass Index among adult respondents of this sample, as reported in Banerjee, Deaton and Duflo (2004a, b). Productive and dry coughs are reported by 11% and 20% of the sample respectively, and are indicative of respiratory illness, known to be the largest cause of death in the state of Rajasthan (Rajasthan Human Development Report, 2002).

4. The pattern could also be due to a concentration of unobserved health conditions at 'middle' levels of SES.

5. Respondents have been asked to report on 29 specific symptoms and 'other' symptoms and ailments.

6. See Table A.

Table 1 : Equation (I)–Linear Regression on Self-Reported Health Status, N=2077, R-squared = 0.28

Independent Variable	*Coefficient*	*Independent Variable*	*Coefficient*	*Independent Variable*	*Coefficient*
1	2	3	4	5	6
Female	-0.136 (0.101)	Cold	–0.009 (0.108)	Upper abdominal pain	–0.248* (0.115)
SES: Log per capita non-health expenditure	–2.435** (0.934)	Dry Cough	–0.499** (0.125)	Lower abdominal pain	–0.172 (0.139)
Squared SES:Squared log per non-health expenditure	0.127** (0.076)	Productive Cough	–0.582** (0.161)	Genital ulcers	–0.336 (0.35)
Literate, unschooled	0.206 (0.535)		–0.571 (0.442)		–0.27 (0.14)
Max. completed class : 1-10	0.324** (0.108)	Blood in spit	0.244 (0.552)	Swollen ankles	–0.388 (0.423)
Max. completed class : 11-12	0.671 (0.451)	Fever	–0.255* (0.108)	Hearing problems	0.093 (0.323)
Graduate or above/Diploma	0.961** (0.313)	Diarrahoea	0.073 (0.134)	Skin problems	–0.339 (0.258)

(Contd. . . .)

(contd. . . .)

1	2	3	4	5	6
		Bodyache	–0.195 (0.117)	Chest problems	–0.059 (0.159)
		Fatigue	–0.589** (0.13)		–0.021 (0.454)
		vision problems	–0.038 (0.149)	Paralysis	–1.359* (0.536)
		Headache	–0.316** (0.103)	Night sweats	–0.442 (0.285)
		Backache	–0.151 (0.118)	Weight loss	–0.353* (0.162)
		Vomit	0.031 (0.164)	Menstrual problems	–0.244 (0.281)
		Worms	–0.212 (0.309)	White discharge	–0.095 (0.208)
		Breathlessness	–0.461* –(0.188)	Other problems	–0.352* (0.153)

Robust standard errors in parentheses.
* significant at 5%; ** significant at 1%.
Age dummies included in regression, Omitted Education Category : Illiterate.

Table 2 : Equation (2)–Linear Regression on Individual Symptions

	Cold	Dry Cough	Productive Cough	Blood in Cough	Blood in Spit	Fever	Diarrhoea	Bodyache	Fatigue	Vision
	(1)	(2)	(3)	(4)	(5)	(6)	(7)	(8)	(9)	(10)
Female	–0.04	–0.098**	0.046**	–0.006	–0.002	0.048*	0.008	0.196**	0.053**	0.036*
	(0.021)	(0.018)	(0.014)	(0.005)	(0.004)	(0.022)	(0.017)	(0.022)	(0.018)	(0.014)
SES: Log per capita	–0.315	–0.04	–0.269	–0.003	0.014	–0.116	–0.19	–0.572*	–0.256	–0.059
non-health expenditure	(0.244)	(0.204)	(0.147)	(0.147)	(0.035)	(0.155)	(0.155)	(0.204)	(0.239)	(0.155)
Squared SES: Squared log per capita non-health expenditure	0.028	0.003	0.021	0.000	–0.002	0.012	0.015	0.049*	0.021	0.004
log per capita non-health expenditure	(0.02)	(0.017)	(0.012)	(0.003)	(0.003)	(0.02)	(0.015)	(0.02)	(0.018)	(0.013)
Literate, unschooled	0.123	0.229	–0.068**	–0.024*	–0.013	0.18	–0.181**	–0.366**	0.275	0.352
	(0.341)	(0.322)	(0.026)	(0.01)	(0.007)	(0.329)	(0.029)	(0.034)	(0.331)	(0.285)
Max. completed class: 1-10	0.057*	–0.021	–0.004	–0.005	0.009	0.001	–0.035	–0.028	0.017	0.025
	(0.027)	(0.023)	(0.016)	(0.006)	(0.006)	(0.026)	(0.02)	(0.026)	(0.022)	(0.016)

(Contd. . . .)

Table 2 : (contd. . .) Equation (2)–Linear Regression on Individual Symptoms

	Head-ache	*Backache*	*Vomit*	*Worms*	*Breath-lessness*	*Upper Abdominal Pain*	*Lower Abdominal Pain*	*Genital Ulcers*	*Painful urination*	*Swollen Ankles*
	(11)	(12)	(13)	(14)	(15)	(16)	(17)	(18)	(19)	(20)
Female	0.128**	0.131**	0.029*	–0.002	–0.016	0.078**	0.034*	0.018**	–0.024	0.017**
	(0.022)	(0.021)	(0.014)	(0.007)	(0.012)	(0.019)	(0.015)	(0.005)	(0.014)	(0.005)
SES: Log per capita	–0.476	–0.860**	–0.069	–0.176	–0.14	–0.524*	–0.247	–0.033	–0.082	–0.005
non-health expenditure	(0.245)	(0.245)	(0.145)	(0.093)	(0.132)	(0.23)	(0.179)	(0.05)	(0.127)	(0.051)
Squared SES: Squared log per capita non-health expenditure	0.039	0.072**	0.006	0.013	0.012	0.042*	0.021	–0.003	–0.006	0
	(0.02)	(0.02)	(0.012)	(0.008)	(0.011)	(0.019)	(0.015)	(0.004)	(0.01)	(0.004)
Literate, unschooled	0.103	0.19	–0.071**	–0.052**	–0.098**	–0.197**	-0.111**	–0.007	–0.129**	–0.002
	(0.356)	(0.35)	(0.02)	(0.013)	(0.036)	(0.037)	(0.024)	(0.008)	(0.02)	(0.008)
Max. completed class: 1-10	0.007*	–0.011	–0.004	–0.014	–0.003	0.006	–0.027	–0.005	–0.01	0.013*
	(0.028)	(0.025)	(0.016)	(0.008)	(0.015)	(0.023)	(0.017)	(0.006)	(0.017)	(0.007)
Max. completed class:	–0.005	–0.183**	0.025	0.026	0.029	–0.156**	0.075	–0.029	0.014	0.002
11-2	(0.101)	(0.053)	(0.061)	(0.044)	(0.054)	(0.035)	(0.083)	(0.031)	(0.062)	(0.004)

(Contd. . . .)

Table 2 : (contd. . .) Equation (2)–Linear Regression on Individual Symptoms

	Head-ache	*Backache*	*Vomit*	*Worms*	*Breath-lessness*	*Upper Abdominal Pain*	*Lower Abdominal Pain*	*Genital Ulcers*	*Painful urination*	*Swollen Ankles*
	(11)	(12)	(13)	(14)	(15)	(16)	(17)	(18)	(19)	(20)
Graduate or above/	0.138	0.039	–0.015	–0.022**	–0.001	–0.159**	–0.092*	–0.002	–0.034	0.025
Diploma	(0.094)	(0.08)	(0.048)	(0.008)	(0.041)	(0.039)	(0.038)	(0.005)	(0.048)	(0.024)
Observations	2514	2514	2514	2514	2514	2514	2514	2514	2514	2514
R-squared	0.03	0.05	0.01	0.02	0.05	0.03	0.01	0.01	0.01	0.02
F-stat (SES variables)	1.90	6.19**	0.15	3.76*	0.63	3.25**	1.00	0.32	0.23	0.49
(Prob > F)	(0.150)	(0.002)	(0.863)	(0.023)	(0.530)	(0.039)	(0.368)	(0.725)	(0.792)	(0.611)

Robust standard errors.
* significant at 5%, ** significant at 1%.
Age dummies in all regiessions. Omitted education category Illiterate.

(Contd. . . .)

Table 2 : (contd. . .) Equation (2)–Linear Regression on Individual Symptoms

	Hearing Problems	*Skin Problems*	*Chest Pain*	*Memory Loss*	*Paralysis*	*Night Sweats*	*Weight Loss*	*Menstrual Problems*	*White Discharge*	*Other Problems*
	(21)	(22)	(23)	(24)	(25)	(26)	(27)	(28)	(29)	(30)
Female	0.16	–0.003	0.007	–0.012*	–0.001	0.009	0.089**	0.059**	–0.084	–0.029*
	(0.009)	(0.009)	(0.015)	(0.006)	(0.003)	(0.007)	(0.013)	(0.007)	(0.008)	(0.012)
SES: Log per capita	–0.217*	–0.156	–0.15	–0.240*	–0.017	–0.059	–0.221	–0.039	–0.007	–0.101
non-health expenditure	(0.109)	(0.109)	(0.142)	(0.096)	(0.036)	(0.067)	(0.172)	(0.072)	(0.122)	(0.124)
Squared SES: Squared log per capita non-health expenditure	0.017*	0.012	0.01	0.020*	0.001	0.004	0.017	–0.003	–0.002	0.009
	(0.009)	(0.009)	(0.011)	(0.008)	(0.003)	(0.005)	(0.014)	(0.006)	(0.01)	(0.01)
Literate, unschooled	–0.043	–0.029**	–0.151**	0	–0.003	–0.029**	-0.088*	–0.006	–0.002	0.383
	(0.36)	(0.013)	(0.05)	(0.011)	(0.004)	(0.011)	(0.035)	(0.022)	(0.021)	(0.351)
Max. completed class: 1-10	0.006	0.025*	–0.007	–0.015*	0	0.012	0.031	0.005	0.005	0.006
	(0.009)	(0.012)	(0.017)	(0.006)	(0.003)	(0.01)	(0.017)	(0.01)	(0.01)	(0.016)

(Contd. . . .)

Table 2 : (contd. . .) Equation (2)–Linear Regression on Individual Symptoms

	Hearing Problems	*Skin Problems*	*Chest Pain*	*Memory Loss*	*Paralysis*	*Night Sweats*	*Weight Loss*	*Menstrual Problems*	*White Discharge*	*Other Problems*
	(21)	(22)	(23)	(24)	(25)	(26)	(27)	(28)	(29)	(30)
Max. completed class:	0.003	–0.023	–0.018	0.004	–0.003	–0.012	0.019	–0.030**	–0.032**	0.035
11 -12	(0.008)	(0.045)	(0.046)	(0.005)	(0.003)	(0.008)	(0.054)	(0.009)	(0.012)	(0.063)
Graduate or above/	0.056	0.043	0.016	0.035	0.02	0.022	0.005	–0.022*	–0.027**	0.171*
Diploma	(0.04)	(0.046)	(0.052)	(0.034)	(0.024)	(0.033)	(0.047)	(0.008)	(0.01)	(0.077)
Observations	2514	2514	2514	2514	2514	2514	2514	2514	2514	2514
R-squared	0.07	0.03	0.03	0.04	0.01	0.01	0.04	0.04	0.06	0.02
F-stat (SES variables)	2.02	1.15	2.35	3.57*	0.12	1.04	1.52	0.58	1.06	0.58
(Prob > F)	(0.133)	(0.316)	(0.095)	(0.028)	(0.885)	(0.354)	(0.219)	(0.561)	(0.346)	(0.560)

Robust standard errors.
* significant at 5%, ** significant at 1%.
Age dummies in all regiessions. Omitted education category Illiterate.

Table 3 : Direct and Symptom Effects

	At 25th percentile SES (=5.52)	*At 50th percentile SES (=5.82)*	*At mean of SES (=5.87)*	*At 75th percentile of SES (=6.22)*
	1	2	3	4
Direct Effect	–0.039 (0.116)	0.091 (0.089)	0.113 (0.085)	0.264*** (0.082)
Total Sypotoms Effect	0.081 (0.058)	0.060 (0.042)	0.050 (0.040)	–0.017 (0.043)
Cold	0.000 (0.003)	0.000 (0.003)	0.000 (0.003)	0.000 (0.005)
Dry Cough	0.003 (0.012)	0.003 (0.009)	0.002 (0.009)	0.001 (0.009)
Productive Cough	0.022* (0.012)	0.014 (0.009)	0.013 (0.009)	0.005 (0.008)
Blood in Cough	0.002 (0.005)	0.002 (0.004)	0.002 (0.004)	0.002 (0.003)
Blood in Spit	–0.002 (0.005)	–0.002 (0.004)	–0.002 (0.004)	–0.003 (0.005)
Fever	–0.004 (0.008)	–0.006 (0.006)	–0.006 (0.006)	–0.008 (0.006)
Diarrhoea	–0.002 (0.005)	–0.001 (0.003)	–0.001 (0.003)	0.000 (0.003)
Bodyache	0.006 (0.007)	0.0060 (0.005)	–0.001 (0.004)	–0.007 (0.006)
Fatigue	0.014 (0.015)	0.007 (0.011)	0.006 (0.011)	–0.003 (0.011)
Vision	0.001 (0.003)	0.000 (0.003)	0.000 (0.003)	0.000 (0.002)
Headache	0.014 (0.010)	0.007 (0.007)	0.006 (0.007)	–0.003 (0.007)
Backache	0.010 (0.010)	0.003 (0.005)	0.002 (0.004)	–0.005 (0.006)
Vomit	0.000 (0.003)	0.000 (0.002)	0.000 (0.002)	0.000 (0.002)
Worms	0.007 (0.010)	0.005 (0.007)	0.005 (0.007)	0.003 (0.004)

(Contd. . . .)

1	2	3	4	
Brathessness	0.003 (0.008)	0.0030 (0.006)	0.0030 (0.005)	–0.004 (0.006)
Upper Abdominal Pain	0.015* (0.009)	0.009 (0.006)	0.008 (0.006)	0.000 (0.005)
Lower Abdominal Pain	0.003 (0.004)	0.0030 (0.003)	0.0030 (0.003)	–0.002 (0.004)
Genital Ulcers	0.000 (0.004)	0.001 (0.003)	0.001 (0.003)	0.001 (0.002)
Painful Urination	–0.004 (0.005)	–0.003 (0.004)	–0.003 (0.004)	–0.002 (0.004)
Swollen Ankles	–0.002 (0.004)	–0.002 (0.003)	–0.002 (0.003)	–0.002 (0.003)
Hearing problems	–0.003 (0.010)	–0.002 (0.006)	–0.002 (0.006)	–0.001 (0.002)
Skin problems	0.008 (0.007)	0.006 (0.005)	0.005 (0.004)	0.002 (0.003)
Chest Pain	0.002 (0.007)	0.002 (0.006)	0.002 (0.005)	0.002 (0.004)
Memory loss	0.000 (0.010)	0.000 (0.005)	0.000 (0.004)	0.000 (0.006)
Paralysis	0.008 (0.006)	0.007 (0.005)	0.007 (0.005)	0.006 (0.005)
Night sweats	0.007 (0.006)	0.005 (0.005)	0.005 (0.005)	0.004 (0.004)
Weight loss	0.012 (0.010)	0.008 (0.007)	0.008 (0.007)	0.003 (0.005)
Menstrual problems	–0.001 (0.004)	–0.001 (0.003)	–0.001 (0.003)	0.000 (0.003)
White discharge	–0.001 (0.003)	–0.002 (0.003)	–0.002 (0.003)	–0.002 (0.004)
Other problems	0.001 (0.006)	-0.001 (0.005)	-0.002 (0.005)	-0.004 (0.005)

Bootstrapped standard errors in parentheses.

*significant at 10% ** significant at 5%; *** significant at 1%.

Four symptoms (blood in spit, diarrhoea, vomit and hearing problems) show positive albeit insignificant associations with self-reported health status. The positive associations could be driven by the simultaneous occurrence of these symptoms with other more disagreeable conditions which have been controlled for in the analysis.

Table 2 reports the coefficients of interest from equation (2) run for each symptom D_i. For twenty three of the thirty symptoms, the association between SES and the probability of reporting the symptom is negative at low levels of SES and positive at high levels of the same. However, the associations are significant for only five of these symptoms (bodyache, backache, upper abdominal pain, hearing problems and memory loss). For seven symptoms (blood in spit, genital ulcers, painful urination, swollen ankles and menstrual problems) the relationship between SES and probability of symptom reporting is reversed, *i.e.* an increase in SES at low levels causes an increase in the probability of reporting the condition while at high levels of SES the association is negative.

Table 3 reports the estimates of the direct and symptom effects of SES on health at the mean and the 25th, 50th and 75th per centiles of log per capita non-health expenditure.

Although the estimates in Table 3 are small and statistically insignificant, they reveal two very interesting patterns. The first of these indicates that the protectiveness of SES on health via the direct effect increases with the level of SES. At the 25th per centile of SES the direct effect is negative–indicating that SES is not protective of health via the direct channel at the 25th per centile of SES – but it becomes positive and higher in magnitude at the mean, the 50th and the 75th per centiles.

However, the total symptoms effects demonstrate the exact opposite trend. While the total symptoms effect is positive at lower levels of SES–suggesting that SES is protective of health at these levels–it decreases in magnitude with increasing SES and becomes negative at the 75th per centile. This suggests that SES is less and less protective of health at higher levels via the symptoms channel.

Recall that the total symptoms effects indicate whether higher SES lowers the probability of reporting the more 'serious' symptoms (i.e. the symptoms that have an adverse effect on self-reported health). The results presented in Table 3 suggest that SES is not necessarily protective of health through this channel. Specifically, the results obtained suggest that at low levels of SES, it is protective of health through the symptoms channel since an increase in SES is associated with a fall in the probability of reporting 'serious' symptoms (*i.e.* the total symptoms effect is positive). However, the protective effect via symptoms diminishes at higher levels of SES so much so that at the 75th per centile of SES, an increase in SES is associated with a rise in the probability of reporting 'serious' symptoms (hence. the total symptoms effect is negative).

There could be several explanations for the observed pattern in total symptoms effects. One explanation could be that the poor are less aware of their health than the rich and hence are less likely to report the more serious symptoms. However this factor seems likely to be operative only for 'other' symptoms since all the rest are very easily observable conditions. It is also possible that the poor under-report the more serious conditions because they can ill-afford to be sick and miss work or because of the social embarrassment associated with certain ailments. Unnithan-Kumar's (1999) description of the health behaviuor of rural women in Rajasthan suggests that women may be inclined to neglect reproductive ailments till they take a turn for the very worst. The study also documents the social embarrassment of publicly acknowledging and seeking treatment for reproductive ailments. This could explain why women from poorer families with fewer resources to devote to health care may choose to ignore their menstrual problems relative to those from richer families. The findings of this paper point to the need for future research to identify the mechanisms behind the SES-health gradient that operates through the symptoms channel identified here.

5. Summary and Conclusion

This paper uses recent data collected in Rajasthan, India, to study the link between SES (measured by log per capita monthly non-health expenditure) and health through the direct and symptoms effects. The direct effect measures the relationship between SES and self-reported health among individuals who experience the same symptoms, whereas the symptoms effect measures if SES is associated with a lower probability of reporting 'serious' symptoms, *viz*. the symptoms that have an adverse impact on self-reported health.

While small and statistically insignificant, the estimated direct and symptoms effects reveal two interesting patterns. I find that the protective effect of SES on health through the direct channel increases with the level of SES. However, the exact opposite pattern holds for symptoms effects. While increased SES lowers the probability of reporting serious conditions at low levels of SES (*i.e.* the symptoms effect is positive) this effect decreases in magnitude at higher levels of SES. At the 75th per centile the symptoms effect is negative indicating that higher SES increases the probability of reporting the more serious conditions. Hence, the symptoms-driven effect of SES on health becomes less protective at higher levels of SES.

There could be several possible explanations for the patterns observed in direct and symptoms effects. The findings of the paper point to the need for future research to identify the same.

REFERENCES

Adler, N. *et. al.* (1994) : "Socioeconomic status and the challenge of the gradient," *American Psychologist*, January 1994, 49(1), pp 15-24.

Banerjee, Abhijit, Deaton, Angus and Duflo, Esther (2004a) : "Health Care Delivery in Rural Rajasthan," *Economic and Political Weekly*, February 28, 2004, pp. 944-949.

Banerjee, Abhijit, Deaton, Angus and Duflo, Esther (2004b) : "Wealth, Health and Health Services in Rural Rajasthan," *American Economic Review*, 2004, 94(2), pp. 326-330.

Case, Anne (2004) : "Does money protect health status? Evidence from South African pensions," In : Wise D (Ed), Perspectives on the Economics of Aging, University of Chicago Press: Chicago; 2004, pp. 287-311.

Chen, Lincoln C. and Murray, Christopher J. L. (1992) : "Understanding Morbidity Change," *Population and Development Review*, 1992, 18(3), pp. 481-503.

Lleras-Muney, Adriana (2005) : "The Relationship Between Education and Adult Mortality in the U.S.," *Review of Economic Studies*, January 2005, 72(1), pp. 189-221.

Rajasthan Health Development Report (2002) : Published by: Government of Rajasthan, Available at: http://hdrc.undp.org.in/shdr/rhdr/dwnld_chap_raj.htm

Sen, Amartya K. (2002) : "Health : Perception versus Observation," *British Medical Journal*, 2002, 324(7342), pp. 860-61.

Smith, James P. (1999) : "Healthy Bodies and Thick Wallets: The Dual Relationship between Health and Economic Status," *Journal of Economic Perspectives*, Spring 1999, 13(2), pp. 145-166.

Strauss, John and Thomas, Duncan (1998) : "Health, Nutrition and Economic Development," *Journal of Economic Literature*, June 1998, 36(2), pp. 766-817.

Thomas, Duncan *et al.* (2003) : "Iron deficiency and the well-being of older adults," May 2003, mimeo, UCLA

Unnithan-Kumar, Maya (1999) : "Households, Kinships and Access to Reproductive Health Care among Rural Muslim Women in Jaipur," *Economic and Political Weekly*, Mar. 6-12, 1999.

6

Poverty, Health and Environment Nexus: A Study of Community Foresty in India

—*Pratap C. Mohanty, Sibabrata Das*

1. Introduction

Environmental degradation is one of the serious problems faced by the people in the country. Rapid population growth, industrialization and urbanization in country are adversely affecting the environment. Though the relationship is complex, population size and growth tend to expand and accelerate these human impacts on the environment. All these in turn lead to an increase in the pollution levels. However, environmental pollution not only leads to deteriorating environmental conditions but also have adverse effects on the health of people. India is one of the most degraded environment countries in the world and it is paying heavy health and economic price for it. In current development discourses it is rather odd to find any discussion about poverty minus the environment or about nature without people. There is much controversy surrounding the poverty-environmental degradation nexus. The predominant school of thought argues that poverty is a major cause of environmental degradation and if policy makers want to address the environmental issues, they must first focus on the poverty problems. Poverty problem is prevalent in most of the developing and underdeveloped countries.

The links between poverty and the environment are conditioned by the interaction of economic, social, demographic and even climatic factors. An examination of India, one of the world's largest and most populous countries, is essentially an examination of a microcosm of the earth. Its populace encompasses the entire range of the income and education spectra, its culture consists of diverse religions, languages, and social systems, and its geography is a sample of almost every terrestrial climatic zone of the planet. It is this variation that makes India's environment so interesting. India holds the dubious honour of suffering from poverty-induced environmental degradation at the same time, pollution from affluence and a rapidly growing industrial sector. In light of this dichotomy, it is a tricky task to understand the complexities behind the state of India's environment. Furthermore, these problems will only be exacerbated in the years to come, as India remains one of the fastest growing countries in the world, in terms of population as well of economy. And what is learned from the Indian development experience will afford other countries valuable insight into the best path to take for environmentally sustainable development.

The first and overriding priority of developing countries is economic and social development and poverty eradication. India, too, recognizes that environmental degradation has social reasons, and that combating poverty is a prerequisite for sustainable development. It has been recognised that the sustainable development approach is the key to a continuous growth of the economy. The government of India has a firm belief that only people's participation can achieve highest level of successful implementation of existing programmes of conservation and environmental protection.

Here we seek to examine the complex interplay of environment, health and poverty in the context of the role of India's Joint Forest Management (JFM) or Community Forestry. The whole analysis is organised into five sections. Section II deals with the basic definitions of poverty, environment, health degradation and, finding the linkages between them. Section III gives the detailed report of community participation and the extent of JFM in India. Section IV examines the advantages of JFM in India. The main findings and the policy suggestions are set out in Section V.

2. Conceptual Framework

Common Definition of Poverty

Poverty is, in absolute term, the inability of an individual to satisfy certain basic minimum needs for sustained, healthy and reasonably productive living. Conceptually, any attempt at quantifying the incidence of poverty in population requires, taking into account the level and pattern of an individual's personal consumption expenditure as well as their access to social transfers and public provisioning. The proportion of population not able to attain the specified level of expenditure is then segregated as poor.

Measures of Poverty

A variety of descriptive indices are used to measure poverty, but the most common are the headcount index (HCI), poverty gap index (PGI), and squared poverty gap index (SPGI). The headcount index, also called the headcount ratio (HCR), is the most widely used index. If a household spends below a pre-defined level, then it is considered to be poor. The index measures the portion of families below the poverty line. The HCI is useful since it allows one to calculate the marginal impact of additional spending, output, etc. on the number of people lifted out of poverty. The HCI is specified by,

$$HCI = \frac{HC}{n}$$

Where n is the total population and HC is the number of households that satisfy the condition $yi < p$, where p be the poverty line and yi be the expenditure level of an individual or household i (both measured in the same currency).

A problem with the HCI is that it ignores concerns about the distribution of income among the poor. Consequently, more sophisticated measurements of the Foster-Greer-Thorbecke form are also used when measuring poverty (Foster, Greer, and Thorbecke 1984).The two most common are the PGI and SPGI. The former measures how far poor individuals are from the poverty line. Individuals above the poverty line have a zero poverty gap. The calculation of the PGI is described by,

$$PGI = \frac{1}{n} \Sigma_{y_i < p} \left(\frac{p - y_i}{p} \right)$$

The HCR and the PGI share a problem : neither is especially sensitive to the destitute. For example, if a poor individual receives an income transfer from a much poorer one (with both of them still below the poverty line), neither index would change.

Higher-order poverty indices such as the SPGI give greater weighting to those further away from the poverty line than the PGI.[1] An observation from Indian poverty research is that the information provided by all three measures is roughly the same.

Present Status of Poverty in India

Using such an approach the planning commission, Government of India has been estimating the head count ratio at state level, separating for rural and urban areas for over three decades.[2] It is currently adequacy norm of 2400 and 2100 kilo calories per capita per day to define state specific using a

1. There are some concerns with the SPGI, even though it tackles distributional concerns among the poor better. Leach and Mearns, (1991) briefly address the issue. The sensitivity of the SPGI to measurement errors tends to be higher than the HCI or PGI. For a more precise mathematical interpretation of the SPGI, see Dasgupta, and Mäler, (1994).
2. De Janvry, Fargeix, and Sadoulet, (1992) discusses the strengths and weaknesses of a calorie-based poverty line. He points out that as average income rises, the correlation between per capita consumption and under-nutrition tends to be lower.

minimum consumption expenditure, anchored in an average (food) energy poverty lines, separately for rural and urban areas. These poverty lines are then applied on the NSSO's (National Sample Survey Organization) household consumer expenditure distributions to estimate the proportion and number of poor at state level.

In 1962 Planning Committee first attempted to define an official poverty line for India. At the national level the incidence of poverty on the head count ratio declined from 44.48 per cent in 1983 to 26.10 per cent in 1999-2000. In absolute terms, the number of poor declined from about 323 million in 1983 to 260 million in 1999-2000. While the proportion of poor in the rural areas declined from 45.65 per cent in 1983 to 27.09 per cent in 1999-2000; the decline in urban areas has been from 40.79 per cent to 23.62 per cent during this period. The Tenth Plan (2002-07) has set a target of reduction in poverty ratio by five per centage points to 19.3 per cent by 2007 and 15 per centage points by 2012. The targets for rural and urban poverty in 2007 are 21.1% and 15.1% respectively.

Poverty, Health and Environment Interactions

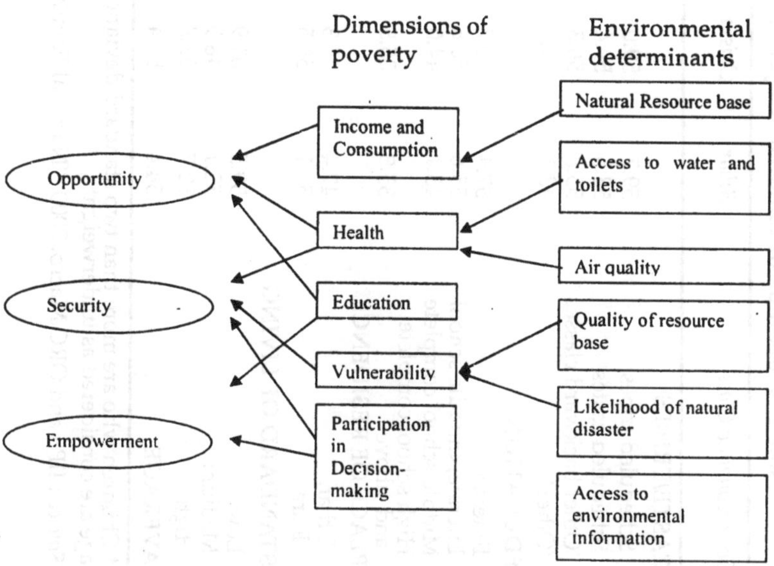

Table 1 : Proportion of Children (< 3 years) Underweight* in Various Socio-economic Classes, 1998-99

Socioeconomic Class	*Bihar*	*Orissa*	*West Bengal*	*Madhya Pradesh*	*Maharastra*	*Gujarat*	*India*
CASTE/TRIBES							
Scheduled tribes	59.7	59.0	57.4	64.5	65.2	56.6	55.9
Scheduled castes	58.5	59.4	56.1	57.5	51.4	45.4	53.5
Other backward classes	55.8	56.3	36.1	55.4	48.4	49.0	47.3
'Other'	43.1	43.0	45.8	40.5	46.3	36.3	41.1
EDUCATION							
Illiterate	57.4	60.7	58.4	61.2	57.3	57.0	55.0
Literate,<middle school	55.6	50.6	46.4	51.0	53.4	41.0	44.6
Middle school complete	43.1	44.0	36.5	41.9	40.3	31.8	36.6
High school complete and above	35.3	35.5	18.9	28.0	36.1	27.5	26.6
PLACE OF RESIDENCE							
Urban	47.4	45.3	31.5	44.3	44.1	38.1	38.4
Rural	55.1	55.5	52.6	58.4	53.2	49.3	49.6
STANDARD OF LIVING							
Low	59.5	61.9	56.5	61.5	60.4	63.0	56.9
Medium	52.1	48.9	44.2	58.0	49.5	46.2	46.8
High	32.7	27.8	21.4	33.6	27.5	25.9	26.8
AVERAGE	54.4	54.4	48.7	55.1	49.0	45.1	47.0

* Children who are more than two standard deviations below the median reference population in terms of weight for age are considered as underweight.

Source : IIPS and ORC Macro. 2000. "National Family Health Survey (NFHS-2)", 1998-99.

Table 2: Proportion of Children (< 3 years) Stunted* in Various Socioeconomic Classes, 1998-99

Socioeconomic Class	*Bihar*	*Orissa*	*West Bengal*	*Madhya Pradesh*	*Maharashtra*	*Gujarat*	*India*
CASTE/TRIBES							
Scheduled tribes	56.4	49.4	46.6	59.9	57.1	46.9	52.8
Scheduled castes	57.6	50.7	45.6	52.7	43.7	48.9	51.7
Other backward classes	54.7	44.2	27.0	51.5	40.3	46.5	44.8
'Other'	45.1	32.4	40.1	37.2	35.0	37.5	40.7
EDUCATION							
Illiterate	56.2	50.1	54.6	57.2	49.3	55.9	54.4
Literate,<middle school	57.2	41.9	34.3	46.6	39.4	43.6	40.7
Middle school complete	42.1	32.8	22.5	32.4	33.0	30.3	34.0
High school complete and above	36.2	21.9	16.2	27.9	27.0	21.3	25.4
PLACE OF RESIDENCE							
Urban	42.2	37.0	25.5	39.8	33.3	38.5	35.6
Rural	55.0	44.8	45.1	54.3	44.2	46.7	48.5
STANDARD OF LIVING							
Low	57.5	50.8	51.8	58.7	52.6	56.5	53.7
Medium	52.4	38.5	33.3	52.2	36.1	47.0	45.3
High	35.7	21.2	14.7	31.2	24.2	25.0	28.5
AVERAGE	53.7	44.0	41.5	51.0	39.9	43.6	45.5

*Children who are more than two standard deviations below the median reference population in terms of height for age are considered as stunted.

Source : IIPS and ORC Macro, 2000, "National Family Health Survey (NFHS-2)", 1998-99.

Table 3 : Proportion of Children (< 3 years) Wasted* in Various Socio Economic Classes, 1998-99

Socioeconomic Class	*Bihar*	*Orissa*	*West Bengal Pradesh*	*Madhya*	*Maharashtra*	*Gujarat*	*India*
CASTE/TRIBES							
Scheduled tribes	33.5	30.5	17.7	24.7	31.0	21.7	21.8
Scheduled castes	23.1	22.8	18.1	19.9	15.6	12.3	16.0
Other backward classes	19.7	24.6	13.7	18.7	20.9	8.8	16.6
'Other'	18.3	19.7	11.5	16.3	20.7	13.4	12.8
EDUCATION							
Illiterate	22.4	26.6	15.8	22.7	24.4	2.1	17.1
Literate, Middle School	17.8	21.1	13.4	15.7	23.4	12.9	15.3
Middle School complete	18.3	22.2	12.2	15.2	13.9	14.3	13.3
High School complete and above	15.5	20.8	4.0	9.8	17.4	11.3	11.0
PLACE OF RESIDENCE							
Urban	17.1	23.6	11.1	17.3	15.7	11.3	13.1
Rural	21.4	24.4	14.2	20.6	24.8	19.2	16.2
STANDARD OF LIVING							
Low	23.4	28.0	15.5	21.6	28.2	26.0	19.7
Medium	19.8	19.8	12.5	20.9	19.0	14.1	14.3
High	11.1	16.9	9.3	13.0	14.7	10.9	10.2
STATE AVERAGE	21.0	24.3	13.6	19.8	21.2	16.2	15.5

* Children who are more than two standard deviations below the median reference population in terms of weight for height are considered as wasted.

Source : IIPS and ORC Macro, 2000, "National Family Health Survey (NFHS-2)", 1998-99.

Poverty is said to be both cause and effect of environment degradation. The poor people, who rely on natural resources more than the rich, deplete natural resources faster as they have no real prospects of gaining access to other types of resources. Poorer people, who cannot meet their subsistence needs through purchase, are forced to use common property resources such as forests for food and fuel, pastures for fodder, and ponds and rivers for water. Clean drinking water facility through taps is available to only 35 per cent of urban households and 18 per cent of rural households in India. Other residents use unsafe water sources like wells, ponds and rivers. Population pressure driven overexploitation of the surface and underground water resources by the poor has resulted into contamination and exhaustion of the water resources. Urban population is also using rivers to dispose of untreated sewage and industrial effluent. The result is that health of those dependents on untreated water resources is increasing at risk. In the absence of capital resources, the poor are directly dependent on natural resources. Moreover degraded environment can accelerate the process of impoverishment, again because the poor depend directly on natural assets. Although there has been significant drop in the poverty ratio in the country from 55 per cent in 1973 to 36 per cent in 1993-94, the absolute number of poor have, however, remained constant at around 320 million over the years. Acceleration in poverty alleviation is imperative to break this link between poverty and the environment. The poverty and rapid population growth are found to coexist and thus seems to reinforcing each other. It also contributes to environmental degradation through over exploitation of natural resources like land, air and water. The deterioration of natural resources and unsafe living conditions affects the environment and health of the poor people.

Tables 1, 2 and 3 give an overview of differences of prevalence of undernutrition between Scheduled Caste, scheduled tribe, other backward classes and non Scheduled Caste/Tribe/OBC ('other' castes). The level of undernutrition by educational level of the mother, place of residence and standard of living of the household are also shown in the tables.

For all the indicators of nutritional status, the level is higher among scheduled tribes than scheduled castes, other backward class and 'other' at the national and also state level. The level of underweight among scheduled tribes and scheduled castes is substantially higher than 'other' category. It is seen that there is not much difference between scheduled tribes and scheduled castes in Bihar, Orissa and West Bengal. The level is quite high among Other Backward Classes than 'other' in Bihar, Orissa and Madhya Pradesh. The gap between ST-'other', SC-'Other' and OBC-'Other' in terms of per centages of stunted children is substantial. But it is seen that the rate of underweight and stunting is higher among 'other' than OBCs. Social group gradient in rate of wasting is also observed. Comparisons with state average figure show that in 'other' category per centage of malnourished children is lower than the state average while it is higher in all the rest of three groups. But in some cases, the figures for OBC are also lower than state average.

Above discussion highlighted that there are considerable variations in per centage of undernourished children across social groups in almost every state. But there are cases where differences are nominal. But there is no doubt that, the prevalence of undernutrition among scheduled tribe is the highest in all the states, though in Orissa, the figures for stunting and underweight is more among scheduled castes than scheduled tribes, but the difference is marginal.

This type of social gradient generally gives an impression that higher rates of undernutrition among children belonging to particular caste/tribe may be attributable to the membership factors *per se*. But then there are certain difference in characteristics such as educational level, place of residence, standard of living etc. associated with caste and tribe that influence the level of undernutrition. Therefore, some or all of the social group differentials in rates of undernutrition could be on account of differentials in one or more of the factors. For example, high level of undernutrition among children from scheduled tribe household may be due to their low economic condition. Given that there is such a strong relationship between socioeconomic factors and nutritional status and there are important differences in the distribution of the socioeconomic circumstances of different caste/tribe, it would seem to make sense to explore how far caste/tribe variations in undernutrition remain, once socioeconomic differences between caste/tribe have been controlled. Such an approach for analysis and interpretation regards socioeconomic position as a confounding factor that needs to be 'controlled out' to reveal the 'true' relationship between caste/tribe membership and nutritional status. If there is an effect of caste-tribe after controlling for the effects of factors such as education, standard of living, place of residence, it could be called a net effect. Hence, an attempt was made to see if the net effect persists after statistically controlling for the effects of other variables through logistic regression technique.

Various poverty reduction strategies and programmes designed by Government of India and individual states may serve as long-term solution to the problem. In the short term, combined food and nutrition supplementation programmes would be most effective to address undernutrition. To this effect, it is important to develop community based interventions giving priority to deprived households as a short term solution. Providing health education messages and interventions for population in general and children, in particular on healthy diets and healthy lifestyles might be effective in reducing the incidence of undernutrition. All major reports on health promotion in recent decades have stressed the importance of community participation programmes for successful health promotion programmes (WHO, 1981, 1986, 1997). It is likely that community participation to promote health varies across social groups. Community participation may increase access to local services. It may also promote rapid transmission of health information, adoption of health behaviour norms and social control over deviant health related behaviour. Besides, the fundamental question that arises in this context is how much of the modern amenities in public health are percolating down to the tribal strata of Indian society. The most important problem in public health among the tribes concerns the shortage of medical personnel and qualified nurses in the face of continued belief in the old system and a steadily rising faith in the new. Another important point to be noted is that even the existing medical staffs are reluctant to work and provide services in tribal areas because of difficulties of housing, education for their children etc. Availability of health services was not included in this analysis; it is known that there is a severe lack of attention paid to health care. It is also important to provide health care facilities and also other infrastructure in order to improve health status of the tribal population.

3. Deforestation

Forests are an important natural resource of India. They have moderate influence against floods and thus they protect the soil erosion. Forests also play an important role in enhancing the quality of environment by influencing the ecological balance and life support system (checking soil erosion, maintaining soil fertility, conserving water, regulating water cycles and floods, balancing carbon dioxide and oxygen content in atmosphere etc.

India has a forest cover of 76.52 million square kms. of recorded forest area, while only 63.34 million square kms can be classified as actual forest cover. This accounts for 23.28 per cent of total geographic area against 33 per cent recommended by National Forest Policy of 1988. Per capita availability of forests in India is much lower than the world average. In the year 1997, as compared to 1993, the total forest cover has decreased by 6710 Sq. Kms. The states, which have shown significant decline in the forest covers, are Andhra Pradesh and Madhya Pradesh. Whereas the states of Gujarat, Maharashtra, Rajasthan and West Bengal have shown an increase in forest cover.

In 1981-83, only 11.2 per cent of country's total land area comprises dense forest with a crown density of more than 40 per cent, thus reflecting a qualitative decline of forests in the country. The total forest area diverted for non-forestry purposes between 1950 and 1980 was 4.5 million hectares, *i.e.* at an annual rate of 0.15 million hectare. To regulate unabated diversion of forestland for non-forestry purposes, Forest (Conservation) Act, 1980 was enacted. It has resulted in reduction of diversion of forest area for non-forestry purposes considerably and the present rate of diversion is 16,000 hectare annually (Economic Survey of India, 1998-99). Continuing deforestation, therefore, has brought us face to face with a major ecological and socio-economic crisis.

4. Community Participation and Joint Forest Management in India

India's national forest policy of 1988 was a landmark policy for local people's rights over forest resources. The policy recognized people's participation in using and protecting forests and suggested the forest communities should develop and conserve forests together with the state forest departments. This reform in forest policy has begun to transform how forests are protected and used in India. Communities that were historically perceived to be encroachers and illegal users of forests by the state were invited to partner with the state in protecting forests. Following national implementation guidelines in 1990, various state governments began implementing their own Joint Forest Management strategies. By 2001, some twenty-two states had adopted JFM[3] (Joint Forest Management) (Agarwal, 2001). JFM was launched in the early 1990s and made it possible for the forestry department to involve people and communities in the management of certain forests. JFM caught on very quickly, and by 2001 some 45,000 JFM groups were protecting approximately 12 million hectares of government forests (Kumar, 2002)[4].

The following figures outline the overall position of forest cover in India. The area under forest cover has been fallen from the year 1987 to 1999 and also from sixth five year plan to ninth

---

3. The terms social forestry, community forestry, joint forest management are used synonymously and interchangeably.
4. The total land area coming under community management is likely to be much higher as the above figures do not include the many traditional groups which are not recognized under JFM.

five year plan in most states. The per capita availability of forest land has been reducing from 1950-51 to 1998-99. Madhya Pradesh is distinctively having the highest forest area cover and this is followed by Orissa, Andhra Pradesh and Maharashtra.

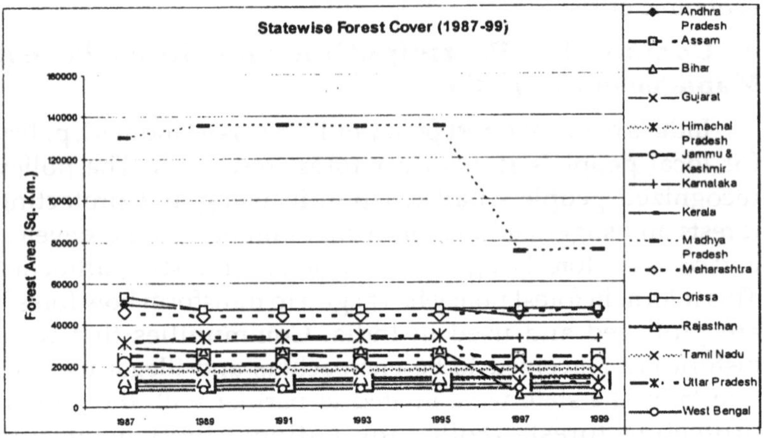

Fig.1 : State-wise Forest Cover India (1987-1999)

Source : State of Forest Report 2001, Forest Survey of India, Ministry of Environment and Forest, Govt. of India.

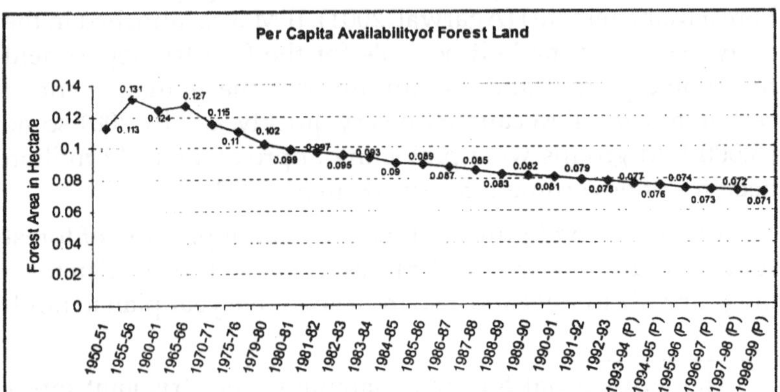

Fig. 2 : Per Capita Availability of forest Land in India (1950-51 to 1998-99).

Source : Selected Socio-economic Statistics 2002, Central Statistical Organisation, Ministry of Statistics and Programme Implementation, Govt. of India.

Under the terms of JFM, Village Forest Institutions (VFI) is given conditional access to specified forest products in accordance with the guidelines laid by the forest department. The products usually include fuelwood, fodder, and non-timber forest products. Forest departments also provide VFI's with information, training, and wage employment related to forest management. Initial community funds may also be provided. In many states, JFM resolutions mandate that villagers be solicited to make micro-plans for forests (Sundar 2000). Organizing into a VFI can result in access to wage employment and fuelwood through forest management activities such as lopping, clearing of debris, and cutting. In return, VFIs agree to certain conditions such as collective protection of the forest against encroachment, poaching or timber smuggling, and, monitoring of restrictions on some types of use. After a period of protection (5 to 10 years or more), the VFI and its members are entitled to 25 to 100 per cent of the net income from the sale of major forest produce, timber (Khare and others 2002).

The organization structure and membership rules of VFIs differ in each state. For example, in Andhra Pradesh, all households living in a JFM village are eligible for JFM membership. While membership is optional for the general population of the village, it is automatic for ST and SC households (GOAP, 1996). In Madhya Pradesh and Orissa, two persons (one of which must be a woman) from each household living in the JFM village are automatically considered members (GOO, 1993 and GOMP, 1996). In Uttar Pradesh, membership to JFM is either automatic to the village residents who are registered in the electoral rolls of the village or those who are existing members of the forest panchayat system. In West Bengal, only "economically backward people living in the vicinity of forests" are considered to be members. However, every family living in the vicinity of the forests has the option of becoming a member (GOWB, 1990). In general, VFIs have an executive committee that makes major decisions. VFIs have no independent legal existence as they are usually registered with the forest department alone[5].Authority to enforce protection varies.

In addition to state supported joint forest management, India has a history of community forest management undertaken either by self-initiated groups, with NGO support, or initiated in colonial times with British support (Khare and others 2000, Ballabh and others 2002, Agarwal 2001, Lise 2000). These 'traditional' groups are particularly evident in the states of Orissa, Bihar, Uttar Pradesh and Jharkhand. For example, in Orissa, only 1,200 out of the approximately 5,000 community forest management groups are estimated to participate in JFM. (Singh, 2002). It appears that these traditional groups are often not officially recognized under JFM rules, and in many cases are compelled to change their structure and functioning in order to be officially recognized and receive benefits associated with JFM (Sundar 2000, Khare and others 2002).[6]

5. Advantages of Joint Forest Management in India

Some theoretical issues underlying the advocacy for community forestry can be analysed by using the *Von-Thunen conceptual framework of rural landscape*. Consider some homogenous landscape with a local community located at the center 'O' in figure-3 below. The horizontal axis measures distance from the community center or market while the vertical axis measures the value of land employed in agriculture and forestry at any distance. Without the loss of generality, we assume that all households and firms face homogenous inputs with cost of access being the only factor explaining the difference in production costs. In this case, land value in agriculture (Va) decreases with decreasing access. As the distance to the market increases, agricultural land value

5. The Village forest Institutions are known by various names in the different states. For example in Andhra Pradesh, they are known as Vana Sanrakshana Samithi (VSS) and as Forest Protection Committees (FPC) in Orissa.

6. The exception is Gujarat, where committees are registered under the co-operative society act (Sundar, 2000).

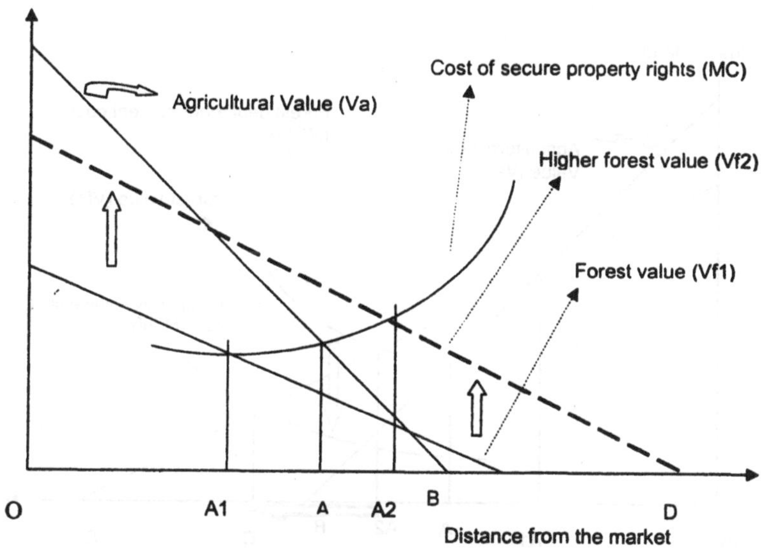

Fig. 3 : Forest Land and Property Rights

function eventually falls to zero at point B. Beyond this point, no single farmer will find it profitable to invest in agriculture because the cost of secure property rights exceeds returns on any agricultural investment on the land. This description also applies to the forest value function (V_f). Households and firms will protect their ownership rights, crops and livestock at some cost. Secure property rights on agricultural land and property is feasible and enforceable for land in the region O-A_1. Although households still take advantage of forest resources in the neighbourhood of O-A, investment in them is unprofitable due to high cost of establishing and enforcing property rights on them. As a result, land in the neighbourhood of OA is often used as communal grazing land and for collecting of timber and non-timber forest products under open access.

At the early stages of rural development, forest products; construction timber, mushroom, firewood, edible caterpillars, etc are plentiful and commands no price (i.e. the shadow value of the resource is zero) and as a result the forest resource is subject to over-exploitation and degradation.

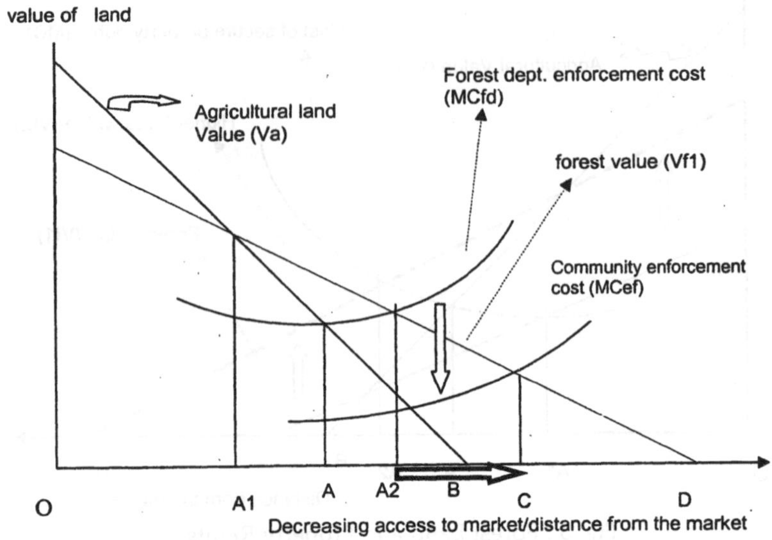

Fig.4 : Advantage of Community Forestry

As the neighbourhood forest becomes degraded, forest products become scarce and therefore economically valuable (*i.e.* the shadow price exceeds zero) and the forest value gradient shifts outwards to V_{f2} from V_{f1}. This shift increases land under enforceable property rights from A to A_2, and the local community can use this additional land either for plantation forestry, agro-forestry or indigenous forest management. Households still rely on open forests for additional forest products for own consumption and for sale. So, they will continue to collect forest products in the region to the right of A_2. This general description illustrates a key point that some private forest management is possible. It is at this point that we begin to examine community or Joint Forest management and discuss its advantages basically for any community that fits this theoretical description. Most natural forests are located on customary lands surrounding local communities and far from government local and central offices, a feature that makes government an 'absentee landlord'. Moreover, government officers including forest officers at district level will not have the same knowledge about the resource and local community that the local landowner has. This means that local forest management will be less expensive if managed by the local community than by any government ministry.

Figure-4 reproduces figure-3 with two cost functions of indigenous forest management, one for the Forest Department (MC_{fd}) and the other for local community management or JFM (MC_{ef}). Apart from its potential to reduce the costs of management, local community management also brings more forest land under sustainable management depicted by distance, A_2-C.

How much forestland can effectively be managed at the local level depends, to a large extent, on the strength of collective action, which in turn depends on factors that influence the marginal cost and benefits of collective management.

The data set is taken from the fifty-fourth round of India's National Sample Survey (NSS), undertaken between January and June of 1998. The fifty-fourth round was the first national survey in which household and village level information was collected regarding common property rights and resources in India. The survey focused only on rural India. (Chopra and Dasgupta, 2003).

To focus on the nature of dependence of the households on natural resources and CPRs, four major states (Bihar, Karnataka, Madhya Pradesh and Maharashtra) are considered. These states are selected on the basis of the level of development, both agricultural and industrial. States are ranked according to per capita income from agriculture and industry respectively. The four states with the highest ranks of income from agriculture are: Punjab, Haryana, Karnataka and Gujarat. The lower ranking states with regard to agricultural income per capita are: Bihar, Tamil Nadu Jammu and Kashmir, Uttar Pradesh and West Bengal. With respect to industry, Punjab, Tamil Nadu, Maharashtra and Gujarat are the most developed and Bihar, Jammu and Kashmir, Orissa, Rajasthan and Uttar Pradesh are the least developed. Using further the criteria of the significance

Table 4 : Distribution of Households Collecting from Commons (Number and Percentage of Households)

State	*Fuelwood*	*Fodder*	*NTFPs*	*State Total*
India	24744 (36)	6450 (9)	9365 (14)	67674 (100)
Bihar	2977 (40)	1117 (15)	582 (7)	7482 (100)
Karnataka	1666 (53)	539 (17)	304 (10)	3161 (100)
Madhya Pradesh	3184 (55)	516 (9)	1408 (24)	5812 (100)
Maharashtra	3222 (60)	679 (13)	514 (9)	5374 (100)

Note : Figures in parentheses denote percentage of households in each category.

Source : NSSO 54th Round.

of CPRs in the economies of the states, we have selected Karnataka and Bihar as the agriculturally developed and backward states, respectively, and Maharashtra as the industrially developed state. Madhya Pradesh, the central Indian state with a large plateau and forest region inhabited by tribal communities is selected as the fourth Indian state.

This table indicates the nature of dependence of households in these states on CPRs as measured by number of households collecting each of the three commodities, fuelwood, fodder and NTFPs. Large numbers collect fuelwood from the commons in all four states, the per centage varying from 40% to 60%, while the average for India is 36%. The per centage of household collecting fodder is lower, ranging from 9% for India to 17% for Karnataka. NTFP collection also involves low per centages of households, with the range varying from 7% to 24%, Madhya Pradesh having the highest per centage at 24%.

Table 5 : NTFPs Collected and Per centage Distribution of Collected Items

State/ NTFP	*India*	*Bihar*	*Karna-taka*	*Madhya Pradesh*	*Maha-rashtra*
1. Fruits	17.86	15.48	31.03	28.21	25.29
2. Roots,Tubers,	9.10	14.22	1.59	7.93	0.33
3. Gums & resins spinach, etc.	0.61	-	-	1.65	0.16
4. Honey	2.96	1.83	9.28	2.21	2.30
5. Medicinal/herbs	2.72	0.69	-	2.38	0.49
6. Fish	16.93	19.72	11.41	4.96	16.91
7. Leaves	26.51	28.78	10.34	43.28	29.72
8. Weeds, Grass, Cane, Bamboo	23.31	19.27	36.34	9.38	24.79

Note : Column Totals Equal 100.

Source : NSSO 54th Round (1999).

Table-5 gives a picture of the range of non-timber forest products collected in the states and in the country as a whole. At the all India level, leaves, weeds, cane grass, bamboo constitute a large part of total collections. These are followed by fruit and fish. Maharashtra and Bihar follow the same pattern but in Karnataka, cane grass and bamboo are more significant than leaves. In Madhya Pradesh where 24% of households are engaged in NTFP collections, 43.28% of the collections consist of leaves (possibly tendu leaves for bidi making contribute significantly to this).

6. Conclusion

To summarize our main household level results, we find that household participation[7] in CF is influenced by state geographic and policy differences, literacy, fuel wood scarcity.

7. For instance in UP, the JFM order of 1997 required the existing Van Panchayats to accept in writing that the Panchayat rules no longer apply under JFM (Khare and others, 2000).

A key policy relevant result is that scarcity is correlated with participation. This suggests that new government guidelines need to be cautiously implemented. Our findings regarding fuel wood consumption reinforce the poverty-environment hypothesis, which suggests that fuel wood collection will decrease with wealth because of increased opportunity costs of labour and changes in preferences (Bardhan and Others, 2002). Community forestry and JFM in India appear to be a case where some participants actively join a village forest institution and are rewarded for their membership. Households who do not join, *i.e.*, those who do not claim to be participants–either because it is not important to them, or because of ignorance, or for some other reason–do not gain in the short to medium term.

We conclude that programmes designed to increase participation in community forestry are important. The analysis reveals that rapid population growth plays an important role in environmental problems of the country, from deforestation to land degradation, air and water pollution to the spread of disease. The considerable magnitude of air and water pollution pulls up the number of people suffering from respiratory and water borne diseases and many a times leading to deaths and serious health hazards. The above evidences and facts suggest that the poor people are very much linked to CPRs, thus the protection of those natural resources is essential for reducing the extent of poverty and simultaneously regenerating the environment, so that sustainable development can be achieved. Scarcity motivates the people more to participate in community forestry and participation improves the welfare of the people. The analysis suggests that there is an urgent need to control population and environmental pollution in the country for better health of present and future generation. In conclusion, it can be suggested that for the success of non-market institutions in reducing poverty and improving the environmental quality and health, one should not only seek the perfect bonding of social capital, cultural institutions, will for participation, decentralisation, participatory governance, administrative reforms and role of international development organisations, but also quite essentially the political will and commitment.

REFERENCES

Agrawal, A. (2001) : 'Common Property Institutions and Sustainable Governance of Resources', *World Development,* 29 (10), pp. 1649-1672.

Ballabh, V. and Balooni, K. and Dave, S., (2002) : 'Why Local Resources Management Institutions Decline : A Comparative Analyses of *Van* (Forest) *Panchayats* and Forest Protection Committees in India', *World Development,* vol.30, no.12, pp.2153-2167.

Bina Agarwal (1997) : "Gender, Environment, and Poverty Interlinks: Regional Variations and Temporal Shifts in Rural India, 1971-91", World Development Vol. 25, No. 1, pp. 23–52.

Chopra and Dasgupta (2003) : *The Nature of Household Dependence on Common Pool Resources : An Econometric Study for India,* Institute of Economic Growth, Working Paper Series, No. E/232/2002, Delhi, India.

Chopra, K. and Gulati, S.C. (2001) : *Migration, Common Property Resources and Environmental Degradation : Interlinkages in India's Arid and Semi-arid Regions,* Sage Publications India Pvt. Limited, New Delhi.

Chopra, K., and Kadekodi, G.K. (1991) : 'Participatory Institutions : The Context of Common and Private Property Resources', *Environmental and Resource Economics,* vol. 1, pp. 353–372.

Chopra, K., Kadekodi, G., K., and Murty, M.N. (1990) : *Participatory Development: People and Common Property Resources,* Sage Publications Limited, New Delhi.

Chopra, Kanchan and Gulati, S.C. (1998) : "Environmental Degradation, Property Rights and Population Movements : Hypotheses and Evidence from Rajasthan, India", Environment and Development Economics, 3, pp. 35–57, Cambridge University Press.

Dasgupta, Partha, and Karl-Göran Mäler, (1994) : *Poverty, Institutions, and the Environmental–Resource Base,* World Bank, Washington D.C.

De Janvry, A., A. Fargeix, and E. Sadoulet, (1992) : 'The Political Feasibility of Rural Poverty Reduction', *Journal of Development Economics,* vol. 37, no. 1/2, pp. 351-67.

Foster, J. J. Greer, and E. Thorbecke (1984) : 'A Class of Decomposable Poverty Measures', *Econometrica,* vol. 3, no. 52, pp. 761–65.

GoI, 1999 : Economic Survey (1998-99), Government of India, Ministry of Finance, Economic Division.

Government of Andhra Pradesh (1996) : *Joint Forest Management,* Order No. G.O.MS.NO.173.

Government of Madhya Pradesh (1996) : *Joint Forest Management,* Notification No. F.16-4-10-2-91.

Government of Orissa (1993) : *Joint Forest Management,* Notification No. 16700-10F (pron) -20/93.

Government of West Bengal (1990) : *Joint Forest Management,* Resolution No. 5062-For/D/IS-1688.

Khare, A., M. Sarin, N.C. Saxena, S. Palit, S. Bathia, F., Vania, M. Satyanarayana, (2002) : *Joint Forest Management: Policy, Practice and Prospects, Policy that works for Forests,* World Wide Fund for Nature-India and the International Institute for Environment and Development, People Series, No. 3. New Delhi.

Kumar, S. (2002) : 'Does Participation in Common Pool Resource Management Help Poor? A Social Cost-Benefit Analysis of Joint Forest Management in Jharkhand, India', *World Development,* vol. 30, no. 5. pp. 65-72.

Leach, Melissa, and Robin Mearns, (1991) : *Poverty and Environment in Developing Countries : An Overview Study,* Insitute of Development Studies, Sussex, UK.

Lise, W. (2000) : 'Factors Influencing People's Participation in Forest Management in India', *Ecological Economics,* vol. 34, pp. 379-392.

Mohanty, P.C. (2007), *Environmental Concerns and Poverty Alleviation in India : The Role of Non-Market Institutions,* paper presented at Singapore Economic Review Conference (SERC), organised by Singapore Economic Review committee in conjunction with Brooks World Poverty Institute, University of Manchester, from August 2-4, 2007, Singapore.

NSSO. (1997) · *Energy Used by Indian Households, Report No. 410,* New Delhi : National Sample Survey Organization, Department of Statistics, and Government of India.

Ravindranath, N. H. and Hall, D. (1995) : Biomass, Energy, and Environment: Developing Country Perspective from India; Oxford University Press.

Repetto, Robert. (1995) : The Second India Revisited : Population, Poverty, and Environmental Stress over Two Decades, World Resource Institute, Washington.

Singh, N. (2002) : 'Federations of community forest management groups in Orissa: Crafting new institutions to assert local rights', *Forests, Tress and People Newsletter,* vol.46, September, pp. 35-45.

Sundar, N. (2000) : 'Unpacking the 'Joint' in Joint Forest Management', Development and Change, vol. 31, pp.255-279.

TERI. (2000) : Teri Energy Data Directory & Yearbook, Tata Energy Research Institute, New Delhi.

7

Poverty, Health and Tribal Development through Joint Forest Management : A Case Study in a Tribal Village of Birbhum

—Arun Kumar Mandal

1. Introduction

West Bengal is among the Indian States where the rate of growth of crop-output has reached a satisfactory level. Rank of west Bengal with regard to agricultural production has improved much. But rural poverty in West Bengal is very high. This high incidence of rural poverty that is higher than that of all India figure of 34.7% (Source-World Development Indicator, 2005) shows west Bengal is placed among the poorest States in the country. There are a large number of tribal population in the district of Birbhum.Due to cause of poverty the tribal people do not have su[illegible] food to eat, water to drink, shelter to live and cloth[illegible] to wear which in turn lead to ill-health of the tribal people. Profs. A.K. Sen emphasized on public health and primary education to increase the efficiency of work-forces which in turn lead to an increase in agricultural and industrial production. Good and free health care services would have a pivotal role in reducing poverty both directly and indirectly through reducing population and healthy work force does have a catalectic role for economic and social development of a country. Hence forest development takes an effective and useful role in the sphere of rural economy providing these basic needs of life as well as alleviating rural poverty, promoting health condition and achieving development to some extent. Researchers extensively in this district did not explore the socio-economic impact of JFM.A very few studies have revealed the social and economic values of forest resources on forest dwellers. The State Govt. did not also pay proper attention for the protection and rejuvenation of forest resources in this district. The district also experienced poverty and unemployment problems due to lack agricultural advancement and industrial development. The State Govt. has also chalked out various types of poverty alleviating programmes in this district. But the programmes did not carry into effect owing to the lack of proper management, organization and integration. In this background, JFM may be an important and useful instrument for poverty amelioration to some extent as well as upliftment of the socio-economic living condition of the forest dwellers, because forests are renewable resources that contribute significantly economic development and improvement in the quality of the life of the people. They provide NWFPS in terms of food, fodder, fuel fibre; raw materials for industries, water etc. and support the agricultural production. Apart from this district has also acquired a much less per cent of forest area as compared to whole WB as well as country. So, this district is lagging far behind of required per centage of forest areas and also violating environmental feasibility and viability having a great alarming Situation. In this backdrop, various types of forestry development programmes and policies under JFM should be adopted for the restoration of degraded forest land which automatically would lead the stepping stone of socio-economic status of forest dwellers. Poverty can be must be tackled using three strategies simultaneously (1) Economic growth, (2) Human development, (3) Anti poverty programmes (Nayyar, Dhiraj, 2000, EPW). UNO (1990) emphasized on human development in terms of infant mortality, life expectancy and literacy rate. Women and girls are mainly responsible for collection of NWFPs (Beck, Tony, 2000).

2. Objectives of the Study

So, it is necessary to explore : (1) about the health status of tribal people in the dimensions of Sex ratio, age at marriage, fertility and mortality, nutritional status, family welfare programmers and scope for modern health care facilities of the study area and the awareness of tribal people about knowledge and nature of forest products (Wood and NWFPS).

(2) To investigate the role of JFM for poverty eradication and Tribal development from the point of view income generation, employment creation and environment protection in a sustainable manner without hampering forest resources.

3. Methodology

The study is based on a randomly selected sample of 35 households at Banavilla, a tribal village. Questionnaire method and Statistical tools *e.g.* correlation matrix, analysis of variance (ANOVA), and multiple regression have been deployed to collect and analyze the primary data. Lastly, Analysis and findings of survey results have been discussed in this paper.

4. Status of the Village (Banavilla)

This village stands very near by the metal road under Illambazar P.S of Birbhum District. The people of this village are facilitated by short distance two towns namely Bolpur and Illambazar. It has 307 population and 70 households belonging to ST and per capita income per month is estimated as Rs. 709.04. The villagers earn their livelihood from farm and non-farm activities having engaged in cultivation for own land, wage labourer and very few are service holders. The village had witnessed some improvement in agricultural production during few years due to introduction of deep tube well of 72.9 hectare land irrigation (48.60 hectare winter crop and 24.3 hectare summer crop). The intensity of cropping is better and agrarian structure is characterized by small and marginal farmers. The average farm size records 0.947 hectare (5.85 bigha). The village possesses 8.1 hectare (50 bigha) area as habitation and 2.43 hectare (45 bigha) as CPRs in the form of vested grazing land scattered here and there. The literacy rate of this village is 45 per cent. Besides, this village at first experienced as pioneer of a forest protection committee (FPC) under Joint Forest Management (JFM) involving local people in the management and protection of forest in the early 1990's in Birbhum.

Analysis and Findings of Survey Results : Details about the Awareness of Local People (Mainly Tribals) Regarding Non-wood Forest Products (NWFP) and Valuation

Let us discuss about the price of various Non-wood Forest Products (NWFP), time engaged in forestry and benefits which the poor people get directly or indirectly at this village. NWFPs are generally the major source of earning for the fringe population in a forest based ecosystem and have either some industrial use as raw material as food item.

Green Sal leaves are collected throughout the year except February and March when the trees remain leafless. Those leaves are used for making Sal leaf plate by hand weaving. These Sal plates are sold in the market with lower price varying a range between Rs. (1.50 – 2.00) / bundle with 20 pieces of Sal plates. One woman respondent reported that she could collect green Sal leaves in a day within 5 hr from 7 AM to 12 Noon such amount by which 320 piece of Sal plates can be easily made. A tribal woman can be employed 10 hrs per day for only collection and making of Sal plates. Various types of Mushrooms grow naturally in Sal forests throughout the year. These are collected by FPC members and other villagers for domestic consumption as well as for commercial gain. The price of Mushroom varies from Rs. 25 to Rs. 30 per Kg. Economically important mushrooms include Kurukuri Mushroom, produced in June-July and Karan Mushroom, produced in August-September.

Mohua is collected from March to June. The flower is used for preparing liquor (Rs. 12 per litre), the puppy portion of the fruit is used as vegetable (Rs. 10 per Kg.) and edible oil is extracted from the seeds (Rs. 30 per Kg.). Kend leaves are used for making "Bidis". Fodder income from forestry is estimated by subtracting expenditure behind a cattle after grazing in forest for 6 or 7 hrs per day from total expenditure incurred by that cattle staying at home throughout the whole day. Although the valuation of fodder income from forestry and other forest products is estimated as imputed value. Employment generation from forestry is calculated on the basis of how much time household's members would enable to be engaged for looking after cattle during grazing in the forestry per day. The time is generally accounted for 5 or 6 hrs from 10 A.M. to 5 P.M. per day. Fuel income from forestry is calculated as Rs. 6-8 per sack filled up dry leaves and small dry twigs. The required time for collection of one sack of dry leaves per candidate is 1 – 1½ hr which is taken into consideration as employment generation for fuel collection in forestry. Prices of other forest products are as follows :

(i)	Forest Potato	Rs. 4 / Kg.
(ii)	Cashew nut	Rs. 30/Kg.
(iii)	Mango	Rs. 10/Kg.
(iv)	Date	Rs. 10/Kg.
(v)	Piyel Fruit	Rs. 12/Kg.
(vi)	Tassar	Rs. 45/piece
(vii)	Honey	Rs. 80/Kg.
(viii)	Resin	Rs. 65/Kg.
(ix)	Gum	Rs. 50/Kg.
(x)	Broom	Rs. 5/piece

Myrobalans is the collective term given to the fruits of Amloki (Embalika officinalls), Behera (Terminalia bellerica) and Haritaki (Terminalia chebula). The fruits are medicinal and also used in manufacturing ink and as mordant in dyeing of cotton. The fruits are collected, dried, bagged and marketed. Other medicinal plants like Anantamul, Satamul, Kamegh, Kruchi etc. are collected and used for improving health conditions. The local tribal people have direct awareness and indigenous knowledge about the NWFPs and its uses.

Table 1 : Average Household Size and Sex Ratio, at Banavilla

Caste	*Total house-hold*	*Total house-hold*	*Average house-hold size*	*Male*	*Female*	*Sex Ratio (Male; Female*	*Life Expectancy*	*Fertility rate*	*Age at marriage*
ST	35	156	4.45	81	75	1 : 0.925 (1000 : 925)	40-50 yrs	3 / woman	14-18 yrs.

Table 2 : No and Percentage of Households Use Various Sources of Drinking, Cooking and Bathing Water

Caste	Sources of drinking water				Sources of Cooking waster				Sources of Bathing			
	GP	TW	W	Pond	GP	TW+DTW	W	Pond	GP	TW	W	Pond
	10	21	4	-	7	19	5	4	3	8	4	20
	(28.57)	(60.00)	(11.42)		(20.00)	(54.28)	(14.28)	(11.42)	(8.57)	(22.85)	(11.42)	(57.14)

Table 1 highlights that the average household size and fertility rate account for 4 and 3 woman respectively. Tribal women get into married within average 14-18 years and estimated life expectancy of tribal people varies within range 40-50 years that is lower expectancy in the tribals than the national average. Sex ratio at this tribal village witnesses 1000 : 925 (Male : Female) following almost national average and medium fertility rate compared to national average. The literacy rate of tribal people records 45% which is lower than that of general as well as SC population.

Table 2 exhibits that most of the households (60.00% and 54.28%) collect drinking water and cooking water from tube-well, deep tube well and pond is the main source of bathing (57.14%) . German project and well play an important role for providing sources of drinking water, cooking water and bathing to some extent. Some respondents report me that they are more conscious about drinking, cooking and bathing water and they do not have any problem for securing three types of water which directly influence the good health of tribal population.

Table 3 : Place of Birth of Children

Caste	*No of Household under care of*			*Hospital*	*Nursing*	*Total*
	Untrained Class	*Trained Class*	*Elderly Relative*			
ST	28 (80.00)	—	—	6 (17.15)	1 (2.85)	35

Figures in parenthesis are the per centages.

Table 3 gives an interesting picture that tribal women give birth their child at home (80.00%) in hospital (17.16%) and in nursing home (2.85%) respectively. They are presently facilitating by ICDS (Integrated Child Development Scheme) and DFID (The Department for International Development), *e.g.* maternity benefit (Rs. 500 – 700, JSY).

Table 4 : Account of Immunization of Children below 6 Years and Haria Drinking

Caste	*Immunization done (no. of household)*	*Immunization running*	*Immunization not done*	*% of Haria drinking*
ST	7 (20.00)	16 (45.71)	12 (34.28)	30 (85.71)

Table 4 depicts that about 20 per cent households have done immunisation, 45.71 per cent are continuing immunisation and 34.28 per cent of households neglect immunisation due to lack of knowledge about good health. *Haria* drinking is common picture among the tribal population and here is also no exception and *haria* drinking has direct bearing on ill health. The tribal population are not aware of this malpractice.

Table 5 measures the following village level survey data. It gives an account of Rs. 7147.70 as AFY; 20.98% of AFY to ATY; Rs. 1718.82 as AFY_{fuel}; 5.04 % of AFY_{fuel} to AFY; Rs. 2454.91 as AFY (fodder); 6.10% of AFY (Fodder) to AFY; 344 as AFLD (Average forest labour days); 45.61% of AFLD respectively. All these accounts visualise the importance of forest resources in the lives and economy of tribal people.

Table 6 brings out that per centage of annual forest income to total income per household varies from 9.92 to 29.1. Per centage of forest labour days to total annual labour days per household varies from 29.23 to 70.1. Maximum and Minimum per capita forest income record Rs. 267 and Rs. 45 respectively. These results visualize the high degree of dependence of tribal households on forest resources for income generation and employment creation.

Table 5 : Average Forest income (AFY) per house hold per annum, percent of average forest income to total average income (%AFY to TAY), Average Fuel Income (AFY), percent of Average Fuel Income to Average Forest Income (% AFY to TAFY), AFY $_{fodder}$, % AFY $_{fodder}$ to AFY, AFY $_{Sal\ Plate}$, % AFY $_{Sal\ Plate}$ to AFY of household

Forest Items / Village	AFY (Rs.)	% AFY to ATY	AFY (fuel) (Rs.)	% AFY (Fuel) to AFY	AFY (fodder) (Rs.)	% AFY (Fodder) to AFY	AFY (Sal) (Rs.)	% AFY (Sal) to AFY	AFLD (Labour Day)	% AFLD to ATLD
Banavilla (N = 35)	7147.70	20.98	1718.82	5.04	2254.91	6.10	2444.86	7.89	344	45.61

Table 6 : Forest Related Information of Household

Forest Items / Village	Maximum Total Forest Income (Rs.)	Minimum Total Forest Income (Rs.)	% of Maximum FY to TY	% of Minimum FY to TY	Maximum Forest Labour Days (FLD)	Minimum FLD	% of Maximum FLD to TLD	% of Minimum FLD to TLD	Maximum FY_{PC} (Rs.)	Maximum FY_{PC} (Rs.)
Banavilla (N = 35)	102356	16510	29.21	9.92	698	218	70.19	20.32	268	45

Table 7 : Per centange of Households Used Forest Products in the Items of Fuel, Fodder, Sal-plate Making at Banavilla

Forest Items / *Village*	*% of Household used fueld*	*Fodder (%)*	*Sal Plate (%)*
Banavilla	97.14	71.42	80.00

Table 7 shows that 97.14 per cent households use dry fallen leaves and twigs of forest as fuel, fodder used by households estimate 71.42% and households make Sal Plate about 80%. So forest resources can be conceived as life blood of tribals economy.

Correlation matrix table 8 reveals that there have some degree of association of forest resource base with non-forest items *i.e.* farm and non-farm activities, family members and no. of cattle etc. This table shows that farm size is without having any reason highly related (X_1X_2 35 : 0.5844) with family members. No. of cattle is highly related; (X_3X_1 : 0.650184) with farm size because big farm size owner brings up more cattle for carrying out agriculture activities and for required milk. Non-forest income is positively and significantly related (X_4X_2 : 0.599447) with no. of family members indicating that given the availability of jobs from farm and non-farm sectors more number of family members can get greater scope for earning more. No. of LD in forest varies positively with some degree of correlation (X_5X_2 : 0.492747) with No. of family members. It seems to indicate having greater number of family members may be helpful for increasing participation in both forest and farm activities. Fuel collected from forest in terms of dry leaves and twigs is also highly correlated (X_7X_2 : 0.678814) with no. of family members and less correlated (X_7X_1 : 0.025204) with farm size but negatively associated (X_7X_3 : - 0.12562) with no. of cattle because higher the no. of family members higher is the day to day fuel consumption. The households holding more farm and more no. of cattle are associated with reduction of fuel collection from forest. This is because having larger number of cattle means larger supply of fuel in the form of cowdung. Households possessing more land and no. of cattle

Table 8 : Correlation Matrix Among Farm Size (X_1) Family Member (X_2), No. of Cattle (X_3), Non-Forest Income (NFY :X_4), Forest Labour Days (FLD :X_5), Non-Forest Labour Day (NFLD : X_6) Fuel Income (X_7), Fodder Income (X_8)

X_iX_j	X_1	X_2	X_3	X_4	X_5	X_6	X_7	X_8
X_1		0.584435	0.650184	0.208949	0.140701	0.37925	0.025204	0.730342
X_2			0.325287	0.599447	0.492747	0.483114	0.678814	0.453327
X_3				0.136394	0.255002	0.378615	-0.12562	0.956272
X_4					0.210127	0.475532	0.447392	0.166842
X_5						0.382661	0.580092	0.310276
X_6							0.26174	0.412643
X_7								-0.92232
X_8								

manage fuel requirement from their own agricultural residual and cow dung. As a result, fuel collected from forest for such households is reduced as compared to less farm- size and less no. of cattle owner households. Fuel collected from forest obviously shows positive and significant relation (X_7 X_5 : 580092) with no. of LD in forest. Fodder income from forest also makes high and positive correlation (X_8X_1 : 0.730342) because with farm size and no. of cattle (X_8X_3 : 0.956272) higher farm size owner possess no. of cattle. This table also accounts for the inverse relationship between fuel collected from forest and fodder income from forest (X_7X_8 : -0.0232) because more fodder income form forest having implied more farm size and more no. of cattle explains to reduction of fuel collection from forest. This table also brings out an interesting feature that non-forest income is less correlated (X_4X_5 : 0.210127) with no. of LD in forest, it seems to indicate the availability of farm and non-farm jobs does not affect in the collection of forest products. The table also exhibits the following less correlation combination.

	$r(X_1X_3) = 0.325287$,	$r(X_4X_5) = 0.210127$
$r(X_4X_8 = 0.16642$	$r(X_1X_4) = 0.208949$,	$r(X_1X_6) = 0.37925$
$r(X_5X_8) = 0.310276$	$r(X_1X_5) = 0.140701$,	$r(X_3X_6) = 0.378615$
	$r(X_3X_4) = 0.136394$,	$r(X_5X_6) = 0.382661$
	$r(X_3X_5) = 0.255002$,	$r(X_1X_7) = 0.025204$
		$r(X_5X_7) = 0.26174$

So, $Y = f(X_1, X_3, X_4, X_5, X_6, X_7, X_8)$, where Y = Forest Income.

Table 9 exhibits that there is negative and significant relationship between forest income and farm size of household. This result shows that higher farm holding households earn less forest income due to farm and non-farm activities. The family members and number of cattle's are positively and significantly associated with forest income evidently.

Table 9 : Forest Income (Y) is a fn of (i) farm size (x_1) (ii) family members (x_2) and (iii) No. of cattle (x_3) ; $Y= a + b_1x_1 + b_2x_2 + b_3x_3 + e$

Regression. output Village	*Const.*	*S.E of EST*	*R squared*	N	*Df*	*x coefficient*	*SE of coeff*	*Value of t*
Banavilla	2006.866	1586.424	0.604668	35	31	*(i)* -152.28 (b_1) *(ii)* 979.3077 (b_2) *(iii)* 505.9534 (b_3)	*(i)* 70.0903 *(ii)* 206.245 *(iii)*127.6027	*(i)* -2.1726 * *(ii)* 4.7482** *(iii)* 3.9650***

* indicates 10% level of significance.

** indicates 5% level of significance.

*** indicates 1% level of significance.

Table 10 : Number and proportion of poor and non-poor households w.r.t. annual income and annual income excluding forest income and taking into consideration for poor household with less than Rs. 20,000 per annum, while non-poor household with more than Rs. 20,000 per annum respectively

Village	*No. of H.H. w.r.t. A.Y.*	*No. of non-poor H.H.wrt A.Y.*	*No. of poor H.H. excluding A.Y.*	*No. of non-poor H.H. w.r.t. without F.Y.*
Banavilla	5	30	11	24
	(14.00)	(86.00)	(31.00)	(69.00)

Table 10 reveals that the no. and per cent of poor and non-poor households with respect to annual income account for 5(14.00%) and 30(86.00%) respectively.

This result signifies low per centage of poor households as compared to non-poor households due to performance of agrarian structure facilitated by better irrigation system uses

Table 11 : No. and proportion of households lie below poverty line according to poverty line (Rupees per capita per month) : NSS report, 1999-2000, Rural : 335.46 and Urban 451.19 is 0% of FY to TY variation with respect to Income group

Income group (Rs.)	*No. of households lies PBL w.r.t. total excluding FI*	*No. of household lies BPL w.r.t.*	*Variation between income group*	*Variation with income group*	*Value of 'F'*
					266.30
10,000-	7(n_1 = 13)	10(n_1=13)	xj = 23.68	28.46	F= 28.46
<30,000		(28.57)	n_1 = 13		= 9.356**
30,000-	0(n_2=19)	1(n_2=19)	x.j = 21.04		
<50,000		(2.85)	n_2 =19		
50,000 &	0(n_3 = 3	0(n_3 = 3)	x.j = 8.90		
above	20.00%–3		n_3 =3, p-1 = 2		
	20%	31.42%	266.30		

**indicates 5% level of significance.

of forest resources in a sustainable way, good communication system, situation from local market, abundant of opportunity to enter into non-farm activities, and well assistance (help) of local panchayat. If the forest income is excluded from annual income of household so no. and proportion of poor households increases from 5 to 11(14.00 – 31.00%) with reduction of no. and proportion of non-poor households from 30-24 (86% - 69%). This result implies that forest resources play an active and useful role in reducing income inequality between poor and non-poor households and alleviation of rural poverty at Banavilla. To some extent symmetrical distribution of income is made possible through forest income among the households.

Table 11 makes a comparison between below poverty line (BPL) households on the basis of per capita per month income taking into consideration of household's annual income and exclusion of forest income from household's annual income. This table represents that as a whole and 20 per cent of households within in group Rs. 10,000 - <30,000 lie BPL while other two groups do not fall under BPL. But it has increased from 20% to 31.42% w.r.t. total annual income without forest income where 28.57% in income group of Rs. 10,000 - <30,000 and 2.85% in income group of Rs. 30,000 - <50,000. The high value of F (9.35 at 5% level) also indicates the proportion of forest income to total income differs significantly between income group. The above results also significantly imply that forest income plays a pivotal role in eradication of rural poverty, an important tool in reducing income inequality between poor and non-poor and between different income groups.

5. Conclusion

Prof. A.K. Sen has also emphasised on Public Health and primary education to increase efficiency of work force. Various N.G.O. have come forward to ensure the improving health condition to some extent. It has been found that illiteracy in tribal, as also in non-tribal population is positively correlated with ill health. Root of ill health lies in poverty. Forest income has a direct bearing on poverty alleviation as well as ensuring good health. Efficiency in work force promotes agricultural and industrial production and accelerates economic growth. Economic growth reduces poverty and unemployment securing human development and quality of life in terms of good health, nutrition, higher literacy education and employment income, high life expectancy, low infant mortality and good communication system to some extent. JFM acts as an instrument to reduce poverty, promote health condition and secure economic development of tribal people.

Major Finding of the Study are :

(i) Tribal's household derives 9.92% to 29.21% of their income from forests.

(ii) Per centage of forest labour days to total annual labour days per household varies from 20.23 to 70.19.

(iii) The tribal people are very conscious about the NWFPs they are utilising in optimum and feasible way.

(iv) The tribal people find that NWFPs are very useful to them during the stressful time in maintaining their day to day requirements.

(v) Tribal women are main responsible for collection of NWFPs.

(vi) There is negative and significant relationship between forest income and farm size of households.

(vii) JFM helps to reduce rural poverty and unemployment and promote health condition.

(viii) There is medium fertility (3/woman) and lower incidence of malnutrition among the tribal people. About 85.71 per cent tribal people drink haria.

(ix) The tribal woman is medium healthy.

(x) The tribal woman is illiterate.

(xi) Low nutritional status of the tribals.

(xii) Medium life expectancy (40 – 50 years) in the tribals.

(xiii) The literacy rate of tribal people shows 45 per cent.

(xiv) The status of the tribal women in the study area can be evaluated by over-work, illiteracy, sub-human physical

living conditions, medium fertility and availability of modern health care facilities to some extent.

(xv) Tribal people suffer from sickle cell disease/anemia.

(xvi) The fruits like Amloki, Bahera and Haritaki are medicinal and medicinal plants like Anantamul, Satamul, Kalmegh, Kruchi etc. are collected and used for improving health status of the tribal people.

In order to the upliftment of tribal economy, health and rejuvenation of forests the following steps should be taken :

(1) Primary health care and health centres must be introduced in the study area.

(2) To afforest the barren lands and reforest the degraded forest land.

(3) To meet the requirements of fuel, fodder fertiliser, fruit of the forest – dwellers in around forest area.

(4) To generate additional labour opportunity particularly to the landless tribal.

(5) Formation of Self Help Group (SHGs) from amongst tribal people including the members of forest protection committee (FPCS) may take an effective role to uplift the social and economic status of the tribals.

(6) It is accepted the fact that ill effects of the chemical fertilizers have set out recently. So the SHGs will be trained for making vermicompost, manufacturing of dishes and/or plates with 'Sal wood leaves'. Forest will be utilized for 'Be-keeping'. A subsidiary project of Goat keeping will also be initiated. Thus, with the introduction of these activities the social and economic health of the tribal in the study area will substantially be uplifted.

REFERENCES

Agarwal, Bina (1989) : Rural Women, Poverty and Natural Resources – Sustence, Sustainability and Struggle for Change. EPW, October 28, 1989.

Agarwal, S.K. (1997) : Poverty and Environment (Environment Issues and Themes).

Beck, Tony (1994) : Common Property Resource. Access by Poor and Class Conflict in West Bengal. EPW, January 22, 1994.

Beck Tony, Madan Ghosh (2000) : Common Property Resources and the Poor – Findings from West Bengal, EPW, March, 2000.

Ballabh, Vishwa (2001) : Forestry and Related Issues. Indian Journal of Agri. Econs., Vol. 56., No. 1. Jan. – March 2001; Pages 29-32.

Chatterjee, Nandini (2001) : Social Forestry and Human perception in Birbhum District ('Environment, population and Development' edited by Prithyishnag Chandra, Shekhar Kumar, Simita Sengupta, 2001.

Chand, Attar (1983) : Economics of Forestry.

Nayyar, Dhiraj (2000) : The Health Status of Tribals, EPW, October, 14, 2000.

8

Poverty and Health in Orissa : An Overview

—Santosh Kumar Behera,
—K.C. Sahoo

1. Introduction

Orissa is a major state in eastern India with an estimated population of 36,804,660 people (2001). Orissa is a reach state with poor people. Orissa is endowed with rich natural resources in the form of vast mineral deposits, with forest, fertile land, plentiful surface and ground water resources, long coastline, and picturesque tourist potential. But, such resources have not been exploited adequately for income generation activities. In that sense, she is poor. The annual population growth is 1.83 per cent, which is lower than the all-India figure of 2.14. Scheduled Tribes and Scheduled Castes, mostly living below poverty line, constitute nearly 41 per cent of the population. . Around 47.13% (all India average is 26.1%) in Orissa lives below poverty line, with limited access to exploitable resources due to a complex interplay of social, economic and cultural dynamics. Frequent droughts, floods, cyclones and other natural calamities not only impoverish the people, but also make them morbidly stoic towards the place of development. When we look the data sets for Orissa, anybody will be astonished. Orissa has the highest infant mortality in the country. Our two-third of the rural population is living in abject poverty and health facility is pretty bad, as we have lowest number of doctors per capita in the world. Most surprising thing is that we have less than 5% of the population having access to subsided food aimed at poverty alleviation. State's economy has in curried huge losses to the extent of Rs. 13,230 Crore due to natural calamities from 1998-2003. More then 90% of the state plan outlay is being financed from borings. The health status of a population is a reflection of the socio-economic development of the country and is shaped by a variety of factors–the level of income and standard of living, housing, sanitation, water supply, education, employment, health consciousness, personal hygiene and by the coverage, availability, accessibility and affordability of health care delivery services. It is widely accepted that the poor health status of low-income countries is the product of inadequate nutrition, lack of a protected water supply, and overcrowded and in sanitary housing conditions. These conditions lead to deficiency diseases, air-borne diseases, and facially related and water-borne diseases, which dominate the morbidity pattern in less developed countries. In brief, these diseases arise from a set of conditions which in themselves represent poverty and deprivation. Health professionals have a key part to play in eradicating poverty. The relationship between health and poverty or health and development is complex, multifaceted, and multidirectional. Poverty in its various dimensions could be a manifestation, as well as a determinant, of an individual's health. Since neither health nor socio-economic development alone, but improvement in both is necessary for overall development, policy makers are baffled as to how much improvement in health is necessary to trigger improvement in the economic front, and *vice-versa*.

Theoretical background of this Paper : Based on the secondary sources of data the present paper attempts to analyze the scenario of poverty and health condition of the state of Orissa. This study also attempts to focus the role of the government of Orissa and India to eradicate poverty and improve the health status of the state.

Poverty and Health Scenario in the State of Orissa as Compared to India—Poverty ratios for rural and urban areas of Orissa and India are given in Table-1. It shows that the poverty ratio in Orissa has declined from 67.28% in 1973-74 to 48.01% in 1999-2000 in rural areas and from 55.62% to 42.83%

in urban areas. But, these figures are much higher as compared to the national average of 27.09% for rural areas and 23.62% for urban areas in 1999-2000.

Table 1 : Per centage of Population below Poverty Line in Orissa and India

Year	Orissa			India		
	Rural	Urban	Combined	Rural	Urban	Combined
1973–74	67.28	55.62	66.18	56.44	49.01	54.88
1977–78	72.38	50.92	70.07	53.07	45.24	51.32
1983–84	67.53	49.15	65.29	45.65	40.79	44.48
1987–88	57.64	41.53	55.58	39.09	38.20	38.36
1993–94	49.72	41.64	48.56	37.27	32.36	35.97
1999–2000	48.01	42.83	47.15	27.09	23.62	26.10

Source : Government of India, Economic Survey 2001-02.

Table 2 : Percentage Distribution of Persons below Poverty Line by Occupation Groups, 1993-94 and 1999-2000 (Rural).

India	Years	Artisans	Agri-cultural labours	Non-Ag. Labours	Self-Employed in Agri-culture	Others	Total
	1993–94	11.2	40.7	08.4	33.2	6.5	100
	1999–2000	12.3	46.8	7.6	28.1	5.3	100
Orissa	1993–94	14.2	45.2	5.3	30.8	4.4	100
	1999–2000	8.2	5.9	4.2	26.6	5.1	100

Source : NSS 50th and 55th rounds data on household consumer expenditure.

Table 3 : Percentage Distribution of Persons below Poverty Line by Caste 1993–94 and 1999–2000.

	Year	ST	SC	OBC	Others	Total
India	1993–94	14.8	27.6	—	57.6	100
	1999–2000	17.5	27.3	—	55.2	100
Orissa	1993–94	36.0	18.5	—	45.5	100
	1999–200	41.1	22.4	—	36.4	100

Source : NSS 50th and 55th rounds data on household consumer expenditure.

The incidence of poverty by social groups shows that there was higher concentration of poverty among the scheduled caste and scheduled tribe population in both rural and urban areas.

Health Systems Performance: An Overview : Health status is a crucial variable which influences the average expectation of life as well as number of persons in the productive age bracket, production, productivity, earning capacity and finally welfare. It may be stated that a country's progress depends on the health of the people, (Ansu Pari, 1998). According to modern concept of WHO, *"health implies a sound mind in a sound body, in a sound environment"*. There have been significant changes in the health scenario over the past two decades. Infant mortality has decreased from 143 to 81 between 1980 and 2002, a reduction of 62, which given the overall situation under which the state has been performing, is not a small achievement. However, it is a matter of concern that over the last four years the infant mortality rate (IMR) has stagnated. Institutional delivery has not increased much, but the deliveries are now taking place in better surroundings than before due to increased awareness of the people supported by the trained birth attendants, anganwadi workers, and auxiliary nurse midwives (ANMs). The immunization programme has been doing well, despite great difficulty in making potent vaccines available in ultra rural inaccessible pockets. Polio has been almost eradicated. After staying polio free for 3½ years, two cases of polio have been detected in one district in the State in late 2002. Orissa was and still continues to be a major contributor in the national figure of deaths due to malaria. Diarrhea diseases are still rampant, but there is a significant reduction in the deaths due to diarrhea. Tuberculosis (TB) detection and treatment has shown promising trends in the last few years.

Table 4 : Neo-natal, Infant and Under 5 Mortality Rates (Deaths for 1000s Lives births):1998-99.

	Neo-natal Mortality Rate (NMR)			*Infant mortality Rate (IMR)*			*Under 5 mortality Rate (U5M)*		
	Rural	*Urban*	*Total*	*Rural*	*Urban*	*Total*	*Rural*	*Urban*	*Total*
India	46.7	31.7	43.4	73.3	47	66.6	103.7	63.1	94.9
Orissa	48.6	49.3	48.6	80.9	81.1	81	104.8	102	104.4

Source: http : / / www.nfhsindia.org / pnfhs2.html.

——

Table 5 : Comparison of Health Status of Orissa with India

Indicators	*Orissa*	*India*
IMR (Infant Mortality Rate)	81	67.6
CMR (Child Mortality Rate)	25.5	29.3
Life Expectancy % of Population	58	60
Below Poverty line	47.15	26.10
Complete Vaccination	57.8	54.2

Source : Health for the millions, December, 2002—January, 2003.

This table above clearly underlines Orissa's position in healthcare as among the lowest possible status. This has resulted in Orissa being part of the infamous BIMAROU states of India. The comparison is done with other states in India, which are doing well to highlight that it is possible for a developing country like India to achieve higher health status. The question being "If it is possible for other states in India to attain better health status why not Orissa?"

Assessment of National Health Programmes : TB/ Malaria/Leprosy/HIV/AIDS

Tuberculosis

The government estimates that there are about 500,000 cases of TB in Orissa at any given time, and that about 25 per cent of these (125,000) are sputum positive. The incidence is estimated at about 80,000 new cases per year, with about 17,500 deaths occurring annually due to TB (State TB Cell, DHS – Status Report 2000-2001). Some of the districts are covered under the RNTCP (Revised National Tuberculosis Control Programme) funded by DANTB, DANIDA. This covers ten districts in north and South Orissa, and is ready to take off in four more districts. These districts have sufficient quantities of anti-TB drugs, chemicals, etc. The laboratory technicians (and in some cases, Pharmacists) have been trained in sputum microscopy, and records and registers are maintained separately. This programme follows the DOTS treatment, and DOTS providers are also trained. Regular programme monitoring takes place and the cure rate is over 85 per cent with low defaulter rates. In the districts not covered by the RNTCP, the regular National TB control programme is functioning. Of this, SCC (short-course chemotherapy) is available in some districts.

Malaria

Malaria is one of the leading causes of death in Orissa, and is a matter of great concern. The number of reported deaths due to malaria (in absolute numbers) has increased steadily since 1993. It is estimated that only about 10 per cent of malarial deaths get reported as such. In 2000, there were 442 deaths reported due to malaria. Who are diagnosing and treating TB patients. The World Bank assisted Enhanced Malaria Control Programme (EMCP) operates in 158 out of the 314 blocks. The total cost of the project in India is Rs. 6758.86 million (1996), and Orissa has the second largest share of the total project budget. The project has been running for the past three years, but according to the departmental report, 'no significant development has been observed in EMCP blocks for control of malaria'. The remaining blocks are covered under the National Anti-Malaria Programme (NAMP). Costs for this are shared equally between the Centre and the states. The salaries of all staff (EMCP and NAMP) are borne by the state. In spite of having Drug Distribution Centers (DDCs) and Fever Treatment Depots (FTDs) in many places smear collection and reporting are much delayed. Availability of chloroquine tablets in the remote hamlets is a problem. Many deaths due to malaria go unreported, or are reported as 'fever' and the state does not accept this as a malaria death if no smear was taken, or the smear was not read. The concept of 'Presumptive Radical Treatment' or PRT was introduced in 1996; it only began being implemented in 1998, that too, in a few areas. Staff in most areas is not aware of this, nor are there adequate stocks of primaquine readily available. There is a need to improve the monitoring of the malaria control programme in Orissa in order to ensure that there is some control over the spread of the disease.

Leprosy

Effective treatment for Leprosy was not available till 1981 when WHO prescribed Multi-Drug Therapy (MDT). After the introduction of MDT, the National Leprosy Control Programme was renamed as National Leprosy Eradication Programme (NLEP). The NLEP is one of the most successfully implemented National Health Programmes in the state of Orissa, with support from Government of India, the World Bank, and several bilateral donor agencies. The extensive use of MDT in the state has completely changed the leprosy scenario of the state within the last 18 years. The disease was highly endemic in the state prior to launching of the NLEP in the year 1983. At that time the prevalence of the disease was 121.4 in 10,000 populations. The endemicity of the disease in different districts varied from 50 to 250 per 10,000 populations. Since 1982–83, 7.6 lakh leprosy cases have already been registered under MDT and of them over 94 per cent cases have already been cured and discharged. The prevalence of the disease came down to only 7.6 per 10,000 populations by 1 February 2001. Orissa has planned to achieve elimination of leprosy, bringing down the prevalence rate of leprosy below 1 case per 10,000 populations by the end of 2004. The leprosy elimination programme in Orissa is supported by the Government of India, the World Bank through the Government of India, WHO, DANIDA, LEPRA, The Leprosy Mission, Hoina, and the German Leprosy Relief Association. The state plans to consolidate the efforts towards elimination of leprosy in the next 3 years with wider involvement of the general health care system, NGOs, and the community as a whole.

HIV/AIDS

The National AIDS Control Programme was started in the state in 1992. However, with several other communicable diseases prevalent in the state, not much importance was given to the programme. Even today, Orissa has few HIV+ and full-blown AIDS cases as a per centage of its population. It is a low prevalence state. Nevertheless, with HIV+ cases at just below

1 per cent of the population, the alarm bells are ringing. In 1999, Phase II of the National AIDS Control Programme was started with the objectives of reducing the spread of HIV infection in the state and strengthening the state's capacity to respond to HIV/AIDS on a long term basis. It plans to reduce HIV infection among high-risk population through targeted interventions, STD Control, and condom programming; and to promote prevention among low risk population through IEC activities, social mobilization blood safety, and counseling. It also plans to build the capacity of the community for low cost care and support of people living with HIV/AIDS (PLWHA). The programme is under implementation. Its success (or otherwise) can be known only after some time.

Poverty Alleviation Programmes : Poverty reduction has been an important goal of development policy since the inception of planning of India. The central and state governments over the last five decades have adopted several poverty alleviation strategies. These could be classified into four broad groups such as *(i)* institutional reforms, *(ii)* empowerment of the poor; *(iii)* development of resource deficient areas; and *(iv)* special employment programmes.

2. Institutional Reforms

Land Reforms : Land reforms constitute one of the major institutional reforms for ushering in egalitarian growth. The main components of the land reforms (LRs) undertaken by the government are: abolition of Zamindaris/jagirdaris and other intermediaries; regulation of tendency; consolidation of landholdings; and distribution of ceiling surplus land to landless and marginal holders. In the 1950s and 1960s, the functionless intermediaries and Zamindaris were abolished in several states.

Decentralization : Decentralization of development administration and planning was one of the major development interventions in the 1950s and 1960s. The creation of a community development block below the district level was essentially viewed as a significant measure to take administration closure to the people. The creation of local bodies, namely, panchayati raj institutions (PRIs) for rural development planning at the instance of Balwant Rai Mehta Committee (1957), was an initiative to facilitate people's participation in planning and implementation.

3. Empowerment of the Poor

Empowerment of women and the socially disadvantaged classes like SCs and STs have been receiving attention of the development professionals during the last three decades. The empowerment of the poor is a multistage process and all the different sections of poor (SCs, STs and Women) should be enabled through a series of measures like leadership building, legal knowledge, livelihood security, and better access to information. The active participation of the poor in the development process has been deemed to be a pre-requisite for improving their socio-economic status.

Self-Help Groups (SHGs) : The field experience in the realm of administering of poverty alleviation programmes (PAPs) during the last few decades clearly points out that groups approach has an edge over an individual oriented one. The development of women and children in rural areas (DWCRA) was introduced in 1982-83 and it promoted groups' activity and helped poor women establish better access to formal credit institutions and markets. It also aimed at sensitizing the women to the socio-economic problems of their environment. Thus, the SHGs of the poor offer great promise for the socio-economic upliftment of the poor in a sustainable manner.

4. Development of Resource Deficient Areas

Poverty has been concentrated in resource deficient areas like desert, drought prone and remote hilly areas. Some of these regions have been experiencing environmental degradation due to soil and wind erosion, loss of vegetative cover, and extreme shifting of sand. To restore ecological balance and also to develop a drought proof mechanism, the Drought Prone Area Programme (DPAP) was launched in 1973.

5. Employment Programmes

Self-employment Programmes : Swaranjayanti Gram Swarozgar Yojana (SGSY) : The SGSY, launched in April 1999, aims at bringing the assisted poor families (Swarozgaris) above the poverty line by organizing them into Self- Help Groups (SHGs) through a mix of Bank Credit and government subsidy.

Food-For-Work Programme—The Food-For–Work programme (FFW) is one of the oldest wage employment programme launched during the 1970s. The programme was designed to ensure employment and food security to rural people affected by natural disasters like droughts and floods. In November 14, 2004, the National Food-For-Work Programme (NFFWP) has been launched in the 150 most backward districts.

Sampoorna Grameen Rozgar Yojana (SGRY)—It launched in 2001, aims at providing additional wage employment in all rural areas and thereby food security and improve nutritional levels.

Rural Housing-Indira Awaas Yojana (IAY)—The IAY operationalised from 1999-2000 is the major scheme for construction of houses for the poor, free of cost.

Rural Employment Generation Programme (REGP)—It launched in 1995 with the objective of creating self-employment opportunities in the rural areas and small towns, is being implemented by the Khadi and Village Industries Commission (KVIC).

Prime Minister's Rozgar Yojana (PMRY)—It started in 1993 with the objective of making available self employment opportunities.to the educated unemployed youth by assisting them in setting up any economically viable activity.

Swarna Jayanti Shahari Rozgar Yojana (SJSRY)—The Urban Self employment Programme and the Urban Wage Employment are the two special components of the SJSRY, which in December 1997, substituted for various extent programmes implemented for urban poverty alleviation.

Jawahar Gram Samridhi Yojana (JGSY)—It works that result in the creation of durable productive community assets are taken up.

National Social Assistance Programme (NSAP)—It provides social assistance benefit to poor households affected by old age, death of the primary breed winner or need for maternity care, through National Old Age Pension Scheme, National Family Benefit Scheme and National Maternity Benefit Scheme.

Employment Assurance Scheme (EAS)—A wage employment programme, which generates additional wage employment opportunities during the period of acute shortage of wage employment through manual work for the rural poor, living below the poverty line. In Orissa, for generating wage employment opportunities for the rural poor, the scheme was introduced initially in 143 Revamped Public Distribution System (RPDS) blocks of 16 districts on 2nd October 1993. **Pradhan Mantri Gramodaya Yojana (PMGY)**—It aims at improving the quality of life of people in rural areas by focusing on village level development in the critical area of health, primary education, drinking water, housing and rural roads.

For children, **the Integrated Child Development Service Programme (ICDS)** has been introduced in the state from the year 1975-76. Presently, the scheme is being implemented through 281 ICDS projects in 269 blocks of Orissa. It offers a package of health care services covering supplementary nutrition, immunization, health check up, nutrition and health education, maternal care, and pre school education to children in the age group of 0 to 6 years.

For women, **Indira Mahila Yojana (IMY)** : which aims at empowerment of women through awareness generation and training.

Balika Samridhi Yojana (BSY) is another national level programme which aims at improving the status of the girl child belonging to the below poverty line (BPL) groups.

Integrated Rural Development Programme (IRDP) : which is being functioning in the state from the year 1979-80, is a centrally supported anti-poverty programme planned for amelioration of rural poverty?

Training of Rural Youth for Self Employment (TRYSEM) : The purpose of the programme is to equip rural youth in the age group of 18-35 years from families below poverty line with professional skills in different trades and vocations so as to enable them to take up self employment ventures in the fields of agriculture and allied activities and in business.

Managing and Rural Poverty Alleviation Water : An innermost interest should be on the correlation between the management of water resources for sustainable rural livelihoods. The central point of the rural development lies in the management of natural resources, and in particular by providing equitable access to resources, including water.

Jawahar Rozgar Yojana (JRY) : implemented in the state of Orissa in 1999-2000.The purpose of the programme is to give hundred days employment to the every BPL families.

Mid-Day Meals Scheme (MDM)—The scheme was operating in 40,697 primary schools covering 45, 03,045 number of students belonging to all the 30 districts of Orissa in 1998-99. The Mid-day Meals scheme is aimed at benefiting the poor and needy primary school going children in the State particularly in rural and backward areas.

6. Conclusion

It is found that the incidence of poverty and ill health were more in northern and southern regions of Orissa as compared to coastal region. Caste-wise, among the scheduled tribe population, the incidence of poverty was higher than that among scheduled caste and other caste population. Further, the per centage of rural families living below the poverty line was found to be much higher in the State. As a result of higher incidence of poverty in the State, the living condition of the people in terms of the development indicators like literacy rate, infant mortality rate, per capita income, per capita food grain production, etc. was much below the national average. Even within the State, composite indices of the socio-economic indicators show that there was greater inter-district variation in the living condition of the people. Moreover, the performances of the welfare activities like EAS, PDS, ICDS and

MDM are observed to be not satisfactory in the State, and these factors are mainly responsible for the poor living condition of the people. In the light of the above findings, it is suggested that efforts should be made to reduce the incidence of poverty among the people of the State at least to the national average through appropriate policy measures.

As the economy grows, poverty diminishes faster when growth is strong, slower when it is not (Allaoua *et. al.* 1997). Economy is related to health. Without economy and health we don't go forward. Economy improves the health condition of the people. But it is not always improving the health. Economy and health are the basic or minimum requirement of once development so far as the human being and area concerned. To improve the living conditions of the people, increase in economic growth is necessary. For this, the values of the development indicators like literacy rate, per capita income, infant survival rate, per capita food grain production, per capita net value added by manufacture, etc. have to be improved through appropriate and adequate investment in the sectors like education, agriculture, health, industry and transport and communication. An integrated approach in all these sectors is very much necessary for the all-round development of the State. To reduce the higher concentration of rural poverty and ill health in the State, adequate funds should be diverted to the rural sector in the form of poverty alleviation programmes and other rural developmental programmes and at the same time, efforts should be made to rectify the present loopholes and problems in the rural developmental programmes. Administration should see that the funds are utilized properly. For better levels of living of the rural poor, increase in agricultural production and stability in food grain prices are highly necessary. With regard to climatic crises like flood, drought, cyclone, etc., the government should take necessary steps to control all these crises, so that, the conjunctural poverty causing mass structural poverty (headcount index) in the State can be reduced. In my point of view not only the role of central and state government but also the role of NGOs and self help groups (SHGs) should take the challenge to eradicate poverty and improve the health status in the state of Orissa.

REFERENCES

Allaoua, Z. *et. al.* (1997), *India—Achievements and Challenges in Reducing Poverty*, The World Bank, Washington, D.C.

Ali, A. (2000a) : *"The Present Health Scenario in India; An Overview"*, Health for the Millions, Vol. 26, no. 2, New Delhi.

Ansu Pari, (1998) : *Diet, Nutrition and Health*, Print Well Publications, New Delhi.

Economic Survey 2005-2006 : Govt. of India, Page 205-207.

Economic Survey 2000 – 2001 : Directorate of Economics and Statistics, Planning and Co-ordination Department, Government of Orissa (2001).

Economic Survey 2001 – 2002 : Directorate of Economics and Statistics, Planning and Co-ordination Department, Government of Orissa (2002).

India Social Development Report : Council for Social Development Oxford University Press, New Delhi, 2006.

Report of Planning Commission : Govt. of Orissa 2001-2002.

Kar, G. C. : *Poverty and Human Development : An Enquiry into the Causes of Rural Poverty in Orissa*, Deptt. Of A. & A. Economics, Utkal University, Bhubaneswar (Mimeo).

Kar, G. C. and R. K. Meher (2001) : *An Evaluation of Anti-poverty Programmes in Koraput District of Orissa* (Mimeo), Nabakrushna Choudhury Centre for Development Studies, Bhubaneswar.

Kar, G. C. and R. K. Meher (2001) : *An Evaluation of Anti-poverty Programmes in Nawarangpur District of Orissa* (Mimeo), Nabakrushna Choudhury Centre for Development Studies, Bhubaneswar.

Khan, M. H. (2001) : *Rural Poverty in Developing Countries – Implications for Public Policy*, International Monetary Fund, Washington D. C., March.

Misra, S. N. and M. Behera (2000) : *An Evaluation of Anti-poverty Programmes in Mayurbhanj District of Orissa* (Mimeo), Nabakrushna Choudhury Centre for Development Studies, Bhubaneswar.

Panda, M. (2000) : *'Changing Poverty Scenario in Orissa'*, Paper presented in the Seminar on 'Social Development Research in Orissa', Nabakrushna Choudhury Centre for Development Studies, Bhubaneswar.

Report of Planning Commission, Govt. of Orissa 2001-2002.

Shankar, K. (1997) : 'Revamped Public Distribution System – Who Benefits and How Much?' *Economic and Political Weekly*, Vol. XXXII, No. 13.

Vaidyanathan, A. (2001) : 'Poverty and Development Policy', *Economic and Political Weekly*, Vol. XXXVI, No. 21, May 26 – June 1.

World Development Report (2000/2001). Attacking Poverty, Oxford University Press, Delhi.

SECTION—II
Health and Development

9

Health and Development–Need for A Healthy City

—*Ranabir Dey*

1. Introduction

Health is an elusive concept, and environmental change is leading us to new health risks and exposure to new forms of danger. Development in its many facets can have very positive but also negative effects on physical and mental health. The notion of development refers to a value-positive concept, which aims at improving the living standards of the people and the general conditions of human welfare in a region. It is a value positive concept because development is an irreversible concept, which can change only for better. Development is mainly referred through its economic sense and has always been highlighted as a quantitative aspect reflected through growth of output and national income. The developmental process has never been neutral nor it is uniformly spread across the regions. The level of economic development is the function of the harmonious interaction between natural environment, technology and the institutions created in a region. However, improvement in health is widely regarded as a vitally important measure of the overall socio-economic development of any country.

In the last four decades, although public health had faired reasonably, which is indicated by improvement in some sensitive health indicators such as rise in life expectancy and reduction in child mortality rates, yet the desired level and standards of medical facilities is still very far from satisfactory. Much of the neglect and failures attributed to health sector in developing nations has been a combination of several strategic or poorly conceived approaches towards socio-economic development. With increasing population growth and resource constraints and environmental degradation, the quality of living conditions in human settlements is deteriorating. Large urban settlements, overcrowding, demographic structure, spatial configuration and lack of urban services have raised several constraints that poses up new challenges in the urban settlements. Environmental health has emerged as the leading concern in the changing mortality and morbidity pattern of many cities. Generally it is argued that developing and less developing nations has woefully under invested in human capital formation, that is, spending on education and health. Furthermore, their priority for human capital formation was and continues to be distorted and questionable.

With respect to health not enough effort was made to promote the *primary health care approach,* often declared as the principal strategy to tackle the many health problems faced by countries. The various health issues that evolve in urban settlement such as environmental degradation resulting from housing shortage and inadequate and ineffective urban services causing health hazards, sedentary life styles and stress related degenerative ail ness, diffusion of several communicable and vector-borne diseases like urban malaria resulting from massive construction and air cooling operations and absence of proper healthy working conditions, are mainly a result of managerial and administrative weaknesses at all levels of the health system. This has resulted to many policies and programmes being poorly implemented leading to widening of the gap between the level of objectives and targets stated and their optimum fulfillment, due to costly inefficiencies and failures. The interrelationships and synergy that seemed to exist between education, housing, fertility control, nutrition, water sanitation and development has not been adequately exploited by the existing policies and programmes.

The model of Health and Socio-Economic Development, as given by *Barlow, 1979* provides a proper understanding about the interaction that exists between the two. There are twenty bivariate relationships shown in the model between health, fertility, nutrition, education and income. The latter represents economic development and can be reflected by growth in per capita income or a similar matter.

The model of Health and Socio-Economic Development, as given by *Barlow, 1979* provides a proper understanding about the interaction that exists between the two. There are twenty bivariate relationships shown in the model between health, fertility, nutrition, education and income. The latter represents economic development and can be reflected by growth in per capita income or a similar matter.

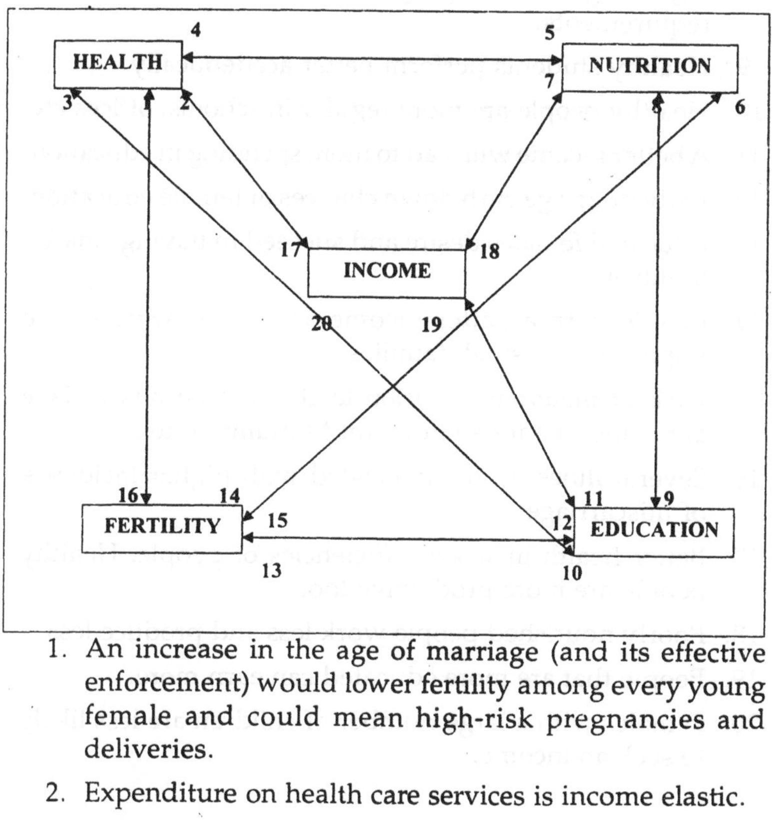

1. An increase in the age of marriage (and its effective enforcement) would lower fertility among every young female and could mean high-risk pregnancies and deliveries.
2. Expenditure on health care services is income elastic.

3. People that are more educated care more for their health.
4. Malnutrition is a primary cause of many illness and disability and often exacerbates other diseases through reduced immunity.
5. Diarrhea often means loss of nutrition.
6. Large number of children and quick succession of birth makes adequate nutrition of each child more difficult and costly.
7. Population in the High Income groups spends for on their diet.
8. People that are more educated are more careful regarding the food preparation and their nutritional requirements.
9. Healthy students perform better academically.
10. Healthy people are more regular in schools, offices etc.
11. A better income will lead to more spending in education.
12. Early marriage curb down chances of female education.
13. Educated females desire and succeed in having smaller families.
14. People with a better income are more aware of the importance of small families.
15. Lack of maternal nutrition leads to more miscarriage and subsequent rise in Infant Mortality Rates.
16. Several illnesses are associated with higher incidence of miscarriage.
17. Better health increases efficiencies of people. Healthy people are more productive too.
18. Poorly nourished people work less and produce less.
19. People that are more educated can earn more.
20. Females with a large number of children are less likely to seek an income.

2. Generalizations

- There should be an increase in medical schools, doctors and hospitals.
- An increase in highly trained health work force and effective role of Government in financing medical schools is ideally desirable.
- There should be a change in the focus on medical education *i.e.* socio-cultural aspects of health, disease and ill ness prevention, health education, management and economic aspect of health care needs to be improved. The role of teamwork should be provided due importance and an integration of medical schools with health care delivery system and planning and evaluation functions of government at local, state and national levels is essential.
- Deficiency in facilities and resources of some medical colleges in respect to medical staff, equipments, library facilities and proper instructors are needed to overcome.
- Tendency of leakage of doctors from public to private sector is a serious concern too.
- Lack of government hospitals seemed to be a chronic problem.
- Biased health spending in favor of urban poor is also an issue to tackle.
- There is an essentiality to provide emphasis on local participation, awareness programmes, proper and effective feed back system, information system on government facilities and an organized community.
- Primary health care approach for resource allocation is the need of the hour to place greater emphasis on education and training of nurses, ANMs and Multipurpose workers.
- There is a need for proper management of primary health care through systematic supervision of staff, greater accountability, better information gathering and

use, training of staff, redefinition of jobs and tasks and improved communication between central and field personnel

3. Healthy Cities

Keeping in mind the above generalizations, it becomes quite evident that every city should have its own strategy to maintain a healthy environment essential for urban sustainability and their own health strategies would reduce health strategies would reduce health burdens in their population. Besides, the continuous growth of urban population due to collective impact of natural growth and continuous influx of migrants to city atmosphere has placed an ever-increasing burden on the social and economic responsibility of the government to maintain the sustainable standards of urban environment. Such a dualistic process all the way impact the city health aspect most adversely. Nevertheless, rapid urban growth had created a sort of panicking pressure on the demand for adequate housing, urban basic services and health care facilities too. The chronic problem with most of such urban growth is its unplanned nature that consequently shoots up a crisis on environment health, over exploitation of natural and human resources and thereby affecting human health. Similarly, rapid scale of industrialization also seems to add health risks. Several diarrhoeal and acute respiratory diseases are its demerits. Besides, the environmental degradation due to uncontrolled waste disposal and its inefficient processing had also created several hiccups. Contaminated food due to inadequate sanitation, misuse of chemicals adds up the disease burden all the way more. An alternative approach, therefore, is usually sought. The Healthy City concept came into the picture only in 1985. It was the title of a speech given at an international meeting in Canada. This presentation involving the role of nurturing environments and healthy cities in maintaining the health of people, offered a set of new and contexts of the place, surroundings, relationships and opportunities and their interactions that affect people's lives. It also suggested the solutions to both community and quality of life problems. It was analyzed that not only good health services or individual lifestyles are important to benefit health but the role of a **supportive environment** seems to be essential too. Supportive environment refers to the physical, economic and social aspects of the surroundings, the settings where people work. *(Man.)*

It was identified that development programmes working in isolation tend to neglect the emerging and existing health concerns. However, the WHO since 1986 has taken initiative to promote the concept of healthy cities, largely in developed countries recently in the developing countries have also come under its influence. Cities were encouraged to target and solve local problems and get people from many parts of the community involved in the Healthy Cities process. WHO then invited practitioners to come together and share strategies, resources and success stories.

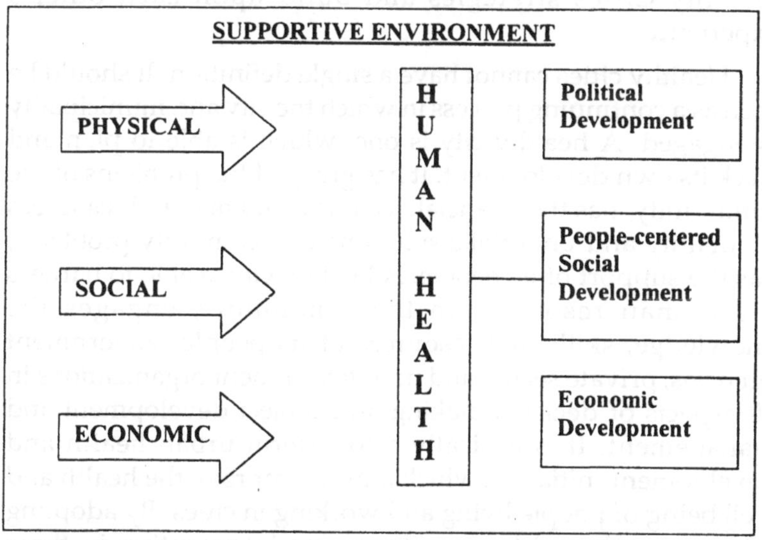

The healthy cities concept seeks to build a strong case for public health at the local level and to put health issues into the agenda for urban policy makers. The major thrust of the concept is that bio-medical approach alone is not enough to solve human health problems and an integrated approach involving social, economic and environmental domains of our settlements for better health has to be considered. The Healthy Cities movement now includes projects in well over 1000 cities and more are starting all the time. Each project defines different goals and activities but all bring a wide variety of people into the community improvement work at hand as when a Healthy Cities project is organized, everyone participates together. The vastness of the concept demands not only governmental initiatives but also NGOs, CBOs, schools, private sector and communities as partners in promoting healthy cities. Achieving Healthy cities means building on each city's own resources and on the skills and managerial capacities of its people and formal and informal institutions. In December 1993, the first global conference on Healthy Cities and Communities was held in California, USA. More than 1400 participants from communities in over 50 countries came together to share Healthy Cities strategies and build upon each other's experience.

Healthy cities cannot have a single definition. It should be seen as a continuing process in which the city and municipality is engaged. A healthy city is one, which is able to plan and track its own development. It has grasp of the problems of the community; has the financial, technical and material resources to identify and undertake solutions to community problems; has the support of its people. A healthy city is able to harness the human resources in the community, engages the knowledge, skills and resources of its people, government agencies, private sector, and non-government organizations in all aspects of decision-making and project development and management. It is basically a long-term urban health and development initiative, which aims to improve the health and well being of people living and working in cities. By adopting this approach and by monitoring an intervention in three domains *i.e.* *(a)* physical and emotional health, *(b)* sustainable environment and *(c)* livelihood and prosperity, the health conditions of all people can be improved and sustained. Healthy city is a place where human beings enjoy sound healthy conditions, good working and living conditions, an environment which is free of all types of pollution, bright, well ventilated homes, with access to clean water, proper recreational facilities for adults and children and a community which maintains common social values. Planning of a healthy city involve improved livelihood strategies, public participation, social thinking and grass root level actions. The following are the key players whose efforts may need to be coordinated in a Healthy Cities project— community members, local, provincial and national politicians, government service providers from a variety of sectors (*e.g.* health, welfare, transport, police, public housing authority, etc.), community service providers, non-governmental organizations, community-based organizations, private enterprise interests, consumer groups, local government authorities, provincial government authorities, relevant national government authorities, ethnic groups , community media and educational institutions.

Health depends in part on our ability to understand and manage the interaction between human activities and the environment. The complex relationship between health and environment extends the responsibility for promoting health to all groups in society. Healthy cities therefore strives to provide health care facilities to all its citizens, operates through commitments and co-operation at all levels, public participation and is achieved by integration of governmental planning, institutional involvements and mutual co-ordination and community involvements. Healthy city is virtually an ongoing process that involves public participation, prioritize health and health issues within planning agenda, considers the future needs of citizens and aims for better future.

Common steps towards achieving the status of a Healthy city will include the following steps—

- Raising Awareness of the Healthy Cities concept and approach is important first steps in developing inter sectoral collaboration and integrated planning. A series of educational workshops can provide people with a chance to explore the Healthy Cities concept and approach and consider its applicability to their context.

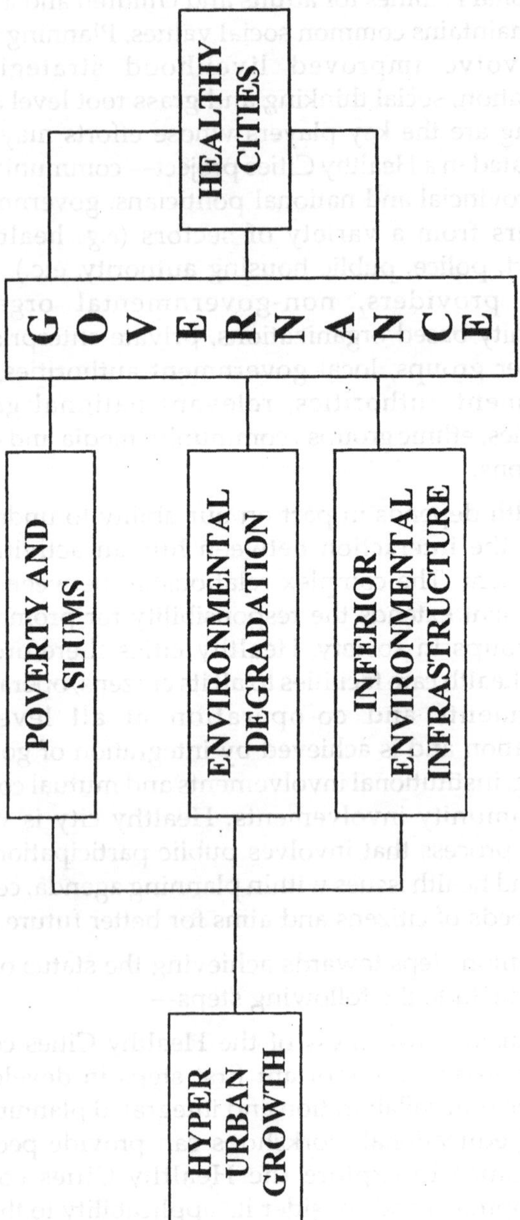
HEALTHY CITIES
GOVERNANCE
POVERTY AND SLUMS
ENVIRONMENTAL DEGRADATION
INFERIOR ENVIRONMENTAL INFRASTRUCTURE
HYPER URBAN GROWTH

- The next step is to find a group of people sufficiently interested in, and willing to spend time for, developing a local Healthy Cities project. A local intersectoral initial task force should be set up with people from this group. Its tasks are to gather information about the city, make a preliminary analysis of the local situation, establish contact with key individuals working on health and urban development, convince potential supporters, and prepare a plan for the full development of the Healthy Cities project, including establishment of a steering committee and allocation of budget for a secretariat.
- Gaining access to, and establishing good communication with, executive decision-making structure of a city is crucial, as these decision-makers can provide resources and legitimacy to the project. Their support is important for achieving integrated planning and action in various settings. Decision-makers in local government play the most crucial role in developing and implementing a Healthy Cities project. National and/or provincial supports in terms of technical expertise available at those levels are also important.
- Gaining a strong commitment of the local (and provincial) government to the project is an important step towards incorporating health agenda into citywide strategies. It facilitates the integration of all concerned departments, attracts various agencies, and involves many supporters.
- Effective implementation of a Healthy Cities project requires the establishment of an organizational structure (usually called a steering committee) at a high level within the city. It should bring together the interests of all the main sectors/actors, such as local government, health authorities, the business society, voluntary groups, and the community. A steering committee functions to delineate priority health issues of a city, develop an action plan, mobilize resources, encourage taking specific approaches, evaluate progress, and make

decisions on operational issues. Ideally, a steering committee should work with different departments of the local government, and consider the different elemental settings in cities (*i.e.* schools, workplaces, markets, healthcare facilities, etc.

- A city health profile gives a comprehensive view and some background information on the health and environment situations of the city. The process of developing a city health profile requires the involvement of multiple sectors, in order to facilitate further intersectoral collaboration in the planning and implementation of the project activities.
- An action plan should address the priority issues identified in the process of developing the city health profile. The plan should be based on the principle of integration of activities wherever possible. The plan should establish a future vision of the city and short- and long-term goals.
- The integration of activities at elemental settings (*e.g.* schools, workplaces, markets, hospitals) helps to focus on the project and develop shared concerns and values of cooperation among people involved in the settings.
- Publicizing the city health profile contributes to raising awareness about the health and environmental situation of the city. Promotion of the action plan raises awareness across sectors.
- To implement activities, resources should be mobilized. Participation from the community, the local government, and other groups and agencies with their resources; introduction of technologies and academic expertise; and training of the participants—all contribute to the expansion of capacity of the project.
- Broad-based participation of various sectors and the community often ensures successful implementation of the planned activities. A range of activities at the city and local levels are implemented. The typical categories

of these activities are environmental improvement (*e.g.* water and sanitation, healthy markets, pollution reduction, etc.); organization reform and change (*e.g.* healthy schools and healthy workplaces which aim to re-orient their organizations towards health protection and promotion); and tackling specific diseases or risk factors (*e.g.* dengue reduction, injury prevention, etc.). In each of these activities, the implementation should use the Healthy Cities processes of working across sectors and involving the community.

- The monitoring and evaluation of results of the implementation of the planned activities are crucial for the management of the project. The outcomes of the monitoring should lead to periodic revisions of the city health profile, and the revised profile should be disseminated to the people involved in the project as well as to the community.
- The action plan for a Healthy Cities project should be revised and amended in light of information from the project evaluation and the changing situation within the city. The planning process should be dynamic. Any feedback from the evaluation should enable the project to be responsive to the changing need and situation of the community.
- Mechanisms to secure political commitment, intersectoral collaboration, community participation, finance, human resources, information sharing, awareness building, and national and international networking assure sustainability. Continuing training programmes and opportunities to develop personal skills of the project staff are essential

Characteristics of a Healthy city will include : *(a)* fixed transit, preferably rail, above and below ground. Subways along all major travel corridors; buses or trams on all secondary corridors; *(b)* Mixed-use, mixed-income neighbourhoods; *(c)* Buildings of different age, condition, and size; *(d)* Living spaces everywhere, especially near downtown; *(e)* Large or small public squares at all significant intersections; *(f)* Lots of people coming and going (immigrants, people moving in from other places, and people moving out to other cities); *(g)* Street trees and rooftop gardens for pleasure, and to ameliorate temperature extremes; *(h)* Light rail or a rapid train connection to the airport. Freight and passenger rail depots in town; and *(i)* Shops that open onto the sidewalk, not onto parking lots. All automobile parking is underground or mid-block, not between street and shop. The Healthy City has a safe and healthy environment for the people, provides a sustainable ecosystem, supports a strong mutually supportive and non-exploitative community, encourages a strong sense of public participation, aims at meeting basic needs for all, promises access to wide range of resources and experiences and a healthy environment and health care facilities for all, holds a diverse and innovative economy and maintains a healthy status for the city.

Health is far too serious to be left to doctors and medical specialists. There is a need to establish a dialogue between urban planners, city managers, medical specialists and environmentalists in order to build an agenda that will strengthen the dialogue between local government and stakeholders and define multi-sectoral approaches for solving city health problems. Achieving the integration of activities is fundamental to the Healthy Cities approach. To an economist, a healthy city might be one that replaces imports in a positive frenzy of creativity and innovation; to an urban planner, a healthy city may be one that has good physical and spatial characteristics in areas such as housing, transport and green patches within the built environment; to a sociologist, a healthy city may be one that that promotes social cohesion; to a health care planner it may have high quality accessible health care services; and for a common man, a healthy city may be one that enables him to ensure a good living and carry out all his functions of life in an efficient manner. Urban Planning is essential for promoting an innovation like Healthy city. However, *Urban Planning and Health* care not new as far as their connection is concerned. Indeed, in many European countries, the interlinkages are quite evident with various health related development. But it is ironical that in modern day planning, several Urban Planning decisions are not considered in health. However, planners can be highly influential in promoting healthiness in a city through improving individual behaviour and lifestyles by shaping a productive physical environment in a précised framework. Besides, urban planners can generate proper and effective social networks through sensitive urban renewal schemes that will influence personal health in a better manner in the long run. Proper planning in terms of provision of local structural conditions *viz.* adequate housing, work environment can help to reduce poverty which will indirectly effect in improving human health. A broader overview relates planning with general socio-economic, cultural and environmental conditions and thereby human and social health. Efforts to improve urban health will be more effective if such integration is achieved, because it will avoid duplication and increase cooperation and coordination among parties involved. Integration will lead to cost-effective solutions, synergy between activities, and substantial benefits in terms of resources sharing. Intensive efforts should be made to incorporate existing community activities/projects, which fit the Healthy Cities concept into the Healthy Cities project. The planning process provides a good opportunity to develop and share the vision of the city and to involve people in the community in various activities as well as to popularize the Healthy Cities concept. A wide range of health determinants usually managed by different government departments, non-governmental and community organizations as well as individuals influences people's health. Health development is closely inter-linked with urban development. Successful urban development supports health development, and the health of the population contributes to the development of the city as a whole focusing on the bringing about the sustainable human development to enable people to mutually support each other in performing all functions of life and in developing their maximum potential. To attain better health conditions and improved quality of life is the operational goal. The inclusion of health concerns into the citywide strategy and the consistency between health strategies must be considered.

REFERENCES

Manga, Pranlal (1991) : *Health and Socio-economic Development in India : An Overview*, Bombay, IGIDR.

Anand, Sudhir (Ed.) : Peter, Fabienne (Ed.) Sen, Amartya (Ed.) (2004) : *Public Health, Ethics, and Equity*, Oxford University Press, New Delhi.

Manual on Healthy Cities, Human Settlement Management Institute, HUDCO, Ministry of Urban Development, World Health Organization.

www.healthycities.org

http://www.doh.gov.ph/HC/healthycity.htm

10

Quality of Governance as a Base for Health and Development

—*Arnold J.J. Hagens,*
—*Kathya Córdova Pozo*

1. Introduction

Many researches have verified the importance of health in the process of development of a country. Indeed, health is a significant evidence for development of a society. However, communities which lack health do not always notice the failure or underestimate the real impact of it as we will present in this research. Developing countries in Latin America have health programmes that tried to improve the status of health in the population controlled by health index. Despite this effort, many populations in Latin American countries still suffer from basic health problems and health access is not yet universal or equal for all the population (CEPAL, 2005a).

This research paper will try to answer the question what is the main determinant for health and development. This determinant is seen as a barrier for the society to not have a good level of health and as a consequence lower development possibilities. The barriers that will be presented add up to a group of variables that participate in the condition to the access the services of health and are determinants for a fair access to all the population. The innovation of this research is that we will cross information with the strength that the government has to accomplish the plans for health in a country. This research examines the relation of the role of the government in the health system and the development that is achieved through a strong intervention.

The research will focus on Latin America, precisely in the smallest countries of the Southern Cone of Latin America that are going to be denominated fragile countries. These countries are : Paraguay, Bolivia and Ecuador. Occasionally we will compare it with some other countries for reference purposes.

The following paper is divided in three parts. The first part presents health issues in developing countries within Latin America. A second part will introduce our theoretical framework that will cross information in health and development through a good governance from the national government. Finally, a third part will present the impact on development for a country taking into account the quality of governance. The paper concludes that if the government has a good organization and possesses quality governance, development can be reached and pushed forward.

2. Health Issues in Developing Countries

This part will present the general index of health and development for : developing countries and fragile countries in Latin America. In the first part we will present the epidemiology of diseases in fragile countries and analyzes the profile of diseases that are persistent in the regions mostly in the poor countries. In the second part we will present evidence on health for development and will try to explain why health didn't improve in the social and economical context.

2.1 Epidemiology of Disease in Fragile Countries

The Latin American countries are having a general transition in their epidemiologic diseases that go from communicable to chronic diseases (Iriarte *et al.*, 2007). This is due to important demographic changes; rapidly shifting models of organizing and financing national health systems; inequitable access to health care for the population. This transition is probably even more serious for fragile countries in Latin America because governments are not well prepared and do not have a good plan to handle them.

According to the statistics of USAID Infant mortality rate has reduced considerable in every one of the southern countries although they still have high rates. The rates for these countries in the last 10 years are in average: Bolivia 52, Ecuador and Paraguay 24. The same goes with the rates of mortality under 5 years old: Bolivia 69, Ecuador 29 and Paraguay 32; and the rates of mortality under 14 years old: Bolivia 18, Ecuador and Paraguay 6. As we can notice, Bolivia is the country with the worst mortality rates for the youngest population. Despite the health programmes that are aimed to protect the children under 5, the rates of mortality are still high and despite the reduction within last 10 years, the rates are still worrisome.

If we take a look at several statistics from Institituto Nacional de Estadistica (INE, 2001) we see that in Bolivia, the illiteracy varies from 5% in the urban areas until 57% in the rural areas. This is a big problem for people to gather knowledge which helps them to improve their lifestyles. Another indicator is number of houses with a room exclusively for cooking purposes and not also for sleeping. In the department of Cochabamba houses with a kitchen vary from 55% to 90%. This results in respiratory diseases since the gases from the cooking are breath by the people. Also in the rural areas people often still use wood for cooking which causes a thick smoke which is more dangerous for health, especially for children. Sickness caused by contaminated water is also originated from the fact that only 8% of the houses have access to the network of potable water and in the best case only 75% of the houses in the city have potable water. As a consequence, people use water from alternative origins (rivers and pits) which might be dangerous to health.

According to the INE, Bolivia has 27.60% of the population between 0-4 years old that is with malnutrition (between light and serious level). This will have an important impact in the life expectancy at birth which in Bolivia is only 65 years. Between the three countries that are analyzed, Bolivia has the lowest life expectancy at birth, having Ecuador in 76 years and Paraguay at 75 years. The same can be observed with lifetime risks in maternal death chances. Out of every 47 deliveries 1 woman will die in Bolivia, in Ecuador 1 out of every 210 and in Paraguay one every 120 (USAID, 2007). Bolivia is behind with social public expenditure in health that goes in average in the last years around 3.9% of the GDP while Ecuador is around 5% and Paraguay 5.7%[1].

Health until now is explained by statistics by countries regions, or municipalities. But these statistics are not capable to show the specific situation of every community in order to understand why some are excluded from health programmes. Because governments take this information as-is they are blind to reality of the people and lacks the capacity to improve them, not only by the side of health programmes but also by the improvement of other programmes that cooperate with their development.

In these fragile countries, health and development cannot only be analyzed by two factors depending one on the other. Health cannot longer be seen as physical illness in the population (such as diarrhea, tuberculosis, etc.) but also should be seen with an integrated analytical view to understand why development has not reached the desired level in these countries. Following, we will present a critical analysis of the indexes of health crossed with other factors that influence both in health and development such as sanitation, water provision, health access and education.

2.2 Evidences on Health and Development

In Latin America, the programmes for promotion of health incorporated in the late 90s have improved health status in the region. Nonetheless, this improvement is far from expected since there are many marginalized groups (from rural and

1. Our special thanks to Dr. Freddy Córdova Chief of the department of Family Medicine of the Faculty of Medicine, Universidad Mayor de San Simon (Cochabamba – Bolivia) for his comments and critics on the text.

urban areas) that do not have access to health. Besides, promotion of health in Latin America has been linked to the will of every government as a political upgrade for them (Salazar, L. de, Vélez, J. A., 2004). Health programmes were based on this will and not on the real determinants of health which go beyond the health sector, including economical and social sectors.

Furthermore, only people with low to medium income assist to public health services. Higher income people often go to private health services. The visit to a doctor involves often a certain amount of money even when the person is insured. In South America more than 25% of the population lives below the poverty line with 1 to 2 dollars per day (World Resource Institute, 2003). Moreover, these countries do not have health insurance for all the population. In Bolivia for example, the ones that have universal health insurance are only the children from 0-5 years old and the pregnant woman within the SUMI programme which started in 2002. This means that people who are not in one of these groups don't have access to free health services. The fee of medical doctors varies from 30-100 Bs. And this will not include any medicaments. Considering that 14% of the population has half of the minimum salary and 34% has the minimum salary (500 Bs/month), the visit to the doctor touches 6%-20% of their income. This is one of the main explanations why people wait too long to go to a medical doctor. It is better for them to believe that their body will heal up by itself than spend 6% of their salary "unnecessarily".

In the survey people also revealed that the main sickness as diarrheas, pneumonias, chagas, or others that mainly affect these fragile countries and societies, are difficult to prevent contrary to what is thought due to other determinant factors. People have difficulties to access basic services as water, sanitation and housing. Diarrhea for example, is easy to be prevented with clean hands before cooking or eating. But in the majority of the urban periphery areas and rural areas potable water is inexistent and rivers that some of these areas might have are so contaminated by the same community's habits[2]. People know the problem but "there is not much that can be done since the river is the only source they have for doing all those activities and the potable water is not available yet" (Survey Answers, 2007). The government doesn't realize well what the reasoning of other people is and what they do in reality. This is why; health programmes lack 'hands on' characteristics on the community.

In Bolivia, the creation of the Law of Popular Participation (1994) and the Law of Decentralization (1994), established in the Supreme Decree 24237 created the Decentralized and participative public system in health[3]. This participative programming for their activities in health for each community was thought as the solution for the problems mentioned before. The system of participation is still valid now-a-days because it answers to equity and fights against poverty; and has been used as a base Universal Insurance in Bolivia (starting by phases from 2008). However, the participation of the community in the elaboration of their Strategically Operative Plans (POA, for Spanish) is almost baseless. This is due to the fact that the community does not understand how to fill in the forms for the POA and they do not know how to include their needs. Therefore, most of the persons in charge of the POA conception do it based on precedent forms (sent by the central government). Unfortunately, for the needs of the population, any activity that was not included in the POA will not be worked out. If they include something important, most of the time small infrastructure projects which can be finished within a year. The ones that are more costly they leave out. Like this, every year is the same despite the "popular participation" in the formulation in the POA. The communities of fragile countries lack a critical education. They are aware of their problems but they don't know the base of the problem.

2. Some habits around the rivers are: washing their clothes, washing themselves, taking the animals to drink from the river, leaving their garbage around, letting the sewage go into the rivers, etc.

3. The participation of the community is done through a representative of a territorial base organization (OTB, from Spanish) and they meet together every month to talk about their problems. They participate in the elaboration of the POA that is a budget plan for the forthcoming year.

According to the survey, they know they lack basic services but they are not aware that for example housing problems are the origin of chagas. Therefore, in their POA, they consider fumigation of vinchucas[4] but this doesn't kill all the insects and it is only a matter of time before the population of the insect has reached again dangerous level. After those types of efforts, people get disappointed with the promises for development because they do not see results. This is a great problem for the community that cannot escape from their illnesses due to poverty and improve development.

Other issue in health is the age-groups of the population. Fragile countries in Latin America are characterized by their young population. In Bolivia around 49% of the population is in between 0-18 years old; and 9.8% of the population is in between 20-24 years, and 36% in between 25-55 years (table 1). This means that 36% of the population that is within Active Working-Age has to sustain the 64% of the population of which more than 50% are so young that they have no financial resources at all.

Table 1 Groups of Age in the Population

Group of the Population	*Percentage*	*Average activities*
0–18	48.76%	Dependent age
19–24	9.83%	Carrying on studies (from 1-5 years)*
25–55	36.12%	Active Working-Age
56–98	5.29%	Passive Age

Fuente : INE Bolivia.

* not all the population in this age goes to study, but it is not possible to know the esxact percentage that goes to.

In general, people are aware that health and education are

4. Vinchucas is the popular name of the insect Triatoma infestans that infect of chagas. This is controlled by vector-borne diseases and normally by only fumigating the houses instead of covering them with cement that will avoid better the incoming of the vector in the houses that are build typically by sand and logs. The control should also go through the cleaning of the house, avoiding farm animals nearby, recovery of holes.

important factors for a good economical sustained life. This is mainly the reason why people hope for having a good health for themselves and their descendents. People are conscious that when one lacks good health, they cannot work and perform well. Just by seeing a handicapped person, people know how much this handicap affects someone's life, social performance and economical future. In the words of Nobel Laureate Amartya Sen, health (like education) is among the basic capabilities that gives value to human life[5]. Knowing all this, the population, still only assist to the health centers when they think it is necessary to go and don't go when it is for prevention This is point where our analysis started. When do people from fragile countries go to the doctor? When do they consider that it is needed to go to a health center? In order to have a good answer to this, our analysis was based on the statistics of health of different countries and a survey carried on the population that assisted to the public health services with primary health attention in Cochabamba (Bolivia). The objective was to know why and when they go to a health center and when they don't. The results show that people are aware of health importance but they do not realize that some recurring problems need to be checked in time by the doctor to determine if there is some illness related to it. Some people walk around with a problem a long time without doing anything about it, until it turns into a real annoyance that prevents them to do normal activities or do their work. People think that going to the doctor before is not worth since; they think that their own body recovers always by itself. Sometimes, they get used to the nuisances of illness that they do not notice the problem anymore, which might lead to worse at the end. The same problem happens with their children, when they have diarrhea or get a cold, parents would not assist to the doctor thinking that children get sick every

5. Sen stresses that certain substantive freedoms ("the liberty of political participation or the opportunity to receive basic education or health care") are "constituent components of development" (essentially, end goals) as well as contributors to economic progress. See Sen (1999), *Development as Freedom*, especially Introduction and Chapter 1.

time but get better soon afterwards. The only reason why they would take a child to the doctor is when the child is in an evident deterioration of his capacities

The working-age block in fragile countries has to support a large group of young people who do not have any financial resources. The problematic age composition represents a great challenge for the social and economical government policies (CEPAL, 2005a, p.104). The threat for the near future is that due to the small amount of working people there are little resources available for the large number of young people to get well prepared. These fragile countries that have the majority of their population between the ages of 0-18 and have no health insurance, no pensions and certainly no actions to tackle these issues which can turn into major problems in the present and endanger their future. This is completely different if we look at European countries that already took actions for their fast growing retired population but that still manage to maintain a retirement pension system.

The drama is not only in the age-group but also in the economical activities that this population has. In Latin America, the informal economy has an important impact on the total income of every country. Although the informal economy is difficult to measure and it is not included in the GDP; there were several efforts to present a general picture of the problem (Soto, 2000). The statistics show that in these fragile countries 51% of the economy is moved by informal activities of non-agricultural origin. Unemployment is one of the main causes for the people in working-age to employ themselves in an informal economy that have not any provision of health insurance. Consequently, the informal economy has an important impact on health status and development by a threefold explanation. The first one is that the people who work in informal economy make money by their own subsistence; thus, they dedicate more time to their business and have no savings for health. This group of people is a potential element of social conflict and confrontation since they see no hope for their future. Besides, there is a group that dedicates to illegal activities in order to sustain their families without measuring the risk involved. Second explanation is linked to the first. The people who are health-insured in fragile countries are the ones that work in very big private companies or public organizations that are heavily controlled by the government and the ministry of work. The small companies (which in a majority are informal) are not controlled and do not have enough money to insure their workers. So in mutual agreement the employer and employee agree to pay directly that money as part of the salary to not have the insurance or others involved with the company (Levy, 2007). Third explanation is based on the migration of the population outside the country[6] where health is not considered as a possibility to access since they live in the black market due to their illegal residence status.

As we mentioned before, for the population, health is an important factor for economic sustainability. However, the amount of deaths and sick people in all the South American countries shows that not all people have access to basic health (CEPAL, 2005c). Public health centers can be found everywhere in the countries but they lack personnel and inputs for being able to attend the patients of the region. In Bolivia, there is one medical doctor per 2500 persons in the main cities and 30% of the total dentist that the city needs, but in the rural areas there is only 1 doctor per 7000+ persons and no dentist (MSD, 2007).

Health then is profoundly influenced by educational, social, economical and institutional factors. Since every analyzed factor needs the participation of the government to tackle the problem, the reality would be different if governments would adjust the health programmes to these factors.

3. Development by Threefold Axis

This second part will present the framework for this research. We will present the relation between health, education and quality of governance to reach development.

6. In between the 2003 until March 2007, around 500 persons/day migrated to Europe (Spain or Italy) searching for better life.

Health is often taken as an important factor for development of a country's economy. World Health Organization (WHO) defines health, "as the state of complete physical, mental and social well-being and not merely the absence of disease or infirmity"[7]. Governments have a lot to do with the provision of health care to the society since they are responsible for the general well-being of the people. Since most of healthcare systems in developing countries are not well supported and managed, it is not surprising that the health situation in these countries is not good.

Some governments in South America have orientated their policies into a socialistic path especially after having too liberalistic phases in their economy. Communism was orientated to serve better the population and to eliminate the difference between rich and poor people. The study of health in Bolivia that is one of the countries orientated to a socialistic path, shows that the government is failing in the equal supply of health, since the results expected by the population are not reached. Bolivia, one of the denominated fragile countries in South America has changed government in 2006. This new government came in to power by the support of the population. It was strongly believed that fast development could be reached with a President from the base of the population. The main problem is that the government does not show any base for strong changes in society and is only pushed on big popular projects which have little impact on the development. Even when the government tried to focus in health and education, the policies seem to lack a vision of development. For example, to fix the problem of accessibility in health, around twelve hundred Cuban doctors were contracted to assist people in Bolivia. However, the origin of the problem of health as we are presenting is not the lack of doctors only, actually, the statistics that the "colegio medico" (medical association in Bolivia) tells

7. Preamble to the Constitution of the World Health Organization as adopted by the International Health Conference, New York, 19-22 June, 1946; signed on 22 July 1946 by the representatives of 61 States (Official Records of the World Health Organization, no. 2, p. 100) and entered into force on 7 April 1948.

that there are around 10.000 medical doctors that have no jobs, doing other activities, like driving a taxi or tending tables in restaurants. Unemployment affects not only the income in a family but also endangers their security and health and creates a social confrontation.

Therefore, we are suggesting the development of a threefold axis framework (figure 1). First one, a *focus on education,* to improve the quality of life based on the vision for development. Second one, a *health focus,* which means the availability of health services to confront and prevent sicknesses. And third point; *focus on quality of governance,* which is needed to make adequate and effective policies. There are other factors which also affect development: infrastructure,

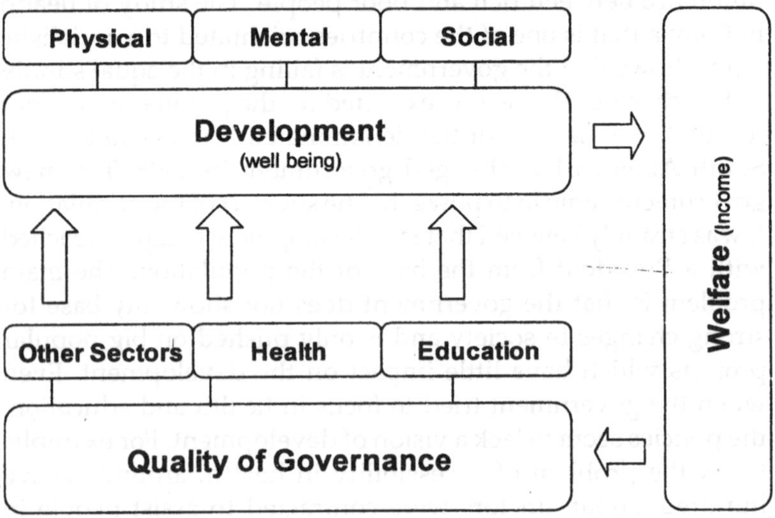

Fig. 1 : Development as a result of the quality of governance.

defense, legal systems, etc. Still, quality of governance can break vicious circles to leap up good functioning economy and better regulated market sector. Without well educated people and no good health, development will be difficult. On one side, this is because there are no human resources to design and implement adequate policies. And second, because the understanding and application of certain regulations will only be understood by people through education.[8]

In the next part we will analyze how health, education and governance actually impact development.

4. Impact on Development

The previous analysis shows that health and development are related. As Jeffrey Sachs explained thoroughly, the burden on the economy of people with a shorter life expectancy and/ or a chronic disability can be enormous due to a diminished productivity (Sachs, 2001). Second mentioned impact of health are the often large poor families in developing countries where poverty is the main cause for a high infant mortality rate since they cannot give the necessary health care to all the children. A third reason is the negative effect on the economy due to diseases which lowers returns of its vital sectors. Furthermore, certain epidemics can have serious effects on social stability of the country. Bolivia saw for example 40.212 cases of cholera between 1991 and 1995, resulting in 814 deaths. Since then, there has been a decline in incidence from 2,068 cases in 1996 to 467 in 1998 and no cases from 1999. This certainly had a great impact in the social stability of the country.

In this chapter, we will focus on governance and education as endogen variables of health and development. Development automatically implies improvement of Governance, education and health. We will discuss the impact of education vs. governance to motivate development first. Then, we will discuss issues of free market and governance. Finally, we will take a look at the impact of the development through health related public sectors and the quality of governance.

4.1 Education vs. Government to Motivate Development

Education is in many cases a government task, or at least it is a strongly regulated sector depending on many laws and quality standards. In many of the analyzed countries, basic

8. The term of education that is used in this research does not refer only to the acquisition of knowledge but the acquisition of wisdom through a critical analysis of their environment.

education is free. In Bolivia, higher education in the university is also free and accessible. However, the model of education in Bolivia is static and of low quality (CEPAL, 2002) and is not focused in the creation of a critical thought and not based in the productivity and development. Education is very passive and only focuses on the teaching of reading and writing.[9] People often ignore the laws where they are realizing their activities. This avoids them to take full advantage of their rights by law. As Jose Marti said "the only way to be free is being cultivated".

Education often is a long term investment; it is difficult to see the results in the short term. If we relate it with indicators of life expectancy and we see a reduction on disease occurrences, this affects directly life expectancy than what education would have. Despite this, education can impact health and development in different ways that will present below.

4.2 Knowledge on Healthy Life

The provision of knowledge on how to be productive will give the possibility to get a sustainable income which can satisfy the basic needs. This at the same time will give the possibility for people to control better their health status. The same, providing a critical way of thinking will improve life and health situation.

One problem that goes along with education is the bandwagon effect. This effect means that people goes along with the mainstream's thought. So a certain idea or habit is considered to be true because everybody thinks like that even without scientific evidence. For example, in Bolivia there are a large number of cultural habits which are believed to be miraculously effective. In some cases patients also decide for

9. The government of Bolivia launched a campaign of alphabetization for adults with the goal of learning how to write and read. This learning implied also the decolonization of the education so they did not read from books outside, but this education did not implied the learning to analyze their own reality with a critical vision.

those believes since they are cheaper and more accessible than the real doctor. A study done in Haiti proved that women thought it would be good to stop breastfeeding the baby in case of diarrhea, which of course could even worse the medical problem. (Kirkpatrick, 1987). The same problem can be observed in the Bolivian cultural believes.

Education also influences the accessibility of people in health services. There is a great unfamiliarity to the rights for health, life and social rights. Lack of education excludes people from health services and a healthier life.

Parents play an important role in the children's education. It has been proven that the parents that have certain behaviour and habits inherit them to children (Andreson, 2004). This can be a threat at the moment of focusing for example on children for health education; they might not accept it, since it contradicts what their parents already taught them. This so-called spill-over (Sachs, 2001) and is an important issue to be taken into account when addressing education and knowledge to parents.

Governments from fragile countries could play an important role in the quality of the different policies needed to educate people for a healthier life.

4.3 Resources, Free Market and Regulation

The creation of health programmes is unilateral. Only the government participates in its elaboration. Consequently, when the population demands for an improvement of health and development, the government thinks that it is time for a health reform or time to do more investments. However, investment issues are not well analyzed since it is not only money that it is needed to develop the sector. Actually, most of the mistakes from donors came from focusing on the lack of money rather than the other factors that were affecting the status of health.

Governments have several tasks related with health and development. First one is the provision of public goods, which cannot be provided by the market Such as roads, military defense, research, etc. Markets in general don't get involved in this. A second task is the paternalistic role. This means the social responsibility to the less fortunate in the provision of health insurance, subsidies, assistance with natural disasters, etc. A last focus is the regulation of the market and filling up the market failures such as: the abuse of market power and dominant position, cartels, imperfect competition, lack of provision of services to the areas where it is not profitable for the market and other failures that can cause inequalities in the economy.

Social and economical factors have serious effects on health. Expenditures on health come from two sides, one is the government and another comes from the private sector. Market failures are presented when private investment is not done in those areas where there would be no benefit. Also, when there is no regulation the private sector can take higher benefits from the population. In figure 2 we can see the total expenditures on Health by the government and private sector calculated over the gross domestic product (GDP). We can see that even in the

Table 2 : Government Expenditures in Health as Part of the Total Health Expenditures

Country	%
Argentina	45.30
Bolivia	60.70
Brazil	54.10
Canada	69.80
Chile	47.00
Colombia	86.00
Cuba	87.80
Ecuador	40.70
Guyana	83.50
Paraguay	33.70
Peru	46.90
United States of America	44.70
Uruguay	43.50
Venezuela	42.00

worst case the health sector takes about 4% of the GDP and in the United States even up to 16%. This percentage reflects a big size of the economy that is moved by health in every country. If we do a further analysis in the expenditures of the government in the total expenditures of health, we can observe that in all countries, public investment in health is the major percentage. This corroborates the fact that private investment will only be made where there is a potential for profit. In order to enhance the data shown in the figure 2, we present a detailed percentage of the public expenditure in health compared with the total expenditures that the health sector has in the country (see table 2). We see that the share of the government on health is important; this automatically implies that if the government doesn't possess a good policy on these large expenditures the effectiveness can be in danger. Furthermore we can not ignore the private expenditures on health which in many cases involve free market mechanisms. If the government fails in regulating well the free market of health we risk high costs, and low quality of health services. Such market failures need to be tackled by governments through strong policies, however if the government doesn't possess the knowledge neither sufficient financial and human resources it is most likely an impossible task. However, this data should be crossed with the expenditure in health by region and making a differentiation between urban and rural areas to have a stronger fact. Unfortunately, our research could not go that far due to the lack of statistical information in all three countries.

Market failures are very likely in health care; main reason is asymmetric information. On one hand, a patient might know very well that he has headache or diarrhea but tries to heal himself instead of having a better solution based on the knowledge of the doctor. On the other hand, a patient could get very expensive treatment while it could be solved with a simple medicament. Nevertheless asymmetry can also be a problem for the doctors treating the patients. These market failures are more likely to occur when the government does not control and regulate health sector. More openness of regulated information by the government would be needed (Birks, 1993).

4.4 Development Level by Quality of Government

We have now seen the significance of health and education for development and how much impact the quality of governance has on both factors. The improvement of the quality of governance improves health and therefore the society can advance their development. We will now take a look at some direct numbers that will present the direct relation between the quality of governance and the improvement of health.

Despite health programmes are valid for all the country; there are some disparities that make the health status different from one region to the other. The first one is in the large difference in the health situation between urban and rural area. About 36% of the population in Bolivia lives in the rural area (WHO, 2007). If we take a look at the countries in the American region, we see that there is a clear relation between the life-expectancy and the region where the people live. In figure 3 we see a positive effect on life expectancy whenever more people live in the urban areas. There is another correlation in

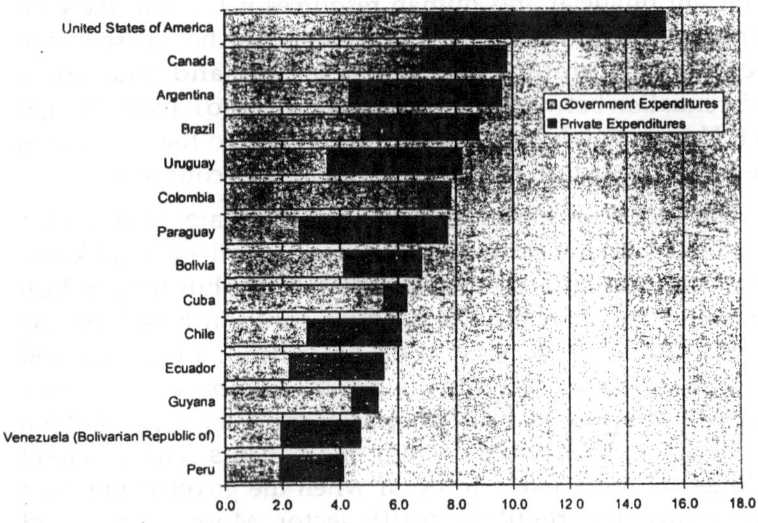

Fig. 2 : Total Expenditure (Divided in Government and other) on Health as percentage of gross domestic product of selected countries.

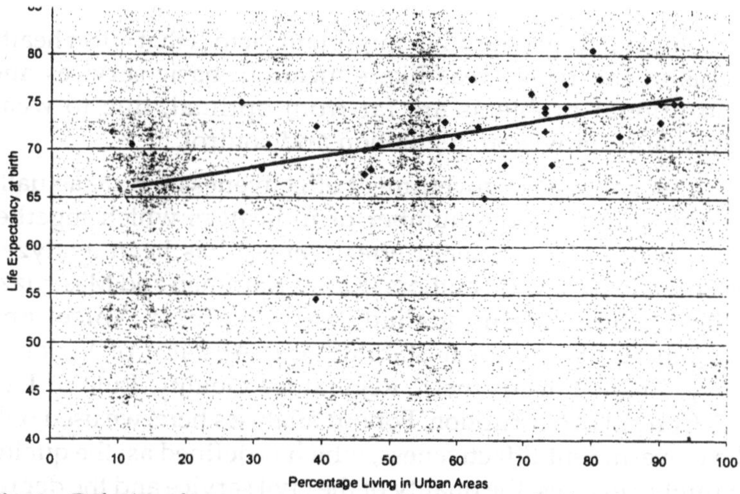

Fig. 3 : Relation between persons living in urban areas and life expectancy (Americas).

between the illnesses of poverty (chagas, pneumonia, diarrhea, etc.) and people living in rural areas. Statistics show that there are more of the mentioned cases in rural than urban areas. Also the frequency is higher with people from peripherical urban areas as we presented in the first part of the research.

With these results, no suggestion is made for people to move to the cities. With this comparison we want to make it clear that the health situation in rural areas is worse off. If the government is the only provider of health systems in the rural areas, the programme should be the same or aimed to improve faster the quality of life of the population. Despite this reality, provision of public health is deficient and people rather make the travel to health centers in the city (Survey, 2007). If we analyze the health provision in Bolivia, we observe that health services are more numerous in the city, public as well as private and are well provided with human resources. Also the perception by the people of the quality of service of the urban health services is higher than of the rural ones. This situation represents a weakness for the government which is not capable of tackling market failures in rural areas by providing a minimum level for health services. Nevertheless, we should certainly not forget the other important factors that affect health status in the rural areas like education, basic services and institutional problems are far from optimal, due to weak governance provision, regulation and control.

If we talk about government effectiveness we are actually talking about a large number of indicators which together express this. Government effectiveness has been analyzed extensively by several authors (Kraay, Kaufman and Mastruzzi, 2006). They distinguished 6 indicators: Voice and Accountability, Political Stability and Absence of Violence, Government Effectiveness, Regulatory Quality, Rule of Law and Control of Corruption. For our analyses here, we used only the Government Effectiveness, which is defined as: the quality of public services, the quality of the civil service and the degree of its independence from political pressures, the quality of policy formulation and implementation, and the credibility of the government's commitment to such policies. Through this indicator we can give a direction on what is the quality of health and education policies in a country.

In figure 4 we see the relation between government effectiveness and life expectancy at birth. Although it might

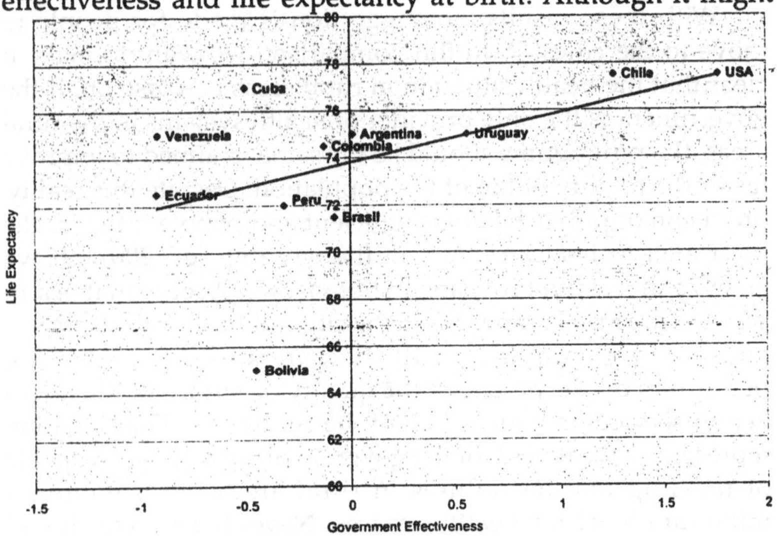

Fig. 4 : Relation between Government Effectiveness and Life Expectancy

not count the same for the all the countries, there is a tendency that *government effectiveness* increases life expectancy. Despite the relation between those two factors, it is interesting to look at the exceptions to mention that income is not a decisive factor for government effectiveness and neither for the Life Expectancy. Chile and Cuba for instance, are two exceptions in our study, with a different political system and GDP per capita. Cuba shows that still is able to reach almost the same life expectancy as Chile, despite the fact that the government effectiveness is worse in Cuba. This can be explained because Cuba has a communistic regime which does focus a lot on health and education status due to political promises to the society. The involvement of Cuba in health can also be seen in Table 2, where the biggest part of health expenditures comes directly from the government. Therefore, although they are not effective they have a good focus on health.

Another extreme case, in line with the regression, is Bolivia. Bolivia does not score high on government effectiveness but is the country with the lowest life expectancy (65 years) when others score higher even with worse government effectiveness. This dramatic number can be explained partly because a large part of the population lives in rural areas where the health and education are of a low quality and the people have low income. Maybe to have a better analysis, we should take into account the other government factors that Kraay, Kaufman and Mastruzzi present. The survey from people in the rural area show, that they often lack good knowledge on simple preventive medicine, often they need to travel far to reach a hospital or a school, and doctors are not hired for full time and neither have sufficient equipment to do a good job. This inequality in access to public services like education and health which is also mentioned by Sachs (2001) creates eventually a big division in the population. One group of the people benefits from the best of health and education services and the other group stays behind, creating a larger gap where it becomes difficult to escape from this vicious cycle. This is a tough task for the government called to create better policies for improving health. Yet, due to corruption, which is higher in poorer (fragile) countries (Kaufman, Kraay, Mastruzzi, 2006) and the ineffectiveness of the government, health can only change bit by bit. Interesting detail is that the governments call themselves socialistic but in reality one cannot see any real change for the poor from the country side. Education did not change and the provision of health is being attacked in doubtful ways.

A last point where we analyzed the relation between quality of governance and health is the management of human resources. As is often mentioned government tasks are often tasks which cannot be covered by the market; but they should still try to be efficient. A problem that was observed in SEDES-Cochabamba (Public Health Department) located in Bolivia, is that the assignment of people to certain positions is not transparent and it is not based on the skills and motivation. For example, people who have contacts in this public organization can have work in the city without a "transparent selection" even when the post designation is for a health center in the rural area. The same can be observed in other public organizations. People who barely finished secondary school become minister of justice (Valdez, 2006). Doctors who just finished the university might get a job faster than other skilled doctors with years of experience just because of the social network. According to law all the selection is supposed to go through exams and proper interviews but in practice there is a lot of corruption which leads to inefficiency in many government tasks like health and education. This has a serious negative effect on development and goes even beyond the health sector.

5. Conclusions and Recommendations

We have analyzed a whole range of effects within developing countries in South America based on the development of a framework that compares the different factors and their impact on health and development. From this framework analysis, the following conclusions can be extracted.

Improving health is not just a matter of removing the financial constraints or following reforms on the health sector only. Many policies based on improving health are just based on adding more money to the sector so that there is more hospital infrastructure or there are more doctors. In this article it is stated that there are other factors that go beyond the health sector as the access to water, sanitary services, housing and education (wisdom) of the people to get involved better in the planning and control of their development. Therefore, it is important to focus clearly on what is the best policy so people can participate better in the creation of a plan for development with real health improvement.

Education is an important factor : *(a)* to know the basic rights for health; *(b)* it can help them prevent diseases and *(c)* is a key to enhance their problem awareness to do a critical analysis of the situation. This all can lead them to assist to a health center in time and can help preparing better plans for development (elaboration of their POA for example). The paper presented several cases where a lot of the health problems are caused by lack of awareness of the people to solve the problem in time. Hence, the critical and analytical education can break bad habits in the people's lifestyle.

A good quality of governance can help to improve health and education. In these fragile countries, governments fail on the side of policy making and implementation. Poor governments lack the capacity for solving the market failures and taking into account the real community needs. This causes problems throughout the country worsening disparities between urban, peripherical and rural areas. The government effectiveness has a direct effect on health and therefore development of the country.

If health and education improves, the country reaches a better level of development. Then, if development improves, people will demand better health services and education which improves the cycle of development.

REFERENCES

Anderson L. (2004) : "Parents teach children healthy living habits". *News and public affaires, Texas University, URL: http:// agnews.tamu.edu /dailynews/stories/CFAM/Feb2304a.htm*

Anonymous (2007) : Evo Morales, *Wikipedia. Accessed August 30th 2007. URL: http://en.wikipedia.org/wiki/ Evo_Morales.*

Arriagada I., Aranda V., Miranda F. (2005) : *"Políticas y programas de salud en América Latina. Problemas y propuestas"*.. Serie de Políticas Sociales *vol 114 CEPAL. Santiago de Chile.*

Birks, S. (1993) : Health Care - Market Or Market Failure?, Paper Presented to Public Health Association of New Zealand Conference, 1993, Wellington, Massey university.

CEPAL (2002) : "Panorama de la Educación en América Latina y sus Principales Desafíos." Presentación de Arturo León en la reunión FNUAP/CEPAL sobre Pobreza y Población, Ciudad de México, 14 y 15 de octubre 2002.

CEPAL (2005a) : "Panorama social de América Latina". Ed. 2004, LC/G.2259-P. Santiago de Chile.

CEPAL (2005b) : "Panorama social de América Latina". Ed. 2005, LC/G.2288-P. Santiago de Chile.

CIA (2007) : The World Factbook – Bolivia, CIA, https://www.cia.gov/ library/publications/the-world-factbook/geos/bl.html, accessed August 28th 2007.

Instituto Nacional de Estadística (2001), : Censo Nacional de Población y Vivienda 2001, INE, La Paz.

Iriarte C., Waitzkin H., Breilh J., Estrada A. And Merhy E.. (2002) : *"Medicina social latinoamericana: aportes y desafíos"*. Magazine Panam Salud Publica. *Vol. 12 no. 2. August.*

Kaufmann, D., Kraay, A. and Mastruzzi, M. (2006) : Governance Matters V: Governance Indicators for 1996-2005. *World Bank Policy Research.*

Kirkpatrick, Sharon Minton (1987) : Health beliefs of women in developing countries (DISS), Graceland College, Independence.

Levy S. (2007) : Can Social Programmes Reduce Productivity and Growth? A Hypothesis for Mexico. 8th Annual Conference. GDN Publishers. Pekin.

Ministerio de Salud y Deportes. *(2007)* : Accessed 10th August, 2007. URL: http://www.sns.gov.bo

Sachs Jeffrey D. (2007) : Macroeconomics and Health : Investing in Health for Economic Development, WHO, Switzerland.

USAID Statistics (2007) : Latin America and the Caribbean. Accessed in August 2007. URL: http://qesdb.usaid.gov/cgi-bin/broker.exe?_program= lacprogs.phn_1. sas&_service=default

Salazar, L. de, Vélez, J. A. (2004) : "Searching evidence of health promotion effectiveness in Latin America",. Ciência & Saúde Coletiva, 2004 (Vol. 9, No. 3) p. 725-730. Sao Paulo.

Sen, A. (1999) : Development as Freedom. Ed. By Alfred A. Knopf. New York.

Soto H. (2000) : The Mystery of Capital: Why Capitalism Triumphs in the West and Fails Everywhere Else. *Basic Books, New York.*

Valdez, C. (2006) : *Entrevista a Casimira Rodríguez: Ministra de Justicia de Bolivia: "Quiero cambiar la cara de la justicia"*, La Época, No. 221, 29/1/2006.

WHO (2007) : World Health Statistics, WHO, Switzerland.

World Resource Institute (2003) : EarthTrends Country Profiles – Economic Indicators – Bolivia, WRI, http://earthtrends.wri.org/

11

Health Care System of Madhupur Subdivision, Jharkhand

—*Manjari Sarkar (Basu)*

1. Introduction

Human Resource Development (HRD) has necessarily to be assigned a key factor for development strategy. The essential factors, which lead to HRD, are health, education, nutrition, sanitation, hygiene etc. In developing country like India where a large section of people belongs to BPL, there is an urgent need for improved Health Care System (HCS). In a social life, health is of paramount importance as a national asset and basis of efficiency. On the other hand health is a prerequisite for increasing productivity. It is directly related to fertility, mortality, life expectancy, education, per capita income etc. and indirectly related to reduction of exploitation. That is why; organized health care system is very essential to achieve broader social goals.

In the Madhupur Subdivision (under the dist. of Deoghar, Jharkhand) more than 91% (2001) of total population lives in rural areas and this SD is also famous for multitribal region. The rate of literacy is not sound in this area (Rural), only 44% are educated (2001) out of total 551368. The HCS of Madhupur SD is very poor. In 2006 total number of organized HCS is only 24 and total number of private medical practitioner is only 15.

So the ratio between doctor & people is 1 : 36758. Where all Indian figures are near about 1: 3800. This region is considered as a backward region of India and Jharkhand itself belong to backward state. The main objectives of this study are appended below :

- To study the existing situation of HCS.
- To study the distributional pattern of HCS.
- To find out the relationship between socio-economic condition & educational status of respondents.
- To find out people's attitudes toward the scientific HCS.
- To find out the implementation of NRHM (National Rural Health Mission).
- To find out the causes of low respondance toward scientific HCS.
- To suggest some remedial measures for improvement of existing HCS.

Study area : Madhupur Subdivision is under the Deoghar District of Jharkhand contains dissected uplands, lowlands, rocky exposure of ancient crystalline basement complex covered with jungle. It represents an erosional surface with residual hillocks and boulders. The average elevation of this region is about 432.5 metres but elevation ranges between 160 m – 705 m from river bed to hill tops. Patharda, Phuljori. Bunchi are the famous hills of this region. Slope also varies between 1.5° to 22° from riverbed to hilly tract. This Subdivision extends between 24° 02′ N to 24° 24′ N latitude and 86° 24′ E to 87° 05′ E longitude. It comprises an area of 1372.5 sq. Km. and consists of four blocks namely Madhupur, Keron, Sarath & Palojori. According to 2001 census, the total population of this region is 551368. In this SD about 91.43% (2001) people live in rural areas and only 8.57% people in urban areas. Most of the people belong to SC and ST categories with low literacy rate (44% in rural areas of the study). The HCS of Madhupur SD is very poor. The ratio between doctor and people is 1 : 36758. Where all India figure is near about 1 : 3800.

Existing situation and distributional pattern of HCS : Existing situation of HCS of Madhupur SD mainly depends upon Govt. Hospital, primary health center, private clinic, registered medical practitioners, some dispensaries and medical out lets(Table 1). All the above facilities are very much inadequate in comparison with total population. Presently total population has become 551368 and approximate no. of medical practitioner is 40. This picture clearly depicts the ratio of Doctors & local people of this region as 1 : 13784. This is vulnerable situation for healthcare management system. On the other hand total no. of existing HCS is not sufficient at all to mitigate the actual needs of the rural masses. Locational position and distributional pattern of HCS is (Table 2) uneven. Most of the people (more than 1000 villagers out of 1356) have to strive 20 Km. to 60 Km. or more to get in touch with HCS. Here, in this study the investigator has taken 10 sample villages, which are situated within 4 Km. to 60 Kms. away from Madhupur Town. It is observed that more or less the situation of the respondents in terms of medical treatment is pathetic and still so grave.

Socio-economic & educational condition of the respondents : Most of the people do not depend upon modern medical science. It is found from the field survey that 64.67% of the total population (Table 3, 4, 5, 6, 7) undergoes *Jaributti* and Ayurvedic treatment. Only 26% peoples do not feel the necessity of any medical treatment (in case of pregnancy, cold and cough, weakness and snake biting etc.). However 18% population undergoes allopathic treatment and 6% peoples visit Homeopathy doctor in case of skin disease and gastric & allied problems. This situation is not uniform throughout the society. It depends upon social caste, educational and economical status. In case of ST groups more than 70% peoples prefer *jaributti* as the only means of health care. More than 64% peoples of this caste undergo treatment from *ojha* or *gunin*. It is found that more than 66% of total population prefers *ayurvedic* medicine mainly who is belonging to lower social strata and SC groups. Only 10% & 6.67% people depends upon allopathic and homeopathy treatment respectively. Near about 16% peoples are not interested about any kind of treatment. However consciousness about modern allopathic HCS gradually develops among general category people. In case of general caste 25% peoples undergo allopathic, 12.5% undergo homeopathy and 55% undergo ayurvedic treatment. Only 7.5% of total population does not consume medicine excepting for acute cases.

Table 1 : Shows the HCS of Madhupur SD

Category of HCS	*Year (1991)*	*Year (2006)*
Govt. Hospital sub-center	06	07
Primary Health Center	08	09
Private Clinic	05	08
Medical Store (Field)	15	30
Dispensary (Field)	10	22

Source : Field Survey Report (2005-06).

This situation very much depends upon social, economical and educational status of local people. In my study area total no. of respondents is 150, out of which 65 persons are illiterate. Among this 65% to 55.38% prefers ayurvedic treatment, 15.38% prefers allopathic and 6.15% under go homeopathy but 25.05% do not cosume medicine in normal case.

Attitude towards scientific treatment : Most of the inhabitants in this region are economically very poor. This region being a dissected plateau, connectivity could not be developed; even Central Govt. plan (PMGSY) fails to repair this situation. It is still so grave, patients and their family becomes helpless in taking the patient of acute condition to Health Centre of Hospital. In my study area 54.56% depend upon *ojha* or *gunin* and 19.34% visit doctor or HCS, however 26% people visit Doctor or Health center on acute condition. They cannot depend upon this Govt. run health centers due to irregular and poor quality of services and amenities they used to receive from these HCS. Apart from these reluctancy and poor attitude of medical staffs and doctors towards the ill fated patients are also a major causes of repulsion among the people of this region towards the HCS (Govt.). Inspite of this, distance and availability of HCS plays a vital role. Some time various illfated patient has to strive more than 20 Km to 60 Km. In the case of private clinic, picture is somewhat different. In this context, people expressed their opinion in a different way. Almost 20% opined that quality of medical treatment and amminities are available in private clinic, even attitude of doctors is better than Govt. Hospital (Table : 8,9), but this type of treatment is very costly to the local people. So they cannot afford to visit private clinic.

Apart from the above mentioned causes it has been seen that most of the inhabitant of this region could not able to get access or to afford modern scientific medical treatment. 58% of population has no faith upon medicine supplied by Govt. agencies. They thought that the medicine as supplied were not upto the mark. However rest 42% expressed their satisfaction on Govt. run Health centers.

The investigator got strange experience at the time of field study when she asked about vaccination and family planning programme, 30% of the population had no concept about pulse polio (Table 11) and other statutory vaccination programme. 32.67% (mainly Muslim communities) believes that family planning programme is contrary to religion and has been forbidden by *Allah*. So health workers avoid visiting in those regions. However 37.33% have got some idea about family planning programme and vaccination. It may be concluded from the above discussion that the attitude of the masses towards modern scientific medical treatment was not favourable.

Ill–Health and work participation : Out of 50 rickshaw puller 60% can work 3-4 hour per day, 36% can work 2-3 hour/day and 04% can worked 4-5 hour/day, but it is not satisfactory, normal performance. When they were interrogated they replied that they could not able to utilize their efforts to the full extent due to some physical hazards like weakness, respiratory trouble, gastric problems (Table 10 & 12) cropped up in the later stage as they ignored health care system at their early stage So they had to loose their income for short duration of working ability span. It is hindrance for development of their personal life, as well as creates social problems by generating pseudo unemployment.

Implementation of NRHM : National Rural Health Mission (NRHM) has been launched on 12th April 2005 by the Govt. of India. The important strategies of this mission include : Strengthening public health infrastructure, increasing community participation, creating village level health workers, for supporting vulnerable groups *i.e.* adolescent girls, pregnant women, lactating mothers children and weaker section. In my study area NRHM is not implemented still now. Social worker, NGO and local people do not know about this mission (Madhupur SD), but on 24.07.05 Red Cross Society started their activity at Madhupur town. Secretary of Red Cross Society Mr. P.L. Gudgutiya said Govt. sent some medicine, which was distributed free of cost among 2.5 lakh people most of them were *bidi mazdur* of this region. Expect this work this society helps local people by conducting various camps like eye operation, immunization, blood grouping and blood donation. This is an important step for local rural and needy people to eradicate some health related problem.

Causes of Low Responses to Heath Care System : In the Madhupur Subdivision, most of the people belong to BPL class. So they face various problems :

(i) They could not able to manage even meal daily. In this situation HCS has become luxurious item to them.

(ii) In most of the cases they had to ignore diseases like respiratory trouble, liver cirrhosis, weakness, heart problem etc. at an early stages. So they do not feel to visit doctors or HCS.

(iii) A large section of people are illiterate or less educated, so, superstition and wrong idea still persists in their mind. In the case of snake biting, hysteria or in acute situation they prefer ojha, (local name : Bura baba) or *gunin*. In most of the cases they avoid modern scientific treatment.

(iv) Persons who have faith in modern HCS avoid visiting HCS for some reasons such as: ? Doctors & Nurses are not readily available.

- Poor infrastructure *i.e.* bed, accommodation etc. are not adequate, apparatus or equipments are not up to the mark. Medicine or other amenities are not availed.
- Medicine as supplied from HCS is of inferior quality.
- Local people could not afford to mitigate the expenditure be incurred in private clinic.

(v) Conditions of roads or link roads are very poor. In most of the cases patients are taken to Health center by *Khatia*, van rickshaw, even on foot.

(vi) Ambulances or carriages are scarcely being seen or not available at all.

(vii) In some cases lack of publicity and awareness on the part of the Govt. regarding special Health Care System has been observed. It makes the people to some extent to miss the opportunity of getting modern scientific treatment.

2. Remedial Measures of HCS

(1) At least one health center to be opened with in a 5 km distance.

(2) Mobile medical Van be introduced which would help to implement different programme like vaccination, family planning etc. It will also help to carry patient of critical condition and pregnant women at the time of labour pain to near by health center.

(3) Number of doctors and nurse be increased and effort should be given to motivate them towards their duties.

(4) Initiatives should be taken by Govt. agencies to make people aware about the function and significance of HCS among the common people.

(5) Action should be taken by Govt. to keep vigilance on various activities of the health centers including distribution of medicine and allied matters.

(6) Instrumental development including transport facility of these health centers should be look into and it will attract the rural masses to get services from HCS.

(7) Local NGOs, social organizations, doctors, teachers, and human right organizations should cooperate and acquainted themselves with the importance of this HCS.

Table 2 : Location of Sample sities and No. of Respondants

Village	*Distance from Madhupur*	*& P.S.*	*No. of Respondence*	*Name of PS*
Pahartali	14	14	10	Madhupur
Bhaluwa	20	20	10	"
Chorkata	6.5	6.5	20	"
Titaritatanr	22	14	10	Keron
Pratappur	4	30	10	"
Churnardi	9	50	20	Sarath
Rajwardih	16	55	10	"
Phuljori	14	35	20	Palojoti
Raghunathdih	20	62	20	"
Jormundi	13	55	20	"
		(Total respondent : 150)		

Table 3 : Types of Medicine Used and Attitude Toward Scientific Treatment (Caste) (%)

Do not use medicine	*Allopathic*	*Homeopathy*	*Ayurvedic*	*Caste wise*	*Doctor*	*Ojha*	*Visit to Dr. in acute case*
7.50%	25%	12.50%	55%	General	37.50%	25	37.5
16.66	10	6.67	66.66	SC. & BC.	13.34	66.66	20
26	4	0	70	ST	12	64	24
Total @ 17.33	@ 12%	@ 6	@ 64.67	Total	19.34	54.66	26

Table 4 : Attitude Toward Scientific Treatment (Education wise)

Do not use medicine	*Allopathic*	*Homeopathy*	*Ayurvedic*	*Education wise*	*Doctor*	*Ojha*	*Visit to Dr. in acute case*
23.05	15.38	6.15	55.38	Illiterate	9.23	46.5	44.61
25.08	32.25	16.13	25.8	Primary	32.25	24.19	43.58
25	41.66	16.66	16.66	Secondary	50	25	25
14.2	42.85	14.28	28.58	Higer Edu.	71.42	0	28.7
				Total	162.9	95.69	141.89

Table 5 : Attitude Toward Scientific Treatment and Types of Medicine Used by Income Groups

Do not use medicine	*Allopathic*	*Homeopathy*	*Ayurvedic*	*Monthly income group*	*Doctor*	*Ojha*	*Visit Dr. in acute case*
66.61	0	0	33.34	1000 & <1000	0	91.66	8.34
50	4	2	44	1000-3000	4	90	6
14.28	42.85	7.14	35.72	3000-6000	35.72	42.85	21.44
16.66	50	16.66	16.66	> 6000	25	58.33	16.66
Note: Gen. 40, SC &BC 60, ST 50,		Illiterate 65, Primary 62, Sec. 12 H.S. 07 12, High. 7					
Income: 60 (1000),50 (1000-3000), 28 (3000-6000), 12 (> 6000)					64.72	289.84	52.44

* Caste wise percentage; Education & Income wise %

@ Percentage to total respondents.

Table 6 : Opinion about Govt. Hospital and Health Center (Total Respondents)

Distance	*No timing*	*No Infrastructure of Doctor*
110	25	15

Table 7 : Opinion about Private Clinic (Total Respondents)

Huge Charge	*Not Well Equipt*	*Distance*	*Availability of Medical treatment*
95	15	20	20

Table 8 : Preference of Treatment & Satisfaction about HCS

No prefe-rence	*Prefer of Govt.*	*Private Clinic*	*Name of Village*	*Satisfied*	*Not Satisfied*
52.66%	41.33%	6.00%		42%	58%
5	5	6	Pahartali	6	4
6	4	5	Bhaluwa	5	5
5	12	10	Chorkata	10	10
6	3	8	Titaritatanr	8	2
2	8	6	Pratappur	6	4
10	8	8	Churnardi	8	12
4	6	5	Rajwardih	5	5
12	8	8	Phuljori	8	12
14	4	3	Raghunathdih	3	17
15	4	4	Jormundi	4	16
Total 79	62	9		63	87

Table 9 : Medicine Used by Respondants

Do not use medicine	26
Allopathic	18
Homeopathy	9
Ayurvedic	97

Table 10 : Ill-health and Work Participation (Among Rickshow Puller)

% Of Rickshow Puller	*Working h./day*
60.00%	3.5
36.00%	2.5
4.00%	4.5

Table 11 : Knowledge about Immunization and Family Planning

Facility availed	*Do not know*	*Not interested*	*Villages*
6	2	2	Pahartali
2	4	4	Bhaluwa
2	2	6	Chorkata
5	5	0	Titaritatanr
4	6	0	Pratappur
6	6	8	Churnardi
5	4	1	Rajwardih
12	6	2	Phuljori
6	6	8	Raghunathdih
8	4	8	Jormundi
56	45	49	
37.33%	30%	32.67%	

Table 12 : Problem about Health (% to respondents)

Respiratory trable	44.67%
Cirroshis of liver	27.63%
Problem after pegnancy	6%
Weakness-malnutrition	15.37

REFERENCES

A. Ahmad & S. K. Shamin (2004) : Evolution of health facilities for social well-being in Meerut District : A strategy for micro level planning, *Indian Journal of Regional Science,* vol. 36, No. 2, pp. 16-24.

K. Kumari, R. Reddy and N.Veni (2006) : A study of health care delivery systems in Kurnool District, Andra Pradesh, *The Decan Geographer*, vol. 44, No. 2, pp. 13-26.

M. Dey (1997) : Impact of malnutrition on women's health in W. Bengal, *Landscape systems and ecological studies*, vol. 20, No. 2, pp. 53-58.

N. Devadasan (2006) : Community health insurances schemes, *Yojana*, June 6, Vol. 50.

P.K. Roy (2001) : Economic Geography—A study of resources, New Central Book Agency (P) Ltd., Calcutta, pp. 139-142.

R. N. Ojha (2006) : National Rural Health Mission, *Kurukshetra*, Vol. 54, No. 8, pp. 29-31.

R. R. Ashrit (2006) : Health status of working women, *Yojana*, March, Vol. 50, pp. 75-77.

S. Saxena and A. Prakash (2006) : Sanitation and health, *Yojana*, June, Vol. 50, pp. 22-24.

Sarkar (Basu). M. (2006) : Literacy, An important measures for regional development—A case study of Madhupur, Jharkhand, Practicising Geography, Vol. 10, Winter.

T. Ghosh and A. Sarkar (2004) : Maternal & Child Health Scenario, *Landscape System and Ecological Studies*, Vol. 27, No. 1, pp. 109-118.

12

Research and Development in Health Education—Focused on Value Clarification among Health Professionals

—Karen Wistoft

Health professionals working in the field of health promotion and education experience certain value conflicts: their professional and personal values, the values of their clients or of the health services clash with pedagogic values such as participation, involvement, learning and competence development. My educational research is concerned with the exploration and development of the knowledge about values and health education related to competence development among health professionals. The purpose is to contribute to systematic knowledge development with a view to support and diversify the significance that is founded in theory and relevant to the practice of working with values within various cultures and selected settings: schools, local communities, educational institutions and political organisations. The research moreover aims to diversify a number of more general concepts and connections relatable to health educational development. The overall value theme is elucidated by two development projects that transform as well as challenge specific health-educational practices. This forms the basis of the development of a critical, constructive and practice-oriented perspective on competence development within health education. Empirical and systems-theoretical knowledge is generated about pedagogical competence within health promotion and disease prevention and the knowledge about how development work and experiments can strengthen this competence. This article contributes to *(a)* a discussion about professional competence development and the qualification for value clarification not necessarily expressed through ethical rules but rather in fundamental views, reasoning, linguification and reflections; and *(b)* a methodological discussion about the developmental approach. The research strategy is finally reflected into a systems-theoretical perspective.

1. Methodology

The general objective of this educational research is to contribute to a systems-theoretical framework of interpretation related to value clarification in health education. Based on investigation of two health educational development projects, the research illustrates the demand for a conceptual understanding of the complexity of values and value clarification among health professionals. To satisfy this demand, the thesis modifies a frame of interpretation to describe the complexity of values in health education. The research suggests a concept of value that is based on systems-theoretical epistemology (Luhmann, 1990, 1993) related to the communicative turn in sociology (Leydesdorff, 2002) and the logic of distinctions (Spencer-Brown, 1971).

Values are interpreted as empirical phenomena in health education and health promotion by describing them as communicative observations in social systems (Luhmann, 1995). The research deals with observations in a doubled-up, second-order perspective through observations of the communication (Luhmann, 1993). Finally the research is concerned with the notion of "being educated" (Bildung) and proposes criteria of observation for building competencies for value clarification in health education as a starting point for a more general theory. The research questions are :

— How do health educators observe and communicate values related to their practice?

— What qualifies health educators to practice value clarification?

The research is a theory-based interpretation of observations of communication from the empirical perspective described above. Before conducting analyses and making interpretations, the research distinguishes between health education and educational research (Luhmann & Schorr, 2000); between those aspects that pertain to developmental work and those that pertain to educational research. The methodological aim is to reflect the developmental projects (educational practices) and the research through hermeneutic interpretations (Rasmussen, 2004). To do so, the idea is to make a possible connection between the communication of scientific knowledge and knowledge in educational practice. The dialogues between researchers, decision makers and educators, represented by public health service nurses, primary care nurses, health promoters, teachers and health promotion supervisors, are crucial to the research approach.

In order to formulate research questions that open for tests of validity, the research separates the aims of research from the aims of the developmental work (Kruse & Wistoft, 2006). Explicating assumptions, methods, strategies of analysis and interpretations (observations), the research strives to achieve transparency. The research oscillates between dialogue research (experimental work and workshops) and qualitative empirical research (interviews, observations, questionnaires) developing relevant concepts and theories. The theoretical framework is based on the general theory of social systems as put forward by the German social theorist Niklas Luhmann (Luhmann, 1995) and leading scholars of systems theory (Andersen, 2003). This is done deliberately to serve one main purpose, namely that of analysis. The intention is to try out systems theory when it comes to practical analysis of value clarification among health professionals. The research aims to modify a model of ethics as second-order cybernetics (Thyssen, 1992; von Foerster, 1992) for reflecting on value complexity. To construct this theoretical model of value clarification, the research addresses two basic assumptions of Luhmann's general systems theory :

A : The epistemological assumption that knowledge (as well as values) is produced by operating with a distinction and by the stabilisation of this distinction within an already existing system of distinction (Qvortrup, 2004b : 17). Values are not conceptualised ontologically; values are not representations of an ideal world – the basis of absolute intrinsic values - or representations of a structural (linguistic or social) reality.

B : the sociological assumption that social phenomena such as values and norms are constituted by communication and not by actions or structures (Leydesdorff, 2002; Luhmann, 1994). Observable values are communicated values. The point is not to observe values as results of actions but as results of communication. This means, first of all, making a clear distinction between learning and education, which makes it possible to formulate a theoretical distinction between individual and social values. Moreover, this communicative concept, in contrast to a large segment of educational research literature, does not restrict value reflection to the formation of the moral self and moral education (Ven, 1998), but considers value as a wider concept inherent in communication in general.

The empirical focus is value complexity in health educational communication. The radical interpretation of "being educated" holds that individuals are formed through self-referential processes; we are always "learning to learn" as part of a lifelong process (Luhmann & Schorr, 2000). This implies that individual values are recognised and appreciated as part of a learning process and an educational process. Moreover, it anticipates that individuals are able to recognise and cope with the values of other individuals. Traditionally, moral education covers values, norms and ethics, but as an implication of the notion of being educated, moral education is no longer thought of as the transfer of norms and values from one generation or human being to another, or from one situation or setting to another. Values are observed as temporal constructs in communication, including educational communication.

2. Development Approach

The development approach is an educational development approach practised as a special research and developmental strategy to promote interplay between research and development. There are several different terms for the strategy : experimental and developmental work, action research, "Mode 2" research, dialogue research, etc. The fundamental idea is to create a possible connection between development of knowledge in practice and scientific knowledge. The relationship between educational development and educational research has been discussed on an ongoing basis for several years (Slavin, 2002). On the one hand, the question is whether educational development work is appropriate as a developmental strategy, and on the other hand it is discussed whether educational development work is appropriate as a research strategy. This discussion is relevant for the research at hand, since the two educational projects that make up the empirical field are also significant for the research method. The purpose of the developmental work is to develop a health educational practice for creating change in a health promoting direction. The interest is especially to develop the employees' competencies with regards to handling health-educational services within the health services. The purpose of the developmental work is to improve the participants' capacity to reflect on and handle the values that come into play in their own practice. The purpose of the workshops and classes is to include the participants' experiences, knowledge and values in the establishment of a space for critical reflection. The overall goals are used as indicators or success criteria for the development work while concrete goals, contents and methods are determined in the individual local projects based on the value conflicts, issues and possibilities for change arrived at the participants.

The development work draws on the interactive dialogue research and thus on a specific concept of dialogue (Storgaard,

1991). Dialogue means to communicate without trying to win each other over to one's own standpoint and without resorting to personal criticism or speaking for or against a cause. Dialogue is seen as a special kind of conversation, namely the kind in which the intention is not to defend a point of view but to study; not to persuade but to explore. Furthermore, the development work draws on an educational concept of participation referring to democratic learning processes (Hart 1997; Jensen & Simovska, 2006). In this context, participation is involvement, co-decision and dialogue related to health promotion. Development work consultants see interactive participation and dialogue as tools for diffusing value conflicts. The orientation in relation to participation and dialogic processes forms the outset for the involvement and engenderment of practical knowledge both on the part of health professionals and on the part of consultants. The value complex of development work is founded in a democratical health educational ideology (Jensen, 1997; Jensen *et al.*, 2000).

The research focuses on what is positively possible to produce knowledge about. The purpose of the development work is new thinking and the development of new strategies in health promotion and disease prevention. With this research and development strategy, the researchers are both consultants and researchers. As researchers they do not find themselves in priviliged positions of observation outside the field they are observing, because they are themselves part of the educational development work. The same holds true when they function as consultants. Thus the research is complex, and should be regarded as such. The field of observation may be seen as two social systems: development work and research; each of these is ascribed a specific role in the systems with their actors as their surroundings. Apart from the roles, which are social constructs, their identities as persons are significant, that is how the researchers see themselves, on the one hand as researchers, where they among other things use specific theories and interpretation models, and on the other hand as development consultants, where they teach, guide and support the health-educational projects.

There are both qualities and problems connected with the roles applied by the research strategy known as educational development work. Let me make it clear that in a systems-theoretical sense it is in principal impossible to take part in developmental communication and scientific communication at the same time. It is not impossible, however, to be ascribed both roles : consultant in the educational experiments and researcher of the academic environment; but it is impossible to take part in different types of communication and thus assume both roles simultaneously. Satisfying expectations for both roles indicates an ability to differentiate and connect different types of knowledge, relations, resources, interests, views and experiences. For example, the way in which the particpants use the consultants will depend on the consultants' degree of involvement. If they wish to be used as consultants, they must participate in development communication and then abstract themselves as researchers in the academic environment, where they can reflect scientifically on their observations. The question is how they may qualify their research as observers while freeing themselves from the meaningfulness by which they are surrounded?

First and foremost, this complexity demands willingness to communicate. As described above, educational development work draws on the idea of dialogue research. As with any other type of communication, dialogue entails a difference between the parties. Without this difference, the dialogue would become meaningless and come to an end. But the research does not have an authority as a dialogue partner in the sense that the participants are led through clarification of their own values by a more qualified and questioning facilitator. Rather, a fluent dialogue becomes a source of knowledge. The empirical insight of the researcher is arrived at both through contact with the other party, intuition and conversation as well as through written communication between participants and researchers. Thereby, knowledge is also changed in the process itself. This change is the potential of dialogue.

3. The Field of Observations

The specific health development research is based on observations made in two educational development projects focusing on participatory approaches : "Values in Health Education and Promotion in Greenland" and "Values in Public Health Nursing at Schools" carried out by the Research Programme for Environmental and Health Education at the Danish University of Education (Jensen *et al.*, 2006; Wistoft *et al.*, 2005; Wistoft & Schnack, 2006). The projects deal with different issues in relation to values in a wide variety of settings and educational challenges ranging from primary care over public health to adult education in several different institutional settings in Greenland and the municipality of Copenhagen. Research on the projects is undertaken in collaboration with a number of organisations in Greenland and Denmark.

The aims of the developmental work are : to reflect on the values of health professionals as part of their contribution to health promotion; to provide a critical view of the often conflicting values facing the field of health promotion and prevention; to set an agenda for sustainable development, participation and education; and to promote health through appropriate educational approaches and the development of professional pedagogical competencies. The purpose is to continue experimenting and to develop and evaluate new strategies in order to identify current ideologies within the field of health promotion and education. The challenges of the differing discourses of health, moral and ethical traditions of various cultures essentially consist in understanding the values and feelings of others by taking the 'participatory perspective'. Health is a key concept and is seen as valuable because health implies that some things in life are better than others. The value of health education includes the concept of health and principles of participation and action. The concepts of action and participation are key elements in an action-competence approach developed in Denmark in relation to health promotion and health-promoting schools (Jensen, 2004; Schnack & Jensen, 1997).

The two projects are based on health education and promotion viewed from a societal perspective that includes environmental aspects and are based on an empirically descriptive and critically constructive theory of health promotion and education (Jensen, 2000; Jensen, 2004). Both projects are designed in three phases : Phase 1 focuses on the identification of values, conflicts of values, and descriptions of the local projects; Phase 2 focuses on experimentally facilitated processes within action and participation in different settings and workshops. In Greenland seven single projects including experiments in different settings are carried out, and in the Municipality of Copenhagen eleven projects at different schools are implemented. Every development project is facilitated by a supervisor and observed by the same person as researcher; Phase 3 focuses on documentation and evaluation of the results with a view to determine new health-educational strategies.

The participants represent different levels of the health systems involved, such as health visitors, local educators and ministerial and municipal officials. Seven ongoing local health projects in the municipality of Nuuk in Greenland are being studied as part of the first project, which runs from January 2004 to December 2006 and involves the participation of health professionals from selected health districts, nurses and health visitors engaged in promotional practices, educators in health education and promotion and supervisors from the Home Rule Government. In the second project, 145 health visitors in the municipality of Copenhagen participated in four-day workshops during the autumn and winter of 2004/2005 and sixteen of them designed their own experience projects together with pupils, teachers and parents at the schools where they work during the period from April 2005 to March 2007.

Dialogue workshops, questionnaires, focus group interviews and in-depth interviews are carried out to clarify values and the challenges they present to future health promotion. At the workshops, which are held in the course of the projects, experiences are exchanged and individual projects are discussed. During all three phases, consultants teach relevant subjects and offer support for the solving of practical, political or organisatorial issues. It is seen as part of the participants' qualification that they learn to relate reflexively to their educational practice. In the final phase, being rooted in health educational practice is the main purpose along with several national health conferences on "Value Clarification & Changes" in Greenland and Denmark.

4. Empirical Findings

With these development projects, a clearly defined field is charted, namely health care in schools and the need to develop new paths within disease prevention and health promotion. These expectations from the surroundings compel health professionals to relate to the conflicts of value that are found in practice. This is done in several ways. For example, the development projects test how a healthcare worker can promote health in her disease prevention work or, inversely, supplement her health promotion work with disease prevention. Through the development work, space for dialogue and reflection is created, along with new ways for health promotion and disease prevention to interplay.

It becomes clear that health educators face value complexity in their health educational practice as well as in their reflections on practice. Actions and decisions are no longer based on traditional norms and values or on objective knowledge. The educators are left in different situations where their educational action and choice of rationale are contingent and subject to discussion. This internal complexity is related to the observation of external conflicting interests and different expectations in relation to health-educational practices. The purpose and outcome of health education are discussed in public as well as in special interest groups.

The question of value complexity is highly relevant when we consider the often conflicting values that prevail in the field of health promotion and prevention. The participants in general (health professionals) refer to WHO-defined health as "a state of physical, mental and social well-being, and not only the absence of disease and disability" (WHO, 1986) and indicate that a healthy life is not only a question of treating or preventing disease but also a question of the quality of life and "living the good life". A good life is not just being alive, but living for the realisation of individual and social values—although they ask, what values?

The health visitors at the schools in Copenhagen are trained nurses with competencies in public health policies and services. Their health promotion practice demonstrates a commitment to "the whole pupil", including their families, and to improving and protecting the health and well-being of the school community. In contrast, the health educators in the Greenland project come to the field of health promotion from different professions, bringing different values, traditions, knowledge and ideologies to the table. They acquire the competencies needed to clarify and relate the values and feelings that are associated with these various settings, cultural (indigenous) traditions and different visions—not to simply leave the values and value conflicts as they are, juxtaposing them, as it were, without attempting to relate them to one another. Inasmuch as the health promotion processes and the dialogues with the indigenous people and pupils occur, different models of relationships relevant to the clarification of health education and health promotion have been defined.

Observation of the communication that occurs at the workshops and listening to the participants' descriptions of several experiments has made it clear that there is such a high degree of value complexity in the field of health promotion and education that it is difficult to differentiate between and prioritise values. A general empirical finding is that the participants find it difficult to separate their 'own values' from their professional values in their communication. And it has become clear from the experiments that they are only able to observe values through their own values. Moreover, an interesting finding is that the participants do not reflect on their own health and health promotion as learning processes through their professional work. Their professional and private concepts of health lead separate, parallel lives. The values they express may therefore tell us more about the social context to which the values are connected than it does about the participants' own values.

Value complexity in the different health educational practices is high – both inside and outside of the professional functions. Thus the participants find contrary and conflicting values in their professional functions, *e.g.*:

(a) Promoting healthy learning processes conflicts with maintaining social control,

(b) Being a public health expert conflicts with working towards participatory health education,

(c) Connecting with powerful guidelines of health behaviour and lifestyle conflicts with participation in decision making,

(d) Having an educational background in biomedical science conflicts with working with a broad concept of health,

(e) Being part of a biomedical disease treatment system conflicts with the ideology of action competence,

(f) Local healthy policies conflict with lifestyle recommendations made by the National Health Service, and

(g) Carrying out national prevention strategies conflicts with aims in regard to participation in health promotion.

Through dialogue with health educators, the supervisors investigate and develop the concept of value and experiment with different processes of value clarification. The first step has been to discuss 'value' and 'clarification' as observations and then combine and reflect on them. The participants are not interested in the term 'value' as such, but in 'value' insofar as it stands for 'valuing' as a process. Moreover, it becomes empirically clear that valuing and clarifying are closely connected. It is, for example, difficult for the health visitors to identify conflicts of values between the adolescents and themselves during the dialogues about health; instead they consider whether or not the dialogue takes place from a participatory perspective. They value the educational activities rather than clarifying the values in the dialogues.

The two projects have developed ways of clarifying not just the concept of value but also that of clarification. It has become clear what the health educators say about values, how they relate value to their concept of health, and how they include the values of their target groups. Furthermore it has become clear how they become observers, how they manipulate communication with the values and how they observe and reflect on values in their health dialogues. The conclusion is that health educational work is to want something with other people: to want them to learn something and to develop positively as humans.

One way to be able to act professionally in health education is to clarify the values connected with health practices and thus create the basis for giving direction to health education. It is therefore crucial to establish the necessary basis for allowing health professionals to relate to these discussions and processes to do with value clarification. For example, many healthcare workers experience a conflict when on the one hand they work with ground rules according to which children must be respected and involved in a discussion about what health is, while on the other hand they are part of a tradition according to which healthy living is seen as pre-defined and not subject to discussion.

In connection with the pedagogical work with children and youths, there is talk of opposite approaches and working methods. The concept of health promotion is often used about processes that activate and develop children's own resources, own quality of life and motivation to act in favour of their own health on a more general level. Within this approach, ideas of involving these target groups in order to increase their ownership and motivation are central. In contrast to this, disease prevention (and treatment) are often seen as initiatives that 1) target specific diseases and 2) are implemented as top-down activities. Health promotion as distinct from prevention and treatment is therefore often presented as participatory and bottom-up as opposed to expert control and top-down. This juxtaposition is seen by professionals as counterproductive, since in both areas of treatment and prevention there is a need to establish processes that contribute to build up the motivation and ownership of target groups, just as there is a need for expert knowledge in the area of health promotion.

5. Educational Development Work as a Research Strategy

In connection with the methodological approach, it has turned out that proximity and involvement have great significance to the researcher role. Furthermore, the results from the development work show that health-educational research today is spread out between tradition and criticism, between respect for the known and a will to think new. Health education is a living and necessary practice, also in the health services, and it is necessary to realise that health and scientific research is not enough to provide disease prevention and health promotion if the knowledge generated is to create practical resonance. The educational researcher is thus ascribed a real role. Health-educational practice first and foremost promotes that the actors, that is the health professionals and the target groups themselves, believe that what they do makes a difference. Researchers must be prepared to employ 'research virtues'. These imply : a real interest in researching, inquisitiveness, and commitment to the target groups and society in general. They must have or develop the ability to evaluate their own observations and, not least when it comes to educational development work, the ability to reflect on their own participation in the field of health education. Furthermore, the individual researcher must involve him or herself in the personal and professional competence development of the project participants, and in his or her own competence development as a researcher.

Getting involved in one's own learning process is not without its risks, and getting involved in that of others is so much more risky. On the other hand, it is important that the project participants encounter true commitment, both reflecting scholarly values related to the basic code of true/false and a respect for the cultural values and ways of living of the outside world, human dignity, integrity and vulnerability. Commitment is the life nerve of any collaboration in new thinking and problem solving in the interest of society. Researchers must constructively take advantage of this by committing and taking advantage of the connection between teaching/development and research in order to deliver the optimal results (new knowledge). By showing personal and professional commitment, the researcher must contribute to making the un-tried attractive and the well-known fascinating, and at the same time create a resonance between research and practice. This is where scholarly ambition starts.

Despite the constructive development approach, some strategic problems related to the two development projects at hand can be identified. First and foremost, the coordination of the relevant research, development and practice interests demands both overview and differentiation. On the one hand it is significant that in communication one may differentiate between research and practice with separate functions. An unclear and absent separation of the functions can lead either to an unintended legitimisation of the educational or educational-policy practice, among other things through reproduction of practice discourses or to make the research normative, ideological, political in its outset and make it get in the way of its primary function : the production of new knowledge. The two development projects have clear political and ideological outsets that have proved difficult to separate from practical, scholarly interests. At the same time, irritation or neglect arises in practice if the research results do not have a form that can support the practical actions. In contrast to the action research tradition (Aagaard Nielsen & Svensson, 2004), which sees research and planning in collaboration between the researcher and practitioner to ensure the commitment of both parties in a common project as a virtue, I believe it is crucial to distinguish clearly between development questions and research questions. This separation is important, among other things for the sake of clarity between the different interests and roles. The empirical analyses show that the role confusion leads to a large part of the communication being about disentangling the different interests.

On the other hand it is crucial that the communication creates connections between research and practice. The empirical problem is that the educational practice focuses exclusively on what may be expressed through usage terminology. For the sake of the practitioners, research ambitions for more or less complicated scientific methods for data collection and interpretation are toned down. However, researchers tend to disregard the usability of their results, and the question of whether new scientific knowledge can support practical and political decisions does not become important. These problems do not repeat themselves in the two development projects. It is my experience that educational development work is a 'risky' research and development strategy because great demands are placed on communication for the handling of several tasks which the participants mutually commit themselves to.

These difficulties can be interpreted as a question of how the differentiation/connection between health educational development and educational research can take place. There must be a clear divide between the various motives and interests, which means, among other things, a differentiation between research issues and development issues, and, for that matter, also between development and non-development tasks, and it becomes relevant to discuss how a connection between educational research and health educational development becomes plausible. The question is if a common theme may be found that can be used as a medium to make the connection more plausible.

6. A Systems—Theoretical Model

What separates research and development is their perspective on knowledge; thus the different camps have different motives for collaborating on knowledge production. What connects them is a common interest in the production of knowledge/theory, since both research and development are knowledge-based (Wistoft, 2007). A solution of the methodological problems above is that the educational experiment considers not only as a media within development work but also as a communicative trick (Luhmann, 1995), making a connection between research and development more probable. The communication must be based on interaction and organisation. Thus I suggest that educational development work as a research and development strategy is seen as (1) interaction, that is the simultaneous sensuous presence of persons with the following roles ; practicians, development consultants and researchers and (2) an organisation that solves special health-educational tasks with decisions made on the basis of values. The educational experiment may be illustrated as so :

	I: Interaction	**II: Organisation**
Characteristic	Presence/absence	Membership
Expectations	Individual and personal values	Roles
Reflection	Proximity principles	Decision base / Values

6. Experiments as a Medium for Reflection

It has been found empirically that educational experiments open up to fertile discussions among the project participants. In this way the experiments serve to connect the communication between the developers, consultants and researchers. *Design Experiments* (Cobb *et al.*, 2003) are a broadly used development model that takes its outset in experiments that are created in collaboration between developers and researchers and are tested in research schools or 'labs'. However, this model results in a number of difficulties similar to those described above. In general as well there are difficulties to simultaneously meeting demands for scientific solidity and demands for development (Burkhardt & Schoenfeld, 2003). I therefore insist that the educational experiment should be carried out in practice and subjected to observation in concordance with educational research and health educational development. As a system of interaction, the strategy may be observed according to its logic about proximity between people. The researchers research, the practitioners practise and the consultants develop. As a system of organisation, the strategy may be observed from a perspective of membership, roles, decision bases and values.

A methodological success criteria for an educational development work to function as a research and development strategy is that a connection is made between scientific knowledge production and the practical goals, actions and changes of the development work. The organization is significant to a number of issues, including which mutual commitments the participants take on in relation to goals, plans, data collection, implementation, etc. Who does what when? And how is it decided? Ideally, practical contributions must be includable in the research, just as scholarly contributions must be includable in the communication of health professionals. My thesis is that these mutual contributions (connections) become more probable through the educational experiment as a *medium of reflection*. Both research and development professionals have an interest in educational experiments as a basis for knowledge production, albeit with differing perspectives and motives.

REFERENCES

Aagaard Nielsen, K., and Svensson, L. (2004) : Action and interactive research–a Nordic approach, *A draft for a book and preliminary version of a first chapter*: RUC.

Andersen, N.Å. (2003) : *Discursive analytical strategies : Understanding Foucault, Koselleck, Laclau, Luhmann*. Bristol: Policy Press.

Burkhardt, H., and Schoenfeld, A. H. (2003) : Improving educational research : Toward a more useful, more influential, and better-funded enterprise. *Educational Researcher, 32*(9), 3-14.

Cobb, P., Confrey, J., di Sessa, A., Lehrer, R., & Schauble, L. (2003) : Design experiments in educational research. *Educational Researcher, 32*(1), 9-13.

Hart, R. (1997) : *Children participation, the theory and practice of involving young citizens in community development and environmental care.* London : Earthscan Publications Ltd.

Jensen, B.B. (1997). A case of two paradigms within health education. Health education research–theory & practice. *Health Education Research, 12*(4), 419-428.

Jensen, B.B. (2000) : Health knowledge and health education in relation to a democratic health promoting school. *Health Education, 100*(4), 146-153.

Jensen, B.B. (2004) : Environmental and health education viewed from an action perspective–a case from Denmark. *American Journal of Curriculum Studies, 36*(4), 405-425.

Jensen, B.B., Roesen, J.V., Glisman, H., & Wistoft, K. (Eds.) (2006) : *Sundhedsplejen ved en skillevej? Erfaringer fra et sundhedspædagogisk udviklingsarbejde*. København : Sundhed og miljø, Københavns Kommune.

Jensen, B.B., Schnack, K., and Simovska, V. (2000) : *Critical environmental and health education. Research issues and challenges.* København: Research Centre for Environmental and Health Education, The Danish University of Education.

Jensen, B.B., and Simovska, V. (2006) : Involving students in learning and health promoting processes: Clarifying "Why?" "What?" and "How?". *Journal of Health Promotion and Education*.

Kruse, S. and Wistoft, K. (2006) : Value complexity in health education —a systems theoretical contribution to value clarification. *Cybernetics and Human Knowing* (in press).

Leydesdorff, L. (2002) : The communicative turn in the theory of social systems. *Systems Research and Behavioural Science* (19), 129-136.

Luhmann, N. (1990) : The cognitive programme of constructivism and the reality that remains unknown. In W. Krohn (Ed.) *Self organisation. Portrait of a Scientific Revolution* (Vol. 64-85). Amsterdam: Kluwer Academic Publishers.

Luhmann, N. (1993) : Observing re-entries. *Graduate Faculty Philosophy Journal, 16*(2), 485- 498.

Luhmann, N. (1994) : How can mind participate in communication? (W. Whobrey, Trans.). In H. U. Gumbrecht & K. L. Pfeiffer (Eds.), *Materialities of communication*. Stanford, California : Stanford University Press.

Luhmann, N. (1995) : *Social Systems* (J. Bednarz & D. Baecker, Trans.). Stanford, California : Stanford University Press.

Luhmann, N., & Schorr, K. E. (2000) : *Problems of reflection in the system of education*. Münster/New York: Waxmann.

Rasmussen, J. (2004) : Textual interpretation and complexity–radical hermeneutics. *Nordisk Pedagogik, 24*, 177-194.

Schnack, K., and Jensen, B. B. (1997) : The action competence approach in environmental education. *Environmental Education Research, 3*(2), 163-178.

Slavin, R. E. (2002) : Evidence-based education policies : Transforming educational practice and research. *Educational Reasearcher, 31*(7), 15-21.

Spencer-Brown, G. (1971). *Laws of forms*. London : Allen Unwin.

Storgaard, K. (1991) : Dialogue research–an approach to scientific and pracical experience. In T. Cronberg, O. M. Jensen & L. Qvortrup (Eds.), *Danish experiments - Social Constructions of Technology* (pp. 157-166). Copenhagen : New Social Science Monographs.

Thyssen, O. (1992) : Ethics as second order moral observation. *Cybernetics and Human Knowing*, 1(1).

Ven, J.A. v.d. (1998) : *Formation of the moral self*. Michigan : W.B. Eerdmans.

von Foerster, E. (1992) : Ethics and second-order cybernetics. *Cybernetics and Human Knowing*, 1(1), 9-18.

WHO. (1986) : *The Ottawa Charter for Health Promotion* (No. Health Promotion, 1, iii-v) : World Health Organization.

Wistoft, K., Jensen, B.B., and Roesen, J.V. (2005) : *Værdier på spil? Mellem sundhedsfremme og forebyggelse i skolesundhedsplejen*. København : Danmarks Pædagogiske Universitets Forlag.

Wistoft, K., and Schnack, K. (Eds.) (2006) : *Værdier og sundhedspædagogik–udvikling af forebyggelse og sundhedsfremme i grønland* (Vol. 1). Nuuk: Paarisa, Peqqissutsimut Pisortaqarfik - Direktoratet for Sundhed, Grønlands Hjemmestyre.

13

Socio-cultural Dimensions Tribal Health : A Challenging Domain of Social Workers in India

Kakali Paul (Mitra)

1. Introduction

The term 'health' assumes a connotation in the common parlance which refers to the (desired) balanced state of body and mind. Thus, 'health' and 'disease' are paired polar concepts (Mahapatra, 1986). The World Health Organization (WHO) seeks to define health as "A state of complete physical mental and social well being and not merely the absence of disease and infirmity." The concept of well being stands for the "the state of being happy, healthy or prosperous" (Websters, 1969). Evidently 'health' includes physical health (healthy), mental health (happy) and social health (prosperous and free of strife), (Behura, 1991). Health and disease are, however, related to biological and cultural resource of a community in a specific environment.

Every culture, irrespective of its simplicity and complexity has its own system of beliefs and practices concerning health and ill-health and treatment of diseases. Each culture also has a particular system of medicine which tries to treat the diseases in its own way. Every culture also has its own way of health care system by which they use their beliefs to look after the diseased persons. As a component of its overall culture, the idea of health of a community is shaped by the interplay of a number of social, political and cultural forces.

The health status of people or group is often determined as much by cultural practices as by biological and by environmental factors. It is a fact that healthy lifestyle is as much a product of health consciousness as the attitude towards life. Attitude of feelings are difficult to modify; particularly when they are deeply rooted in cultural myths and beliefs. "Cultural" causes are, however may not always be easy to be separated from "medical" causes.

Health has always been a major concern of community development. It is a basic requirement, not only for the fulfillment of the human aspirations, but also for the enjoyment of all mankind of a better quality of life. It is also indispensable for a balanced development of the individual within the family and as part of the community of the nation.

In India there is an immense heterogeneity of medical beliefs and practices all over the country. Besides the well known and wide spread medical system such as Ayurvedic, Unani, Homeopathic and allopathic, there are various types of localized folk and tribal medical beliefs and practices often based on magic and sorcery. Besides, there are other socio-psychological reasons too. Health to a tribal community by and large, is a function of the interaction between socio-cultural and socio-biological practices, the genetic attributes and environmental condition. The widely varying prevalent health practices of the tribal community include use of indigenous herbal drugs, taboos, superstitions and magico-religious beliefs. Excluding any of these can not determine the health and health status of the tribal community. Polgar (1962), pointed out that it is not true that primitive groups are lacking ideas about health and how to care for it. The tribal communities have a system of health care of their own and by which they have survived for a long. The system is however, must be judged as adequate at least for their purpose. G. M. Carstairs (1955), refers to the importance attached to "confident prognosis' as an attribute of the role of the healer. Traditional medicine establishes 'faith' and 'assurance' to the patient. Marriot (1955), has also emphasized the cultural definition of medical roles. Trust, responsibility, charity, power, respects are the important aspect of interpersonal relations in medical sphere. It is not so much his technical skill that gives prestige to a healer but his spiritual power gained through communication with supernatural entities.

It is thus apparent that health is not the exclusive domain of medical science. It needs the co-ordination between social scientists, medical practitioners and the social workers to deal effectively in both prevention and cure of diseases. As a matter of fact more studies covering different facts are urgently necessary to understand some of the realities of health problems and their world view particularly for the tribal communities.

In this paper however, an endeavour has been made to explore different aspects of health culture of the tribal people. An attempt has been made to know the tribal notions regarding health, ill-health and *vis-a-vis* way of treatment. An elucidation on their traditional belief system of health care and way of treatment is made which will make a comprehensive understanding about how the tribals are swinging between indigenous belief system and practices and modern ideas of health care system. It gives a new dimension of health work for the culture bound tribal people.

2. Tribal Concept of Health and Ill-health

Tribal society is normally conceptualized as clan-lineage based segmentary system characterized by mechanical solidarity. Beteille (1977), described the tribe as a society; further society based on kinship, where social stratification is absent. Broadly tribe is an aggregate of people sharing social values, common dialect, territory and culture. But in a restricted sense, tribe means "a group of people under a chief and maintaining distinct cultural traits". The ways of livelihood of Indian tribe are several and it is true that they cannot be exclusively placed in a particular typology in its strict sense. They use all available means to eke out its subsistence and make complex economy, though the tribesmen of India have their primary means of economy that grading from hunting and gathering stage to settled agricultural stage according to varied environmental circumstances of the country. Thus, over 8 percent of India's total population, the tribals have a variety in their culture, lifestyle and above all different customs and worldview of their own. Today despite their adaptation and exposure to the culture of larger society, modernization, industrialization; live in a world of dynamic isolation that helps the tribal to maintain its distinct socio-cultural identity. Tribal concept of health, disease or treatment of life and death is as varied as their culture. Apparently in majority of the tribal areas it appears so from the surroundings of the village which exhibits lack of sanitation and drainage system, in adequate supply of safe drinking water, non-airy rooms, coexistence of cattle shed with the living rooms, unplanned growth of hamlets etc. But inspite of such ecological habitation pattern, tribals have their own concepts of health care, cleanliness and diseases. Normally tribals are strenuous and hardworking. They niggardly provided in life in the remote and often inhospitable environment. Generally to the tribals good health means 'active condition of the body', *i.e.*, the proper functioning of the body. Those, who can do manual work, can take normal food and can do domestic work, are considered to be healthy. That means, the general index of a threat to health is expressed through withdrawal from work. Along with this they also have a positive concept of health which implies a good physical and mental health to carry out work. Tribal concept of health is however, functional one and not clinical. That is why the tribal people having scabies, itches or ringworm are still considered themselves to be capable of normal daily work like any normally healthy person. An occasional headache, stomachache or body pain or weakness is not considered seriously as symptoms of any dieses or ill health. Even fever or body pain of the children is considered quite normal and healthy for their physical growth. If any one takes it seriously may be ridiculed in the family and by the neighbour. It is not unknown to them that health implies a sufficient reserve of physical strength, ability and endurance as well as mental equilibrium to meet demands of life. Therefore, the good health is only the perfect combination of physical and mental constitution. This idea is not so far from the definition of WHO.

On the other hand tribal people believe in order to keep sound health; one has to maintain a balanced relationship with natural and supernatural world. Natural world comprises of dietary habits and nutritional status, drinking habits, surroundings and state of cleanliness, hygiene of the people etc.; while the supernatural world is the combination of evil eye, ancestral spirits and *Bongas* (spirit). Tribal people think that one individual may bring some affliction by committing or omitting certain acts, may also cause some affliction harmful for the whole village, clan or larger group. But such conceptualization is not mediated through an intervening variable like sanitation. Normally tribal people do not associate certain diseases or epidemics with insanitory conditions of community living. This does not mean that some specific tribal people do not like or create clean or sanitary settlement. For example, Santal or Ho houses are neatly plastered with colour earth and the glistening metallic utensils cleaned everyday by them. Most of the tribal people even food gathering Kadar and Kharia or semi-nomadic Birhors are found to restrict their habits of cleanliness in their personal level. They clean their clothes and body regularly which indicates their sense of cleanliness and beauty. But above this aesthetic sense how these act of personal hygiene are positively correlated to their community health and inversely how their lack or infringement is responsible for several diseases or epidemics is not formulated in their concept of health. To a tribal mind, the real enemies of human health and prosperity are the gods and the spirit of the dead. Thus, to become healthy and disease free, one has to maintain a three way relationship *viz.* man-man, man-nature and man-supernature. The fate of individual and community at large depends on their relationship with unseen forces which intervene to human affairs. If men offend them, the mystical power punish by sickness, death or other natural calamities.

The tribal people believe that the supernatural power who for certain things provide for the protection and remedial measures are of malevolent and benevolent types *i.e.* some supernatural elements are responsible for sickness and at the same time it can drive away the root cause of sickness or help the diseased person to come round. Santals, the largest tribal community of India, are usually spirit-ridden tribe and their life pattern based on belief in personalized and impersonalized supernatural being. It is believed that at the time of birth they are allotted a certain span of life by the supreme god, *i.e. thakur*. Death comes only at the end of this allotted span of life. But besides supreme god, the Santhals also believe in a number of *Bongas*, mostly malevolent who are supposed to harass humanity. As a result they suffer from diseases. They have strong belief that the supernatural beings, particularly various *bongas* enter into the body of a person causing diseases. When such spirit or *bonga* becomes angry on the community as a whole it causes epidemics.

Beside hostile spirits, ghosts or dead, another cause of disease in tribal society is the breach of some taboos. Tribe regard taboo as 'holy dread', an objectified fear of demonic power thought to be concealed in the tabooed objects. When a taboo is violated, the tribal believe it may result in disaster in human life. To them diseases are sometimes attributed by human agencies such as evil eye, or touch of persons who have some magical power and even magical spell by the sorcerer. The children are believed to be mostly affected by these powers. Thus, it is to be said that the nature of tribal health concept is an unique culture-bound constellations.

3. Diagnosis and Treatment of the Diseases

To a tribal as the causation of the diseases are either the displeasure of the supernatural being or the intrusion of malevolent spirit into the body; recognition of evil eye, evil touch or air and types of supernatural power is significant for the diagnosis of the diseases. Disease is caused by bad spirits and the spirits are bad either because one has not properly propitiated them. Generally the concerning village priest in addition to his religious functions acts as the mediator between the people and the mystical power. By propitiations and prayers he tries to maintain the good relationship between the people on the one hand and mystical powers on the other, which intervene human affairs. Thus magico-religious treatment of disease is resorted to.

Before treating the diseased person, the root causes of the disease, forces behind the sickness, as believed by them, are to be found out. The particular spirit or deity responsible for the sickness has to be identified. This identification of the spirit usually is done by the magico-religious specialists or some traditional medicine man. Sometimes different types of specialists exist in a particular society. All the specialists are not alike. They have different specializations which they acquire from their parental generations as well as personal practice. They are called in different names vary from one tribe to another (like *ojha, gunin, dehari* etc.). It is a general trend among the tribal people, when somebody falls ill he will prefer to wait and see how it will go. If, however, disease continues and dose not respond to domestic medicine, service of the concerning specialists is called. He can see the cause of the disease and have the power to identify the evil spirit or evil eye responsible for causing harm to him through magical ritual.

Classification of diseases is culturally articulated in simple and traditional tribal societies. Grown up people through their experiences have rounded knowledge of all diseases that occur in their societies. But the specialists in their societies, regarded as the experts are supposed to have some comprehensive knowledge about the disease. They prevail to an indigenous disease classificatory system though it may less systematized, less specialized and also less articulated from the standpoint of recognized taxonomic system of modern medical science. Their classification is more or less generalized and the special attention in categorization of diseases are given on the basis of age *i.e.* child and adult, sex and age and seasonal variations round the year. Generally to them Worm and rickets are the diseases of the children. Leprosy, Tuberculosis, Piles, Hernia and Anemia are some common adult diseases. On the other hand menstrual problems, leucorrhoea or amenorrhea are the diseases exclusively of the females. Cough or cold-cough, diarrhea, cholera, dysentery, headache, fever, pox, gout etc. are some common seasonal diseases. Beside these they could also classify some diseases as malnutritional and infectious. Generally dental carries, sores on tongue are identified as malnutritional diseases. Infectious diseases are measles, pox, and malaria. Though among most of the tribes it is interestingly noted that they know the mosquitoes as the root cause of malaria but for measles and pox their faith still laid on wrath of goddess.

Some tribal communities working in the city or town areas as industrial labourers, daily labourers or in any other jobs and even as maidservants in domestic households or in lodges and hotels of tourist spots are found suffering from various venereal diseases and even HIV Aids. Unfortunately, these are completely new and above their classification from their generation after generation experiences.

Traditional tribal method of treatment is generally two ways. One is magico-religious treatment and another one by herbal medicines. Main way of magico-religious treatment is the expulsion of evil or angry spirit or *bonga* from the body of the patient. The magico-religious practitioner treats the patient through the process of magical spell or incantation with the assistance of his own *bonga*. He takes up different processes of appeasing the evil or cruel *bonga* by offering some sacrifices or he takes the recourse to coerce the evil *bonga* with the help of a higher *bonga*. He also utters *mantras* (hymn or verse) and performs some magical rituals. Finally when the spirit is believed tó be invoked from the body of the patient; the shaman confined the spirit to a distant outside the village. When illness is caused due to harmful magic of the sorcerers or witches then it associates with both causing and curing of diseases. Thus, the sorcerers and witches are often utilized to take revenge on the enemies. Usually in these cases they are treated by administering some enchanted edible objects like salt, rice etc. The medicine-man or shaman also detects the sorcerer who is believed to cause the illness. In some cases it leads to some counter magic or even physical fight. When the casting of evil eye afflict the children more seriously he performs certain rituals and at last offers some enchanted roots, shoots or leaves of the locally available herbs for eating. For some minor diseases the medicine-man are generally found to utter some magical spells and prepares some enchanted roots and salt for eating, enchanted water for drinking or enchanted oil for massaging.

When magical methods, enchanted objects, or ritual performances satisfy their psychological sense and patients are believed to be free from the disease then in order to relieve the pain, strain and other secondary symptoms, a variety of herbal medicines are prescribed by the tribal medicine man. Treatment by herbal medicine is, however, also very much practiced as a popular method of treatment. Though the tribal people of India in general do not have any record of their method of treatment and medicines required to cure different types of ailments, they possess oral knowledge which has been transmitted to the posterity. As a matter of fact they have a good awareness of herbal medicines and most of all senior persons are found to be quite knowledgeable of the herbal medicines. The medicines specialists kept stock of these medicines and supplied the people whenever needed. The herbs, roots, leaves and other ingredients used in the medicine are generally available in their locality. In certain cases herbs might be given in their natural form, while in complex diseases modifications and enchantment according to need are provided. The medicine man is, however, only the knowledgeable person for perfect composition and doses of the medicines.

4. Present Scenario

Yet the tribal people tend to cling more to the indigenous medicine but exposure to modern medicine is not a very recent one. They perceived a change, sometimes not completely in beliefs but in practices regarding health and medical care. Tribal people of all over India, have to maintain a regular contact with mainstream people for their livelihood. It makes them highly exposed to modernization as well as to modern medicinal treatment. On the other hand, Government of India, in the year 1985 committed to achieve "Health for all by 2000 A.D." through the universal provision of comprehensive primary health care services. In the overall health development programme Government promised, emphasis will be laid on preventive and promotive aspects and on organizing effective and efficient health services which are comprehensive in nature, easily and widely available, truly accessible, and generally affordable by the people. As a result large number of tribal villages even living in isolated areas is now having minimum a primary health centre and sometimes also some private medical practitioners. Thus, a trend to shift in the scale of preferences towards modern medicine is not uncommon especially to the new generation. But sometimes interestingly their preference is found to restrict for some diseases like typhoid, cholera, gastro intestinal diseases, skin diseases etc.; those require immediate relief. For abortion and sterilization, they are increasingly turning to gynecologists to minimize risks of life. At the time of complicated cases of delivery, sometimes after failing of traditional midwife, women are sent to the health centre or hospital. But in most of the cases their preference is home as the traditional procedure for child birth is more preferable and comfortable also to her though it is inconvenient to the hospital.

It is a common feature among the tribal that after fall ill they are waiting for two to three days to watch the progress of illness and after preliminary judgment of their own regarding the types and importance of the disease they decide where to go; to the traditional medicine man or to the health centre? They consider medical aid to be futile when the disease is believed to be caused by supernatural agency. Pox, emaciation of children, insomnia, dog, fox or snake bite are some conditions for which they fall back completely to traditional magico-religious therapy. Leprosy is one of such diseases considered by the tribal people as the most dangerous contagious disease. Initially when any one is attacked by this goes to the local shaman or medicine man. When it becomes out of his reach he announce it as an awful disease and nothing but a result of his sin. Thus it not only afflicts the body, but also affects the social position of the patient. As they believe, leprosy can be transmitted from generation to generation and, therefore, the patient is supposed to leave the village. As this disease is also believed to be a contagious one, even the family members of the patients do not accompany them. The patient has to leave his/her family, village and spent rest of the life by begging. Some diseases which require long term treatment like tuberculosis, cancer etc. tribal people are found to make a two way treatment. Modern medicinal treatment is at the one hand and traditional magico-religious and herbal on the other hand. As they belief that medicine can make temporary relief but without blood sacrifices to appease the deity or incantation of magical spell to drive out evil spirits, complete cure will never be possible.

Thus, the reality is that though impact of modernization has given momentum to change in most of the tribal society of India and they are more and more prone to modern medicines and even surgery, their indigenous practices will hardly die in near future. Their belief in faith healing will persist.

5. Role of Social Workers

Traditions die hard and people find relief by clinging to old ages. The situation has its irony, because the consequence of what they do often is in fact to preserve the traditional order or at least its facade. Social workers should start from here. Health work to a social worker specially for the tribals should not be a part of philanthropy but must be seen as part of the overall framework of their society and culture. Within the limits of their own respective world view the tribals are capable of identifying and nomenclaturing various kinds of ailments and diseases. They seem to be quite aware of the causative factors of the diseases but it is completely in their own way. Their belief in the existence of supernatural powers, evil touch or spell of witch behind the diseases or intrusion of poison (*tejo* called by the Santals) by the witches through food; all are arisen from their experiences of certain unexplainable diseases and death. It has led tribal people into believing in other than material visible world, *i.e.* invisible spirit world.

Therefore, for the development of tribal health, social workers have to make them understand that the causative factors are different types of germs, viruses, bacteria etc., those are really invisible without a microscope but they are not unexplainable. Tribal people have to learn to identify the right and the wrong. Evil spirit, witch or sorcerers are not the bearer of diseases but their wrong ways of day to day life like habitation pattern, sanitation, drinking water, food habits, bathing habits, and even early marriage are more harmful and causes of diseases. It is, therefore, necessary to aware them about proper hygiene which will be more effective to prevent the wrath of *bongas* than animal sacrifices.

Social workers have to make them aware that problems for one are problems for all. Thus, a systematic organizational effort is required to maintain a communal hygiene. Best effort has to be given for awakening the 'limited want' tribal people to know what the better health is and want for it and to know the thing they can do to improve their health.

There should not be a wide gulf between the thinking, experience and idea of a social worker from the tribal people. The knowledge of beliefs and practices give a social worker more insights in understanding their world views. Differences in the view point, contrasts and conflicts between the social workers or the roles assumed by the traditional and modern medical practitioners may result in obstacles to the acceptability of modern ideas and medicines also. Identification of all categories of traditional medicine man, magico-religious practitioners and village priests is very much essential and make them well aware and trained about the reality behind their beliefs and myth. Identification should not be restricted within a particular village but it should be extended to what extent they go for a better magico-religious practitioners or medicine man. Only they have the power to make a pragmatic bent in the attitudes of the tribal people.

Ayurveda is the very foundation of ancient medical science in India and the earliest use of medicinal plant is found in *Atharveda* and *Rigveda,* the sacred scripture of *Hindus*. India's ancient scriptures bearing ample proof of highly developed scientific concepts of Ayurvedic system and systematic utilization of herbals in treatment of human diseases. It is, therefore, no harm to encourage the tribal habits for using certain herbs for the control of diseases or undesirable fertility. It is quite possible to achieve effective and safe methods of cure and fertility control through the herbal materials used by the tribals. But now the non-availability of the indigenous herbs, possibly due to wanton destruction of forest and dearth of knowledge among the current generation of the local medicine man have possibly created aversion to such system of treatment among the tribal of India. Not only that, it as much as associated with sorcery, magic and superstition that discarded since its effect as it is more imaginary than real. Ethno botanic and phytographic investigation is required to explore the medicinal herbs. Considerable amount of information on the traditional uses is available with the tribals. It is, however, systematic research work on these plants, pharmacological experiments or clinical tests are required to promote positive knowledge and more accuracy of the application of herbal medicine. To achieve full potency and dissemination of knowledge among the traditional medicine men, training and awareness camps have to be organized for a comprehensive intervention between health workers, medical practitioners with folk medicine men and the community. In this way, the health workers or social workers be able to reach the unreached. On the other hand, people's participation should be assured and self confidence of the people be developed to explore the innovative ideas among themselves. Tribal people have to be inspired to boost up the missing medicinal plant resources in their area. The people will also take the responsibility to learn themselves about proper health care and build up capability to judge the required treatment when fall ill. Thus, it is not an exclusive domain of social workers or medical practitioners but a coordination of anthropologists, botanists, biochemists, medical scientists, social workers and above all the tribal people.

REFERENCES

Behura, N.K.; 1991 : "Anthropology of Disease, Treatment and Cure" in *Man and Life*, Vol. 17(1-2), pp. 35-40.

Beteille, Andre, 1977 : "The definition of Tribe", in *Tribe Cast and Religion in India*, Ed. by Thapar Ramesh, The MacMillan Company of India Limited, Delhi.

Bhattacharya, S. & Sengupta, Shyamal Kanti, 1986 : "The concept of Disease and its Treatment among the Birhor of Purulia", in *Tribal Health : Socio-Cultural Dimensions*, Ed. by Budadeb Choudhury, Inter India Publications, D-17, Raja Garden Extn., New Delhi-110015 (India).

Bhowmic, P.K., 1955 : "Treatment of Diseases among the Lodhas of West Bengal", *Man in India*, 35(4), 287-298.

Bodding, P.O., 1925 : "The Santals and Diseases : Studies in Santal Medicine and Connected Folklore" in *Memories of the Asiatic Society of Bengal*, Vol. X(1), pp. 1-132.

Carstairs, G. M., 1955 : "Medicine and Faith in Rural Rajasthan" in *Health, Culture and Community*, Ed. by B.D. Paul, Russel Sage Foundation, New York.

Choudhury, Buddhadeb, 1986 : "Cultural Dimentions of Health : A Study on West Bengal Villages" in *Tribal Health : Socio-Cultural Dimensions*, Ed. by Buddhadeb Choudhury, Inter India Publications, D-17 Raja Garden Extn., New Delhi-110015 (India).

Das, Jagannath, 1986 : "The Concept of Disease and Treatment in Tribal Orissa" in *Tribal Health : Socio-Cultural Dimensions*, Ed. by Buddhadeb Choudhury, Inter India Publications, D-17, Raja Garden Extn., New Delhi-110015 (India).

Dube, S.C., 1976 : *Tribal Heritage of India*, Vikas Publication, New Delhi.

Elwin, V., 1955 : *The Religion of an Indian Tribe*, Oxford University Press, London.

Guha, Anita, 1986 : "Folk Medicine of the Boro-Kacharies – A Plains Tribes of Assam" in *Tribal Health : Socio-Cultural Dimensions*, Ed. by Buddadeb Choudhury, Inter India Publications, D-17, Raja Garden Extn., New Delhi-110015 (India).

Gupta, S.P., 1986 : "Tribal Concept of Health, Disease and Remedy" in *Tribal Health : Socio-Cultural Dimensions*, Ed. by Buddhadeb Choudhury, Inter India Publications, D-17 Raja Garden Extn., New Delhi-110015 (India).

Kabir, M. & Krishnan, T. N., 1996 : "Social Intermediation and Health Change : Lessons from Kerala", in *Health, Poverty and Development in India*, Ed. by Monica Das Gupta, Lincoln C. Chen, T.N. Krishnan, Delhi University Press, YMCA Library Building, Jai Sing Road, New Delhi, 110001.

Mahapatra, L.K., 1977 : Concept of Health Among the Tribal Population Groups of India and its Socio-Economic and Socio-Cultural Correlates in *Tribal Health in India*, Ed. by Salil Basu, Manak Publications Private Ltd., Delhi.

Mann, R.S. & K., Mann, 1986 : "Religious Attributes and Cure in Tribal India" in *Tribal Health : Socio-Cultural Dimensions*, Ed. by Buddhadeb Choudhury, Inter India Publications, D-17 Raja Garden Extn., New Delhi-110015 (India).

Marriot, Mckim; 1955 : "Western Medicine in a Village of Northern India" in *Health, Culture and Community*, Ed. by B. D. Paul, Russel Sage Foundation, New York.

Polgar, S., 1962 : "Health and Human Behaviour : Areas of Interest Common to the Social and Medical Sciences", in *Current Anthropology*, Vol. 3, pp. 159-205.

Prasad, P. Durga, 1997 : "Socio-Cultural Determinants of Health Status of Rural Women" in *Health Planning in India*, Ed. by G. Ramchandrudu, A.P.H. Publishing Corporation, 5, Ansari Road, Darya Ganj, New Delhi – 110 002.

Sing, S.P. & Sing, V.L., 1986 : "Folk Lore Claims by Tribals and Experimental Evaluation of Some Medicinal Plants with Special Reference to Contraception" in *Tribal Health : Socio-Cultural Dimensions*, Ed. by Buddhadeb Choudhury, Inter India Publications, D-17, Raja Garden Extn., New Delhi-110015 (India).

Verma, K.K., 1992 : *Health Care and Family Welfare (Alternative Strategies)*, Mittal Publications, New Delhi – 110 059 (India).

Vidyarthi, L.P. & Rai, B.K., 1985 :*The Tribal Culture of India*, Concept Publishing Company, New Delhi.

WHO; 1978 : The Promotion and Development of Traditional Medicine, WHO, TRS No. 622, Geneva.

14

Spiritual Health : An Agent of Human Development

—Raja Ghosh

1. Introduction

"Health is the basis of Virtue (*Dharma*), Wealth (*Artha*), Desires (*Kama*), and Emancipation (*Moksha*)". The words from Charaka Samhita prove the needs and reasons behind building a good health of human being, which leads towards making him a 'complete man' in society. But to make him complete, upliftment the quality of his health condition is an important factor as it was realized that the ill health is symptom of social disequilibrium. Because the ill health caused towards the malfunctioning of the social system in terms of poverty, ignorance, population explosion, un-employment, old age, un-hygienic living conditions, bad housing, poor nutrition and incompatible dietary habits, poor quality of drinking water and sanitation facilities etc. According to the Hindu scripture, the complete man is a person, who is loyal to every stages of his life till to death for reaching up to his optimum goal for which the maintenance of good health is one of the important preconditions. The ancient Indian myths and scriptures including the history of yoga, which is basically a process of controlling the body system including the respiration, established that health is an important contributor in achieving the success of a human life.

According to the Oxford Dictionary—the health is *(i)* "a person's physical and mental condition or *(ii)* the state of being well in body or mind and *(iii)* soundness esp. Financial or morale." From this, the question raised in our mind that whether health means only the biological and mental component of the human being or something else? To solve the tension in our mind the World Health Organization (WHO) came forward in four decades ago and define health as - "is not the mere absence of diseases but essentially conforms to the social, physical and mental well being", It is quite clear that health represents not only the physical condition of the human being but the entire conditions of the human being, which includes his physical, Physiological, Financial, Morale and Mental or Psychological status. In support of this several studies have been conducted on health as it is realized that behind making the nation successive, the good health conditions of the human being plays a pivotal role. P. K. Bajpai (1998) also state that the health means "not only the absence of illness, but the prevalence of congenial, social, psychological and physical conditions where a person can achieve his optimum and enjoy life peacefully and successfully."

2. The Holistic Approach of Health and its Relation with Development

The definition given by WHO indicates that health is an expression of total condition of human life *i.e.* physical, genetic, chemical, environmental, cultural, economic, psychological, mental, intellectual and spiritual, which support the ancient 'Indian concept of Health' given by the 'Ayurveda'. It termed health as 'Swasthya' and indicates that it is a state of equilibrium between a human's external and internal environments. The above-mentioned documents proved health is one of the basic necessities of life, which needs continuous improvement and considered as one of the fundamental right of the human being.

The United Nation's declaration also re-established the health as a holistic approach and the human's right through its statement–"*Everyone has the right to a standard of living adequate for health and well-being of himself and of his family, including food, clothing, housing and medical care and necessary social services, and the right to security in the event of unemployment, sickness, disability, widowhood, old age, or other lack of livelihood in circumstances beyond his control"* (UN General Assembly in December 10, 1948, article 25.1). Thus health would be considered a holistic approach, which is associated with the quality of life of the human being and intimately correlated with the development.

Development is a very broad term, which includes the key word 'develop'. The dictionary meaning of development is 'a stage of growth and advancement.' During the course of civilization it was realized gradually that the human beings are most valuable and precious resources of the society who will play a pivotal role in Nation's development. The quality of a state depends upon the efficiency and quality of its human resources. Thus numerous kinds of efforts were taken into consideration for the overall development of human being, which includes his physical, social, economic and psychological development that leads to make him a chief contributor in the National Development.

Frequent programmes on development of the above sectors have been taken by the government and non-government organizations on the basis of "Right to Development", which is presently termed as 'human development'. In simple sense the human development is a Process of Developing the Human Potential in terms of his social status, economic and physical conditions, psychological/mental strength & spiritual entity that leads towards achieving the optimum goals of human's life. The Encyclopedia of Britannica define this particular term- "A complex concept of development based on the priority of human well-being and aimed at ensuring and enlarging human choices which lead to equality of opportunities for all people in the society and empowerment of people so that they participate in and benefit from the development process."

But it was realized that until and unless the people become spiritually developed the full amount of development could not be achieved. And thus at present, the National as well as the International organizations emphasizing on developing the *'Spiritual Health'* of the human being as it was revealed that the eternal spiritual entity is the key ingredients for overall and sustainable human development. Presently, the term development associated with different areas like–economic, physical, community, social, urban, rural etc., which means the upgradation of the existing 'quality' of these sectors, that directly contributes in the national development.

The above notes make it clear health of the human being is an essential parts of his development process. Even the United Nations also thrust upon the development of health as the member countries of the UN unanimously agreed on improvement of health in achieving the progress of the nation. Subsequently in September 2000 the member state adopted the UN Millennium Declaration, which endorsed by 189 countries, which is popularly known as Millennium Development Goals (MDGs). There are eight MDGs build on the agreements at UN Conference in 1990s set before the state to make them committed for reducing the poverty, hunger and to tackle ill health, gender inequality, lack of education, lack of access to clean water and environmental degradation that to be reached by 2015. The following comments made by the Director General of WHO Dr. LEE Jong Wook established the link between the health and development.

"Improvements in health are essential if progress is to be made with the other Millennium Development Goals".

If we examine the MDGs we may see that three out of eight goals, eight of the 16 targets and 18 of the 48 indicators relate directly to health, which is also an important contributor to several other goals. The MDGs provide a vision where health and education are squarely at the centre, which emphasized the importance of effective health systems as an essential factor for development as well as remind the civil society to reconsider the concept of development which is not equal to just the economic growth only. Therefore, we may said the MDGs as a form of shorthand for some of the most important outcomes that development should achieve :

- Fewer women dying in childbirth;
- More children surviving the early years of life;
- Dealing with the catastrophe of HIV/AIDS;
- Making sure people have access to life-saving drugs;
- Better health–in all its forms–making a major contribution to the reduction of poverty.

But when we speak about the development programme on health, we may see that several kinds of plans are taken up where emphases are given on materialistic achievement like introduction of several health related schemes, infrastructure development in rural and urban areas, information dissemination and so on. A very few words are there related to the developing the attitude of the human being, which is one of the precondition to receive the materialistic support, because the other factors will contribute towards the development only when the motivated and committed people area ready to use it. Thus several International and national organizations presently underlining the concept of developing the spirituality among the human being, which would be act as the catalytic agent in coordinating the external support and inner effort of the human being.

3. Spirituality : The Change Agent for Human Development

What is spirituality? It is a million dollar question before the human civilization. Is it some kind of religious in nature or something else? During the elongated period of civilization, the people are trying to find out the answer of this question. It is an admitted fact that each human being is a combination of body and spirit (physical and mental), which is complementary to each other. The sprit of the human being guided his biological instruments to act accordingly. The word 'spirit', which represents the courage or the strength of the mind is eternal in the human being. The Encyclopedia of Britannica explicates spiritualism as "the philosophy of higher reality". Several philosophers around the world also define the term in their own way like- "immaterial reality", "a universal mind", "a supreme being" etc., which is exists in the human being since his birth, and by examining the thoughts, it would be said that it is beyond the materialistic world. Spirituality relates to matters of sanity and of psychological health. The spirituality aimed at :

- simultaneously improving one's wisdom and willpower.
- achieving a closer connection to Deity/the universe.
- removing illusions or "false ideas" at the sensory, feeling and thinking aspects of a person.

The concept of spirituality in India is not a new concept. It has a long past. According to some Indian scriptures, spirituality (Sanskrit: *adhyatma*) relates to the *'self'*. Several philosophers, philanthropists, religious leaders as well as social reformers, made an attempt to know the concept and concluded that spirituality is nothing but the inherent quality or entity of the human being for knowing the self. It is one of the key ingredients for linking up physical activity of the human being with his thinking. Spiritual entity helps the human being to become self-less, self-dependent, self-confident, self-actualized, and self-powered, which will develop and enrich his inner beliefs as well as empowered him physically, socially, economically and psychologically to act as a sound development partner, who can be yoked to service of society leading towards achieving the ultimate ambition of a civil society.

The above noted points clarify that spirituality is an essential and important component of individual's holistic health and well-being, which was supported by the World Health Organization and many others. It can also be said that spirituality is the manifestation of the divine quality of the human being, which is eternal and used in understanding, realizing and implying the techniques of life for overall development.

The Indian scriptures and mythological stories describe the spirituality or spiritual health as developing the 'self power'

(*Sanskrit- Atman*), which is nothing but the control of body and mind. The *Upanishad, Bhagvad Gita, Ramayana, Mahabharata* and other scriptures are always emphasized on developing the self power and generation of self-realization, which is presently considered as one of the key ingredients of development by the developing as well as the developed societies. From the ancient writings, we came to know that spiritual health represents the inner quality and potentiality of the human being, which would be nurtured and cared. In support of this, Swami Vivekananda, the great social reformer rather than a religious leader also described that the people are in need of such type of education through which they become, self-dependent, build their morale character, develop their mental strength as well as develop their IQ towards fulfilling the objectives of human life. It would very appropriate to quote his dictum—"*Atmono Mokshartha Jagat Hitaya Cha*", which means the liberation of the soul for development of the world and be considered as the best example of human development in a stressful world at present.

The same can also be found in the Upanishad where stress have been given upon the developing the self which is termed as "*Atmanang Biddhi*" *i.e.* 'to know the self first then the others'.

Since over a long period, the philanthropists, educationists, petitioners and the social reformers put their utmost effort in developing the 'self' or the spiritual entity of the people. Because they felt that the spiritual entity helps the individual to develop their inner values, which directly help in achieving the peace and justice; become self-dependent and self-powered; obtain the respect and dignity from others. This is a process of human development, which established equal rights and justice in the society and help the human being to make him analytical in the way of his life. Rabindranath Tagore the first Noble laureate of India and Asia was also in favour of developing the spiritual entity of the human being as he measured it a matter of human development. In many of his writings he expressed about the nurturing and caring for spiritual development like.

"Bipade More Raksha Karo E Nahe Mor Prarthana
Bipade Ami Na Jeno Kari Bhay
Dukhho Tape Byathito Chite Nai Ba Dile Swantana
Dukhhe Jeno Karite Pari Joy"

This indicates to develop the self-power of the human being so that he may able to win the pain of sorrow and not be fearful in any trouble. By emphasizing on development of appropriate educational system of India Rabindranath clearly differentiate between two systems such as–there is a method of education where the people think and work independently and there is also an other system where the people obey the other's order, work on the basis of other's thought and above all act as a helper of others work (simple translation from the fiction– "Siksha").

The *"Bharat Sevashram Sangha"* is an organization founded by *Swami* Pranabananda *Maharaj* with the objective of self-help and self-development. Presently this organization has many branches in all over the India and work in hand to hand with governmental and other non-governmental organizations like– running of schools, hospitals, mobile health unit, services to the pilgrims and so on. The followings are the ideology of the organization, which speaks itself about the spirituality among the human being that make him a complete man.

Aim of life Liberation of soul and self-realization.

Objective of life	Self-abnegation, discipline, truth and *bramhacharya*.
Death in Life	Self-oblivion.
Reality in Life	Realization of Self, self-consciousness.
Piety in life	Valorous, Prowess, Humanity, desire of salvation.
Sin in Life	Debility, cowardice, illiberality or narrow minded, selfishness.
Power in Life	Patience, firmness, tolerance.
Resource in Life	Self-confidence, self-dependence, self-esteem.

Enemy in Life	Laziness, oversleep, drowsiness, inanimateness, six inherent vices, the sense organs.
Friends in Life	Encouragement, Enthusiasm, perseverance.

The above dialogues indicates that the spirituality is very rampant in every walks of our life, which is basically a organized life style of a human being and related with the development of core human values such as- Right Conduct; Peace; Truth; Love & Non Violence.

The British Institute of Sathya Sai Education described the above as follows :

Values Related to Right Conduct

Self-help Skills
Care of Possessions
Diet
Hygiene
Modesty
Posture
Self reliance
Tidy appearance

Social Skills :
Good behaviour

Good manners
Good relationships
Helpfulness
Not wasting

Ethical Skills
Code of conduct
Courage
Dependability
Duty
Efficiency
Ingenuity
Initiative
Perseverance
Punctuality
Resoucefulness
Respect for all
Responsibility

Values Related to Truth

Accuracy
Curiosity
Disarmament

Reason
Self Analysis
Self Awareness

- Faimess
- Fearlessness
- Honesty
- Integrity
- Intuition
- Justice
- Optimism
- Purity
- Quest for Knowledge
- Sincerity
- Spirit of enquiry
- Synthesis
- Trust
- Truthfulness
- Determination
- Unity of thought
- Word & deed

Values Related to Peace

- Attention
- Calm
- Contentment
- Dignity
- Discipline
- Equality
- Equanimity
- Faithfulness
- Focus
- Gratitude
- Happiness
- Harmony
- Humility
- Inner silence
- Optimism
- Reflection
- Satisfaction
- Self-acceptance
- Self-confidence
- Self-control
- Self-discipline
- Self-esteem
- Self-respect
- Sense control
- Surrender
- Understanding
- Virtue

Values Related to Love

- Acceptance
- Affection
- Care
- Compassion
- Interdependence
- Kindness
- patience
- Patriotism

Consideration	Reverence
Dedication	Sacrifice
Devotion	Selflessness
Empathy	Service
Forbearace	Sharing
Forgiveness	Sympathy
Friendship	Thoughtfulness
Generosity	Tolerance
Gentleness	Trust
Humanness	

Values Related to Non-Violence

Psychological	Social
Benevolence	Appreciation of other cultures & religions
Compassion	Brother/ Sisterhood
Concern for others	Care of Environment
Consideration	Citizenship
Forbearance	Equality
Forgiveness	Harmlessness
Good Maners	National Awareness
Happiness	Perserverance
Loyalty	Respect for Property
Morality	Social Justice
Universal Love	

(*Source* : website of the British Institute of Sathya Sai Education)

It would be said from the above that development of

spiritual health signify the coordinating the above mentioned human values in our daily learning system and if needed that may be incorporated in our educational syllabi. It would also be appropriate to quote Sri Sathya Sai, where he links up the human values with the educational system for the overall growth of the human being– *"If human values take root in the educational system, the emerging individuals will have the following attributes : they will want peace and justice in a world that acknowledges the rule of law and in which no nation or individual need live in fear; freedom and self reliance to be available to all; the dignity and work of every person to be recognized and safeguarded; all people to be given an opportunity to achieve their best in life; and they will seek equality before the law and the equality of opportunity for all"*.

If we diversify our vision in to present industrial setting we can see that the corporate world also in favour of developing the spiritual health of the human being, which they named as stress management system. Stress is a very common and unavoidable for a human being in the world. It is the prime duty of a modern manager who should poses some qualities, which are helpful in developing a stress free workplace. It would not be possible for a factory worker to release all his stress just out side the factory premises. It is a psychological phenomenon caused due to many reasons but would be manageable with some physical, psychological and spiritual exercise that ultimately directed towards higher productivity, employee satisfaction, bonding of employee-employer relationship etc. Following this rule the corporate world introduces the meditation, yoga etc. as a regular activity in their corporate as well as in the factory life by developing a new dimensional Human Resource Policy. The following chart describes the reasons of stress in human life, which has a great impact on his health.

4. Conclusion

It could be said that the concept of spirituality or development of spiritual health has diversified from the hypothetical world in to the reality of life by establishing itself as a fundamental component of higher standard of living. Considering the above-mentioned notes on spirituality and its development, we may state that spirituality is an important operational system in human health, which is nothing but a search towards universal truth, which includes–the wonder of the universe, a feeling of the unity, the desire to improve the quality of life for everyone, developing a sense of being part of a larger whole or belongingness, a feeling of oneness of the planet and love for everything on it, an awareness of an underlying order to Creation and love and respect for the diversity of the human family.

Spirituality among the human being is simply a divers thinking of the people from the materialistic world, which helps them to control their repressed willing and directed them in living in a healthy, peaceful and loving environment. If we glance through the dictums of Sri Bhagwad Gita, we may see the reflection of the same thing :

"Dhyoto Vishayana Pungsya Sangastesupajayate

Sangath Sanjayate Kamath Krodhovijayate

Krodhadbhavati Sammoho Sammohath Smriti Bibhramah

Smritibhranshad Buddhinasho Buddhinashath Pranashyati"

Bhagwadgita- 2/62-63

The above dictums advised us that thinking on several aspects of the materialistic world as well as on the vices and the organs directs the human being to become addicted and gave the birth of desire to get it. But our materialistic world could not allow to fulfill these desire in every moment due to many reasons, which resulted the human being become turned to angered, loss of temper, inhuman in nature and narrow minded, developing selfishness and above all self-oblivion. Therefore, spirituality may be referred as the eternal divinity or goodness among the human being by developing which the he is able to learn the life-skill instead of job-skill only.

The human is the most precious and valuable creature in this world who is unique in nature. The human being is the authority of having a majestic power, which may termed as 'spiritual power'. By proper nurturing and caring of this power he is also able to act as a catalytic agent between his thoughts and works. Spirituality is nothing but a process of searching the source of the influence, which boost up the human being to do his work. This searching is eternal, which we found in the dictums of Upanishad :

> *"Om Keneshitang Patati Preshitang Mana Kena Prana Prathama Pariti Yukta*
>
> *Keneshitang Bachamimang Badanti Chakshu Shrotrang Ka Yu Debo Junakti"*

Kenopanishada- 1

Who will operate our mind to perform? Who will control our life and speech and eyes to perform? And to find out the answers of the above is the process of developing the spiritual health. Lastly but not the least, to conclude it can be said that spiritual health empower the person in.

1. Realization of own as well as others potentialities.
2. Developing entrepreneurship to shoulder the responsibility.
3. Developing leadership quality to come forward.
4. Developing the other-oriented approach instead of self-centered approach.

REFERENCES

Ghosh Raja : Work in Health Care–Scope and Experiences with Special Emphasis to Rabindranath Tagore's Creativity", Perspective in Social Work, Vol. XIX, No. 1, Jan.-April 2004, Nirmala Niketan College of Social Work, Mumbai.

Poddar. B. B. Building A Stress Free Work Place, *Workers Education*, March, 2003, Central Board for Workers Education, Nagpur.

Purkait. K. Smt. : The Art of Stress Management, *Workers Education*, September-December, 2004, Central Board for Workers Education, Nagpur.

Swami Someswarananda : How to build your Child (in Bengali), Ramakrishna Mission Lokasiksha Parishad, Narendrapur, Kolkata.

Tagore Rabindranath : *'Geetanjali'*, Rabindra Rachanabali (Sulabh), Vol. 6, Visva-Bharati, Kolkata.

Tagore, Rabindranath : *'Siksha'*, Rabindra Rachanabali (Sulabh), Vol. 6, Visva-Bharati, Kolkata.

The Complete Works of Swami Vivekananda, (Bengali) Vol., 1, *Udbodhan*, Publisher, Kolkata.

The Complete Works of Swami Vivekananda, (Bengali) Vol., 4, *Udbodhan*, Publisher, Kolkata.

The Complete Works of Swami Vivekananda, (Bengali) Vol., 5, *Udbodhan*, Publisher, Kolkata.

The Complete Works of Swami Vivekananda, (Bengali) Vol., 6, *Udbodhan*, Publisher, Kolkata.

Upanishad (Bengali), Gita Press, Gorakhpur.

15

Radon Exposure in Homes and Environmental Health Problems : Causes and Solutions

—Manorama Bhattarai,
—Keshab Bhattarai

1. Introduction

Exposure to radon gas contributes to approximately 50% of the total annual natural radiation exposure in the UK(Hughes *et al.* (2002)). A recent collaborative study involving nine European countries also concludes that radon exposure accounts for approximately 2% of all deaths from cancer in Europe (Darby *et al.* (2005)). It is thought to be the second most common cause of lung cancer worldwide, after cigarette smoking (EPA (1992)).The fact that we cannot see or smell this gas might explain why there is little public awareness about radon as compared to other volatile gases. Therefore the health hazards of radon, especially when it accumulates indoors have been a major focus of research over the years. This paper highlights not only the current evidence regarding the hazards of high residential radon concentrations but also outlines the major remediation efforts that could be employed to reduce it. More specifically, the major objective of this paper are to review the current literature and draw a conclusion on whether or not radon is detrimental to health. Before summarising and evaluating literature, some background on the properties of radon is discussed along with an explanation of how radon gets inside the homes of individuals.

2. Properties of Radon

Radon, a colourless, tasteless and odourless gas is ubiquitous. It is all around us in nature; in the rocks, earth's crust, and soil (IARC (1998), EPA (1992)). Thus, it is not hard to guess how it gets inside the homes of individuals; this will be explained later on in this review. This chemically inert gas usually arises from uranium-238 present in the earth's crust. It then emits an alpha particle while it undergoes radioactive decay yielding short-lived radioactive progeny such as polonium-218 and polonium-214. Most of inhaled radon is exhaled back out; however the little that remains could disintegrate into solid radon progeny that travel and deposit themselves in the sensitive cell linings of the lungs. These solid products then disintegrate emitting alpha radiation which has carcinogenic properties in the lung cells (EPA (1992)). High amount of polonium radiation damages tissues and organs as seen in Mr. Litvinenko's assasination in November 2006 in London by polonium 210; Ramola *et al.* (1999) report on incidence of radon in drinking water in Dehradun India.

A general overview of the process of radon disintegration is explained by a diagram.

3. How does Radon Enter the Homes of Individuals?

The major ways that environmentally occurring radon gas enters houses and buildings are through foundation cracks in floors and walls, joint slabs, water sources, gaps in service pipes, and entry through open windows or doors from the air outside (EPA (1992)). The usual process involves diffusion along a concentration gradient from the soil where there is high concentration, to the floors or air above where there is low concentration. Radon starts to build up and reach high levels especially in ground and basement floors. If ventilation is very poor then the chance of build up is dramatically increased. Radon levels may be particularly high in rural areas as there might be greater exposure to direct soil and the water sources

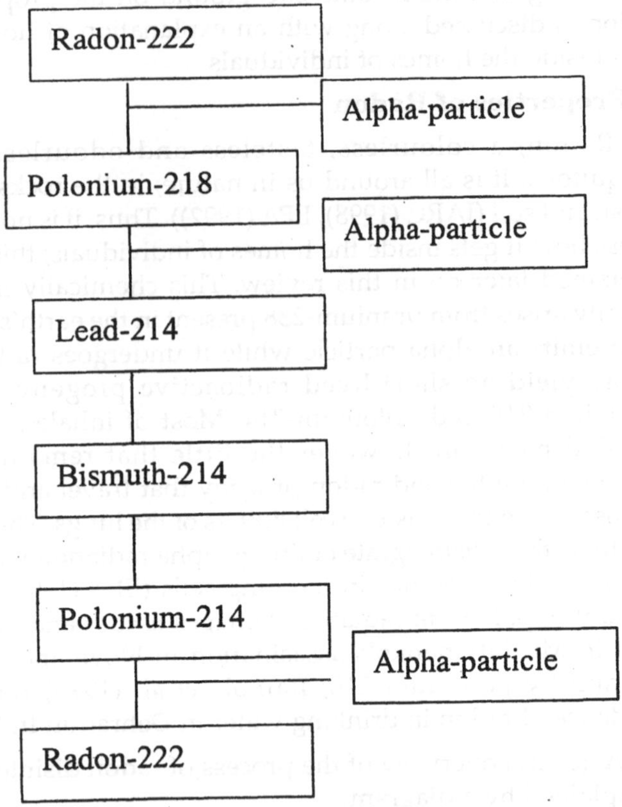

Fig.1 : The Disintegration of radon gas, adapted from HPA (2005)

such as wells drilled in rock. It is also important to bear in mind that the concentration of radon in homes varies according to time such that there is not only seasonal and daily variation but also hourly variation. Changes in the air pressure and weather outside homes might explain seasonal and daily variation. The opening and closing of doors and windows might account for hour to hour differences (HPA(2005)).

4. Results from the Critical Review of Literature

Although, it is known that there is a strong link between radon and lung cancer in miners (IARC(1998)), the focus of this review will be on the risks caused by radon accumulation inside homes. Only a few studies were found that aimed to find any link between radon exposure and diseases other than lung cancers including leukaemia, stomach, and liver cancer; however the results for risk values were deemed inconsistent (WHO (1996), Kohli *et al.* (2000)).Therefore, the focus of this paper remains on reviewing articles that have linked radon with lung cancer. Papers that discussed residential exposure to radon included either ecological studies or case-controls. Ecological studies were helpful in order to explain differences in lung cancer incidence between groups of individuals living in areas with different levels of radon exposure. They are however unreliable as most often studies are based on estimated data obtained from radon potential maps which usually assume that people in a certain geographical area all are likely to have the same levels of exposure. There is no guarantee that all people living in highly affected areas will actually be exposed to high levels as individual variations in exposure occur because of occupational or leisure activities which should be accounted for and it is usually difficult to assess this in ecological studies.

Case-control studies were more popular than ecological studies as they allowed a more direct method to detect any differences between those with lung cancer (cases) and those without (controls). However, they did have limitations due to recall bias, whereby the cases would possibly think harder about past exposures to radon than controls. This means that the cases might over-exaggerate past exposures, therefore resulting in misleading values for relative risk. There is also a chance to miss out important confounding variables which inevitably affect the final results. Combining results from several case-controls are useful in eliminating effects of confounders; therefore a few studies included in this review are meta-analyses. The results of some studies are briefly summarised below along with possible limitations and strengths.

An ecological study examining the relationship between lung cancers in small areas across Scotland (Pearce *et al.* (2005)) concluded that there was a significant relationship between radon and lung cancer in individuals under 55 where lung cancer rates were higher in those that were exposed to higher levels of radon. There was no significant link in older individuals. However, the over generalisation of radon measurements meant that the results did not take into account local variation and use of radon potential maps lead to further uncertainty as they were only based on predicted radon exposure levels rather than true values. The results could be unreliable in that it is possible that in rare cases, houses having high radon potential might truly have low levels and houses having low radon potential could actually have high levels. Other confounding variables such as ventilation in the house, migration or mobility history, type of housing, and exposure other than in homes were not considered and so might have given misleading results.

An Italian meta-analysis (Pavia(2003)) including 17 case-control studies suggested a dose-response relationship between radon and lung cancer with odd ratio (OR) of 1.33(1.15-1.54) when exposures were about 200 Bq/m^3. At 150 Bq/m^3, OR for lung cancer was 1.24 (1.11-1.38) and at 250 Bq/m^3, OR was 1.43 (1.19-1.72); thus proving a linear dose-response relationship. The study had its limitations as it did not completely adjust for potential confounding variables such as outside exposures and residency history. The results might have been affected by misclassification errors and individual variation. The fact that it involved collaboration of different studies might mean that there is still a likelihood that some amount of heterogeneity cannot be ruled out.

A collaborative study consisting of 13 case-controls from Europe with 7148 cases and 14208 controls was conducted by Darby *et al.* (2005). Although this study involved a large sample size, it still had problems with uncertainty of relative risk values. For example, some homes could not measure radon concentration levels (demolished or houses undergoing renovation) so values had to be estimated indirectly. The paper also didn't account for radon concentration according to time variability. For instance, the data could have been collected at times when the radon levels were generally high or low leading to uncertainty in the results. There is also the limitation of not knowing exactly how much time each individual decides to spend downstairs or in a certain room where levels might be higher than in other rooms. So exposure rates are not entirely accurate. The paper did however adjust for important confounding variables such as age, region of residence, smoking, and study. For smoking, full stratification involved age of starting to smoke, number of cigarettes and for ex-smokers duration of smoking. The strength of the study is definitely reflected in its very large sample size which most case-controls do not have. The study gave the result of excess risk of lung cancer for indoor exposure to radon to be 16% for 100Bq/m^3 after adjustment for smoking. This study also shows a dose-response relationship as suggested by the study above.

Another meta-analysis study (Lubin *et al.* (1997) involving eight epidemiological studies including 4263 lung cancer cases and 6612 controls gave an estimated relative risk (RR) of 1.14 (95% CI = 1.0-1.3) at radon exposure of 150 Bq/m^3. However this study had implications of misclassification, heterogeneity, and uncertainty due to possible potential confounding variables that remained unaccounted for. This might be why the RR for lung cancer obtained from this study is much less that of others. The fact that the 95% confidence interval also overlaps 1.0 RR indicating no association at all. Nevertheless, a pretty much narrow confidence interval might mean that this result is likely to be reliable.

An American model (Warner *et al.* (1996)) also showed that there is correlation between radon and lung cancer. This study looked into factors of mobility in US residents and found that mitigation or reduction methods applied in one home throughout life in permanently residing individuals' results in a higher reduction of lung cancer risk compared to mitigation of several places in mobile individuals. It should be noted that mitigation does not completely remove the risk of lung cancer as the individual has already been exposed and the effectiveness of mitigation is also dependent on other factors such as age, sex, outside exposure at work or leisure, and smoking history. For instance it was found that the older the smoking individual is, the less the reduction of risk when mitigation is carried out. Having said this, it is suggested that mitigation of homes in an individual who is routinely exposed to high levels of radon might be successful in reducing their overall risk of lung cancer.

A German case control study (Wichmann *et al.* (2002)) suggested a link between radon and lung cancer. It consisted of two studies in East and West Germany. The East Germany study included 1053 cases and 1667 controls while the West Germany study consisted of 1449 cases and 2297 controls. The large sample size means that results are more likely to be reliable. In West Germany, no correlation was found for the entire area. However, for radon-prone matching areas there was a positive exposure-response relationship with OR of 1.13 (95% CI =0.8-1.46) per 100Bq/m³. There was a slight link for the entire of East Germany with OR of 1.04 (95% CI = 0.96-1.12) at 100Bq/m³. Radon-prone matching areas in East Germany had OR of 1.05 (0.97-1.15) at 100Bq/m³. The fact that the 95% CI results overlaps 1.0 RR could suggest the possibility of no association. The results may have been affected by measurements errors and also by the higher rates of smoking in the urban areas as compared to rural areas.

A Spanish case-control study (Barros-Dios (2002)) with a total of 163 cases and 241 controls, suggested that even with radon concentrations well below the action levels, the risk of lung cancer was increased by 2.5 fold. The study also proved a radon-smoking synergy. The high risk value given by the study, however, cannot be entirely relied upon as the sample size is relatively small and factors such as mobility history was not considered. Also, using next of the kin to take interviews might have a slight implication even though results were done analytically. The strength of the study does however lie in the fact that it adjusted for most confounding variables such as sex, age, lifetime tobacco use, family history and habitat, and even the number of hours spent at home.

A Swedish study (Yngveson (1999)) investigated the association between residential radon exposure and p53 mutations in lung tumour. This involved comparison between

83 non-smoking and 250 smoking lung cancer patients. The results for exposure over 140 Bq/m^3 gave OR of 1.4(95% CI, 0.7–2.6) and 2.8 (95% CI, 0.8–9.3) for radon exposure of atleast 400 Bq/m^3. The OR for mutation in smoking cases against non smoking case was 2.1 (95% CI, 0.9-5.0). Investigation of passive smokers vs. non-smokers in 9 cases gave a much higher OR of 3.1(95% CI, 0.5-18.3); though the large CI implies uncertainty. Yhe fact that 95% CI overlaps 1.0 RR means that there is a chance that there is no association between radon exposure and lung cancer. The limitation of this study could be errors in p53 mutation detection, bias of case-only study and relatively small number of cases.

An American study based in Iowa (Field *et at.* (2001)) demonstrated a link between cumulative radon exposure and lung cancer. Iowa was chosen as this was where a substantial proportion of the population lived in the same home for at least 20 years; this is a positive point of the study. Iowa also has a good cancer registry system making it easy to detect new cases of lung cancer and also has the highest mean screening levels of radon, meaning studies taken here would be more likely to give representative results. The case-control study included 413 cases and 614 controls. A major part of the study involved face to face interviews which could not be possible in all the cases as only 69% of them were still alive for the home visit. Therefore data was obtained from their next of the kin. This might have altered the results as they might not know much about missing information. For instance, they might not know of the individual's past exposures, mobility history or so on. Therefore some results might have had to be estimated; leading to less reliable results. Another limitation of the study is that its size is relatively small when compared to most collaborative studies with thousands of subjects. Another factor to take into account is that this study was only done on females aged 40-84, so results were not representative for younger people and for males. The study did give very conclusive results for continuous measurements with excess odds of 0.24 (95% CI = -0.05-0.92) for all cases and 0.49 ((5% CI 0.03-1.84) for all live cases that were exposed at 11 WLM_{5-19}(this is roughly equal to 148 Bq/m^3 for 15 years). For categorical estimates the results were slightly higher with excess odds of 0.50 (95% CI 0.004-1.80) for all cases and 0.83 (95% CI 0.11-3.34) for all live cases at 11WLM$_{5\text{-}19}$. The study confirms that cumulative exposure to radon is indeed a risk factor for lung cancer.

One study from Finland (Auvinen *et al.* (1996)), however, gave a contradictory result to the rest. It concluded that there was indeed no link between exposure to indoor concentrations of radon and lung cancer. The results are given Table 1.

Tablel : 1 OR (Odds Ratio) for lung cancer According to Radon Concentration Range (Coskeran et al (2002))

Radon concentration (p Ci/L)	*Radon concentration (Bq/m³)*	*OR (95% CI)*	*association*
1.4–2.6	50–99	1.03 (0.84-1.26)	Very weak
2.7–5.3	100–199	1.00 (0.078-1.29)	significance
5.4–10.7	200–399	0.91 (0.61-1.35)	no significance
10.8–34.5	100–1277	1.15 (0.69-1.93)	no significance

The OR values show that there is no relationship between radon concentration and lung cancer risk. It is clearly demonstrated that the values for OR do not follow any linear pattern, *i.e.* it is lower at the range (200-399) Bq/m^3, 0.91 as compared to 1.0 at (100-199) Bq/m^3, the values showing no association whatsoever between high radon levels and lung cancer risk . The OR of 1.15 seen at (400-1277) Bq/m^3 is weak and the 95% CI overlaps 1.0 which could imply no significant association. Therefore, the OR of 1.15 might as well be due to chance.

5. Detection

High levels of radon exposure can be detected by using either short term monitors or long term monitors. Short term monitors are used only if quick results are needed but are likely to give faults in measurements because radon levels fluctuate. It is recommended therefore that the short term monitors are used for at least three months. Short term monitoring devices include charcoal canisters, electric ion chambers, alpha track detectors, continuous monitors, and charcoal liquid scintillation detectors (EPA (1992)). Long term monitoring is more likely to provide reliable average radon levels and last much more than three months. They mainly include alpha track detectors and electric ion chambers.

6. Remediation

Various remediation methods could be carried out in order to reduce radon levels in households having levels equal to or greater than the Action Level (see EPA(1992), HPA(2005), Radon Council (2005) and Lee *et al.* (1999)). These include :

- Passive methods : improved ventilation, seal cracks in concrete floor walls, joints, radon proof barrier between soil and floor; dig sumps (a small cavity beneath the floor) or holes to collect radon; airbricks. This method is cheaper due to no running costs but less effective than active systems.
- Active methods: electric extractor fans, radon meter. It is easier to detect, more effective at reducing radon levels but has higher running costs and subject to mechanical wear.

While conservative methods mentioned above might be very efficient ways to reduce radon levels, an even more productive way may be to increase general public awareness and get householders to do something about increased radon levels in their home rather than to sit down and consider it a minor problem. As like smoking, radon seem to have synergistic effects in inducing radon cancer (Lee *et al.* (1999), Barros-Dios (2002), Yngveson(1999)), smoking cessation programmes would be beneficial in reducing lung cancer incidence.

The Parliamentary Office of Science and Technology report that according to the Radiation Protection Division of the HPA only about 10% of householders with levels above 200 Bq/m^3 actually take part in remediation efforts (POST(2005)). This figure highlights the importance of perhaps introducing strict legislation regarding levels allowed in homes of individuals.

More importantly, this might illustrate either the lack of public awareness on the hazards of radon or general perception that radon could possibly do no harm. Therefore public health measures must be developed and implemented in order to ensure that remediation work is carried out in all homes that have high radon concentrations. Individuals should be warned that although this problem might not be as significant as cigarette smoking in inducing lung cancer, the long term effects of exposure to high concentrations to radon is indeed alarming. Finally, implementation of public awareness programmes on the hazards of radon is definitely well worth the cost if it will influence people to mitigate their homes and reduce their lifetime risk of lung cancer.

Websites of various government organisations such as the EPA (Environmental Protection Agency), HPA (Health Protection Agency) and the Radon Council can be used to gather information about detection and remediation. In the USA, the Action Level[1] value is 4pCi/L which is equal to approximately 148 Bq/m^3; in Britain, the Action Level is slightly higher at 200 Bq/m^3 (Coskeran *et al.* (2002)).

7. Conclusion

Having looked at the evidence suggested by the literature observed, it could be concluded that radon does indeed pose as an environmental hazard in the form of a lung-cancer inducing carcinogen. There was a general increase in odd risk ratios as the concentration of radon exposure in the homes increased. More research needs to be done into this field before any link can be ascertained although the results from all studies except one seemed to be consistent in suggesting a significant association between residential radon exposure and lung cancer. This field is in need of high quality research with greater analytical power and more efficient methods of data standardisation. This might help to produce results with narrow 95% CI that doesn't overlap 1.0 RR. A homogenous approach should be applied to all studies, especially if they are to be collaborated. Similar methods should be adopted for adjusting for confounding variables for all studies to reduce any measurement errors or misspecification. If we find a way to get rid of miscalculations due to all possible confounding variables, we would obtain a higher relative risk value for each study. In this way, not only could we provide evidence for a mere association but we could also establish a more definite casual link. There is always likelihood of random errors for which nothing can be done. Government organisations should possibly be encouraged to provide funding for the conduction of even larger scale case-control studies with better statistical power. It is vital that current focus is put on reducing radon exposure in homes currently with high levels of it.

REFERENCES

Auvinen A., Makelainen I., Hakama M., Castren O., Pukkala E., Reisbacka H., Rytomaa T. (1996) : Indoor radon exposure and risk of lung cancer: a nested case-control study in Finland Journal of the National Cancer Institute., Vol. 88(14) : 966-72, Jul 17.

Barros-Dios J.M., Barreiro M.A., Ruano-Ravina A., Figueiras A. (2002) : Exposure to Residential Radon and Lung Cancer in Spain : A Population-based Case-Control Study Am J Epidemiol 156 : 548-555.

Coskeran T., Denman A.R., Phillips P.S., Gillmore G.K. (2002) : A critical comparison of the cost-effectiveness of domestic radon remediation programmes in three counties of England. Journal of Environmental Radioactivity. Vol. 62(2) : 129-44.

Darby S., Hill D., Auvinen A., Barros-Dios J.M., Baysson H., Bochicchio F., Deo H., Falk R., Forastiere F., Hakama M., Heid I., Kreienbrock L., Kreuzer M., Lagarde F., Makelainen I., Muirhead C., Oberaigner W., Pershagen G., Ruano-Ravina A., Ruosteenoja E., Rosario A.S., Tirmarche M., Tomasek L., Whitley E., Wichmann H.E., Doll R. (2005) Radon in homes and risk of lung cancer: collaborative analysis of individual data from 13 European case-control studies. BMJ. 330(7485) : 223, Jan. 29.

EPA (1992) : Technical support document for the 1992 citizen's guide to radon, EPA 400-R-92-011.

Field R.W., Steck D.J., Smith B.J., Brus C.P., Fisher E.L., Neuberger J.S., Lynch C.F. (2001) The Iowa radon lung cancer study, phase I : residential radon gas exposure and lung cancer The Science of The Total Environment, Volume 272, Issues 1-3, Pages 67-72, 14 May.

Health Protection Agency (HPA(2005)) Radiation Protection Division, Radon at a Glance http://www.hpa.org.uk/radiation/understand/at_a_glance/index.htm accessed on 28/12/2005

Hughes J.S., Watson S.J., Jones A.L., Oatway W.B. (2005) : Review of the radiation exposure of the UK population Journal of Radiological Protection Vol. 25 : 493-496.

International Agency for Research in Cancer (IARC(1998)) : Man-made Mineral Fibres and Radon. IARC Monographs on the Evaluation of Carcinogenic Risks to Humans, Volume 43, 1988 last updated 21/01/1998.

Kohli S., Noorlind Brage, H., Löfman, O. (2000) : Childhood leukaemia in areas with different radon levels : a spatial and temporal analysis using GIS. Journal of Epidemiology Community Health 54 : 822-826.

Lee M.E., Lichtenstein E., Andrews J.A., Glasgow R.E., Hampson S.E. (1999) : Radon-Smoking Synergy : A Population-Based Behavioural Risk Reduction Approach Preventive Medicine, Vol. 29(3) : 222-227, September.

Lubin J.H., Boice J.D. Jr. (1997) : Lung cancer risk from residential radon : Meta-analysis of eight epidemiologic studies. Journal of the National Cancer Institute. Vol. 89(1) : 49-57.

Parliamentary Office of Sciences and Technology (2005) : Reducing radon risks in the home URL:http//: www.parliament.uk/post/pn158.pdf accessed on 28/12/2005.

Pavia M., Bianco A., Pileggi C., Angelillo I.F. (2003) : Meta-analysis of residential exposure to radon gas and lung cancer. Bulletin of the World Health Organization. Vol. 81(10) : 732-738.

Pearce J., Boyle P. (2005) : Examining the relationship between lung cancer and radon in small areas across Scotland Health and Place Vol.11 (3) : 275-282 , Sep.

Radon Council (2005). The Radon Council's guide to Radon.

URL: http://www.brad.ac.uk/acad/envsci/radon_hotline/radonguide.html accessed on 28/12/2005.

Ramola R.C., Choubey V.M., Saini N.K., Bartarya S.K. (1999) : Occurrence of Radon in the Drinking Water of Dehradun City, India, Indoor and Built Environment; 8 : 67-70.

Warner K.E., Mendez D., Courant P.N. (1996) Toward a more realistic appraisal of the lung cancer risk from radon: the effects of residential mobility. American Journal of Public Health. 86(9) : 1222-7, Sep.

Wichmann H.E., Heinrich J., Gerken M., Kreuzer M., Wellmann J., Keller G., Kreienbrock L. (2002) : Domestic radon and lung cancer-current status including new evidence from Germany International Congress Series 1225 (247– 252).

World Health Organisation Regional Office for Europe (1996)), Indoor Air Quality- A Risk-Based Approach to Health Criteria for Radon Indoors, 1996

Yngveson A., Williams C., Hjerpe A., Lundeberg J., Soderkvist P., Pershagen G. (1999) Mutations in lung cancer associated with residential radon exposure. Cancer Epidemiology, Biomarkers & Prevention. Vol. 8(5) : pp. 433-438.

16

Assessing the Health Impacts of Air Pollution : A Case Study of Mumbai

—*Archana Patankar*
—*Pushpa Trivedi*

1. Introduction

Developing countries, in the second half of the 20th century, have experienced the dynamics of economic growth, industrialization and urbanization coupled with rapid population growth, leading to environmental degradation and problems like air pollution. There is a growing awareness and concern in these countries about the threat of air pollution, its impact on human health and economic and social costs involved therein. Many studies have been carried out in recent years to study the health impacts of outdoor air pollution, some notable examples of which are, Jakarta (Ostro, 1994), Santiago (Ostro *et al.*, 1995), Delhi (Cropper *et al.*, 1997) and Mexico City (MAQMT, 2002). India has seen very few studies of this kind so far. Our research aims to carry out such a study, using locally obtained data, to examine the link between air pollution and respiratory and cardiovascular morbidity and estimate the economic costs, for which, Greater Mumbai (hereafter referred to as Mumbai in the text) has been selected as the study area.

Mumbai, as the commercial capital of the country, plays

host to a number of big industries, particularly, chemical and fertilizer plants, oil refineries and so on. It is experiencing rapid population growth, mainly due to large-scale migration from all parts of the country in search of employment. There has been a massive construction boom in recent years to meet the needs of housing and basic infrastructure. The vehicular traffic is also on the rise to meet the growing demands of transport. These factors have contributed to severe air pollution in the city. It, therefore, becomes necessary to examine the health impacts of air pollution for its residents and provide a policy foundation for implementing better air quality programmes for the city. This study assumes importance not only from academic perspective but also has bigger policy implications for other expanding cities in India and elsewhere.

Earlier studies conducted for Mumbai, URBAIR (Shah and Nagpal, eds., 1997) and Joseph *et al.* (2003), extrapolated the concentration-response (CR) estimates from studies conducted in other parts of the world. Study done by Kamat *et al.* (1980, 1992) examined the incidence of respiratory morbidity and not its causal link with air pollution. Our study goes further and conducts a cross-section analysis to analyze the link between air pollution and morbidity effects by developing CR estimates from the local data. For this purpose, the data set was made available to us by the Environmental Pollution Research Centre (EPRC) at King Edward Memorial (KEM) Hospital, Mumbai.

The outline of the paper is as follows. Section Two creates a profile of the study area, whereas, Section Three describes the characteristics of the data set obtained from the EPRC to gain a better understanding of the variables, which are then used in the regression model. The methodology used in the analysis is also detailed in this section. Results and discussion are presented in Section Four and the subsequent section summarizes the key findings of this study.

2. Profile of Mumbai City

Mumbai is located on the western seacoast of India on the Arabian Sea. It was originally a cluster of seven islands, which were later joined to form the present city. It occupies an area of

468 sq. kilometer (km) and its width is 17 km east to west and 42 km north to south (MMRDA, 2006; MPCB, 2003). It is one of the largest mega cities in the world in terms of population, which has been growing steadily from about 3 million in 1951 to 8 million in 1981 to the present day 12 million or 1.2 crores as per the 2001 Census (MMRDA, 2006), with a density of about 25600 people per km^2. Municipal Corporation of Greater Mumbai (MCGM) as the civic authority is responsible for providing basic amenities like safe drinking water and safe disposal of sewage and garbage. Like any other mega city, Mumbai is typically faced with the problems of air, water and solid waste pollution caused by industrial development, heavy vehicular traffic, unprecedented growth of slums, etc.

As of 2003, there were about 7800 large, medium and small-scale industries operating in Mumbai (MPCB, 2003). Most of these units are located in mixed areas; *i.e.*, there is no clear demarcation between residential, commercial and industrial zones. Large and medium-scale units are mainly in pharmaceuticals, thermal power, fertilizer plant, oil refineries, textiles and dyes. Many textile mills have closed down in recent years giving way to a construction boom for residential and commercial complexes, thereby changing the land use pattern. Small-scale units are in engineering, electronic, electrical business and mainly located in industrial estates and other areas. Industries, particularly, fertilizer and oil refineries are responsible for air pollution in some parts of the city. To prevent air and water pollution, Government of Maharashtra has banned opening of new polluting industries in Mumbai city and suburbs, thus making them shift to adjoining districts of Thane and Raigad (MPCB, 2003).

Mumbai, with a large population to cater to, needs basic infrastructure, mainly an efficient transport network. Transport network in Mumbai comprises a huge railway and road network. The length of the railway tracks joining Western and Eastern suburbs with the island city is more than 30 kms respectively. The total length of the road network is more than 1940 kms. The number of two-wheelers and three-wheelers in the city has gone up by more than 100% between 1995 and

2004 whereas the number of passenger cars in the same period has gone up by more than 62% (Shinde, 2005). The massive railway and road network, however, is not sufficient enough for such a large population, which results in congestion during peak business hours. Most commercial activity is concentrated in the island city in the South. The movement between South and North for business purposes in the peak hours, therefore, places a huge burden on the transport network and also contributes to air pollution in the city.

Mumbai, being on the seacoast, experiences a tropical climate with a heavy southwest monsoon rainfall of around 2166 millimeters a year (MPCB, 2003) and temperatures range from 21.5^{0}C to 35^{0}C with marginal differences between summer and winter months. The relative humidity is found to be in the range of 47-86% (MCGM, 2003). Air pollution levels in Mumbai are quite high compared to the national ambient air quality standards (NAAQS) given by the Central Pollution Control Board (CPCB). Air pollution monitoring is done in Mumbai on a regular basis by MCGM. Four pollutants, namely, suspended particulate matter (SPM), nitrogen dioxide (NO_2), sulfur dioxide (SO_2) and ammonia (NH_3) are monitored regularly and their monthly averages are reported. There is a definite seasonal pattern for air pollution in Mumbai, particularly in case of SPM. Higher concentrations are found in winter months (November to February) and lower levels in summer and rainy season (May to September). SPM levels in almost all the areas are above the 24-hour standard for residential areas (200 mg/m^3). One of the most polluted areas is Chembur, mainly because of the fertilizer plant and oil refinery nearby. Here, SPM levels are above the standard for industrial areas (500 mg/m^3). The levels of SO_2 are below the ambient standards for all the areas. SO_2 concentration in Mumbai has gone down in the last few years due to policy initiatives like introduction of low-sulfur diesel for vehicles. NO_2 levels are still high and above the ambient standards in areas like Chembur and Khar. A definite seasonal pattern can also be observed in case of NO_2 levels. NH_3 levels are low in all the areas except Chembur. Here, the NH_3 concentration can

Table 1 : Profile of the Six Areas in the Survey

1 Paper presented at the National Seminar on "Poverty, Health And Development", scheduled on 10-11 March, 2007 at the Department of Palli Charcha Kendra, Visva-Bharati University, Sriniketan, West Bengal.

Area/Profile	*Worli*	*Borivali*	*Khar*	*Bhandup*	*Andheri*	*Maravali*
Population in Lacs (2001 Census)	4.39	12.00	9.06	3.30	12.98	13.69
Municipal Ward	E	R-South R-North	H-East H-West	S	K-East K-West	M-East M-West
Type of Area	Residential and Commercial	Residential and Commercial	Residential	Residential, Commercial and Industrial	Residential, Commercial and Industrial	Residential, Commercial and Industrial
Study period	Sept. 2003	Sept.-Oct. 2003	Feb.-Mar. 2004	Jan. 2004	Mar.-Apr. 2004	Feb. 2003
Total no. of respondents	357	229	278	330	311	307
No. of respondents considered in analysis (% of total population)	302 (0.07)	203 (0.02)	245 (0.03)	258 (0.1)	264 (0.02)	252 (0.02)

Source : Municipal Corporation of Greater Mumbai (MCGM), http://www.mcgm.gov.in

sometimes go up to 1200 mg/m^3. Given the severe air pollution levels in the city, it is essential to examine the resultant health impacts.

3. Data and Methodology

As mentioned earlier, our study aimed at examining the link between outdoor air pollution and morbidity effects as proxied by respiratory and cardiovascular symptoms and diseases for which we used the data collected by the EPRC, attached to the Department of Chest Medicine at KEM Hospital, Mumbai. KEM Hospital is a renowned public hospital run by the Municipal Corporation of Greater Mumbai (MCGM) and has been a pioneering institution for conducting studies on health impacts of environmental pollution. The EPRC team conducted a survey of six areas in Mumbai from February 2003 to April 2004 for creating a representative environmental health profile of the city residents. The selection of these areas–Worli, Borivali, Khar, Bhandup, Andheri and Maravali–was primarily guided by the fact that the MCGM–run air quality monitoring stations are located here. Table 1 below gives details about the six areas including the number of respondents and the time period of the survey. We selected 1524, among 1812 respondents for our analysis; age being the main criterion for selection. Those above 11 years were administered the entire questionnaire schedule by the EPRC and therefore, were selected for our analysis

The questionnaire schedule of the EPRC was quite comprehensive in coverage. It covered the socio-economic details, occupational and travel pattern, indoor and outdoor exposure of respondents and the details pertaining to the actual clinical examination done as part of the survey. Table 2 below lists the dependent and independent variables we selected from this questionnaire for our analysis.

Table 2 : Variables Selected for the Analysis

Variable	*Response*
Dependent Variable	
Symptoms (presence or absence of) :	
Cough	Yes/No (1 or 0)
Phlegm	Yes/No (1 or 0)
Breathlessness	Yes/No (1 or 0)
Wheezing	Yes/No (1 or 0)
Cold	Yes/No (1 or 0)
Diseases (presence or absence of):	
Bronchitis	Yes/No (1 or 0)
Asthma	Yes/No (1 or 0)
URTI	Yes/No (1 or 0)
Cardiac	Yes/No (1 or 0)
Other chest illnesses	Yes/No (1 or 0)
Allergic rhinitis	Yes/No (1 or 0)
COPD	Yes/No (1 or 0)
Independent variable	
PM_{10} (Particulate Matter < 10 μg)	_____ $\mu g/m^3$
NO_2 (Nitrogen dioxide)	_____ $\mu g/m^3$
SO_2 (Sulfur dioxide)	_____ $\mu g/m^3$
NH_3 (Ammonia)	_____ $\mu g/m^3$
Age	_____ years
Gender	Male/Female
Smoking habit	Yes/No
Place of work	Indoor/Outdoor
Occupation	Ranging from not working to doing outdoor activities
Width of the adjacent road	__________ feet
Presence of pollution industry near residence	Yes/No
Hours spent in the kitchen	______ Hrs
Quality of indoor kitchen ventilation	Good/Moderate/Bad
Type of cooking fuel used	LPG/Kerosene

We also obtained pollution data for the survey period of 2003-04 from the air pollution monitoring laboratory of MCGM and selected the levels of pollutants for analysis on the basis of the survey period in each area. Although, MCGM monitors do not record PM_{10} (particulate matter of size less than 10 microns), it is a significant pollutant for health impacts compared to SPM as indicated by the clinical literature. Therefore, an attempt was made to take average levels of PM_{10} – about 57% of SPM based on the literature which states that these levels vary between 45-70% (Ostro, 1994). The pollution levels considered in the analysis are shown in Table 3 below. In case of Andheri, due to the non-availability of pollution records for the survey period, pollution levels for the same month in the previous year were taken after ascertaining similar pollution trends in the last few years in this area.

Table 3: Average Monthly Concentration of Pollutants During the Survey Period

Area/ Pollutant ($\mu g/m^3$)	*Ambient Standard ($\mu g/m^3$)*	*Worli*	*Borivali*	*Khar*	*Bhandup*	*Andheri*	*Maravali*
SPM	200	269	55	427	342	293	579
PM_{10}	100	153	31	243	195	167	330
NO_2	60	51	24	83	64	55	127
SO_2	60	39	9	23	31	22	39
NH_3	400	29	28	43	48	48	149

Source : Air Quality Monitoring & Research Laboratory, Khar, MCGM.

As far as the characteristics of respondents are concerned, the age-wise distribution shows that around 20% were in the age groups of 11-20 and 31-40 years and around 15% or more were in 21-30, 41-50 years and 61 and above. Thus, all the age groups were fairly equally represented in the data set. Further, it contained 43% of male and 57% of female respondents. In case of total monthly family income, over 39% earned between Rs. 5000-15000 and 37% had an income of more than Rs. 15000 per month. Significant area-wise differences were found here. For instance, in Borivali, 63% earned incomes more than Rs. 15000, whereas in Bhandup, 46% earned less than Rs. 5000. Occupational distribution of respondents indicates that overall 40% were housewives and 21% were students. This is not surprising given the fact that 57% of subjects in the survey were females and 21% belonged to the age group of 11-20 years. 27.5% was the total working population out of which more than 15% worked indoors in reportedly pollution-free environments. Only 7.8% worked in outdoor environment and were regularly exposed to outdoor pollution. Around 86.7% turned out to be non-smokers. 6% smoked cigarettes and 8.6% reported smoking other forms of tobacco.

As regards outdoor pollution near residence, in four out of six areas, respondents reported a heavy vehicular traffic on the adjacent roads. Again, in the absence of separate industrial and residential zones, both in Bhandup and Maravali (Chembur), 100% of surveyed houses were close to an industry of a polluting nature. This percentage was slightly lower at 89.4% in Worli. Borivali, Khar and Andheri households, however, were not close to any industry. We also considered exposure to air pollution indoors due to cooking fuel used, smoke in the kitchen, etc. Since the kitchens were reportedly located indoors and 40% were housewives, it was pertinent to look at the hours spent in kitchen everyday. Typically, more than 56% reported spending between 3-5 hours in the kitchen everyday and more than 27% spent 6 hours or more there. Another important aspect was the type of cooking fuel used. Here, 92% respondents reported using LPG cylinders for cooking and only 8% used kerosene. Overall 90% denied presence of kitchen smoke, due to the obvious use of LPG for cooking.

The most important part of the survey was the health assessment of individuals and clinical examinations done to diagnose the respiratory and cardiovascular symptoms and diseases. Maravali (Chembur) as the highly polluted area in the survey reported greater than average percentages for respiratory symptoms like cold, wheezing, cough and phlegm. The most common respiratory symptom among all the respondents appeared to be cold. The percentage of people reporting cold about 4 times a year or less was very high at 68.5% in Worli followed by 46.8% in Maravali. Similarly, Khar and Bhandup had high percentage of people reporting breathlessness while walking on the ground level. Around 16% respondents in Maravali and 14.3% in Bhandup reported cough, whereas, wheezing was also higher than average for respondents in Bhandup, Khar and Maravali. An important point to be noted here is the symptoms reported by respondents in Borivali. It is supposed to be the least polluted area in Mumbai. It, however, had a high percentage of respondents reporting cold, breathlessness, asthma and allergic rhinitis. This might be partly due to the fact that more than 44% were above 51 years of age here. As regards diseases, Maravali had the highest number of patients suffering from bronchitis. There were also more number of patients diagnosed with asthma and COPD (Chronic Obstructive Pulmonary Disease). Asthma seemed to be prevalent in all the six areas; even the least polluted area of Borivali had 10 patients suffering from it. The highest number of respondents suffering from URTI (Upper Respiratory Tract Infection) was found in Worli. In case of COPD, greater number of patients was found in Bhandup, Andheri and Khar. Allergic rhinitis has surprisingly very few patients in Maravali but higher number of patients in Bhandup, Andheri and Borivali. Borivali also had more respondents reporting cardiac and other chest ailments compared to other areas, except Worli in latter case.

Since our objective was to examine the relationship between air pollution and morbidity effects, the null hypothesis used in our analysis was as follows :

"There is no significant relationship between outdoor air pollution and the health effects."

Our study sought to test the validity of this hypothesis by conducting statistical analysis on the given data set. The survey done by EPRC followed a cross-section study design. Even though the data set did not offer a time perspective to see how the instances of symptoms and diseases varied over time with changes in air pollution, we got information on the incidence of morbidity across areas which experienced varying levels of air pollution. This also influenced the choice of our regression model to examine the air pollution-morbidity association.

The nature of the data set was such that only the presence or occurrence of a particular symptom or disease could be tested against the varying air pollution levels. We, therefore, used logistic regression analysis and interpreted the results based on the significance tests like Wald Statistic and psuedo R^2 to infer about the possible association between air pollution and morbidity. Logistic regression is a form of regression put to use when the dependent variable is binary (1 or 0) or dichotomous. It seeks to maximize the log likelihood (LL), which reflects how likely is it (the odds) that the observed values of the dependent variable can be predicted from the observed values of the covariates or independent variables (Garson, 2006).

The logit model used in this analysis takes the following form :

$$\ln [p/(1-p)] = a + bX + e \quad \ldots.(1)$$

where :

- ln is the natural logarithm, $\log_e$ where e = 2.718....
- p is the probability that an event Y occurs, *i.e.*, p(Y=1)
- p/(1-p) is the odds ratio, *i.e.*, the probability of the event divided by the probability of the non-event
- ln [p/(1-p)] is the log odds ratio or logit

The data analysis was conducted using the windows-based statistical software SPSS 10.0. The results of the regression analysis were expressed as odds ratios, which could be interpreted to predict the changes in odds of the occurrence of a symptom or disease due to an increase in a specific air pollutant. A similar methodology was used in cross-section studies conducted in Taiwan (Chen *et al.*, 1998; Hwang *et al.*, 2006). A statistically significant odds ratio for a health effect associated with a particular pollutant would mean that for a specific unit increase in the pollutant, the odds of occurrence of the effect would increase by a certain percentage as given by the odds ratio.

The significant logit coefficients obtained through the model were used as the concentration-response (CR) coefficients for the respective symptoms and diseases as previously done in some studies (Quah and Boon, 2002; Aunan and Pan, 2004). These CR coefficients were then used to measure the percentage change in the health effect under consideration, given the change in the pollutant concentration and the susceptible population. This methodology was first explained by Ostro (1994) and since then, the subsequent studies have made use of it in quantifying the health effects. The following equation was used to quantify the health effects associated with different pollutants under consideration.

$$DH_{ij} = b_{ij} * POP_i * DA_j \qquad \ldots.(2)$$

where:

- DH_{ij} is change in health effect i due to pollutant j
- b_{ij} is the CR coefficient for health effect i related to pollutant j
- POP_i is population at risk of health effect i
- DA_j is change in the concentration of pollutant j

4. Results and Discussion

In this study, the dependent variables, namely the presence (or absence) of symptoms and diseases were used in the logistic regression framework to examine their relationship with the independent variables. In case of logistic models, odds ratios are reported to predict the odds of changes in the dependent variable given the independents and not the actual magnitude of change in the dependent as such. Likewise the odds ratios reported here are an indication of changes in the odds of occurrence of a symptom or disease given the covariates. Significance tests were applied to these models; for example, the model chi-square test was used to test the overall significance of the model. Similarly, the Hosmer-Lemeshow test was applied to test the goodness of fit of these models. For the 'b' coefficients, Wald statistic was used to test their significance. Based on the literature on logistic regression, the obtained results have been interpreted to establish the link between air pollution and different symptoms and diseases.

A preliminary look at the odds ratios reveals that for most respiratory symptoms and a few diseases, the association with air pollution is quite evident. The most important pollutants in terms of health impacts are the PM_{10} and NO_2. SPM or PM_{10} is the most crucial pollutant in Mumbai whose levels are far above the ambient standards almost throughout the year. NO_2 levels are above ambient standards in some areas. But overall, these levels have been on the rise in the last few years, making it a pollutant of concern in terms of health effects. The levels of the other two pollutants are below ambient standards in most cases.

In case of single pollutant models, there is evidence of a link between PM_{10} and cough, phlegm and bronchitis. The same is true for NO_2 and NH_3. In case of SO_2, there seems to be an association with cold, Upper Respiratory Tract Infections (URTI) and other chest illnesses. However, these odds ratios by themselves may not be useful for estimating the changes in health effects for given changes in pollutants, the reason being the simultaneous exposure to all pollutants and need to know the link with health effects given the presence of all these pollutants in outdoor air. Again, PM_{10} and NO_2 have a very strong correlation, probably due to the similar source of emissions, *i.e.*, vehicles in Mumbai. Therefore, they have not been used together while running the models, as it would distort the results due to near-perfect multicollinearity. These two pollutants have thus been considered separately, albeit with the other two pollutants and the odds ratios have been obtained accordingly, which are shown in Table 4 and 5.

PM_{10}, which is calculated in the analysis as approximately 57% of SPM, seems to be associated with the respiratory symptoms of cough, breathlessness and wheezing and with the illnesses like allergic rhinitis and Chronic Obstructive Pulmonary Disease (COPD). The odds ratios reveal that a given increase (about 50-mg/m^3) in PM_{10} would lead to 0.7% more incidences of cough (0.3% - 1.2% being the confidence limits), 0.9% increase in instances of breathlessness and 0.6% more cases of wheezing in the susceptible population. In case of diseases, a given increase in PM_{10} would lead to 1.4% more cases of allergic rhinitis and 2.7% increase in cases of COPD. There are other factors though, which are significant besides pollutants for these health effects. For example, in case of cough, age and

Table 4 : Odds Ratios Obtained for PM_{10} after Inclusion of SO_2 and NH_3

Health Effects	*Model 1*	*Model 2*	*Model 3*
Symptoms			
Cough	1.007 (1.003-1.012)*	1.007 (1.004-1.010)**	1.004 (1.000-1.007)*
Phlegm	0.998 (0.991-1.005)	1.004 (1.000-1.008)*	0.998 (0.933-1.004)
Breathlessness	1.009 (1.006-1.012)**	1.003 (1.001-1.005)*	1.004 (1.001-1.006)*
Wheezing	1.006 (1.001-1.011)*	1.004 (1.000-1.007)*	1.004 (1.000-1.008)
Cold	0.993 (0.990-0.996)**	0.997 (0.995-0.998)**	1.002 (1.000-1.005)*
Diseases			
Bronchitis	1.002 (0.995-1.010)	1.007 (1.003-1.012)*	1.002 (0.996-1.008)
Asthma	0.997 (0.990-1.003)	1.001 (0.997-1.006)	0.998 (0.993-1.003)
URTI	1.024 (0.996-1.052)	0.986 (0.977-0.996)*	1.030 (1.008-1.053)*
Cardiac	0.993 (0.985-1.002)	0.994 (0.989-1.000)	1.001 (0.995-1.007)
Other chest illnesses	0.985 (0.975-0.994)*	0.995 (0.990-1.000)	0.997 (0.990-1.003)
Allergic Rhinitis	1.014 (1.005-1.023)*	1.006 (1.000-1.012)	0.997 (0.994-1.001)
COPD	1.027 (1.020-1.033)**	1.006 (1.003-1.010)**	1.009 (1.005-1.012)**

Notes : 1. *p<0.05, ** p<0.001.

2. Values in parentheses are 95% confidence intervals.
3. Model 1 includes both so_2 and nh_3, model 2 includes only so_2 and model 3 includes only nh_3 along with pm_{10}.
4. All odds ratios adjusted for age, gender, smoking habit, place of work, occupation, width of road adjacent to the house, presence of a polluting industry nearby, hours spent in kitchen, indoor kitchen ventilation and type of cooking fuel used.

Table 5 : Odds Ratios Obtained for NO_2 after Inclusion of SO_2 and NH_3

Health effects	*Model 1*	*Model 2*	*Model 3*
Symptoms			
Cough	1.021 (1.004-1.038)*	1.016 (1.008-1.023)**	1.011 (0.998-1.023)
Phlegm	0.993 (0.968-1.020)	1.013 (1.003-1.023)*	0.995 (0.975-1.015)
Breathlessness	1.028 (1.016-1.040)**	1.003 (0.997-1.008)	1.010 (1.001-1.018)*
Wheezing	1.020 (1.002-1.039)*	1.008 (1.000-1.016)	1.013 (0.999-1.027)
Cold	0.970 (0.960-0.981)**	0.992 (0.988-0.997)*	1.006 (0.998-1.014)
Diseases			
Bronchitis	1.006 (0.979-1.034)	1.018 (1.007-1.028)*	1.005 (0.984-1.027)
Asthma	0.985 (0.961-1.010)	1.005 (0.994-1.016)	0.992 (0.974-1.010)
URTI	1.111 (0.982-1.256)	0.952 (0.918-0.986)*	1.145 (1.035-1.266)*
Cardiac	0.972 (0.942-1.002)	0.984 (0.967-1.001)	1.001 (0.981-1.022)
Other chest illnesses	0.943 (0.908-0.978)	0.990 (0.977-1.004)	0.987 (0.964-1.011)
Allergic Rhinitis	1.047 (1.013-1.082)*	1.005 (0.992-1.018)	0.989 (0.974-1.003)
COPD	1.088 (1.062-1.114)**	1.005 (0.998-1.011)	1.024 (1.012-1.036)**

Notes: 1. * $p<0.05$, ** $p<0.001$.

2. Values in parentheses are 95% confidence intervals.
3. Model 1 includes both $_{so2}$ and $_{nh3}$, model 2 includes only $_{so2}$ and model 3 includes only $_{nh3}$ along with $_{no2}$.
4. All odds ratios adjusted for age, gender, smoking habit, place of work, occupation, width of road adjacent to the house, presence of a polluting industry nearby, hours spent in kitchen, indoor kitchen ventilation and type of cooking fuel used.

smoking habit are important confounding factors. Similarly, in case of breathlessness and wheezing, type of cooking fuel is significant. For allergic rhinitis, age is significant, particularly the lower age groups, given the level of pollution. In case of COPD, age, place of work and type of cooking fuel are potential confounders.

Similarly, the odds ratios for NO_2, given the other two pollutants (SO_2 and NH_3) reveal a significant association with cough, breathlessness, wheezing, allergic rhinitis and COPD. However, the odds of occurrence of these symptoms or illnesses are more with a given increase in NO_2 compared to PM_{10}. For instance, for a given increase of about 50-mg/m^3 in NO_2, the incidence of cough is likely to go up by 2.1% with a range of 0.4%-3.8%. In case of breathlessness, the incidence is likely to increase by 2.8%, whereas it is 2% for wheezing. Allergic rhinitis incidence would increase by about 4.7% and COPD by about 8.8% with an increase in NO_2. Again, age, smoking habit, place of work and type of cooking fuel are the confounding factors.

Results obtained for SO_2 and NH_3 have not been shown here. In case of cold, an increase in SO_2 (about 20-mg/m^3) would lead to higher incidence of cold by about 16%; the increase in cardiac cases would be by about 12% and that for other chest illnesses would be by about 17%. Similarly, an increase in NH_3 (about 100-mg/m^3) would lead to an increase in incidence of cold between 0.7% and 1.7%. In case of other chest illness, this increase in odds would be between 2.4% to 4%.

For the odds ratios found significant in the analysis, the corresponding CR coefficients related to respiratory symptoms and diseases have been reported in Table 6. These coefficients have further been used in equation (2), given above, to quantify the percentage change in the health effects related to given change in pollution concentrations. For instance, in the table below, the percentage change in health effects has been calculated for a corresponding change of 50-mg/m^3 in PM_{10}, 50-mg/m^3 in NO_2, 20-mg/m^3 in SO_2 and 100-mg/m^3 in NH_3.

Taking the significant odds ratios for symptoms and diseases related to different pollutants into account, Table 6

Table 6 : Concentration-response Coefficients and Change in Health Effects

Health effect	*Pollutant*	*CR Coefficient (%)*	*Change in Health Effect (%)**
Symptoms			
Cough	PM_{10}	0.007	0.35
	NO_2	0.021	1.05
Breathlessness	PM_{10}	0.009	0.45
	NO_2	0.028	1.40
Wheezing	PM_{10}	0.006	0.30
	NO_2	0.020	1.00
Cold	SO_2	0.155	3.10
	NH_3	0.012	1.20
Diseases			
Cardiac	SO_2	0.126	2.52
Other chest illnesses	SO_2	0.163	3.26
	NH_3	0.039	3.90
Allergic rhinitis	PM_{10}	0.014	0.70
	NO_2	0.046	2.30
COPD	PM_{10}	0.026	1.30
	NO_2	0.084	4.20

*The percentage change in health effects has been calculated for a corresponding change of 50 mg m^{-3} in PM_{10}, 50 mg m^{-3} in NO_2, 20 mg m^{-3} in SO_2 and 100 mg m^{-3} in NH_3.

develops the concentration–response (CR) coefficients for the same. As shown in the table, percentage change in health effects has been calculated using the CR coefficient (%) and the given change in pollutant concentration. The estimated changes in health effects can be interpreted as follows. For cough, an increase of 50-mg/m^3 in PM_{10} can bring about 350 additional cases among a population of 1 lac (100,000). For a given increase of 50-mg/m^3 in NO_2, the expected increase in cough incidences would be about 1050 per 1 lac population. Similar estimates can be obtained for other symptoms too. In case of illnesses, a 20-mg/m^3 increase in SO_2 would mean 3260 additional cases of other chest illnesses given the presence of other factors among 1 lac people; whereas a 50-mg/m^3 in NO_2 would result in 4200 more cases of COPD. Interpreting these estimates in an opposite manner, a given reduction in the pollutant concentrations would mean the number of avoided cases of the given symptom or illnesses. For instance, a reduction of 50-mg/m^3 in PM_{10} could possibly result in 450 avoided cases of breathlessness and 1300 avoided cases of COPD among a population of 1 lac. Such estimates are important in calculating the avoided burden of disease by controlling the air pollution levels. The coefficients obtained in this study are intended for further use in monetary valuation of these health effects.

5. Conclusion

In summary, the problem of air pollution and its impact on human health is a subject of growing concern for mega cities like Mumbai in the developing world. Many studies have been conducted across cities in developing countries in recent years. However, most of them have relied on estimates obtained from studies conducted elsewhere and mostly in the developed world. It is essential to examine the relationship between air pollution and health impacts using the local data and come up with some estimates that can be used as a rationale for better air quality management programmes in urban areas.

Mumbai has seen very few studies in the past to examine the link between outdoor air pollution and health effects. The previous studies estimated changes in mortality and morbidity as related to air pollution by extrapolating the concentration-response (CR) functions from other studies conducted elsewhere. Our study has attempted to develop the CR coefficients based on the local data. The cross-section analysis conducted on the data set made available by the EPRC has enabled us to develop these coefficients and calculate the percentage change in health effects for the given change in pollutants. The logistic regression model in this study indicates a statistically significant association between air pollutants and some of the health effects, thus invalidating our null hypothesis of no association between air pollution and health effects. The results seem to show significant association between pollutants like PM_{10} and NO_2 and some respiratory symptoms and diseases and given the CR coefficients obtained through the analysis, some estimates of increase or reduction in the number of instances for these health effects have be calculated. These estimates are indicative of the likely impact of air pollution on public health.

However, while looking at these results, some points need careful consideration. Firstly, logistic coefficients are partial coefficients calculated by controlling for other variables in the model. They only reveal the impact of a particular variable given the values of the other independent variables. In case of pollutants, it is really difficult to calculate the exact impact of a pollutant in isolation on the health effect under consideration when partial coefficients are reported. Secondly, a high correlation among pollutants would again make it very difficult to separate the effects of individual pollutants and the evidence given by odds ratios would sometimes be inconclusive. The results reported here should be treated as indicative of the likely association between air pollution and health effects for Mumbai city. Our study is an attempt to build on the locally available information to develop the CR coefficients, which will be used further for economic valuation of health impacts in the subsequent phase of our study. The entire exercise is not only of academic importance to us but would also have larger policy implications in terms of ensuring cleaner air to the urban residents.

REFERENCES

Aunan K., Pan X.C., (2004) : Exposure-response functions for health effects of ambient air pollution applicable for China–a meta-analysis, *Science of the Total Environment*, 329, 3-16.

Brace *et al.*, (2003) : *SPSS for Psychologists : A Guide to Data Analysis using SPSS for Windows*, Versions 9, 10 and 11, Houndmills, Palgrave Macmillan.

Central Pollution Control Board (CPCB), India, http://www.cpcb.nic.in.

Chen P.C., Lai Y.M., Wang J.D., Yang C.Y., Hwang J.S., Kuo H.W., Huang S.L., Chan C.C., (1998), Adverse effects of air pollution on respiratory health of primary school children in Taiwan, *Environmental Health Perspective*, 106, 331-335.

Cropper M.L., Simon N.B., Alberini A., Sharma P.K. (1997) : The health effects of air pollution in Delhi, India, Policy Research Working Paper 1860, Development Research Group, World Bank, Washington D.C.

Garson D. 2006 : Logistic Regression, http://www2.chass.ncsu.edu/garson/pa765/logistic.htm.

Hosmer D., Lemeshow S. (1989) : *Applied Logistic Regression*, Wiley Series in Probability and Mathematical Statistics, Wiley Interscience, New York.

Hwang B.F., Jaakkola J.J., Lee Y.L., Lin Y.C., Guo Y.L. (2006) : Relation between air pollution and allergic rhinitis in Taiwanese schoolchildren, *Respiratory Research*, 7 : 23.

Joseph A.E., Sawant A.D., Srivastava A. (2003) : PM_{10} and its impacts on health – a case study in Mumbai, *International Journal of Environmental Health Research*, 13, 207-214.

Kamat S.R., Godkhindi K.D., Shah B.W., Mehta A.K., Varsha N., Gregrat J., Papewar V.N., Tyagi N.K., Rashid S.S.A., Bhiwankar N.T., Natu R.B., (1980) : Prospective 3 Year Study of Health Morbidity in relation to Air Pollution in Bombay, India, *Bombay Air Pollution – Health Study*, KEM Hospital, MCGM

Kamat S.R., Patil J.D., Gregrat J., Dalal N., Deshpande J.M., Hardikar P., 1992 : Air pollution related respiratory morbidity in central and north-eastern Bombay, *Journal of Association of Physicians, India*, 40, pp. 588-593

King Edward Memorial (KEM) Hospital, Mumbai, http://www.kem.edu.

Maharashtra Pollution Control Board (MPCB), http://www.mpcb.mah.nic.in.

MAQMT (Mexico Air Quality Management Team), (2002) : Improving air quality in Metropolitan Mexico City: an economic valuation, Policy Research Working Paper 2785, Environmentally and Socially Sustainable Development Sector Unit, Latin America and the Caribbean Region, World Bank, Washington D.C.

MCGM (2003) : Environment Status Report 2002-03.

MPCB (2003) : Report on Environment Status of Mumbai Region.

Mumbai Metropolitan Region Development Authority (MMRDA), Basic statistics on MMR, http://www.mmrdamumbai.org/basic_information.htm.

Mumbai on the Net, http://www.mumbainet.com.

Municipal Corporation of Greater Mumbai (MCGM), http://www.mcgm.gov.in.

National Environmental Engineering Research Institute (NEERI), http://www.neeri.res.in.

NEERI (2004) : Particulate Matter Reduction Action Plan for Greater Mumbai.

Ostro B. (1994) : Estimating the health effects of air pollution: a methodology with application to Jakarta, Policy Research Working Paper 1301, Policy Research Department, World Bank, Washington D.C.

Ostro,B., Sanchez J.M., Aranda C., Eskeland G. (1995) : Air pollution and mortality : results from Santiago, Chile, Policy Research Working Paper 1453, Policy Research Department, World Bank, Washington D.C.

Quah E., Boon T.L. (2003) : The economic cost of particulate air pollution on health in Singapore, *Journal of Asian Economics*, 14, 73-90.

Shinde S.D. (2005) : Action Plan for Control of Air Pollution in Mumbai: Transport Sector, Office of the Transport Commissioner, High Level Conference on Strategies for Control of Air Pollution in Mumbai, March 1-2, 2005.

URBAIR, Shah J. and Nagpal T. (Eds.), (1997) : Urban Air Quality Management Strategy in Asia : Greater Mumbai Report, World Bank Technical Paper No. 381, World Bank, Washington D.C.

17

Environmental Impact on Health and Health Support Systems on the Tribal People of Kullu District, Himachal Pradesh

—Guru Prasad Chattopadhyay,
—Anupriya Chatterjee

1. Introduction

Himachal Pradesh, a relatively small state in India nestled in the lap of the Himalaya, is truly considered a travellers paradise for its unique canvas of lofty ice-capped mountain summits ranging from 1,500′ to 20,000′ ft, glaciers, turbulent rivers, picturesque meadows with orchards, ethnic settlement and culture of ancient tribes. This Western Himalayan states embraces a vast mountainous terrain between the rivers Ravi in the northwest and the Tons-Yamuna in the southeast. This state occupies an area of 55,673 km^2 and a total population of 60,77,900 as per 2001 census. The latitudinal extent is 30°22′ and 33°10′ N and longitudinal extent is 70°46′ E to 79°00′ E. The state came into existence in April 1948 and in November 1966 it was enlarged to the present geographic and political entity. Considering its distinctive physiographic and political framework it is named as the Himachal Himalaya.

Kullu district of Himachal Pradesh forms a transitional

zone between lesser and Greater Himalaya. Beas River is the main lifeline of the district with most of the settlement located alongside the river. However a number of tribal settlements exist in the secluded pockets of the mountains. In general the economy of more than 80% of the people in this district is agriculture.

Despite being among the top states in the country in terms of quality of life, having one of the highest per capita income (Rs. 18,912/- at current prices, *2001 census*) and also having fairly extensive network of health institutions, Himachal Pradesh still lacks proper medical facilities and awareness which is a great constraint to the overall health standard of the state. Health problem and occurrence of diseases are particularly acute among the tribal people, many of whom live in the desolate parts in the mountain terrain.

Status of health in Himachal Pradesh is measured mainly by 3 types of indicators :

(1) Life expectancy, crude death rate and infant mortality rate

(2) Demographic indicators such as crude birth rate, total fertility rate, and general fertility rate

(3) Socio economic indicators such as population below poverty line, literacy rate and sex-ratio.

2. Significant Health Problems among the People of the State

Health problems arising due to communicable diseases : In Himachal Pradesh most of the people suffer from three major groups of communicable diseases :

(1) Respiratory problem—Bronchitis, Tuberculosis, ARI.

(2) Water and Food borne diseases – Diarrhea, dysentery, amebiosis, worm infestation and hepatitis.

(3) Contact diseases such as skin diseases, RTI, STDS including HIV/AIDS.

A. Tuberculosis: This is the major killer in the state. The state launched the revised tuberculosis control programme *i.e.* to detect at the earliest stage in 3 districts (Kangra, Mandi and Hamirpur) in 1998 followed by 3 more districts in 1999. The rest of 6 districts would be covered in 2000.

B. Leprosy : The problem of Leprosy was quite high in the state, being 26 per 1000 population in 1971. But now the prevalence rate has been reduced to 0.47/10000 as on March 2000 with the successful conduct of M-LEC in the state and now the disease is likely to be eliminated soon. The current decrease in prevalence rate is shown in the figure below.

C. Malaria : The number of Malaria cases has been declining in the state in the past few years which declined to 1.5 in 1985 and 0.1 in 1999. The problem of malignant malaria is negligible.

D. Diarrhoea : is responsible for a large number of infant deaths. NFHS-2 has estimated as 31% among children under age 3 years. The prevalence of parasitic infection in children below 14 years was at 13.8%.

E. RTI/STDs : The problem of RTI/STD is also quite high in the state. The prevalence is higher in women; overall prevalence of RTI, STD is quite high which calls for intensive efforts in managing the diseases at all levels.

F. HIV-AIDS : Himachal Pradesh is also affected with HIV-AIDS epidemic. As on 03.09.2000 out of 25935 persons screened 254 were found as HIV positive which includes 82 AIDS cases. On the basis of HIV sentinel surveillance data collected in 1999 it is estimated that there might be around 3500-4000 HIV positive cases in the state.

Health problems arising due to non-communicable diseases : Prevention of Blindness programme was launched in the state in 1977-78. The objective is to reduce the prevalence of blindness to 0.3% . In the year 1999-2000 a total of 180 eye camps were organized in which 217397 patients were examined for various types of eye ailments and 14318 patients were operated for cataract. The current state target per year is 24000 cataract operations which are based on the prevailing blindness rate and backlog.

Health problems arising due to nutrition deficiency : As per nutritional survey conducted by women and social welfare department, Government of India covered 10 districts of state. 0.5% of infants were found to be suffering from Marasmus. 81% of children suffered from mild to moderate malnutrition and 4% from severe degree of malnutrition. 8% of adults suffered from chronic energy deficiency. As per NFHS-2, 40% women and 67% children are suffering from anaemia, which is high and warrants focused attention.

Health problems arising due to iodine deficiency : Being a sub Himalayan belt Goitre is still a nutritional deficiency disorder. Prevalence of Goitre was high up to 1974. Now it has come down to 2-13% in1996 for various age groups.

Immunization : Immunization coverage in the state has been high, more than 90% coverage as per National Family Health Survey-2 (1998-99). The state is free from Polio. Incidence of other vaccine preventable diseases is negligible except tuberculosis in children. The survey estimates that only 3% children remained uncovered in the state. 83% received all antigens vaccine specific coverage are 95% BCG, 89% polio and 89% DPT and 89% for measles. Considerable proportion of drop-outs has been reported for polio and DPT.

Disability : Himachal Pradesh sadly has a disabled population higher than the national average. The foremost reason for this are :

- Difficult terrain of the state that hinders treatment in remote areas
- Lack of proper medical facilities
- Lack of awareness, which is the biggest handicap.

One of the States which have disabled population higher than the national average is Himachal Pradesh (2.57). The census data also reveals that the figures are more skewed in favour of rural areas and males as compared to urban areas and females.

3. Health Status of the Women

Maternal and reproductive health problem : Himachal Pradesh is the leading State in Northern India with regard to quality of reproductive health. However, it is far behind Kerala with Reproductive Health Index at 84.6 followed by Tamil Nadu 63.6. 34% of currently married women report of reproductive health problem as per NFHS-2. In 1996 safe motherhood and child health services were incorporated into the Reproductive Child Health and fertility regulation interventions with reproductive health programme. The important elements of the programme are :

(1) Provision of antenatal care including at least three antenatal visits, detection and treatment of anaemia in mothers, management and referral of high risk pregnancies.

(2) Encouragement of institutional deliveries or home deliveries assisted by health trained personnel.

(3) Provision of postnatal care including at least three postnatal visits.

(4) Identification and management of reproductive tract and sexually transmitted infections.

Due to the measures taken we see that for India, average mothers of only 20% of births received all of the required components of antenatal care, where as in Himachal Pradesh 30.2% of births received all the required components of antenatal care which is just above the national average. Yet in Himachal Pradesh births delivered in medical institutions is poor and below the national average.

The survey made by SUTRA an NGO reveals that there are no special programmes to empower women to safeguard their Sexual and Reproductive Health initiated either by the Health services or by Women & Child Development, though the WCD, is busy in organizing women into self help groups, but these issues don't figure into their Agenda. Nor the Health services are getting gender sensitized – as there are no programmes/ trainings for them.

The following table gives disease burden age wise which corroborates our argument :

Other maternal conditions becomes second biggest disease burden for the women of 15 to 44 age group coupled with Anemia as top one.

Anemia and under nutrition : It is a real fact that for the girls attending elementary education (age group 5-14) and for the young and adult women (age group 15-44) the major problem is iron deficiency and anemia whilst the production of food has grown, domestic per capita income has risen, still the girls, young and adult women continues to be deprived from enough nutrition.

Till recently, this state kept on refusing to provide mid-day meals in the primary schools on the plea that there is no drop-out and the nutrition level amongst the children is better than other parts of the state, it is only due to the pressure from the Supreme Court which has made the State to provide the Mid-day meal. But the question of iron deficiency-anemia has not been answered through the mid-day meals as it contents only *Khichadi* and one knows how much iron is available in *Khichadi*.

The whole issue of understanding the strategic gender needs and initiate processes to enable women to lead a life without discrimination and ensuring their Reproductive Rights is lacking in perspective of the policy makers as they feel very proud of accomplishing the Euro-centric development (enrollment of girls in schools, least drop-out rates, low TFR, Low IMR and low MMR) in much better fashion than their neighbouring states. What is missed out is the gender gap. For example, in IMR, the gender gap in Himachal is 17 (next to Haryana), no wonder we have a constant decline in girl child sex ratio.

The consumption of wide variety of nutritious foods is important for women health. In Himachal Pradesh milk consumption by women is 87% in form of milk or curd. The national average is 55%. So Himachal Pradesh is well above the national average. In Himachal Pradesh they consume 94.3% of pulses or beans and 98.8% of green leafy vegetables respectively. In Himachal Pradesh chicken, meat or fish consumption is very low, being only 6.2% which is below the national average of 31.9%. However, this state 71.7% of women consume the amount of fruits which is double the national average *i.e.* 33%.

Anemia usually results from a nutritional deficiency of Iron and B12 and some other nutrients. Anemia may have detrimental effects on the health of women and children and may become an underlying cause of *maternal mortality* and *prenatal mortality* as well as *increased risk of premature delivery* and *low birth weight*.

The lowest prevalence of anemia is found in Kerala with 22.7% while Himachal Pradesh is having 40.5% anemia. The national average is 51.8% so Himachal Pradesh prevalence is below the national average.

4. Observations on Health Problems among the Tribal People with Reference to the Malanese Tribe of Kullu

The Malanese, a relatively small tribal community, lives in the upper Malana river valley in Kullu district. This tribal village is located at an altitude of about 8,000 ft, and till the late 19th century existence of this community remained completely unknown to the other people living in the Himachal Himalaya. Existence of this tribe, comprising hardly one thousand people, was explored in 1868 when A.F.P. Harcourt, the then District Magistrate of Kullu arrived in this part of the mountain on a reconnaissance survey mission for preparation of the first gazetteer of this district. It remains, as ever a matter of conjecture how this small ethnic group, who remain completely cut-off from the neighbouring parts of the Kullu valley as well as from the rest of the civilised world, developed an entirely independent cultural and socio-political system within their small territory. Till the 1970s this tribal people remained almost in seclusion as decided to be so under the instruction of their village god *Jamlu,* through their traditional village headman, the *Gur.* Under the constraints of the local environment they developed on their own their rituals, food habit and health control systems. Over the last two decades he Kullu administration, as well as some NGOs and anthropological researchers have extended activities in this village and have explored some remarkable aspects of social life and food habit which found to have contributed significantly in their health status.

These authors through their several visits to this village have found out some characteristic habits of food clothing and family maintenance which distinctly influenced their health status. In common with many other remote villages in the mountain maintenance of hygiene has always been ignored. Due to the lack of space their own traditional belief almost all families reside with their domestic animals under the same roof and consume food polluted with discharge of the animals. Moreover, since they never learned the art of making cotton clothes the only dress they wear is made of raw wool, the direct contact of which with their body often bring chronic skin disease. The only grain crops they produce in their territory are *Kathua* and *Mandua* (typical in the high altitude environment) with low food value as compared to wheat, rice and maize. Hence malnutrition causes ill health from their very childhood.

As far as the marriage system is concerned these people have no other alternative but to select their life partner within their same community. This brings serious health problem among the generation. Another remarkable matter is related with their system of marriage. The Malanese, by tradition has maintained marriage system in which a young man of 18-20 years gets married to a woman with above 35 years of age. So most of the families here are found to have only one child or two children.

However, as these people gradually started being exposed to the civilized world particularly since the 1980s, some changes in the philosophy of their life have become ostensible. They have now changed their notion towards many social systems they continued to maintain so far. Their marriage system has changed to a certain extent; the health services rendered to them by the district administration of Kullu (they refused so far) has now been accepted partially. Thus the health status of the Malanese tribe in recent years has improved, although not appreciably, but to a notable extent.

5. Existing Condition of Health Care Services under Government Enterprises

Use of health care services is strongly influenced by standard of living of the household 79% of the household with high standard of living in Himachal use private medical sector compared with 63% of household with low standard of living. Majority of the household (59%) in Himachal normally uses the public sector when a household member gets seek utilization of private sector services is much lower in Himachal (41%) then of India (69%) as a whole. Over all, 5 types of health providers are used as sources of treatment by 95% of household. They are private doctors 31%; government dispensaries 18%; CHC, PHC & Rural Hospitals 18%; Private Hospitals or Clinics 10%.

In urban areas 51% households seeks care from Govt. or Municipal Hospitals. Reproductive health services are available through Govt. or Municipal Hospitals, private nursing homes and nursing homes operated by NGO's.

In rural areas 20% household seek care from CHC, PHC and Rural Hospitals, 20% from govt. dispensaries, 14% from govt. or municipal hospitals. Reproductive and other health services are delivered by a network of PHC's and sub-centers and other govt. facilities. Female health workers are posted at sub-centers to provide basic maternal health, child health and family welfare services. Pregnant woman and children can also obtain services from private maternity homes, hospitals and NGO's.

6. Concluding Remarks

In order to correct the imbalances in the health sector and build a healthy society both quality and quantity health care facilities are required. Therefore, the sectors of concern for the state should encompass :

- Increasing proportion of underweight children at birth and slow decline in % of underweight children.
- Chronic energy deficiency is high among the adults, particularly among women.
- Identifying the cause of anemia, high incidence of gastro-intestinal diseases, respiratory infections, lac of safe drinking water and poor access to health care.
- To enhance the socio-economic status and awareness among the people regarding timely health check up and intake of balanced nutritional diet.

The opinions of the *Child Development Project Officials* to enhance the nutritional status of the people of Himachal have been given in the following table :

The Himachal Govt. Health Dept. have envisaged a road map 2008, which aims to provide the people.

- Equal and increased distribution of primary health care services.
- Rationalize the distribution of manpower to increase the utilization and access of services.
- Increase the number of specialists in the state to take care of complicated cases and provide specialized services.
- Continuous training of health personnel to meet the new emerging challenges and increased patient satisfaction.
- To synergize efforts with indigenous system of medicine to increase the outreach and extension of services.
- To increase involvement of community and NGO participation.

If all these measures adopted are enacted religiously, then we can truly curb premature mortality at all stages of life cycle and reduce non-fatal health outcome, mainly of the poor tribal people of Kullu district.

REFERENCES

Himachal Pradesh Human Development Report, 2002 : *Govt. of Himachal Pradesh, Shimla, 2002.*

International Institute of Population Sciences. *National Family Welfare Survey, 1998-99,* Mumbai, India, October 2000.

Annual Report of Rural Center for Human Interest, 2005 – 2006. (www.ruchin.org).

Official websites of Government of Himachal Pradesh.

http://hphealth.gov.in

http://hpkullu.gov.in

http://hphealth.nic.in

18

The Cultural and Industrial Context of Health : An Anthropological Study of the Kharwar Tribes of Uttar Pradesh

—*Neeraj Kumar Thakur*

1. Introduction

Developing countries have sometimes been influenced in their approaches to health care problems by the developed countries that have had a role in their history. The countries in Africa and Asia that were once colonies of Britain have educational programmes and health-care systems that reflect British patterns, though there have been adaptations to local needs. Similar effects may be observed in countries influenced by France, The Netherlands, and Belgium.

Despite variations from country to country, a common, if somewhat idealized, administrative pattern may be drawn for developing countries. All health services, except for a small amount of private practice, are under a ministry of health, in which there are about five bureaus, or departments—hospital services, health services, education and training, personnel and research and planning. Hospital and health services are distributed throughout the country. At the periphery of the system are, dispensaries or Primary Health Centers, often manned by a Doctor and one or two persons with limited training. The dispensaries are often of limited effectiveness and are upgraded to full health centers when possible. Health centers and their activities are the foundation of the system. Health centers are usually staffed by auxiliaries. All health services are under the responsibility of the district medical officer, who, assisted by other professional and auxiliary personnel, integrates the health efforts into a comprehensive programme.

The distribution of responsibilities between auxiliaries and professionals is of central importance. The auxiliaries, by handling the large number of relatively simple problems, allow the professionals to look after only the more complex problems, to supervise and teach the auxiliaries, and to plan and manage the programmes.

The district hospital is dependent on a regional hospital, to which patients with complex problems can be referred for more specialized services. Administrative direction of both regional healt'ˈ services and regional hospital services can be combined at this level under a regional medical officer. The central administration of the ministry of health provides policies and guidance for an entire health service and, in some instances, also provides a central planning unit.

Nonetheless, the public health services developed in African and Asian countries have generally provided a sound basis for future development within the framework of national development. The Uttar Pradesh has traditionally been the center of diverse castes, tribes, communities, religions and traditions. However, the tribal people have been occupying the fringes of consciousness of the people living in this state. It is true that the culture of developed people are accepted and assimilated by these tribal people with time, but still they are at the primitive stage.

It may sound strange to many but the fact remains that there were no scheduled tribes in Uttar Pradesh before 1967. It was only in the year 1967 when five tribes declared as scheduled tribe under Article 342 by the Hon'ble President of India. They were :

1. Tharu
2. Bhoksa
3. Jaunsari (Khasa)
4. Bhotia (Shauka)
5. Raji (Banrawat)

But after the division of Uttaranchal from Uttar Pradesh all these tribes and tribal region are separated and those, which have been left out in Uttar Pradesh, are very few to count on fingers. But recently the Government of India declared the ten "Non-scheduled Tribes" of Uttar Pradesh as Scheduled Tribe by the *Government Order Number 25-3-2003[7]/2003*. (See the footnote on page number-6).

The normal health of the tribal people cannot be said to be very bad but their condition become chronic after repeated infection. The tribes of Sonebhadra face a great deal of hardship in medical treatment. Problems of transportation and communication over great distances, shortages of doctors, staff and other resources, and inadequacies in staff preparation and motivation often lead to malfunctions in the system. Although the tribesmen have their own indigenous medicine but most of the times these medicines are ineffective to their severe diseases and many of these tribes does not have its proper knowledge, how to use it?

The tribes suffer from many chronic diseases, but main cause of these diseases is their changed traditional occupation, so that they are bonded to work in unhealthy, unhygienic and undesirable conditions. The second main cause is pollution borne diseases. The reason of pollution in Sonebhadra is the presence of several chemical industries, hydro-electric and thermal power stations, alluminium factories, cement factories and lime stone factories *et cetera*. Therefore, all the tribal communities along with Kharwars are suffering from these problems in Sonebhadra. The objectives of this present study are to study the impact of society and culture on health and illness and to study the effect of industries on the health of Kharwars.

2. Area of Study

The study has been done in the District Sonebhadra, Uttar Pradesh. This area is situated in southern direction of the state and approximately 200 Km. far from the district Allahabad. The district Sonebhadra is surrounded by four states *i.e.* Madhya Pradesh, Chattisgarh, Bihar and Jharkhand from three sides.

Three villages *i.e.* Chakadi, Kadiya and Arangi were selected for this study. The gram panchayat Panari consist 21 villages including Chakadi, Kadiya Arangi villages. The total population of the gram panchayat *Panari* is 9955. Out of 9955 people 8016 is the Scheduled Caste and Scheduled Tribe Population. The total Population of Kadiya is 615 and Chakadi and Arangi have the population 907, 976 respectively. Approximately 80% population of these villages are SC and ST. the main communities of these villages are Gond, Baiga, Kharwar, (STs) and Kurmi, Kols (BCs and SCs).

List of Ten Newly Declared Scheduled Tribes of Uttar Pradesh

1. **Gond** (Dhuriya, Nayak, Ojha, Pathari, Rajgond) in District Sonebhadra, Mirzapur, Varanasi, Gazipur, Baliya, Jaunpur, Azamgarh, Mau, Devariya, Basti, Gorakhpur, Siddharthanagar and Maharajganj.
2. **Kharwar** (Khairwar) in district Sonebhadra, Varanasi, Gazipur, Baliya and Devariya.
3. **Sahariya** in District Lalitpur.
4. **Pahariya** in District Sonebhadra.
5. **Baiga** in District Sonebhadra.
6. **Pampa** (Panika) in district Sonebhadra and Mirzapur.
7. **Agariya** in District Sonebhadra.
8. **Patari** in District Sonebhadra.
9. **Chero** in District Sonebhadra and Varanasi.
10. **Bhuiya** (Bhuniya) in District Sonebhadra.

3. Methodology

For this present study the villages were selected by purposive sampling. The primary information regarding society, culture, environment and health were collected by interview, observation and genealogy while secondary data has been collected from primary health centers, offices of industries and Block office Chopan, District Sonebhadra, (U.P.). The respondents selected form the Kharwar community by random sampling.

4. Result and Discussion

The difficulties of providing health services for the people of the developing nations involve a cluster of interrelated problems. These arise from the nature of the diseases and hazards to health, insufficient and mal-distributed resources, the design of health service systems, and the education of health personnel in those systems. Woven through the health programmes of the developing nations and complicating them at both family and national levels are the pressures associated with rapidly growing populations.

There are differences not only in the kinds of diseases of different countries but also in the rates at which they occur and in the age groups involved. Life expectancy in some countries is less than half that in others, principally because of high death rates among small children in the developing countries. In much of Southeast Asia, for example, 40 per cent of children die by their fourth year.

The principal causes of sickness and death among small children in the developing world are diarrhea, respiratory infections, and malnutrition, all of which are intimately related to *culture, custom,* and *economic status*. Malnutrition may result from food customs when taboos and simple oversight lead to deprivation of children. Gastroenteritis (inflammation of the lining of the stomach and intestines, usually with accompanying diarrhea) and respiratory infections are often due to infectious organisms that are not susceptible to antibiotics. The interrelationships of these diseases increase the complexity of treating them. Malnutrition is often the underlying culprit; not only does it cause damage itself, such as retardation of physical and mental development, but it also seems to set the stage for other illnesses. A malnourished child develops gastroenteritis, inability to eat, further weakness, and then dehydration. The weakened child is susceptible to a lethal infection, such as pneumonia. Or, to complete the vicious circle, infection can affect protein metabolism in ways that contribute to malnutrition.

Another factor that contributes to this is *family size*. Malnutrition, with associated death and disability, occurs most often in children born into *large* and *poorly spaced families*. The resulting high death rate among small children often reinforces the tendency of parents to have more children. People are not inclined to limit the size of their families until it is apparent that their children have a reasonable chance of survival. Thus, there is a fertility–mortality cycle in which high fertility, reflected in large numbers of small children crowded into a poor home, leads to high childhood mortality, which, in turn, encourages high fertility. This is the basis of the belief that population-control programmes should include effective means of reducing unnecessary deaths among children.

Among limitations of resources, shortages of trained personnel are among the most important; ratios of population to physicians, nurses, and beds provide an indication of the seriousness of these deficiencies and also of the great differences from country to country. Thus, the proportion of population to physicians in developing countries varies drastically.

Money is a crucial factor in health care—it determines how many health personnel can be trained, how many can be maintained in the field, and the resources that they will have to work with when they are there. Governmental expenditures on health care vary greatly from country to country.

As it attempts to provide health care for its people, a nation, on the one hand, must meet the urgent and complex problems, such as obstetric and surgical emergencies for which hospital care is essential. On the other hand, it must reach into the communities and homes to find those who need care but do not seek it and must discover the causes of such diseases as malnutrition and gastroenteritis.

(A) IMPACT OF SOCIETY CULTURE AND TRADITION ON BODY HEALTH AND ILLNESS

There is a new field of Anthropology known as "Anthropology of Body". It investigates the ways in which human body is affected by social, cultural and environmental factors. Human body is deeply affected by its experiences, as well as by norms and values of the group to which it belongs. It is only recently that Sociologists and Anthropologists have begun to recognize the profound nature of the interconnections between socio-cultural factors and the body.

One major theme concerns the effect of social change on health. The rapidly transforming tribal world presents new risks and challenges that can affect the health of tribes. The society, culture and environment have great influence on pattern of health and illness. The improvements in overall public health over the past century cannot conceal the fact that health and illness are not distributed evenly throughout the population. Researches have shown that certain groups of people tend to enjoy much better health than others. Such health inequality can be found at all levels of society.

Most of the scholars acknowledge the correlation between health and social inequalities. One of the main areas of the debate concentrates on the relative importance of individual variables, such as lifestyle, behaviour, diet and cultural pattern versus environmental or structural factors such as income and poverty.

The health pattern of Kharwar tribe of Sonebhadra according to social factors such as economy, social class, gender, geography and some other factors are discussed here :

Relation between Health and Economy

As the common people thought that the tribes are non-scientific is completely wrong; because they know every technical point of their ecology and every other thing related to their life and survival.

However, various new types of circumstances have emerged and polluted ecological conditions are beyond the knowledge of tribe like Kharwar. To cope with these new health problems evolved by this new ecological condition, the Kharwars are struggling hard.

The economy of Kharwar is based on Catechu tree to produce Catechu for sale. Catechu is an astringent water-soluble substance obtained especially from an Asian acacia tree and is used in medicine and dyeing. They know everything about this work from selection of tree to the collection of sap of Catechu. But the new forest policy of the Government and the threat of tree-smugglers of this area have great negative effect on the tribal people and their life. Now-a-day they are bounded to work as daily wage laborers in stone crushers, coalmines, road making, power plant, chemical factories *et cetera*.

Relation between Social Class and Health

There is a clear-cut relationship between pattern of mortality and morbidity and individual's social class. Similarly, there is trend towards better health in society as a whole, significant disparity exists between various classes, affecting health indicators from birth weight to blood pressure to risk of chronic disease. Individuals from higher socio-economic categories are on average healthier, stronger and live longer than an individual from a depressed class. Differences are greatest in respect to infant mortality and child death, but poorer people are at greater risk of dying at all ages of life than more affluent people.

The Kharwars are living in industrial area of Sonebhadra and showing a clear class gradation to health. This investigation reveals some points, which can explain the correlation between class and health. First, the life style of individual is very important for his health. Such as smoking, poor diet and higher consumption of alcohol are the damaging factors of good health. Secondly, the causes of health inequalities in higher social structures are poverty, wealth, unemployment, housing, pollution and poor working conditions *et cetera*. The pattern in health inequality between various classes is the result of material deprivation and poor ecological conditions.

Relation between Gender and Health

Disparities in health between men and women have a very broad field to work. On the whole women enjoy longer life expectancy than men in almost every country in the world. At the same time, women also suffer from a higher incidence of illness than men do particularly in latter part of life. Women are more likely to seek medical attention and have higher rates of reported illness than men. Women in industrial area reported two times more cases of anxiety and depression as compared to men. The overall picture of women's health in developed world is one in which women live longer than men but are sicker and experience more disability.

Among Kharwars, the cause of death pattern of illness shows some differences between men and women. Heart and lungs related diseases are also most frequent killer of both men and women in Sonebhadra, but men suffer from higher rates of death from accident and violence and are also more prone to drug and alcohol dependency. On the whole, men tend to be ill more infrequently, but the illness which do afflict men tend to be more life threatening.

Relation between Institution of Family and Health

The family structure of Kharwars of Sonebhadra is changing from extended family to nuclear family. This pattern shows that after the marriage of the children the parents become bounded to live alone. Then the old parents are suffering from various problems like psychological insecurity and to work more than their capacity, the feeling to negligence *et cetera*. All these factors causing the fast decaying of their health show that the male and female of above than 65 years showing high frequency of problem related with their loneliness than any other age group of Kharwars of Sonebhadra. In this way the family structure is also a very big factor which affecting the health.

(B) EFFECT OF INDUSTRIES ON THE HEALTH OF KHARWARS

Industries and industrialization have literally brought about revolutionary changes in various parts of India on both tribes and caste groups. The tribes of Sonebhadra are very much affected by several industries present in this area. The agriculture and forest based economy of these tribes has been replaced by the *industry based economy*. The desire of cash money has attracted thousands of local tribals.

District Sonebhadra is famous because it is the highest electricity-producing district in Asia. But the original people of this area have paid a lot for this fame. The whole district is suffering from various types of heath problems, specially the people living nearby the factories. The list of some very important industries present here in district Sonebhadra near the villages of tribal concentrations is as follows :

1. Hydro-Electric and Thermal Power Station, Obra.
2. Thermal Power Station, Anpara.
3. National Thermal Power Corporation, Shaktinagar.
4. Vindhya Nagar Thermal Power Station, Vindhya Nagar.
5. Hydro-Electric Power Station, Renusagar.
6. Hindustan Aluminium Company (HINDALCO), Renukoot.
7. Kanoriya Chemicals, Renukoot.
8. Hi-Tech Carbon, Renukoot.
9. Dala Cement Factory, Dala.
10. Churk Cement Factory, Churk.
11. Stone Crushers of Obra, Dala, Chopan and other areas of District Sonebhadra.

These industries are certainly playing a very important role in the economic development of the common people and tribes, but certain kinds of byproducts and waste products of these industries, which are injected in the biosphere in high quantities, are affecting the man and ecosystem adversely. The

Kharwars of district Sonebhadra with other several tribes are suffering from the problem of working in unhygienic and noisy condition, problem of several air-born diseases and water-born disease *et cetera*.

Brief information about various types of industries and there impacts on the health of tribals in general and on Kharwar tribes of Sonebhadra in particular, are as under :

Hydro-Electric and Thermal Power Stations

The power stations of this area are chiefly based on coal for thermal power and some on water for hydro-electricity. This district Sonebhadra has the five big power plants of the country. These are supplying electricity to a large portion of the country.

The coal consumption of these factories is several million tones per day. The chief pollutants of coal burning are fly ash, SO_2, other gases (CO, NO_2), aldehydes and hydrocarbons *et cetera*.

The problems to tribal people and Kharwars are dizziness, headache, eye irritation, coughing and shortness of breadth, sore throat, lung cancer, other lung diseases, chest pain and increased cold allergies *et cetera*.

Chemical Based Industries

Chemical based industries like aluminium companies, carbon-producing companies, various chemical compounds producing companies *et cetera*, of this area dispose off their waste products in the river *Renu* and on the open space near the factories, which is very much fatal and hazardous to the rural people living in these interior areas.

The industrial waste of these industries include metals (copper, zinc, lead, mercury *et cetera*), acids, alkalis, phenols, carbamates, alcohol, cyanides, arsenic, chlorine and many other inorganic and organic toxicants. These are polluting the water of river *Renu* and river *Sone* of the Sonebhadra.

The chief air pollutants of these industries are Ammonia, Carbon Dust, Carbon Monoxide, Chlorine, Hydrogen Cyanides, Phosgene (Carbonyl chlorides), Aldehydes, Hydrocarbons and Acid vapors *et cetera*.

The problems to the common people and the kharwars of this area by these pollutants are irritation in nasal and respiratory tract, inflammation in upper respiratory passage, reduced oxygen carrying capacity of blood, problems in nerve cells, indistinct vision *et cetera*. The people of this region, who use the river water for drinking, are suffering from diseases of eye, skin rashes and anemia.

Cement Factories and Stone Crushers

Both of these are emitting plenty of dust particles, which have the potential of health hazard. The SPM (Suspended Particulate Matter) levels of these areas are found to be five times of industrial safety limits. These are producing chiefly air related problems.

The dust fall and suspended particulates may be of smaller than 10 micron. They are generated by various industrial processes and combustion processes. In polluted air, their concentration may reach up to 100,000 per cubic centimeter. Particulates emitted by the cement manufacturing units of this area cause in plants fall of seedlings, higher puberty of leaves, formation of more stomata and trichomes, reduction in weight of seeds and increase in number of infertile seeds. Dusts from stone crushers, limekilns and slate making units of Sonebhadra are also hazardous to health of plants, animals and human beings. Particles of coal dust released from factories can cause several diseases in human, plant and animals. Coal dust and asbestos found to cause necrotic lesion, reduction in fruit set in plants and silicosis, asbestosis and lung cancer in humans. The common dust particles sometimes become health hazards as they may lead to disease such as allergic asthma, bronchitis, emphysema and even fibrosis of lungs. Pulverized Fly Ash (PFA) is getting accumulated in such large quantities particularly in this area where thermo-electric generators are established that it has proven to be one of the major sources of solid wastes. Since it contains Boron, its deposition by wind in agricultural tract often results in deleterious effect.

7. The Contribution of Health to Human Development

As in case of the Kharwars, bad health is directly and profoundly affecting the economic situation and well-being of every individual of their society and *vice-versa*. This is particularly true in the lower income groups (because their social safety nets are weaker or non-existent) and for the absolute poor, due to the vicious circle of poverty and ill health.

Conversely, better health will boost the individual's level of income (lower treatment costs, increased revenue, longer term increase in revenue due to better work opportunities, increase in revenues due to longer life expectancy, *et cetera*); increase the individuals capacity to acquire education; increase the family's productive opportunities; and increase substantially the psychological well-being of both the individual and the family. The benefits of good health will be even greater for the absolute poor, as they may transform the vicious circle of poverty into a virtuous circle, with better nutrition, lower risks of unemployment or underdevelopment, better housing, better use of training opportunities, higher productivity and , overall, better control over their life situation and that of their family. The whole process is complex and difficult to quantify, but even conservative estimates suggest that health investments often yield the highest rates of return compared to other public investments.

Health status, of tribesmen of Uttar Pradesh in general and of the Kharwars in particular, can be improved through health promotion activities, by means of burden prevention or by interventions geared at burden reduction or cure. The health status of a population is determined by the factors like *Individual* (genetics, exposure to health hazards, behaviour, risk taking), the *Family* (divorce, parental skills, family planning, human reproduction, family violence, care for disabled members) and the *Community*. The community, greatly influence the population's health status through local decisions on sanitation, education, shelter, unemployment and handling of violence. The fact that choices and options are far more restricted for the poorest people provides one of the important linkages between poverty and ill health, and points to the health gain benefits that are associated with poverty-reduction programmes. Therefore, the development and health status are complementary to each other and the development of any tribe/community/society can not be expected, without the supplementation of good health facilities and gain of a better health status.

6. Conclusion

Thus, society, culture and environment have its severe impact on the health and illness of the rural and tribal people. The socio cultural factors such as: culture, social class, behaviour, materialistic culture, social environment, gender, family structures etcetera are influencing the health of Kharwars and other tribal populations of District Sonebhadra

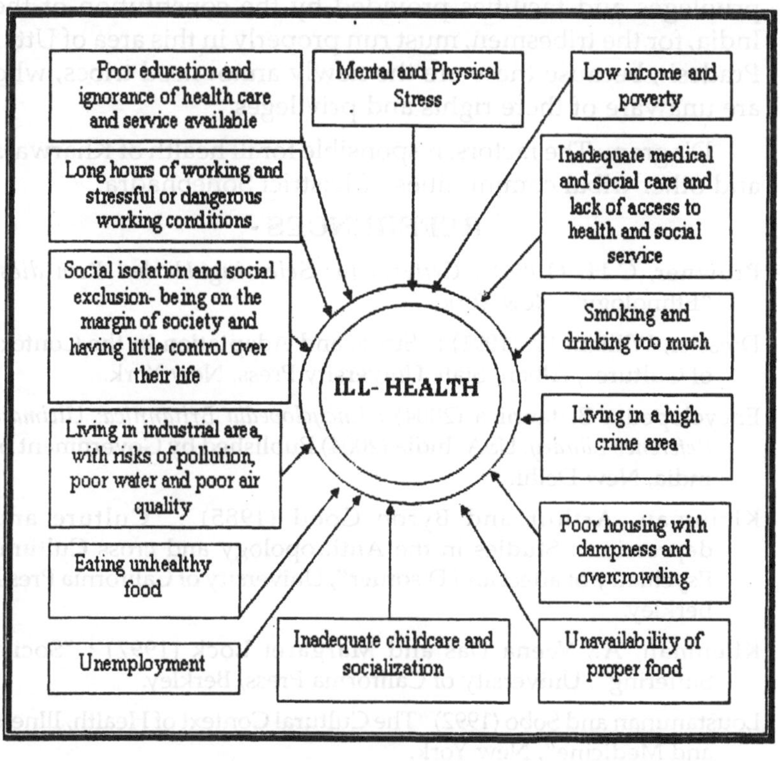

(U.P.). One of the major theme is the change in their economic system, has a very specific and significant impact on their health. The industries of this area are very important and large scale producers of various necessities. But these industries are not controlling the pollutions, produced by their own and disposing off their wastes, systematically, which are very hazardous to whole environment and fatal to the plants, animals and human beings. Tribesmen, who are not capable of making themselves unaffected by these toxic gases, dust particulates and liquefied wastes of the factories, becomes the victims of various chronic diseases, this further cause worst situation for rural and tribal people including the Kharwars.

The shortsightedness, of the management of these industries and government officials, has full responsibility for this situation. The government should assure that all the privileges and facilities provided by the constitution of the India, for the tribesmen, must run properly in this area of Uttar Pradesh, because these are the newly announced tribes, who are unaware of there rights and privileges.

Diagram: The factors, responsible for ill health of Kharwars and other tribal communities of District Sonebhadra.

REFERENCES

Browner, C.H. (1984) : *Criteria for Selecting Herbal Remedies*, "Ethnology", New York.

Dressler, William W. (1991) : "Stress and Adaptation in the Context of Culture", Albani State University Press, New York.

Encyclopedia Britannica (2004) : *Encyclopedia Britannica: Ultimate Reference Library*. USA. India (2004) Published by Government of India, New Delhi.

Kleinman, Arthur and Byron Good (1985) : "Culture and depression : Studies in the Anthropology and cross Cultural Psychiatry of affect and Disorder", University of California Press, Berkley.

Klienman, A., Veena Das and Margaret Lock (1997) : "Social Suffering", University of California Press, Berkley.

Loustanunan and Sobo (1992) "The Cultural Context of Health, Illness and Medicine", New York.

Murdock, G.P. (1980) "Theories of Illness: A World Survey", University of Pittsburgh Press.

Murray C.J.L., Lopez A.D. (1996) : *A Global Burden of Disease: A Comparative Assessment of Mortality and Disability from Disease, Injuries and Risk Factors in 1990 and Projected to 2020.* Harward University Press, Cambridge, USA.

Robert, A.H. (1995) : "Sickness and Healing : An Anthropological Perspective", New Haven C.T., Yale University Press.

Robert, B.E. (1992) : "Sick Societies: Challenging the Myth of Primitive Harmony", Free Press : New York.

Sinha, R.K. & S. Sinha (2001) : "Ethno-Biology", Surabhi Publication, Jaipur, India.

The World Health Report (2002) : *The World Health Report 2002 : Reducing Risks, Promoting Healthy Life.* Geneva : WHO, 2002.

Trehan, A.K. (2004) : *Rural Health,* "Journal-Kurukshetra", Publication Division, New Delhi.

United Nations (2000) : *Millennium Development Goals.* UN General Assembly Resolution A/55/1.2, 18 September 2000.

Wallace, Anthony F.C. (1992) : *Mental illness, Biology and Culture,* "Psychological Anthropology", Cambridge University Press.

World Bank (2000) : *World Development Report 2000-2001 : Attacking Poverty.* World Bank and Oxford University Press, Washington DC.

SECTION—III
Gender and Health

19

Nutritional Status of Women and Children in Three States of India

—Maitreyi Chaudhuri

1. Introduction

In recent years India's economic development has been remarkable. However such economic development has not been able to bring about social development for all sections of population, particularly for women and children of our country. India is one of the countries where males significantly outnumber females. Due to limited access to food and medical treatment undernourishment and malnourishment are high among women. Women's health and nutritional status are influenced by various social, cultural and economic factors. Ill health of women reduces their productivity not only at the household level but also in the formal and informal productive sector.

Women's health is important not only for their own well being but also for the well being of their children. Although infant and child mortality has declined significantly during the past two decades, over 30 per cent of all deaths in India occur among children under five years of age (Tinker, 1996). In India another serious problem is malnutrition that is caused by inadequate or inappropriate food intake, various types of childhood diseases and improper care during illness. Earlier researches also show that there are significant regional disparities in the health and nutritional status of women and children. The northern part of India is characterized by low sex ratio and high infant mortality rate as compared to the southern part. The following table gives the important demographic features of Uttar Pradesh (U.P.), West Bengal (W.B.) and Kerala.

Table 1 : Important Demographic Indicators

Demographic Indicators	*India*	*U.P.*	*W.B.*	*Kerala*
* Sex Ratio (Total Population)	933	898	934	1058
*Juvenile Sex Ratio (Population Aged 0-6 Years)	927	916	960	960
* Literacy rate	64.8	52.3	68.6	90.9
** Birth Rate	25.4	32.1	20.5	17.2
**Infant Mortality Rate (IMR)	66	82	51	11
** Death Rate	8.4	10.1	6.8	6.6

Source: * Census of India 2001; ** Sample Registration Bulletin, 2002.

U.P. is characterized by low sex ratio for the total population, low juvenile sex ratio (age group 0-6 years), low literacy rate, high birth, death and infant mortality rates as compared to W.B. and Kerala. In respect of the demographic indicators considered here, Kerala is in the most favourable position. In Kerala the overall sex ratio is more than 1000, *i.e.* females outnumber males. The juvenile sex ratio in Kerala is also higher than the national figure. However W.B. and Kerala have the same juvenile sex ratio. Of the three states Kerala has the highest literacy rate which is much higher than the all India rate. Literacy rate of W.B. is also higher than the corresponding national rate. U.P. has the lowest literacy rate which is also below the national literacy rate. In respect of birth rate, death rate and infant mortality rate Kerala occupies the highest position. In W.B. and Kerala these rates are below the corresponding national figures. In U.P. these rates are much higher than the all India rates. Thus, in terms of human development indicators, Kerala occupies the highest and U.P. the lowest position

Since maternal and child health is an important aspect of social development, the government has launched several programmes to provide improved health care facilities to women and children. Integrated Child Development Services (ICDS) programme is aimed at improving health and nutritional status of children below 6 years of age and also of the pregnant and lactating mothers. Non Government Organizations (NGOs) are also providing health care interventions to women and children belonging to the disadvantaged section of population. However more remains to be done.

In order to provide health care intervention to women and children, the first and foremost necessity is to have authentic data on the status of health and nutrition of women and children in India. With this aim in view, National Family Health Survey (NFHS) was first conducted in the year 1991-1992 (NFHS 1). The second survey NFHS 2 was conducted during 1998-1999 and the third one *i.e.* NFHS 3 was conducted in the year 2005-2006. The detailed report of NFHS 3 was not available when this paper was finalized. The present paper aims at examining the nutritional status of women and children in three states of India – Uttar Pradesh (U.P.), West Bengal (W.B.) and Kerala. The impacts of various social, economic and demographic indicators on the nutritional status of women and children have also been examined in this paper.

2. Second National Family Health Survey

Second National Health Survey (NFHS 2) was conducted in the year 1998-1999 by the International Institute of Population Science, Mumbai, India and ORC Macro Calverton, Maryland, USA. The survey was conducted in 26 states by following a multistage stratified sampling method. For the present purpose the respondents are ever-married women in the age group of 15-49 years and children below three years of age. The following table gives the sample size considered in the survey for West Bengal, Uttar Pradesh and Kerala.

Table 2 : Sample Size

States	*WomenWomen*	*Women Children*
U.P.	5744	2387
W.B.	3982	1111
Kerala	2653	576

Source : NFHS 2 Report (2000).

Body Mass Index (followed by WHO 2003) has been used to measure the nutritional status of women. Body Mass Index (BMI) has been measured by the ratio of weight and height. A women is said to be undernourished if her BMI is less than 18.5 kg/m^2. Nutritional status of children has been measured with the help of three anthropometric indicators, *e.g.* height for age, weight for age and weight for height. The first indicator shows the percentage of stunted children. The second indicator gives the percentage of underweight children and the third indicator measures the percentage of wasted children. Each of these measures has been expressed in standard deviation (SD) from median value of WHO reference population (Dibley *et al.* 1987 a, 1987 b, Martorell and habcht 1986). NFHS 2 has reported the percentage of children below –2 SD and also below –3 SD. In the former case the children are undernourished and the later case the children are regarded as severely undernourished. In the present study only the weight for height indicator has been used.

NFHS 2 report has furnished data on the nutritional status of women and children according to various background characteristics. The characteristics are residence (rural/urban), sex, religion, caste/tribe, standard of living, educational status, work status, BMI of women/mothers and birth order of children. Data on the nutritional status of women show percentage of women having BMI < 18.5 kg/m^2 and data on nutritional status of children show percentage of undernourished children.

3. Data and Results on the Nutritional Status of Ever-married Women

NFHS2 reports for U.P., W.B. and Kerala furnish the following data on the nutritional status of ever-married women.

Table 3 : Percentage of Ever-Married Women (Age group 15-49 Years) with BMI below 18.5kg/m² by Background Characteristics

Background Characteristics	*U.P.*	*W.B.*	*Kerala*
Residence			
Total	35.8	43.7	18.7
Rural	23.3	24.5	14.7
Urban	39.1	49.8	19.9
Religion			
Hindu	35.6	42.2	21.6
Muslim	38.6	47.6	17.1
Other*	10.7*	52.6	12.4**
Caste/Tribe			
SC	41.3	49.4	27.6
ST	32.6	64.2	29.4
OBC	37.3	35.3	19.8
Other	31.9	39.9	15.8
Level of living			
Low	44.9	57.1	33.1
Medium	36.8	38.4	19.2
High	20.9	16.8	10.1
Education			
Illiterate	40.3	53.0	26.6
Less than middle school	32.9	41.5	19.6
Middle school complete	29.7	34.3	17.2
High school and above	17.9	15.3	16.1
Work Status			
Family business	41.6	51.4	19.0
Employed by some-one else	40.8	55.8	24.5
Self employed	38.1	41.8	18.0
Not worked for the last one year	34.2	40.8	17.4

ST – scheduled tribe; SC – scheduled caste; OBC – other backward caste.

* The 'Other' group in U.P. contains the Sikhs. ** The 'Other' group in Kerala contains the Christians.

The table shows that almost in all categories WB's performance is the worst as compared to U.P. and Kerala. Kerala, however, performs the best in respect of women's nutritional status.

NFHS 2 report gives the total number of women surveyed in all levels of each background characteristic. With the help of these total number of undernourished as well as well-nourished women have been calculated for all levels of each characteristic. For each background characteristic a two-way contingency table has been prepared on two attributes. One attribute is the nutritional status of women having two levels-undernourished women and well-nourished women. The other attribute is one of the background characteristics with levels as shown in table 3. On the basis of each of these contingency tables, a Chi-Square (c^2) test has been performed to test the null hypothesis

H_0 : The background character does not affect the nutritional status of women against the alternative.

H_1 : The background character affects the nutritional status of women.

If the test statistic is found to be significant at 5% level then H_0 is rejected implying that the background character affects the nutritional status of the women. In this case a coefficient of association between the background character and the nutritional status of women is calculated by using the formula $f = \{c^2/(c^2+n)\}^{1/2}$ where n is the sample size (Gun, Gupta and Dasgupta, 2002). Table 2 shows that n differs from state to state. However *n* has also differed for some of the background characteristics within a state because responses have not been available for all women and children in the sample in respect of the background characteristic under consideration. .

Table 4 : Pair-wise Coefficients of Association between the BMI and other Background Characteristics

Background Characteristic	*U.P.*	*W.B.*	*Kerala*
Residence	* .134	* .218	* .057
Religion	* .048	* .053	* .084
Caste/tribe	* .079	* .140	* .090
Standard of living	* .169	* .279	* .173
Education	* .134	* .217	* .077
Work Status	* .060	* .114	* .068

* c^2 is significant at 5% level; *i.e.* H_0 is rejected.

Table 4 reveals that all the c^2s are significant at 5% level of significance. The table also gives the coefficients of association between the nutritional status of women and background characters.

Rural-Urban Disparity : Percentages of undernourished women are higher in rural areas. The rural-urban disparity is the highest in W.B. and the lowest in Kerala. This is evidenced by the coefficients of association in the three states.

Religion : Religion has a significant effect on the nutritional status of women in all the three states. The Sikhs in U.P. and the Christians in Kerala are in a better position as compared to other religion groups in the states. In W.B. the group termed 'Other' has the highest percentage of wasted women. The Hindus in Kerala and the Muslims in W.B. are in a worse position. The coefficient of association between religion and the nutritional status of women is the highest in Kerala and the lowest in W.B.

Caste/Tribe : Caste/tribe factor has significant impact on the BMI of women. In all the three states the ST group has the highest percentage of women with BMI below 18.5 kg/m^2. In W.B. this percentage is very high. In U.P. and Kerala the upper caste group (termed as 'Other') and in W.B. the OBC group have the smallest percentages of undernourished women. The coefficient of association between the caste/tribe factor and nutritional status of women is the highest in W.B. and the lowest in U.P.

Standard of Living : Standard of living has significant impact on the BMI of women. As the standard of living improves the percentage of undernourished women decreases in all the states. The coefficient of association between the standard of living and the nutritional status of women is the highest in W.B.

Educational Level of Women : Education has a significant impact on the BMI of women. In all the three states the percentage of undernourished women decreases as the women's educational level improves. Compared to other two states, W.B. has the lowest number of undernourished women in the highest educational category. In all other categories W.B. has the highest percentages of undernourished women. Coefficient of association between the educational level and the BMI status of women is the highest in W.B..

Work Status of Women : This factor has significant effect on the BMI status of women. In all the three states, the percentage of undernourished women is the lowest among the nonworking women. The reason may be that these women come from the richer class and hence enjoy better nutritional status. In all the three states the status of self-employed women is better as compared to the women employed by someone else or working on family farm or in family business. The coefficient of association between work status of women and their nutritional status is the highest in W.B..

In all the three states the nutritional status of women is found have the highest association with the standard of living index. In U.P. and W.B. education and residence are the next important factors so far as their association with BMI status is concerned. In Kerala religion and caste/tribe factors have higher association with the Nutritional status of women as compared to education.

4. Data and Results on the Nutritional Status of Children below 3 Years

Table 5 gives the data on nutritional status of children (below 3 years) in U.P., W.B. and Kerala. Here under-nutrition implies wasting measured by weight/height. West Bengal has the highest percentage of wasted children in most of the categories discussed here. Rural areas have higher percentage of wasted children as compared to the urban areas. An interesting feature in all the three states is that the percentage of wasted boys is more than the percentage of wasted girls in all the three states. The sample shows that the Muslims in W.B. have the highest number of wasted children. The situation is just the reverse in other two states. Caste-wise, the percentage of the wasted children is the highest among the SCs and the STs and lowest among the upper caste people. For Kerala, however, the percentage of ST children has not been reported. As the standard of living improves the percentage of wasted children decreases in all the three states. The percentage of wasted children also decreases as the education level of the mothers increases. The percentage of wasted children among the mothers with the highest level of education is the lowest in W.B.. In kerala the percentage of wasted children is less for the working mothers. The situation is just the reverse for U.P. and W.B. In all the three states mother's BMI has a strong influence on the nutritional status of children in all the three states. Birth order of the children does not show any systematic impact on their nutritional status in U.P. and W.B. However, in U.P. the percentage of wasted children is high among the children of birth order higher than three. In Kerala this is true even for the children of birth order between two and three.

Table 5 : Percentage Distribution of Undernourished Children (Below 3 Years) by Background Characteristics

Background Characteristics	*U.P.*	*W.B.*	*Kerala*
1	2	3	4
Residence			
Total	11.1	13.6	11.1
Rural	9.5	11.1	10.9
Urban	11.4	14.2	11.2
Gender			
Male	11.4	14.8	12.5
Female	10.8	12.3	9.7
Religion			
Hindu	11.7	13.4	13.0
Muslim	8.8	14.3	10.6
Caste/Tribe			
SC	11.5	18.1	12.3
ST	13.7	17.7	—
OBC	13.6	13.7	12.5
Other	9.3	11.5	9.2
Mother's education			
Illiterate	11.0	15.8	—
Less than middle school	13.4	13.4	18.3
Completed middle school	10.8	12.2	8.6
High school and above	9.4	4.0	9.5
Mother's work			
Family farm or business	13.1	15.4	—
Employed by someone else	12.0	15.2	4.0
Self employed	20.1	11.9	—
Not worked in the past 12 months	10.5	13.4	11.6
Standard of Living			
Low	13.4	15.5	16.2
Medium	10.2	12.5	11.2

(Contd. . . .)

1	*2*	*3*	*4*
High	9.8	9.3	8.8
Mother's BMI			
<18.5 kg/m^2	14.6	16.3	20.2
>18.5 kg/m^2	9.0	10.6	8.3
Birth Order			
1	12.4	13.6	8.6
2–3	9.3	13.8	12.7
4–5	11.4	15.1	—
6+	13.5	8.9	—

Next task is to test whether the effects of various background characteristics on nutritional status of children, as revealed by the sample, are statistically significant or not.

For each background characteristic this is done by testing.

H_0: The background character does not have any impact on child nutrition against the alternative

H_1 : The background character has impact on child nutrition.

As in the case of women's BMI, here also, H_0 is tested with the help of c^2statistic. If the statistic is significant for any background character then the coefficient of association between this character and the nutritional status of children is calculated.

Table 6 : Pairwise Coefficient of Association between Child Nutrition and Background Characters

Background Characters	*U.P.*	*W.B.*	*Kerala*
1	*2*	*3*	*4*
Residence	ns	ns	ns
Gender	ns	ns	ns
Religion	ns	ns	ns
Caste/Tribe	ns	ns	ns

(Contd. . . .)

1	2	3	4
Standard of living	ns	ns	ns
Mother's education	ns	ns	.089
Mother's work status	ns	ns	ns
Mother's	*	*	*
BMI	.268	.180	.166
Birth order	ns	ns	ns

* c^2 significant at 5% level, *i.e.* H_0 is rejected; ns – not significant at 5% level, *i.e.* H_0 is accepted.

The above table shows that in Kerala mother's education has significant impact on the nutritional status of children. In all the three states BMI has significant impact on the nutritional status of the children. All other background characteristics do not have any significant impact on child nutrition when all the levels of a character are considered. A detailed analysis, however, shows that the disparity in the percentage of wasted children is significant between the lowest and the highest levels of living in all the three states. In the case of the mother's education, if only two groups are considered, *i.e.* the illiterate and those having the highest level of education, this characteristic has significant impact on the nutritional status of the children in W.B. Thus the key factor influencing the nutritional status of the children is mother's BMI which, again, is influenced by all the background characteristics shown in the table 4.

5. Conclusion

Though West Bengal is in a better position than U.P. in respect of some human development indicators as shown in table1, the state's performance is poorer than U.P. in respect of the nutritional status of ever-married women (in the age group of 15-49 years) and children (below 3 years). Kerala's performance is far better than the performance of either W.B. or U.P.. In Kerala public health delivery system and the Anganwadis have been rendering very good services for a long time. In W.B. performances of both of these two systems are poor. As a result, large percentages of the mothers and the children are suffering from undernutrition and ill health in W.B..

In all the three states child nutrition is found to have statistically significant association with mother's BMI which is an indicator of the nutritional status of these women. Nutritional status of evermarried women is most strongly associated with their standard of living. Ranking of the background characteristics according to their coefficient of association with the BMI of evermarried women shows that in W.B. and U.P. Standard of living plays the most important role and the next important factor is mother's education. In fact, in all the three states all the background characteristics affect mother's BMI significantly. Thus all these factors indirectly affects the nutritional status of children.

The most important way to improve the nutritional status of children is to improve the nutritional status of their mothers measured by the BMI. Education is very important to raise the level of awareness of women regarding the rules of health and family planning programme. Since poverty lowers the BMI of the women and since in India a majority of the SC and the ST people live in abject poverty, the government should take proper care to ensure that its health delivery system reaches the women and the children belonging to the poorer and the disadvantaged sections of the population. The women should be made aware of the Reproductive Child Health (RCH) programme of the government and the Anganwadi Workers should play their role properly in this respect. Women should be given special care regarding health and nutrition even from their childhood if a nation likes to have a healthy future generation.

REFERENCES

Dibley, M.J., J.B. Goldsby, N.W. Staehling and F. L. Trowbridge (1987a) : Development of Normalized Curves for the International Growth Reference: Historical and Technical Consideration. American Journal of Clinical Nutrition 45 (5) : 736-748.

Dibley, M.J., N.W. Staehling, P. Neiburg and F. L. Trowbridge (1987b) : Interpretation of z – score Anthropometric Indicators Derived from the International Growth Reference : American Journal of Clinical Nutrition 46(5) : 749-762.

Gun A.M., M.K. Gupta, B. Dasgupta (2002) : Fundamentals of Statistics, Volume One; The World Press Private Limited.

International Institute for Population Sciences (IIPS), Mumbai (1995) : National Family Health Survey (NFHS1) 1992-1993.

International Institute for Population Sciences (IIPS) and ORC Macro (2000) : National Family Health Survey (NFHS-2), 1998-99 : India, Mumbai : IIPS.

International Institute for Population Sciences (IIPS), Mumbai (2006) : National Family Health Survey (NFHS-3) 2005-2006, Provisional Data.

Martorell R. and J.P. Habicht (1986) : Growth in early Childhood in Developing Countries : In Frank Falkner and J.M. Tanner (eds) Human Growth : A Comprehensive Treatise, vol. 3, New York : Plenum Press.

Tinker Ann (1996) : Improving Women's Health in India, Washington D.C., World Bank.

World Health Organization (WHO) (2003) : Diet, Nutrition and the Prevention of Chronic Diseases. Report of a Joint WHO/FAO Expert Consultation. Technical Report Series No. 916, Geneva : WHO.

20

Poverty, Gender and Reproductive Health : A Case Study of Self-help Groups in Burdwan District, West Bengal

—Gopa Samanta

1. Introduction

'Poverty' and 'inequality' are two issues of deep concern in the process of development of countries like India. These are more influenced by socio-economic and cultural factors rather than physical one. Unequal distribution of income creates unequal power equations in society. The concept of development, therefore, has been broadened from just rising incomes to the overall well being of people (Rustagi, 2000).

The need for Poverty alleviation was first felt in the late 1960s and early 1970s when a number of studies revealed that economic growth in developing countries benefited relatively developed areas and better-off sections of population, and more or less bypassed backward areas and poorer sections of the population. Since then poverty became the subject matter of core concern in several studies and reports in India (Minhas, 1970; Dandekar and Rath, 1971; Lal, 1973; Mellor, 1976; Chakraborty, 1987; Singh, 1994; Kumar and Yadav, 1994; Rao, 1994; Eswaran and Kotwal, 1994 etc.) being treated as a major cause and effect of many crucial problems. It was therefore, thought that 'a strategy of direct attack on poverty', which aimed at providing productive assets and credit to buy assets and skills/training, directly to the poor would be necessary to enable then to participate in economic growth and to access the benefits of growth (Hirway, 2003).

In the developmental efforts of the first two decades of planning in independent India, no special emphasis was given to the development of women. As a result of the male-biased development intervention, women's position in the society changed in a negative way with the improvement of the economy as well as social status of their family. In the poor and low income families women have access to valued productive activity which is often invisible in the middle class families. Since 1970s, many studies especially the Towards Equality report in 1974 started to highlight the gender discrimination and consequent impoverishment of women, their low status despite growing work burdens, their oppressions, and their invisibility in the productive economy as well as in development programmes.

To remove the gross inequalities between men and women in the society, the Indian government started to take U.P. separate policies and plans for women from mid 1970s (Madhok, 2003). This was partly due to the international pressure created by United Nations and partly as the response to the Towards Equality report of 1974 (Rajagopal and Mathur, 2000). The policies and programmes are many in number, among them the followings deserve special mention.

a. National Plan of Action for Women – 1976

b. National **Nutrition** Policy – 1983

c. National **Health** Policy - 1983

d. National Policy on Education – 1986

e. National Policy on the **Empowerment** of Women – 2000

f. Institutional Support

1. An Exclusive Department of **Women and Child** Development - 1985
2. National Commission for Women – 1992
3. Rashtriya Mahila Kosh (RMK)
4. Parliamentary Committee on Empowerment of women – 2001

Despite a long history of plans and programmes since independence, the Indian women still remain marginalized. National policies on Nutrition and health were taken in 1983. However, not much success has been achieved in these two fronts among the poor people. A large segment of poor especially women suffer from malnutrition, under age marriage and pregnancy and lack of health facilities during child birth. The rate of infant mortality and the death of women during child birth are still significant among rural poor. This poor health status of women is again related to their non-productive role in the family. There is a general consensus among the academics and policy makers that women's reproductive health status is positively related to their levels of literacy, income generating capacity and financial contribution to the family. The health issue is also related to the issue of women's empowerment, which received much attention of the policy makers especially of Microfinance Institutions (MFIs) in the development discourse of the recent past.

In the above context, the poverty alleviating and livelihood generating SHG schemes put more emphasis on women SHGs to make their contribution visible in the family and to empower them in economic as well as social aspects of life. The Indian government and NABARD have started microfinance schemes since 1990s to raise poor women and their families above the poverty line through collective sustainable livelihood projects. The impact of such microfinance programmes on poverty situation and on reproductive health of women are analysed in this paper in the context of Burdwan district. More specifically, the objective of the paper is to analyse the role of self-help groups (SHGs) in bringing changes in the lives of poor rural women especially in their reproductive health status.

For this study five Rural Development Blocks (Burdwan-I, Burdwan-II, Memari, Khandaghosh and Kanksa) have been selected from the eastern part of Burdwan District. This region belongs to one of the rich agricultural economies prevailing in different parts of West Bengal. The flat alluvial plain of lower Damodar valley, well integrated irrigation network consisting of canals, small and minor irrigation schemes and HYV package together have brought a dramatic increase in the agricultural production of the region since late 1980s. Still rural poverty exists in different parts of the district at significant level.

The paper is based on the information collected from extensive field survey in five Rural Development blocks of Burdwan district, West Bengal covering 43 SGSY and 21 SHG women groups, and 500 individual women. The self help groups having at least 3 years of work experience are selected for the study to understand the impact of self-employed livelihood generation schemes on the reproductive health status of poor rural women. The field survey was based on both quantitative and qualitative methods. To complement quantitative information gathered through structured questionnaire survey, qualitative data are obtained through participatory research methods such as long informal interviews and focused group discussions.

2. Gender, Poverty and Development

In south Asian countries the GDP per capita for women is extremely low and is often less than half, or one-third of that of men. In India it is only 38 per cent (Kelkar, 2005). Raju (2005) identified the reasons for this low GDP per capita for women. According to her, the reporting of women as economically less active, which is again determined by their low social status, is the reason for the low GDP of women in India. In most of the developing countries, the productive role of women is not acknowledged, rather remained invisible (Bòserup, 1970). Bhatty (1987) argued that this invisibility of women's work is to the elusive definition of 'work' given by economists and Census Commissioners. She also identified another reason for the non-recognition of women's economic contribution, which is the neglect of the household economy and the unorganized sector, in which women play an overwhelming role. According to Mazumdar (1985), unless the economic and social utility of women in the eyes of their families and the nation to take part in socially and economically productive roles is recognized, the national neglect of women will continue.

Yet, when both household and "productive labour" for market are considered, women work considerably longer hours than men do. This gap is particularly pronounced in poor households. In India, women account for 60 per cent of unpaid family workers and 98 per cent of those, engaged in domestic work (Acharya and Ghimire, 2005). Even after the experience of women's access to income, arguments are being made by scholars that economic independence of women does not convert easily into empowerment. Gulati's (1996) study on the outskirts of Trivandrum noted that women who had supplemented their family income, and in some cases were the 'principal earners' as their husbands were unemployed neither rose in status within the social groups to which they belonged nor did they acquire the condition of being equal with their men folk. Following Waylen (1996), it can be said that production, reproduction, sexuality and socialisation of children are the key factors which together make women powerless in patriarchal societies.

In developing countries, women are always perceived as mothers and/or housewives, their needs were determined to be maternal and child health, and nutrition. The national or state machineries for women, ministries and government departments, in almost all Third World countries reflect this approach to women's issues in their nomenclature; in India for example, the ministry is still known as Ministry and Women and Children's Welfare, Malaysia Ministry of Women, Family and Community Development, and in Bangladesh Women and Children's Affairs, putting women and children's concerns in the same category. However, in recent years, there are few changes and the Pakistan government now calls it the Ministry of Women Development, Indonesia Ministry of Women's

Empowerment, and Sri Lanka Ministry of Women's Empowerment and Social Welfare.

3. Reproductive Health

Health is the second indicator of the Gender Development Index, which is measured as life expectancy at birth. However, life expectancy is a stock variable and is not sensitive to short-term changes (Charmes and Wieringa, 2003). Therefore, we have studied the status of reproductive health of women, which is a good parameter of the levels of women's well being in the society. It has multiple dimensions. In our study we have tried to look at the reproductive health of women with the help of indicators such as age of marriage, age at birth of first child, no of children per women, adoption of family planning methods, no. of children died per women, stages of child death, place of delivery, miscarriages, abortions, and access to health facilities.

The Self Help Groups were supposed to be used by women as a space for discussions, including voicing their personal problems. But in reality it hardly acts as such a common and democratic forum for women. The issues discussed in the group meeting are predominantly related to transaction of loan and its recovery (Table 1). The second major issue which they often

Table 1 : Subjects Discussed in Group Meeting

Issues of discussion	*SGSY*		*SHG*		*Total*	
	no. of Groups	*Percentage*	*No. of Groups*	*Percentage*	*No. of Groups*	*Percentage*
Loan sanction and recovery	43	38.39	21	46.66	64	40.76
Health & Nutrition	18	16.07	8	17.78	26	16.56
Family matters	14	12.50	3	6.67	17	10.83
Education of children	27	24.11	8	17.78	35	22.29
Member's personal problem	10	8.93	5	11.11	15	9.56

discuss in the group meeting is their children's education. This might be attributed to the successful literacy mission in Burdwan district in the 1990s. Sometimes they discuss about the other family matters besides their financial discussion. Health and nutrition related issues are discussed sometimes in the group meeting but does not get high priority (Table 1).

4. Age of Marriage

The average age of marriage for women engaged in self help activity (for about 63.51 per cent of them) is 15 to 18 years. This indicates that the girls are married even before they become adult. About one fourth of women got married below the age of 15 years. This low age of marriage is the result of poverty, illiteracy, and lack of awareness among parents about the problems related to the early age of marriage for women. The women of poorer community in rural areas rarely get married above the age of 22 (Table 2). Due to this early age of marriage, women become mother at a very early age and thereafter often suffer from reproductive health related problems.

Table 2 : Age of Marriage

Age of *Marriage*	*SGSY*		*SHG*		*Total*	
	No.	*Percentage*	*No.*	*Percentage*	*No.*	*Percentage*
Below 15	100	26.60	19	17.43	119	24.54
15–18	236	62.76	72	66.06	308	63.51
19–22	38	10.11	13	11.93	51	10.51
23–26	2	0.53	4	3.67	6	1.24
Above 26	0	0	1	0.91	1	0.20
Total	376	100	109	100	485	100

Coming to the question of choice, these women had no option in life during their marriage time. About 16 per cent of them were not willing to marry at that lower age but their parents did not listen to them. Poverty, dowry and parents' obligation of getting daughter's marriage put them in position to undergo the system without any argument.

5. Age at Birth of First Child

Early pregnancy and giving birth of child at lower age is very often found among women of poorer communities. It has high negative impact on the health of women at different stages of their life cycle. In our survey of women SHG members, it is observed that some women (about 5 per cent) became mother even before their 15 years of age (Table 3). About 48 per cent of women became mother at the age varying between 15 and 18 *i.e.*, before being adult. At the age of 19 to 22, the proportion of women becoming mother is about 40 per cent. The proportion is very low *i.e.* around 7 per cent above the age of 22. From the initiation of DWCRA programme in Burdwan in early 1990s, high emphasis was given on women's heath awareness and problems related to early motherhood. It is also one of the various objectives of SGSY programme. However, no significant impact of all those awareness campaigning is found among our participants. Practically, majority of women have stated that their voices have never been heard – whether the issue is of marriage or of having children.

Table 3 : Age at Birth of First Child

Age groups	*SGSY*		*SHG*		*Total*	
	No. of Women	*Percentage*	*No. of Women*	*Percentage*	*No. of Women*	*Percentage*
Below 15	20	5.42	3	2.83	23	4.84
15-18	180	48.78	47	44.34	227	47.79
19-22	145	39.3	46	43.41	191	40.21
23-26	15	4.06	8	7.56	23	4.84
Above 26	9	2.44	2	1.86	11	2.32
Total	369	100	106	100	475	100

6. Family Planning

Among the married women, about 66 per cent use contraceptives as family planning measures to control the number of child births. The rest 34 per cent of women do not have any access to contraception. It has been observed that women are fully aware of the financial problems related to bringing up of children and therefore not willing to take more than two children. However, in most cases they do not have the power to take decisions regarding the birth as well as the number of children. They are compelled to follow the decisions taken by their husbands regarding the number of children. The issue of adoption of family planning in our case study is not only related to the decisions but also to the access to family planning measures. Pöor people can not provide the cost of purchasing contraceptives.

There is long debate among the scholars on the relation between women's educational level and decision of child birth. Tapan (2000) noted that apart from good medical services, education plays an important role in changing women's attitude towards population decisions. However, a group of scholars (James, 1999; Visaria and Visaria, 1994; Bhat, 2000; Agnihotri, 2002 etc.) disagrees with this common notion. According to them, although most studies have emphasised the role of female education as a factor contributing to lower fertility, the widespread adoption of contraception by illiterate women in the 1990s has raised serious questions about the role of education as a prime mover in the fertility transition. Whatever are the arguments made by the scholars, it has been observed in our survey that the number of children decreases with the increasing levels of education among women.

7. Fertility Rate

Fertility is an important measure of the reproductive status of a population. Fertility rate is measured by the number of children born to women of childbearing age. In our study area women have two children on an average. More specifically about 43 per cent of the women have two children. One child per women has also been noted in 12 per cent cases. However, this relatively high percentage of single child is due to the higher proportion of young women who have chance of second and third child later. Kelkar (2005) noted that women's education, economic independence, increase in remunerative employment, and political mobilization always have substantive effects in reducing the number of births. However, the women in our study are neither economically independence nor much mobilized through political participation. Above all they are not yet empowered to take decisions regarding the birth of child. Therefore, the single or two child decisions are mostly taken by their male counterparts.

Table 4 : No. of Children per Women

Children Per Women	*SGSY*		*SHG*		*Total*	
	No.of Women	*Percentage*	*No. of Women*	*Percentage*	*No. of Women*	*Percentage*
1	42	11.79	13	12.15	55	11.57
2	155	40.73	47	43.93	202	42.53
3	99	26.97	31	29.91	130	27.37
4	40	11.24	10	9.35	50	10.53
Above 4	33	9.27	5	4.66	38	8.00
Total	369	100	106	100	475	100

About 27 per cent and 10 per cent of women have 3 and 4 children respectively (Table 4). This higher number of children is noted in poorer and illiterate couples who have less awareness about the problems related to higher number of children. The number of children also depends on the sex of the first and second child. In most cases of three to four children per women, the first two or three are girl child respectively. Until a male baby is born, the women have to undergo the system of reproduction repeatedly. This preference of son is due to the perception of male baby as the future bread earner for the family. The son is considered as the only asset to the family. We rarely came across women who have no son. About 12 per cent of women, who have single issue, most of them have son as the first child.

8. Child Mortality Rate

Infant and child mortality rates are flow variables and can change within short term period. Dijkstra and Hanmer (2000) advocates that these can be used as good indicators of women's health and are better able than life expectancy to capture gender differences in health conditions. Child mortality rate is also a good indicator of poverty and lack of access to health facilities for poor women. Scholars (see Kelkar, 2005; Dreze and Sen, 2002; Deolikar, 2005) show a clear correlation between women's educational status and the infant and child mortality rates for both girls and boys. Kelkar (2005) has emphasised the role of women's economic independence in reducing child mortality rate. In our study, it is noted that child mortality rate is directly related to poverty, malnutrition and limited access to health facilities.

Child mortality rate among the women SHG members is still relatively high *i.e.* 247 children per 1000 women. About 80 per cent of women did not face the situation of child death. The rest 20 per cent experiences child death after births either once of twice (Table 5). The proportion of child death is more among women in SGSY groups rather than SHG groups. This is because of the fact that the poverty is more acute among women of SGSY groups than that of SHG groups. Therefore, it can be stated that the child mortality rate is directly linked to the poverty levels of women.

Table 5 : No. of Children Died

No. of children died per women	*SGSY*		*SHG*		*Total*	
	No.of Women	*Percen-tage*	*No. of Women*	*Percen-tage*	*No. of Women*	*Percen-tage*
1	56	15.18	6	5.66	72	14.85
2	20	5.42	1	0.94	21	4.33
3	2	0.54	0	0.00	2	0.41
Nil	291	78.86	99	93.40	390	80.41
Total	369	100	106	100	485	100

In the analysis of the stages of the death of child, it has been observed that 31 per cent child death is post-natal in nature (Table 6). These deaths are mostly related to the unscientific mode of delivery by local untrained midwife. The child mortality rate is 22 per cent and 13 per cent in case of children in the age group of one to two months and three to six months respectively. The 23 per cent death of children has also occurred in the age group above one year. These deaths are always related to certain sickness and not getting access to treatment due the poverty. In some cases the parents go to the local quack and the destiny becomes death.

Table 6 : Stages of Child Death

Stages	*SGSY*		*SHG*		*Total*	
Age groups	*No.of Child*	*Percentage*	*No. of Child*	*Percentage*	*No. of Child*	*Percentage*
Post-natal death	32	31.68	4	28.57	36	31.30
1–2 month	25	24.76	0	0	25	21.74
3–4 month	10	9.90	1	7.14	11	9.57
4–6 month	4	3.96	0	0	4	3.48
6 month–1 year	9	8.91	3	21.43	12	10.43
Above 1 year	21	20.79	6	42.86	27	23.48
Total	101	100	14	100	115	100

9. Miscarriage and Abortion

Incident of miscarriages are noted among 13 per cent of women. In a few cases (about 2 per cent), it is more than twice. The miscarriage often takes place among younger women. This may be due to the very early age of marriage. About 51 per cent of women become mother at the age of below 18. Besides, malnutrition often becomes the reason of miscarriage among poor women.

The abortion especially the sex-selective abortion is increasing rapidly in different states of India. According to Bardhan and Klasen (1999), although some 100 million women are 'missing' globally through the methods of female infanticide or sex-selective abortions, there is still underestimation of the 'missing women' in GDI and the GEM. However, the cases of abortions noted in our study, are not sex selective in nature. The people living below poverty level do not have the financial strength to go for a test of the sex of foetus. The overall rate of abortion is very low among the women. Only 3 per cent of women have experienced abortions, of which nearly 50 per cent have gone through the process of abortion twice. In case of these abortions, again the decisions are not taken by women. In most cases the male counterparts have taken the decision of aborting unwanted child conceived due to non practicing family planning programme. In most cases the abortions are done by local quack.

10. Disease and Access to Health Facilities

In an enquiry on the incident of disease among women it is found that 36 per cent (183 out of 500) of women suffered from various health problems in the last two years. About 27 per cent of women (*i.e.* 10 per cent of total) who were affected by health problems did not get any kind of health care or medicine to get recovery of the problems. Among the women who got the access to health facilities, 62 per cent are treated by the local quack (Table. 7). About 14 per cent and 24 per cent of women are treated in nearest health centres and in hospitals respectively. None of them have been able to afford the health care provided either by private medical practitioner or by the private nursing home.

Table 7 : Access to Health Facilities

Type of health service	*SGSY*		*SHG*		*Total*	
	Total	*Percentage*	*Total*	*Percentage*	*Total*	*Percentage*
Health centre	43	11.26	25	21.19	68	13.60
Hospital	88	23.04	32	27.12	120	24.00
Local Quack	249	65.18	61	51.69	310	62.00
Nursing home	2	0.52	0	0	4	0.40
Total	382	100	118	100	500	100

The place of delivery is another significant parameter in the study of access to health facilities for women. On an average, 80 per cent (Table 8) of women beneficiaries of SHGs gave birth of their children at home with the help of local *Dhais* (untrained midwife). This percentage is higher in case of SGSY group members than that of SHG members. This is due to the difference in the levels of poverty for SGSY and SHG women.

About 19 per cent of women gave birth of their children in public hospitals. The proportion is only 1 per cent in case of local health centres as most of the health centres do not have in-patient beds and labour room equipments.

Table 8 : Place of Delivery

	SGSY		*SHG*		*Total*	
	No. of Women	*Percentage*	*No. of Women*	*Percentage*	*No. of Women*	*Percentage*
Home	309	83.74	71	66.98	380	80.00
Health center	6	1.63	0	0	6	1.26
Hospital	54	14.63	35	33.02	89	14.74
Total	369	100	106	100	475	100

No significant impact of access to income is observed on women in the decisions of childbirth. Regarding the birth of child the decision is often taken by their husbands. Very insignificant proportion (1.5 per cent) of women has reported to take decisions of child birth on their own (Table 9). However, more than half of women have reported that they are often consulted by their husband and take decisions together regarding childbirth. The inclusion of women in the decision making process have increased after they have started to contribute to the family income.

Table 9 : Decision Making Regarding the Birth of Children

Decision maker	*SGSY*		*SHG*		*Total*	
	No.of women	*Percentage*	*No. of women*	*Percentage*	*No. of women*	*Percentage*
Self	6	1.63	1	0.94	7	1.47
Husband	166	44.99	47	44.34	213	44.84
Joint	197	53.38	58	54.72	255	53.69
Total	369	100	106	100	475	100

11. Women Empowerment

Autonomy is a multidimensional concept related to empowerment. Dyson and Moore (1983) has been defined autonomy as the capacity to manipulate one's personal environment. Gandhi and Shah (1999) viewed it as a process with continuous involvement rather than a state. They also stated that autonomy should not only incorporate individual beliefs, desires, and choices, but also the social context in which they are made. For example, female autonomy has been found to change over the course of a women's lifetime in some societies. In India, particularly in the North, women acquire more autonomy as they age and produce sons, and then lose autonomy when they are elderly or widow (Das Gupta, 1996).

Ultimately autonomy in different aspects of life empowers women to develop their authority both within and outside households. It would appear that control over the family purse must automatically give women a degree of authority, and this is often assumed to be so (Dixit, 1998). However, some sociologists like Hollensteiner and Burcraff (1975) have pointed out that control over cash does not confer power, since poverty dictates expenditure until income are high enough to give some options. Sometimes women also do not use their economic status to push for their preferences in an overt manner, instead maintaining their relationships through compromise (Kabeer, 1999). Kelkar (2005) opined that there are also women who keep quite and show nothing but compliance to male dominance; this is done as a result of fear of insult and physical assault.

Table 10 : Health Related Authority Index

	Types of Decision Making			
Issues of Decision Making	*Husband*	*Wife*	*Joint*	*Total*
Family planning	160	9	331	500
Family expenditure	257 (51.35%)	43 (8.7%)	199 (39.87%)	500 (100%)
Medical Treatment	207 (41.32%)	63 (12.63%)	230 (46.05%)	500 (100%)

Following Ruhul (1997), we have tried to understand the levels of authority achieved by women after joining SHGs with the help of authority index. Women rarely enjoy independent authority in health related aspects such as family planning, family expenditure and medical treatment (Table 10). Women's decision making in family panning is of insignificant level *i.e.* only around 2 per cent. Nearly 8 per cent of women take decisions regarding family expenditure which covers the purchase of food items. The proportion of women taking decisions regarding medical treatment is slightly better (12 per cent) in comparison to other two aspects. However, one positive aspect is that women are often being included in the decision making. The rate of joint decisions in household affairs has increased after women started to make financial contribution to the family through SHG related activities.

From the study it can be concluded that the impacts of SHGs on the reproductive health status of poor women have started to change, where women have achieved success in livelihood generation as well as in contributing income to the family. But the change is not of that scale as perceived and demanded by the state agencies. Nowadays, MFIs are more concerned only with credit related activities rather than the overall well-being of poor rural women including the health production potential. However, there is no doubt that these schemes may play a good role in health production and are highly dependent on two key elements – female autonomy at the individual level and social solidarity at the group level. Lastly following Mohindra (2003: 35) it can be stated that if existing poverty requires not only raising income levels, but also achieving good health, and poverty remains the main cause of ill-health, comprehensive strategies are required to improve the well-being of poor women. Initiatives through SHGs to improve the health production potential can increase the effectiveness and efficiency of outcomes in well-being, and overall equity impacts of interventions involving social change.

12. Acknowledgement

The author is indebted to ICSSR for funding the research project 'Women's Self-help Groups, Poverty Alleviation and Women's Empowerment: A Case Study of Burdwan District', from which the data are used in the paper.

REFERENCES

Acharya, Meena and Puspa Ghimire (2005) : 'Gender indicators of equality, inclusion and poverty reduction: Measuring programme/project effectiveness', *Economic and Political Weekly* 40(44&45) : 4719-4728.

Agnihotri, S.B. (2002) : 'High female literacy, low child population : Is there a threshold effect?' *Economic and Political Weekly* 37 (39) : 4054-4059.

Bardhan, Kalpana and Stephan Klasen (1999) : 'UNDP's gender-related indices : A critical review', *World Development*, 27 : 985-1010.

Bhat, M. (2000) : 'Returning a favour: Changing relationship between female education and family size in India.' Paper presented for the workshop on Fertility Change in Developing Countries held at King's College, Cambridge, UK, May 25-26.

Bhatty, Zarina (1987) : 'Economic contribution of women to the household budget : A case study of the Beedi Industry' in Singh, Andrea Menefee and Anita Kelles-Viitanen (eds) *Invisible Hands : Women in Home-Based Production, Women and the Household : in Asia Series*, Vol.-I, New Delhi : Sage Publications.

Boserup, E. (1970) : *Women's Role in Economic Development*, Allen and Unwin, London.

Chakraborty, S. (1987) : *Development Planning : The Indian Experience*, Oxford : Clarendon Press.

Charmes, Jacques and Saskia Wieringa (2003) : 'Measuring Women's Empowerment : An Assessment of the Gender-related Development Index and the Gender Empowerment Measure', *Journal of Human Development* 4(3): 419-435.

Dandekar, V.M. and N. Rath (1971) : *Poverty in India*, Pune : Indian School of Political Economy.

Dasgupta, R. (2006) : 'An architectural plan for a microfinance institutional network', *Economic and Political Weekly* 41(11) : 1095-4872.

Deolaikar, Anil B. (2005) : *Attaining the Millennium Development Goals in India*, Oxford University Press and the World Bank.

Dijkstra, Geske A. and Lucia Hanmer (2000) : 'Measuring socio-economic gender inequality, towards an alternative to the UNDP Gender-Related Development Index', *Feminist Economics*, 6(2) : 41-75.

Dixit, Maitreya (1998) : *Women and Achievement : Dynamics of Participation and Partnership*, New Delhi : Kanishka Publishers.

Dreze, Jean and Amartya Sen (2002) : *India Development and Participation*, Delhi : Oxford University Press.

Dyson, T. and B. Moore (1983) : 'On kinship structure, female autonomy, and demographic behaviour in India', *Population and Development Review* 9(1) : 35-60.

Eswaran, M. and A. Kotwal (1994) : *Why Poverty Persists in India*, Delhi : Oxford University Press.

Gandhi, N. and N. Shah (1999) : 'Organizations and autonomy' in N. Menon (ed.) *Gender and Politics In India*, New Delhi : Oxford University Press.

Gulati, Leela (1996) : *In the Absence of Their Men : The Impact of Male Migration on Women*, Buckingham : Open University Press.

Hirway, Indira (2003) : 'Identification of BPL households for poverty alleviation programmes', *Economic and Political Weekly* 38 (45) : 4803-4808.

Hollnsteiner, M.R. and R. Burcraff (1975) : 'The role of women in the Philippines', technical paper presented at International Conference on Women, Mexico City.

James, K. S. (1999) : 'Fertility decline in Andhra Pradesh : A search for alternative hypothesis,' *Economic and Political Weekly*, February 20-26.

Kabeer, Naila (1999) : 'The conditions and consequences of choice : Reflections on the measurement of women's empowerment', *Discussion Paper* 108, UNRISD, Geneva.

Kelkar, Govind (2005) : 'Development effectiveness through gender mainstreaming : Gender equality and poverty reduction in South Asia', *Economic and Political Weekly* 40(44 & 45) : 4690-4699.

Kumar, A. and C.P. Yadav (1994) : 'Poverty Alleviation Through Employment Generation' in A. Kumar (ed.) *New Approach in Rural Development*, New Delhi : Anmol Publications Pvt. Ltd.

Lal, D. (1973) : *New Economic Policies for India*, London : Fabian Society.

Madhok, Sumi (2003) : 'A limited women's empowerment : Politics, the state, and development in northwest India', *Women's Studies Quarterly*, 31(3/4): 154-173, Academic Research Library.

Mohindra, K.S. (2003) : 'A report on self help groups (SHGs) in Kerala state, India: a public health perspective', Report prepared for FCRSS/IRSC, Universite de Montreal.

Mazumdar, Veena (1985) : *Emergence of Women's Questions in India and the Role of Women*, New Delhi : Centre for Women's Development Studies.

Mellor, J.W. (1976) : The New Economics of Growth : A Strategy for India and the Developing World, New York : Cornell University Press.

Minhas, B.S. (1970) : 'Rural Poverty, Land Redistribution and Development Strategy : Facts and Policy', *Indian Economic Review*, April.

Rajagopal, S. and K. Mathur (2000) : 'Women's empowerment through state benevolence', *Economic and Political Weekly* 35(33) : 2908-2910.

Raju, Saraswati (2005) : 'Limited options-rethinking women's empowerment "projects" in development discourses : A case from rural India', *Gender, Technology and Development* 9(2) : 253-271.

Rao, C.H.H. (1994) : Agricultural Growth, Rural Poverty and Environmental Degradation in India, Delhi : Oxford University Press.

Ruhul, Amin (1997) : *Development Strategies and Socio Demographic Impact of Non-Governmental Organizations : Evidence from Rural Bangladesh*, Dhaka : The University Press Ltd.

Rustagi, Preet (2000) *Gender Development Indicators : Issues, Debates and Ranking of Districts*, Occasional Paper No.33, New Delhi : Centre for Women's Development Studies.

Singh, A.K. (1994) : 'Role of IRDP in Eradicating Rural Poverty' in A. Kumar (ed.) *New Approach in Rural Development*, New Delhi : Anmol Publications Pvt. Ltd.

Tapan, Neeta (2000) : *Need for Women Empowerment*, Jaipur & New Delhi : Rawat Publications.

Visaria, P. and L. Visaria (1994) : 'Demographic transition : Accelerating fertility decline in the 1980s' *Economic and Political Weekly* 24 (51 & 52): 3281-92.

Waylen, Georgina (1996) : *Gender in third world politics*, Buckingham: Open University Press.

21

Reproductive Health of Poor Urban Women in Indore

— *Rahul Banerjee*

A sixteen year old unmarried girl from a slum in Indore city in Madhya Pradesh was recently taken to a quack doctor for an abortion when she was five months pregnant. The quack gave her some potion to drink and also pressed her lower abdomen with his hands continuously and aborted the foetus. Later on after coming home she began bleeding profusely and had to be rushed to a government hospital where the doctors removed her uterus and saved her. This horrendous incident on analysis brings out the following serious obstacles that prevent poor urban women from successfully addressing their reproductive health problems—

1. A taboo on discussing reproductive health problems unless matters go out of control.
2. A taboo on discussing sexuality issues with adolescents leading to unwanted pregnancies among unmarried girls.
3. The lack of access to good and certified reproductive health treatment.

This alarming situation has prompted an NGO in Indore, Aarohi Nyas, to try and do something towards improving matters. As a preliminary step the NGO undertook a desk review of the status of reproductive health in India and that of poor urban women in Indore as a prelude to devising a suitable action research programme to address this problem area. Detailed below is a report based on this desk review.

1. Status of Women's Reproductive Health in India

Current thinking among feminists broadly defines the discipline of reproductive and sexual health as the social and clinical study of those problems and diseases that arise from the social asymmetries influencing human sexuality and reproduction. Specifically a reproductive health approach has been defined as that which "enables women and men, including adolescents, everywhere to regulate their own fertility safely and effectively by conceiving when they desire, terminating unwanted pregnancies and carrying wanted pregnancies to term; to remain free of disease, disability or death associated with reproduction or sexuality and to bear and raise healthy children." (Germain & Ordway, 1989). In reality, however, this ideal state of affairs does not prevail anywhere in the world and especially in India most women have to suffer from serious reproductive and sexual health problems. Feminist sociology has pinpointed the dominance of men in society as the prime reason for this and termed this phenomenon as patriarchy (Lerner, 1986). Analysing all the main institutions of society like the family, marriage, kinship groups, media, religious hierarchies and the state, they have shown that all these play a role in maintaining the overall patriarchal structure of society. Over thousands of years this structure has become so well entrenched that to most people including women it seems quite natural instead of being a social construct as it really is.

As a result traditionally women have had to work more, they have been denied the right to inheritance of property, they have had to assume total responsibility for house work and the care of children and the elderly and this work is not counted as of being of any economic value, they have had to go underfed and have been subjected to domestic and external violence of the worst kind. As a consequence of this secondary status women have to bear more babies to ensure that there are male progeny who will inherit the property and provide security in old age. Along with this there is social control over the sexuality of women so that men can be assured that the children born to their wives are truly theirs and so ensure the purity of their descent. Naturally all this affects the overall health of women and especially their reproductive and sexual health. Since there is a taboo on the discussion of these issues women have to suffer their troubles in silence and this leads to mental problems. Thus there is a deafening culture of silence surrounding women's reproductive and sexual health problems (Dixon-Mueller & Wasserheit, 1991). The biggest irony is that the menstrual cycle which is an integral part of the reproductive process is considered in the prevailing patriarchal system to be the cause of various negative things and given a dirty connotation in this country. This affects the ability of women to maintain personal hygiene and results in their being afflicted by various diseases of the reproductive tract.

Analysing the history of health policy in India Prakash has shown how patriarchal social structures have resulted in the marginalisation of women in the health system in this country (Prakash, 1984). Right from the time in the late nineteenth century when for the first time women's health problems were addressed the concentration has been on the provision of maternal health services like safe delivery practices. Even though as a consequence of the efforts of Pandita Ramabai and Lady Dufferin pregnant women began to get access to institutional health services the general reproductive health and associated psychological health problems of women remained unaddressed. Thus continuously ante-natal and post natal care has been provided and the problems of the reproductive tract and sexuality have been neglected. Health policies have been silent about the negative effects of patriarchy on the physical and mental health of women. Thus it is no surprise that the sex ratio which was 972 females to 1000 males in 1911 had declined to 930 by 2001. Matters have been compounded by the use of pre-natal diagnostic techniques to abort female foetuses and this is done mostly by higher income groups indicating that patriarchy is prevalent throughout society irrespective of various divisions (Mari Bhat & Francis Zavier, 2007).

The report submitted by the Health Survey Committee headed by Sir John Bhore in 1946 did stress that the whole gamut of health problems of women should be addressed instead of just concentrating on safe motherhood but there was no specific mention of the problems or reproductive health and sexuality and the ways in which these could be solved. Immediately after independence the economists engaged in the preparation of the First Five Year Plan did not consider the work put in by women inside the home to be of a productive nature and so made no allocation for the overall health of women and concentrated only on providing for safe motherhood. The stress on maternal health over the first half of the twentieth century did produce a number of female doctors and nurses who were also abreast of the latest developments in reproductive health but only the women of rich households had access to the benefits of this knowledge and the vast majority of poor women in this country remained without access to quality reproductive health services.

Government policies for women largely centred around putting most of the responsibility for family planning onto them. Completely ignoring the ground reality that in the patriarchal social structure that prevails in India there is a preference for male children which forces women to bear more children and so the thrust of the programme should be towards mitigating patriarchy the government family planning programme concentrated on doing sterilisations of women given the reluctance of men to get sterilised irrationally fearing a loss of their sexual powers. Thus in addition to the suffering from poor reproductive health women had to shoulder the burden of family planning also. All kinds of dubious experiments involving injectables were carried out during this campaign (FWH, 1995).

Consequently when a joint study group of the Indian Council of Medical Research and and the Indian Council of

Social Science Research conducted a review of women's health in 1980 it found that the main reasons behind high maternal mortality rates and the decline of the sex ratio were the malnutrition and poor reproductive health of most women. The group also averred that this had happened because the government had looked at women only as prospective mothers neglecting their exploitation within and outside the home in a highly patriarchal social setting. However, despite this scathing report there was no improvement in the health policies with regard to women. This despite the fact that the government had endorsed the declaration of the First World Women's Conference organised by the United Nations in Mexico in 1975 which exhorted both governments and the people at large to—"recognise the health needs of women of all ages and situations, those with children, girls who were yet to reach child bearing age and women who had passed the child bearing age range and also those living singly or as couples, give women the right to choose the number of children they wish to have and also the spacing between them and prevent any such discrimination and violence that is against the welfare of women, that prevents them from taking active part in the social, economic and political development of their societies and that violates their human rights" (Whitaker, 1975).

The first effective steps towards improving the status of women's reproductive health in India were taken by NGOs in the 1980s. The pioneer in this respect is the NGO SEARCH in Gadhchiroli district of Maharashtra. In the course of their work among the adivasis they found that all women were not reporting their gynaecological problems properly. So they decided to conduct a detailed study which has now become a landmark in this field (Bang, 1989). The study revealed that 55% of the women surveyed admitted to some gynaecological problem or other but when they were tested clinically this percentage rose to 92. The most disturbing finding was that only 8% of these women had come to the NGO for treatment of their problems indicating a tremendous level of reticence to confront their serious reproductive health problems. Many other studies later have confirmed these disturbing findings (Jeejeebhoy, 1997).

The decade of the nineteen nineties saw a concerted effort by feminists all over the world to improve this sorry state of affairs. The basis of this campaign was the establishment of the reproductive and sexual rights of women (Correa & Petchesky, 1994). According to this view there are four aspects of reproductive and sexual rights—

1. **Bodily Integrity**—All women have the right to protect their bodies and have control over them. Thus women cannot be deprived of their sexual and productive abilities by men or the state and they cannot be made to use these abilities according to the latter's whims and fancies.
2. **Personhood**—Women will take their own decisions regarding reproduction and sexual behaviour and nobody can interfere in this.
3. **Equality**—Women are equal to men in all respects and so the gender division of labour under which women have been given the work of exclusively tending the children and the elderly and also doing housework has to be abolished and men should also take up these responsibilities. Apart from this women's health issues should be better addressed on par with those of men.
4. **Diversity**—The differences arising from difference in values, culture, religion, class, nationality and the like should be respected.

The International Conference on Population and Development organised by the United Nations in Cairo in 1994 and the World Women's Conference in Beijing in 1995 finally led to the adoption of this feminist viewpoint and an appeal was made to all governments to tailor their women's health programmes to meet these parameters. In consonance with this the Government of India made a revolutionary change in its population policies and replaced the sterilisation target oriented family planning programme with a more comprehensive reproductive and overall health programme in which the participation of women was made mandatory (DoFW, 1996).

This new programme charted out a major role for NGOs assuming that the government machinery was incapable of ensuring the participation of women. As a result throughout India a number of NGOs became active in this field and adopted the reproductive and sexual rights approach to women's health. One such is the Stree Hitkarini in Mumbai working among poor slum women. In order to assess the extent of the reproductive health problems of the women in its area of work before embarking on a programme of amelioration this NGO conducted a reproductive health survey among 750 slum women. This study too revealed that 73% of the women suffered from some reproductive health problem or other and they did not seek any remedy for them (Parikh *et al.*, 1996).

However, since NGOs have only a limited reach they have not been able to make much of an impact on a national scale and so even after a decade of the adoption of the new reproductive health approach the status of women has not improved much. The recently concluded National Family Health Survey III has confirmed this (IIPS, 2007). Given in the table below are data for selected characteristics from NFHS III for the whole of India and they are quite disappointing—

Table 1 : Selected Reproductive Health Characteristics of Indian Women

Characteristic	*Female*	*Male*
Adults with below normal Body Mass Index (%)	33.0	28.0
Adults with anaemia (%)	56.2	24.3
Mothers with complete Ante-Natal Care (%)	50.7	
Mothers with complete Post-Natal Care (%)	36.4	
Institutional Deliveries (%)	40.7	
Women 20-24 yrs. married before 18 years of age (%)	44.5	
Women15-19 yrs. who were pregnant/had child (%)	16.0	
Women who have suffered Domestic Violence (%)	37.2	
Total Fertility Rate (%)	2.7	

Source : National Family Health Survey III conducted by International Institute of Population Sciences, Mumbai.

A recent comparative study of the data from the first, second and third National Family Health Surveys has come up with an extremely disturbing finding (Shrinivasan *et al.*, 2007). Even though the spending on family planning by the Government of India after the initiation of the new reproductive health approach in 1996 in the years 1998 -2004 has been double that in the earlier period from 1992 - 1998 the improvement rate in the case of many characteristics given in the table above has been less during the later period. This clearly means that not enough is being done to tackle the deleterious effects of patriarachy which is at the root of most of the reproductive and sexual health problems faced by women.

2. Status of Women's Reproductive Health in the Slums of Indore

The women living in slums in Indore have largely remained outside the purview of qualified medical help and have had to rely mostly on quacks as borne out by the story of the girl related in the beginning. Thus it has been left to NGOs to deliver what little service they can to them. The most important of such efforts is that being undertaken by the Urban Health Resource Centre, New Delhi with funding from USAID in collaboration with five local NGOs of Indore (Agarwal & Bhanot, 2004). The main thrust of this programme named the Environmental Health Programme is on involving the community in the accessing of the government's reproductive and child health services and so improve the health of women and children and reduce the infant, child and maternal mortality rates. 87 Community Based Organisations (CBO) have been formed in the slums and these have then been grouped together to form 9 Lead CBOs. Apart from creating health awareness among the people the NGOs also hold monthly health camps in which doctors come and do check ups and provide medicines to the women. However, this programme too following the general trend in India provides only help for maternal and child health and skirts the larger issue of reproductive and sexual health and patriarchy. Indeed the programme had initially begun with interventions only in child health and has taken up maternal health also because it found that this was imperative if child health was to be improved (Agarwal *et al.*, 2005).

Another NGO, Family Planning Association of India, also provides reproductive health services to poor urban women. However, this organisation too has not done any work on the issues of reproductive and sexual health of women and the larger issue of patriarchy which gives rise to problems in this area. There are a number of other NGOs that work on the livelihood aspects of slum dwellers and their rights as citizens to proper housing, civic amenities and other benefits. One such NGO, Deenbandhu Samajik Sansthan, did an extensive study of the vulnerability of the slum dwellers in Indore in 1997-98 (George *et al.*, 1998). This study found that 63% of the population of Indore lives in slums and 50% of these slum dwellers live in houses of less than 35 sq meter area. 78% of these people have only kuccha housing and 70% have no ration cards. 43% of the households do not have access to any toilets either individual or community and have to defecate in the open. 88% of the households depend on public taps for their water supply. None of the women surveyed at that time had any access to government health services and relied wholly on quacks.

Thus it is clear that the status of reproductive and sexual

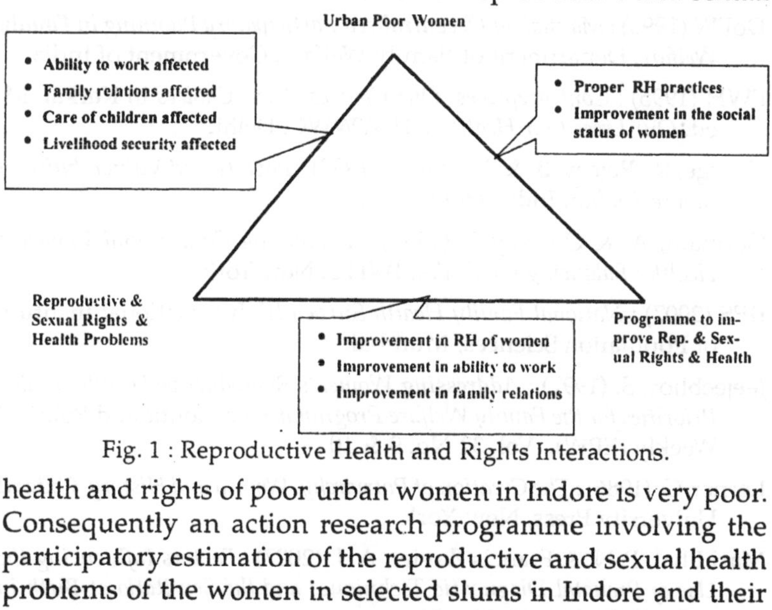

Fig. 1 : Reproductive Health and Rights Interactions.

health and rights of poor urban women in Indore is very poor. Consequently an action research programme involving the participatory estimation of the reproductive and sexual health problems of the women in selected slums in Indore and their redressal through community involvement has been initiated. The general interactions that will be addressed in this action research programme are depicted in the figure above–

REFERENCES

Agarwal, S. & Bhanot, A (2004) : *Participatory Community Health Enquiry and Planning in Urban Slums*, Urban Health Resource Centre, Delhi.

Agarwal, S., Bhanot, A., Kumar, S., Rao, S., Jha, P., Gupta, M. & Shrivastava, K. (2005) : *Partnerships for Improving Health in Vulnerable Slums of Indore*, Urban Health Resource Centre, Delhi.

Bang, R. (1989) : *High Prevalence of Gynaecological Diseases in Rural Indian Women*, Lancet 337 : 85-88.

Correa, S. & Petchesky, R. (1994) : *Reproductive and Sexual Rights : A Feminist Perspective* in Sen, G. & Germain, A. & Chen, L. ed *Population Policies Reconsidered : Health, Empowerment and Rights*. Harvard University Press.

Dixon-Mueller, R. & Wasserheit, J. (1991) : *The Culture of Silence: Reproductive Tract Infections among Women in the Third World*, IWHC, New York.

DoFW (1996) : *Manual on Decentralised Participatory Planning in Family Welfare*, Department of Family Welfare, Government of India.

FWH (1995) : *Contraceptives: Our Choices, Their Choices* in Karkal, M. ed. *Our Lives Our Health*, CUIWWWC, Delhi.

George, R., Rajeev, B. & Sarwal, T. (1998) : *Poverty and Vulnerability in Indore*, Oxfam India Trust, Delhi.

Germain, A. & Ordway, J. (1989) : *Population Control and Women's Health : Balancing the Scales*, IWHC, New York.

IIPS (2007) : *National Family Health Survey III*, International Institute of Population Sciences, Mumbai.

Jeejeebhoy, S. (1997) : *Addressing Women's Reproductive Health Needs : Priorities for the Family Welfare Programme*, Economic and Political Weekly (EPW), Vol. 32 No. 9 & 10.

Lerner, G. (1986) : *The Creation of Patriarchy: Women and History*, Oxford University Press, New York.

Mari Bhat, P. N. & Francis Zavier, A. J. (2007) : *Factors Influencing the Use of Prenatal Diagnostic Techniques and the Sex Ratio at Birth in India*, EPW, Vol. 42, No. 24.

Parikh, I., Taskar, V., Dharap, N. & Mulgaonkar, V. (1996) : *Gynaecological Morbidity Among Women in a Bombay Slum,* Stri Hitkarini. Mumbai.

Prakash, P. (1984) : *Who Controls the Health of Women : Health Policies and the Medical Profession* in Bhaiyya, A. & Bhasin, K. ed *Aspects of Women's Development,* FAO, Delhi.

Shrinivasan, K., Chandra Shekhar & Arokiaswamy, P. (2007) : *Reviewing Reproductive and Child Health Programme in India.* EPW, Vol. 42, No. 27 & 28.

Whitaker, J. S. (1975) : *Women of the World: Report from Mexico City,* Foreign Affairs.

22

The Changing Face of Gender Gap in Health

Mausumi Manna

1. Introduction

Among the various necessities in life- biological, economic, social, cultural and so on- the most tangible gender gap may be observed in health and education. The gender gap in health easily unfolds in women's poorer access to health care and treatment in comparison with men, manifested in higher female mortality including maternal mortality, high prevalence of illness, morbidity and other symptoms. Basu (1993) comments that we now have passed the stage of establishing that gender difference in health and mortality does exist, especially in the South Asian region, which may even have widened over time in some areas. Researches on whether the gender gap in health is being narrowed in specific regions and among certain population groups, while it is widening in other regions and among other groups have been inconclusive (Dyson, 1984). Studies on women's health in India have noted some improvements in disease prevention and treatments, and in maternal care. But they also highlight the inadequacy of low-cost services as well as poor health status of women belonging to low-income categories. Datta Gupta (1998) comments that even after 50 years of independence medical help does not reach the female child as often as it should, and female child mortality remains higher than that of the male child. While researches on women's health confirm the existence of a gender gap in health, few questions remain pertinent. What is the nature of the gender gap in health and what explains its existence? In the classical sense, for gender gap to exist, women must be subjected to this gap as a block, as a sex-based class. The existence of the gender gap somewhat presupposes that men and women exist as two differently identifiable category. It is not just the biological difference that creates the gap; though the health need is essentially linked to biology at least as far the reproductive health is concerned. The gender gap in true sense must be independent of all the background variables like family income, religion, language, culture and others that determine the position of an individual. In other words, women must suffer common deprivation only as women, irrespective of their religion, language, culture etc. It need not only be about deprivation, but can refer to common decision-making, or interest-sharing where women participate as a block to differ from men, considering men also as a block, like women's voting block in having a decisive role in the national election in U.S. (Mueller, 1988).

When we are talking about the gender gap in health, are we really talking in the classical sense of the term? In this article we suggest that the gap is no longer independent of all other background variables, which it was half a century back. Rather the gender gap in health is becoming increasingly depended upon the income gap and the rural-urban gap. I refer to this phenomenon as the changing face of gender gap in health. My exposition is like this—as the health service sector is becoming increasingly dual in nature with substantial rural-urban gap, with profit acting as the major force in disbursing health goods in the upcoming private sector health market and the public sector being burdened with the responsibility of providing health services to the poor, the income gap and the rural-urban gap are becoming highly powerful in determining access to health care and treatment. Given this changing scenario women no longer suffer common deprivation in health care as a block. The gender gap in health is narrowing in the upper segment of the society, while it is widening in the lower segment. Reduction of gender gap in health does not necessarily mean end of all gender inequalities, even among the richest population. But this change in the nature of the gender gap is important to note both from the theoretical perspective, and from the point of view of policy formulation. Besides, it complicates the question–what determines the gender gap in health. The purpose of this article is to highlight this change and discuss its importance with respect to the women's question.

The article is organised as follows. In the next section I have dealt more elaborately on the definitional aspect of the gender gap. In the following section I have discussed how the gender gap in health is changing face over time. Here I have used the health experiences of women in West Bengal, owing to my familiarity with the region. Before I proceed further, few clarifications and notes on future research need to be mentioned. A full quantitative exercise on the proposition made in this article requires reliable access to health data in the private sector, which is slowly accumulating. Such an exercise can be taken up as future research. The proposition we have made, *viz.* the gender gap in health is changing face presupposes a democratic set up, where the health market is open to all. We assume that there is no autocratic control over women's movement in accessing health care services. We assume that the barriers faced by women are economic, or socio-cultural, but not dictated by militancy or similar coercive forces. The experiences of the women in West Bengal need not prompt us to generalise on the nature of the gender gap in health all over India, but it does provoke a rethinking on the state of gender gap in health in the country and on the factors that determine the gender gap in health. A comparative study based on micro level experiences in different regions and cultures in India is expected to provide us with a better insight in this regard.

2. Defining the Changing Face of the Gender Gap

We have argued that a gender gap really exists if it is present independent of other variables. Let us clarify this with the help of an imaginary society, which contains six members : 3 males and 3 females. These people belong to three income categories–upper, middle, and lower. Let us present the income-wise and sex-wise classification of the members in this imaginary society in the following format :

Income	*Female (% share in family income)*	*Male (% share in family income)*
Upper	A [50, 75, 65]	B [50, 25, 35]
Middle	C [50, 75, 55]	D [50, 25, 45]
Lower	E [50, 75, 75]	F [50, 25, 25]

The share in the family income enjoyed by these six members is denoted in the parentheses with the help of imaginary percentages. We have asigned the members three different percentages of shares, which we suggest decide their access to the family income. Under situation 1, where the share in family income is 50 per cent for both the man and the woman in the family, there is no gender inequality in the distribution of family income among the different members of the society. We can comment that this society has no gender gap in terms of distribution of family income. But there exists an income gap in the society, whereby B, D, and F, the three women, enjoy varying standards of living. The variation in the standards depends upon the magnitude of the income gap. Situations 2 and 3, where the percentage share in the family income is different for the man and the woman in the family, presence of both income gap and gender gap are reflected. Here we have taken the distribution of the family income to be unfavourable to women under situations 2 and 3 by assumption, but it could have been otherwise also. In that case we could have noticed a gender gap unfavourable to men as a block. However, the distribution of ownership of resources in the world is grossly unfavourable to women as a block, which is a determining factor in creating a gender gap in health. The difference between situation 2 and situation 3 is that in situation 2 the gender gap is of equal magnitude in all the three income categories, but it is of varying magnitude under situation 3. The most important fact is that under both the situations women as a block are subject to a common deprivation, *viz*. unequal share in the family income. However, materially speaking, B must be better off than D, who is better off than F.

Now the question is, does there exist a gender gap in all major requirements of life, which may be considered necessary for free and good living? This is a difficult question to address. There is no standard definition of freedom and good living to cut across geography and culture. Individual's preference and philosophy of life is also important. However, researches on the status of women all over the world have identified a number of status indicators in which a gender gap is usually identified. We may produce a non-exhaustive list as below :

(i) access to health care and treatment
(ii) opportunities to education and training
(iii) access to market
(iv) wage, promotion, and skill training
(v) land rights, property rights, inheritance
(vi) leisure, recreation
(vii) social mobility, participation in public life
(viii) reproductive and sexual freedom
(ix) decision making in personal , familial and social life
(x) politics

The gender gap with respect to all the above is likely to vary under different socio-cultural set up, and may not share the same relation with the background variables. For example, lack of social mobility can be positively related to family income: richer the family is, lower is the social mobility of the women. On the other hand lack of opportunities to education can be inversely related to family income: richer the family is, women have better chances to receive education. For instance in the 19th Century Bengali women from elite Hindu and elite Muslim families were under purdah, but many of them learned at home to read and write, an opportunity which working class women with greater mobility did not receive. Despite this difference in experience in life shared by the elite and non-elite women, we may say that there existed a gender gap in social mobility and opportunities to education in 19th Century Bengal because women as a whole trailed far behind men in all socio-economic categories with respect to both these components of good living. For gender gap to exist throughout the society, women as a whole must be subject to similar gender discrimination in each stratum and sub-stratum of the society. However, the gender gap can also be confined to any specific stratum or sub-stratum, say only the poor women are victims of gender gap in education, but rich women are not. In that case gender gap no longer remains an independent variable, but depends upon the income gap.

In this imaginary society there can be a gender gap in health if B, D and F always get less attention to their health needs, or do not receive proper treatment to illness in comparison with A, C and E. But health being a costly good, the capacity of the three families to spend on health is likely to be different. We assume that each family is able to spend 10 per cent of their family income on health goods. Let us now consider a situation where 10 per cent of income for the upper income group is adequate to cover the health expenditure required in time of illness for both A and B. Even if we assume that each member has to pay individually from their own share in the family income for their personal health care, under the most gender unequal distribution of family income assumed in situation 2, B can spend a sum equivalent to 5 per cent of the total family income out of her share of 25 per cent, which can adequately cover the required health expenses. But if the income gap is too wide in this society, F's share may not be adequate to cover her required health expenses. B, D and F may, however, share similar gender discrimination with respect to the other status indicators. But if the cost of health goods is fully bearable by A & B, only partially by C & D, and not at all by E & F, in our society there exists no gender gap in health in the upper income group, which may be there in the lower income groups if the distribution of the health goods among the family members is subjected to gender discrimination. The gender gap in health in this case depends upon the magnitude of the income gap, and the cost of health services in relation to the family's ability to bear them. We here argue that in our country the gender gap in health is becoming increasingly dependent upon the income gap, as well as the rural-urban gap because of the lop-sided development of health infrastructure, and growing income inequality.

Private investment in health is rapidly increasing, which is making health a costly item of consumption, going out of the reach of poor consumers like E and F. Since higher purchasing capacity is concentrated in the urban areas, especially in the metropolis which are well connected and communicated, the rural-urban gap in health infrastructure is widening. However, better facilities are no guarantee of absence of gender gap in health. Awareness and attitude are two important factors which may act as constraints in denying all sections of women access to health care at par with men. Our assertion that the gender gap in health is changing face assumes an adequate level of awareness regarding the importance of health care for both men and women, as well as some special need for women in reproductive health. Our assumption is based on the observation that in India since the late 19th and early 20th Century there has been an organised and conscious effort in generating awareness regarding women's health need. Since independence there have also been governmental efforts in adopting special programmes in maternal and child health, and in recent years in reproductive health. There have also been initiatives in spreading awareness and information taken by both government and non-government organisations, though these can still be considered inadequate. If lack of awareness and information does not pose itself as serious constraint, the interdependence between the gender gap and the income gap can be more minutely examined. In order to see how the gender gap in health may be changing face, we can refer to women's experience in Bengal, where there has been a long history in both intellectual exercise and activism in relation to women's health.

Gender gap in health in pre and post independent W. Bengal

Studies on the state of women's health in colonial Bengal point out a gender gap cutting across all social and economic classes. In the city of Calcutta women from wealthy, elite families lacked proper attention to health needs. Missionary women working in Calcutta have drawn a depressing picture of the state of women's health here. As an illustration we can mention Margaret Urquhart's observations regarding the health and hygiene in the kitchen and labour room of elite families. She found them dirty, full of dust, cobwebs, bugs and insects (Urquhart, 1925). In the 18th and 19th Century the state of public health in the city of Calcutta was worse than that in the districts. Shibnath Shastri's *Ramtanu Lahiri O Tatkalin Bango Samaj*, Kali Prasanna Sigha's *Hutom Penchar Naksa* and other contemporary literary accounts in Bengali gives a good account of the open drains, latrines and unsafe drinking water in the city. Similar picture was also portrayed in contemporary periodicals run by both natives and the Europeans. The state of public health in Calcutta gradually improved through the establishment of the Sanitary Board and city hospitals. But till the late colonial period, women all over Bengal suffered ill health in comparison with men, mainly owing to total neglect of proper reproductive health care. The age of marriage and first motherhood being too low, usually within 12-15 years of age, the rate of maternal mortality was too high. Macivor (1920) blamed the physical confinement of the *purdahnasins* in the monotony of the home to be responsible for the poor physical health and low mental spirit of the Indian women. She observed that in the city of Calcutta where the purdah was most strict, the mortality of women was 40 per cent higher than that of men.

Since the publication of the Census statistics from 1872 onwards the high incidences of maternal mortality drew sharper attention. The reports of various Census Commissioners in Bengal observed that the whole of the excess female mortality occurred amongst the young women in the prime of their life. O'donnel, the Commissioner of the 1891 Census blamed the excess female mortality on maternal mortality alone, as huge deficit of females were observed in the 15-50 age group, but there were excess females in the age groups below and above that. The unhealthy conditions in the labour rooms even in the elite households in Calcutta have also been reported in Borthwick (1984). She noted that the *sutikagriha* or the *aturghar* (labour room) was always the smallest and the darkest room in the house, a physical embodiment of the impurity associated with child birth. Fire was lit in the room immediately after the delivery, creating suffocating condition not conducive to the good health of the mother and the infant.[2] Even when modern western medicine and institutionalised delivery facilities were made available, there was reservation among the *bhadralok* class to use them. Doctors studying in the Calcutta Medical College took up mid-wifery as part of their training. Borthwick reported that only the poorest low-caste women entered hospitals for child birth, and mostly when sent by the mid-wives after complications had developed. The *bhadramohilas* gave birth in the *sutikagriha* in their own home. Risley and Gait (1901) observed that the higher caste Hindus usually had fewer women than those of the lower castes, and the Muslims had slightly larger proportion of females than the Hindus. Porter (1931) observed that the high rate of population growth in Bengal since 1921 had been achieved through high cost of deaths, mainly in terms of high infant and maternal mortality.

The gender gap in health in colonial Bengal was independent of the difference in income and social status of the women. This is not only revealed through the European eyes. The women's periodicals in the 19th and 20th Century Bengal like *Antahpur, Mahila, Bangalakshmi, Jayasree* and others regularly published notes and articles drawing attention to the dismal state of maternal and infant health in Bengal. A passage from a short story by Rabindranath Thakur, titled *Sampatti Samarpan* interestingly describes the patriarchal mindset which was largely responsible for the gender gap in health. The story runs as follows. Jnagyanath Kundu was a wealthy man. When the wife of his only son Vrindaban was seriously ill, Vrindaban requested his father to arrange for the treatment of his wife.

The father replied that if consumption of expensive medicines could save life, no King or Nawab would have ever died. He then asked Vrindaban–'the way your mother has died, your grandmother has died, do you expect your wife to die in a more extravagant way?'

But things were fast changing. Educated men were realising the need for protection of women's health. Dwarakanath Ganguli was an important educationist in Bengal who admitted his wife Kadambini to study medicine in the Calcutta Medical College because he felt that unless some women studied medicine and took up the medical profession, the various health complications suffered by women in our country could not be given proper care (Bandyopadhayaya, 1357 B.S.). The Bengali periodicals like *Bamabodhini Masik Patrika O Samalocana* since the 19th Century regularly published notes on high maternal mortality and female mortality in the city of Calcutta. It was initially through the efforts of Bengali *bhadralok* that a consciousness was generated towards the protection of women's health. A pioneering task in this regard at the all India level was taken up by the All India Women's Association founded by Annie Besant, Margaret Cousins and others. Since the very beginning women's health and education were two priority areas in AIWC activities. A consciousness regarding the unequal gender relation in all spheres of life gradually emerged not only in Bengal, but all over India, where the traditional gender roles started being analysed and questioned (Chattopadhayaya, 1939). All these acted as catalyst in reducing the gender gap in health at least at the upper stratum, and increasing women's access to health care.

We argue that this long history in facilitating improvements in women's health could not sustain because the public health infrastructure could not cope with the tremendous pressure it had to bear. The dualism in our health service sector is becoming more apparent in the post globalisation new liberal economic order. There have no doubt been some improvements in women's overall health status. The National Family Health Surveys in 1992-93 and 1998-99 (NFHS–I and NFHS-II) have shown improvements in antenatal and post-natal care as well as increase in institutionalised deliveries (Manna, 2004). A short statistical portrayal can be made as follows :

Women in West Bengal surveyed	NFHS I	NFHS II
Women receiving ante-natal care	75.4 per cent	90 per cent
Ante-natal check up by doctors	60.4 per cent	76 per cent
Institutional deliveries	31.6 per cent	41 per cent

The Government publications at the national and state level also show improvements in important health indicators for both men and women. As the Central Bureau of Health Intelligence data presented below show, in India there have been growth in the basic health facilities available for the general population, but inadequate to cater to the need of the growing population.

Public Health Facilities in India	1951	1981	2002
Hospitals	9209	23555	38031
Rural Health Centres	725	57363	163196
Hospital beds	117198	569495	914543
Doctors practicing modern medicine	61800	268700	625131

In West Bengal there has been very slow growth in rural health infrastructure. The numbers of primary health centres increased from 1251 to 1268 during 1990-91 to 1999-2000, which has remained stationary up to 2005. The number of sub-centres remained stationary at 8126 during the 1990s. The number of government hospitals including those run by voluntary agencies rose from 392 in 1990-91 to 433 in 2004-05 and number of hospital beds rose from 54447 in 1990-91 to 58312 in 2004-05. The doctor-population ratio rose from 0.000601 doctors per head to 0.0006099 doctors per head during 1990 to 2000 (Manna & Jana, 2002). Despite this improvement, the overall health status of poor women and female children are still very low. The expenditure on public sector health as percentage of total state expenditure has shown marginal increase in West Bengal. During the 8th Plan the share of health expenditure in total expenditure in the state was 1.39 per cent which rose to 3.39 per cent during the 9th Plan, but have shown substantial improvement under the 10th Plan (first five years), rising to 5.53 per cent.

Researchers have highlighted the growing economic inequality in the post-globalisation era, which is creating huge income gap in accessing health care. Women's organisations opposing new economic order have focused on the deterioration in women's health status. AIDWA (1998 conference report) argue that to show that women's health status has improved; international funding agencies and the government have quoted the increased longevity of women's lives in the last few decades. However, they have ignored the chronic illness and other medical problems crores of women are facing. As the women rarely spend the meagre family incomes on medicines and doctors' fees for their own illness; which are continually increasing, their health needs remain grossly unattended. The National Sample Survey (1999) observes that the failing of the public health system in our country is leading to rising demand for private health services.

The overall health expenditure in India is 6 per cent of the GDP, 80 per cent of which are spent on private health care. Although the World Bank Report (2000) finds that private delivery in health is expanding rapidly to public in general and even to the poor, there is huge qualitative difference in the health care and service purchased by the rich and the poor. The slow growth of public health sector, which still constitutes the main source of low cost health care to the poor, is largely responsible for greater reliance on more expensive private services. The private sector investment in health is observed to be mostly concentrated in building 'state-of-the-art health clinics' and hospitals in large metropolitan centres, where the services are affordable only to the richer section of the population. The glossy hoardings that advertise the modern facilities and comforts available in these centres do not reveal the dismal state of health in public health centres and hospitals attended by the poor.

However, there is a growing unmet need for health care among both urban and rural women belonging to low income groups. I worked as a voluntary worker for Centre for Development Activities, a local NGO based in Kolkata, in a number of health awareness camps and reproductive health counselling clinics for poor women in north Bengal, mainly around Siliguri and Haldibari during 1999-2000. My interview with the doctors and counsellors attending the clinics, as well as the case records in the clinics exposed large unmet need among the women who attended the clinics. Also contrary to popular belief young husbands accompanied wives on second visits requested by the counsellor, when symptoms of sexually transmitted diseases and urinary tract infections were detected among the women. Our interviews with quack practitioners in the Siliguri town showed that for their reproductive and sexual health needs, poor couples depend more upon the private sector despite the high costs. In a number of cases recorded in the clinics, the couples discontinued treatment after a few visits mainly owing to lack of affordability to purchase medicines. We observed a felt need which is remaining unmet owing to the lack of parity between purchasing capacity and cost of treatment.

3. Epilogue

If gender gap loses its status as an independent variable, do the factors determining the gender gap in health undergo changes? There exixts a popular belief that the gender gap in health and survival is attributed to women's low economic status in the family and the society. Women have poorer access to health care because women's life is less important than that of men, the bread winner. A rich body of empirical research on women's work have validated that women's productive services remain unrecognised; equal payments do not necessarily exist for equal job by men and women; and unpaid family labour by women are regular features. Also lack of rights over land and property are argued to reduce the economic value of women's life. Most of the status indicators mentioned in the previous section can be related to low economic status. Agarwal (1996) argues that the gender gap in the ownership and control of property is the single most critical contributor to the gender gap in economic wellbeing, social status and empowerment. Lingam (1998) reviews studies from different parts of India to reveal a gender gap in intra-household distribution of health goods and services, which are observed to be linked to low economic status of women. The view that apparent non-participation of women in the productive sphere is the factor determining the gender gap in all spheres of life has come from the orthodox Marxist approach to the issue of women's subjugation, stemming from Engels's *Origin of the Family, Private Property and State*. Feminist critiques of this view long felt that Engels's pronouncement was derived from the ideological illogicalities of male supremacy, rather than the real world of history (O'Brien, 1981). A more acceptable theoretical compromise based on a Marxist-feminist synthesis should give recognition to women's productive contribution, as well as reproductive labour, going beyond the narrow approach in which biology is considered destiny for women.

The death of young mothers in unhealthy labour rooms originate from this mindset, in which women's productive roles are ignored, and the reproductive responsibilities are considered their only worth. There has been an increase in the age of marriage and first motherhood among the educated women in our society. But mortality among young mothers from low-income families is still alarmingly high, more alarming in the rural sector in comparison with urban areas where more private facilities are available. Despite a growing feminist consciousness, women's productive as well as reproductive labour is still to be valued at par with that of men's. This tendency is certainly responsible for growing dowry demands, neglect of female child, and in extreme case the growing incidences of female foeticide. If the value of women's reproductive labour is not recognised, the family may not be encouraged to spend unnecessarily on women's reproductive and other health needs. Given this orientation, high maternal mortality and morbidity can easily be blamed on biological weakness of the female sex. However, the better access to health care availed by women from the upper and middle income groups do not always imply greater recognition of women's labour, complying with the standard theoretical explanation of women's lower health (and other) status. While the link between the importances attached to female life and the value attached to women's economic contribution can not be denied, the role of public investment and government monitoring in inducing development of the health sector in a gender-equal term remains compulsive. Affordability and availability become more powerful factors in explaining the varying magnitude of the gender gap in health in different income categories. The narrowing of the gender gap in health for A and B in our imaginary society presented in the earlier section can occur even if B has no direct access to family income, but if her health expenses are affordable to the family. F can be the sole bread-earner in her family, yet unable to meet the small expenses for her health needs. Market economy need not ensure access to health care for all in a gender-neutral manner, the responsibility lies elsewhere.

REFERENCES

Agarwal, B. (1996) : *Gender and Command Over Property : An Economic Analysis*, Kali for Women, New Delhi.

Basu, A.M. (1993) : 'Women's Roles and Gender Gap in Health and Survival', *Economic and Political Weekly*, October 23, pp. 2356-2362.

Borthwick, M. (1984) : *The Changing Role of Women in Bengal, 1849 – 1905*, Princeton University Press, Princeton.

Bandyopadhayaya, B. (1357 B.S.) : *Dwarakanath Gangopadhayaya*, Vangya Sahitya Parishad, Kolkata

Chattopadhayaya, K. *et al.* (1939) : *The Awakening of Indian Women*, Everyman's Press, Madras.

Datta Gupta, B. (1998) : The Status of Women in India in the Fiftieth Year of Independence, Purnamasi Bandyopadhayaya memorial lecture, Rabindra Bharati University

Dyson, T. (1984) : 'Excess Female Mortality in India-Uncertain Evidence on a Narrowing Differential' in Srinivasan *et al.* (ed.) *Dynamics of Population and Family Welfare*, Himalaya Publishing House, Bombay.

Government of India, (annual, 2000 – 2006) : *Health Information of India*, Ministry of Health and Family Welfare, New Delhi.

Government of West Bengal (Annual, 1990–2006) : West Bengal Economic Review, GOWB, Kolkata.

Lingam, L., (ed.) (1998) : *Understanding Women's Health Issues–A Reader*, Kali for Women, New Delhi.

Macivor, A.R. (1920) : 'Women of India–Some Characteristics,' *The Calcutta Review*, No. 300, pp. 101-123.

Manna, M. & Jana A. (2002) : 'Primary Education and Primary Health Scenario in West Bengal in the 1990s', *Artha Beekshan*, Vol. 11, No. 3, pp. 61-73.

Manna, M (2004) : 'Women's reproductive Health Status : West Bengal in Comparison with Other Indian States' in D. Mukherjee (ed) *Social Sectors of West Bengal*, St. Paul's C. M. College, Kolkata, pp. 329-347.

Mueller, C.M. (ed) (1988) : *The Politics of the Gender Gap : The Social Construction of Political Influence*, Sage Publication, Newbury Park.

National Sample Survey Organisation (1999) : *Survey on Health Care*, Department of Statistics, Government of India, New Delhi.

O'Brien, M. (1981) : *The Politics of Reproduction*, Routledge & Kegan Paul, Boston.

Porter, A.E. (1931) : The Problem of Population Growth and an Estimate of Future Population in *Census of India 1931*, Vol. V. Government of India, Delhi.

Risley, H.H. & Gait, E.A. (1901) : *Census of India, 1901*, Report, Chapter III, Government of India, Calcutta.

Urquhart, M.M. (1925) : *Women of Bengal–A Case Study of the Hindu Pardanasins of Calcutta*, Association Press, YMCA, Calcutta.

Wally, S. (1986) : 'Reflections on the Domestic Labour Debate and Prospects of Marxist-Feminist Synthesis' in Hamilton and Barret (ed) *The Politics of Diversity*, Verso, London.

World Bank (2002) : *India : Reducing Poverty, Accelerating Development*, Oxford University Press, New Delhi.

23

Time Allocation, Overlapping Activities and Work Intensity : Implications for Well Being of Women Workers

—*B. Vaithegi*

1. Introduction

In the process of economic restructuring, there has been a trend towards informalisation of employment observed in high and low income countries (Mehra and Gammage 1999, Beneria 2001). One form of informal employment is through subcontracting arrangements and there is growing representation of women in subcontract work. Several studies indicate women's high representation in different home based and subcontract arrangements adopted by the shoe industry, garment industry, fishing net industry, carpets and plastics industry (Benton 1989, Chen *et al.* 1999, Carr *et al.* 2000, Unni and Bali 2002). They show that low wages, poor working conditions, and long hours of work, irregularity and instability of employment characterised subcontract work. Labour legislations were inapplicable to this nature of work. Even though they have employment, women workers are still kept at a very disadvantaged position.

Women take up paid employment because women's

earnings have become crucial for the household income (Khattak 2002). Since women also have the major responsibility for carrying out reproductive activities even as they contribute to productive activities, the pressure on women's work has increased.[1] Women's participation in productive and reproductive work increases their workload. To cope with and manage intensification of work arising from time allocation to market work and domestic work, women may extend their working time but may also employ other strategies such as the performance of overlapping activities. While the latter do not extend the number of hours worked, they add to the intensity of work per unit time. Both the lengthening of working hours and the intensification of work through the performance of overlapping activities could have adverse effects on women's health.

Early efforts to understand the allocation of time by men and women to different kinds of work developed what has come to be known as the new household economics framework. These scholars sought to explain sexual division of labour in terms of comparative advantage and probed into the kinds of incentives that may alter this division of labour. Gary Becker laid the foundations of "New Household Economics" by explicitly incorporating women's time in home activities into the traditional analysis of labour supply and time spent on work.

In recent years have seen renewed interest in time use surveys as a mode of capturing women's work through an enumeration of activities that fall under three broad categories : They are (1) System of National Accounts (SNA) activities, (2) extended SNA and (3) non-SNA activities. The

1. Productive or market work is defined as income generating activities through their links with the market. Reproductive activities or non-market work refer to unpaid responsibility for care and development of people, including children, the aged, the sick as well as the able-bodied. These activities include among others food preparation, health care, cleaning and sanitation, collection of fuel and water (Cagatay *et al.* 1995).

SNA activities are those covered in the system of national accounts and falling within the SNA production boundary. The SNA activities include (1) primary production activities, (2) secondary activities, (3) trade, business and service activities. The extended SNA activities are those falling outside the SNA production boundary but within the general production boundary consisting mainly of unpaid services. The extended SNA refers to the care economy and includes household maintenance, management and shopping for own household, care for children, the sick, elderly and disabled for own household and community services and help to other households. The non-SNA activities are those which need to be performed by people themselves, and cannot be delegated to others. It includes learning and leisure activities, social and cultural activities, mass media etc. and personal care and self-maintenance (Hirway 2002, Bhatia 2002). Time use surveys, have been employed to collect information on the number of people involved in each activity and how much time a person spends on each activity in the course of a day. The information so collected can be used to understand women's work much of which is invisible; unlike the traditional methods of data collection, a time use survey collects information about the productive activities in the household and thus captures the unstructured work patterns (UN, 1991 cited in Bhatia 2002).

Our study attempts to understand the quantitative and qualitative dimensions of women's time allocation behaviour in two segments of the leather footwear industry in Pondicherry, India. It is essential to understand the quantitative dimension of time use which deals with how much time women workers spend for different activities, outside the household and within it, and qualitative dimension deals with the organizational aspects of work intensity, especially the strategies by which women cope with a heightened work load. We have attempted also to look at women's perceptions of their health in the context of time allocation behaviour and well being. In this paper we attempted three things: *(a)* capture women involvement in work under different categories – productive and reproductive; *(b)* examine the ways in which women organise their work and overlap activities in order to cope with work pressure; and *(c)* relate these aspects with women's perceptions of their own health.

The paper is organised in 5 sections. Section 1 deals with the description of area of study, sample selection procedure, socio-demographic characteristics of the sample and methodology used to collect the time use data. Section 2 discusses the time spend by women workers to productive or market activities, reproductive or non-market activities and for leisure, personal care and self-maintenance activities. This section also provides the empirical estimation of determinants of time allocation to market work. Section 3 examines the qualitative dimensions of time use by women workers like pattern of work organization, performance of overlapping activity. The possible linkage between work intensity and well being is examined through women's perception of their health in section 4. Section 5 gives the summary of the study.

2. Area of the Study and Sample Selection Procedure

The study was conducted in Pondicherry, which is a Union Territory comprising four districts, Pondicherry, Karaikal, Mahe and Yanam. The present study is based on factory and subcontract women workers linked to a footwear industry in Pondicherry.

We surveyed 15 out of 75 women workers (20 per cent of the population) in the factory of a firm A making shoe uppers.[2] Due to the nature of industrial homework, we did not know the universe of subcontract workers. In the firm A, there were 15 subcontractors and under each subcontractor there were 5 to 25 women workers. We surveyed in total 100 subcontract women workers who are linked to firm A and firm B.[3]

2. The 'firm' includes the formal factory unit and informal small units and subcontract units linked to it. Firms name has changed to preserve confidentiality.

3. Firm B manufactures full shoes and subcontracts the hand stitching for shoe bottom to women workers. Since we were unable to access information on the formal factory unit of firm B, our sample includes only women workers involved in hand stitching for shoe bottom linked to firm B.

We categorised the subcontract women workers into piece rate workers (shoe bottom, shoe upper workers), and time rate workers (factory workers, saddle makers). Although saddle makers are paid time rate, they are made to do work like piece rate workers. Hence, we cannot treat them entirely as time rated workers since they receive a combination wage.

The 15 factory women workers were involved in different types of work like machine stitching, packing, pasting, punching, skiving and as in charge. Out of 100 workers, 46 were doing shoe bottom stitching, and 34 were doing shoe upper stitching, 14 were involved in stitching and saddle making and 5 were involved in pasting for saddles. One woman worker in the sample from a shoe bottom making unit falls in the supervising category.

3. Socio-Demographic Characteristics of the Sample

The mean age of factory workers (35) is higher than that of subcontract workers (27).[4] Importantly, there are no unmarried girls among factory workers and no factory workers are in the age group of less than 30. In case of subcontract workers 30 per cent are unmarried girls in which 29 per cent are in the age group of less than 24 years and 65 per cent of the married workers are above 24 years of age. Besides 46 per cent of married factory workers belong to the 30-34 age group and 27 per cent are above 35 years. Most of the women workers in the sample have up to middle and secondary education, almost 30 per cent of subcontract workers have less than this and only 2 per cent of subcontract workers have higher than secondary education. While there are no illiterates among factory workers, 3 (20 per cent) of them have higher than secondary education. On the other hand, 8 per cent of the subcontract workers are illiterate. Almost 90 per cent of the total number of women

4. The factory workers are distributed in higher age group (35 years) because, factory stopped recruitment of new workers ten years ago and in the period has also cut down its workforce. Hence women workers in the factory at the time of the survey have been working there for 10 years or more and younger women have not had entry.

workers in our sample belongs to the backward caste called "kavundars".

All the factory workers and 82 per cent of subcontract workers are from urban areas. A small proportion of subcontract workers are from the surrounding villages. Since the work place is located in Pondicherry, these subcontract workers commute to the work place everyday by bus. Most of the women workers (76 per cent) live in nuclear families. However, there is a relatively higher proportion (25 per cent) of joint families among subcontract workers. Nuclear families are more pronounced among factory workers. Significantly, despite the predominance of nuclear families, family size is higher among factory workers. Also the number of earners is lower and the number of dependents higher (4.60 as against 2.80 for subcontract workers) compared to subcontract workers.

The structure of household according to marital status shows that, unmarried workers have higher family size (4.80) and number of earners (2.73) but fewer dependents (2.07) compared to the ever-married workers. Most of the unmarried workers are young and are in subcontract work emphasising the importance of their incomes to their families. This reflects the income pooling strategy of the family whereby each member of the household has to work to meet her/his own expenses and contribute to family expenditure. It could be because of this that the number of earners among unmarried workers' families is higher than in the families of ever-married workers.

4. Methodology : Time Use Survey

As we seek to understand how women workers allocate their time between different activities we collected information on time use pattern. Firstly, very informally, the respondents were asked about their activities from the time they woke up in the morning until the time they went to sleep. In order to gain a detailed picture we did six case studies focussing on the pattern of work organisation of women workers. Then with a list of stylised activities, based on existing literature on time use, all respondents were asked about how much time they allocated for each activity in the last 24 hours of a normal (working) day. The selection of a normal (working) day was done randomly, implying each weekday of the reference week had an equal chance of getting selected (Hirway 2002). However this was supplemented with the detailed interviews to garner activities that may have been missed out.

To survey the factory workers we went to the factory during the working hours and the survey was conducted in the factory. Whereas to survey the subcontract workers we went to the work place (subcontractor's house, shed behind factory of firm A) as well as to the homes of women workers. We observed that subcontract workers worked through out the week and there was no notion of a holiday in a week. Based on the 24 hour recall period, women workers were asked the time spent on each detailed activity by minutes, in an hourly time slot[5].

Our study's special focus is on overlapping activities as an expression of work intensity and its possible association with women's health. But time use survey hitherto has taken into account only one activity at one point of time. We introduced certain questions in the structured schedules containing the list of activities to capture work organisation and overlapping activity.

5. Time Allocation of Women Workers

The study collected information on time allocation to market work, non-market work or domestic activities and leisure, personal care and self-maintenance. Market work is defined as income generating activities through their links with the market (Cagatay *et al.* 1995). The study considers women workers time allocation to factory and subcontract work as

5. As mentioned earlier in this section that time use data was collected for a normal working days and it did not include non working days. It is because factory workers have holidays in weekends and subcontract workers did not have concept of holiday. Since the comparison of time allocation is made between factory workers and subcontract workers, the study did not include time use pattern of factory workers on non working days.

market work. For non market work or domestic activities, the study collected time allocation to certain activities like cooking, cleaning vessels, washing clothes, purchase vegetables, purchase provisions, buying milk, household poultry, kitchen garden, collection of firewood, collection of drinking water, preparation of snacks, pickles, grinding of food grains, community services and help to other households, child care activities.[6] Following the definition of Cagatay *et al.* 1995 the study considers the above mentioned activities as non-market or domestic activities.

The study categorise time allocation to watching TV, music, personal care-personal hygiene, eating/drinking, dressing up, reading, games, hobby, time with friends, prayer, sleeping as leisure, personal care and self maintenance activities.[7]

We have categorised women workers according to work status as well as marital status. Marital status tends to be associated with distinct patterns of time allocation by women, owing to differences in reproductive responsibilities. Unmarried workers figure only among subcontract workers, hence they are examined separately within subcontract workers. The study discusses the comparative picture of average time spent on productive or market activities, non-market or domestic activities and for leisure, personal care and self maintenance activities in a day by an ever-married factory worker, subcontract worker and unmarried subcontract worker.

---

6. In Indian time use survey, the activities like household poultry, kitchen garden, collection of firewood, collection of drinking water, preparation of snacks, pickles, grinding of food grains are classified as primary production activities. Since the present study classified the market work as purely income generating activity, we did not include these unpaid activities as primary production activities. The words reproductive activities, non-market work and domestic work are used interchangeably.
7. The study mentions these activities in a single word as leisure activities in order to avoid the repetition of words.

6. Time Spent on Market Work

Table 1 gives the comparative picture of time spent by the three categories of workers (ever married factory worker, subcontract worker and unmarried subcontract worker) in market work.

Table 1 : Average Time Allocation (in hours) to Market Work by Work Status and Marital Status

Women workers by work status/marital status	*Market Work*	*Percentage of time spent on market work*
Factory workers	8.73	36.38
Subcontract workers		
Ever-married	8.99	37.48
Unmarried	9.68	40.34

Source : Field Survey 2002.

A comparison of average time spent by ever-married factory worker and subcontract worker reveals that, an ever-married subcontract worker spends more time on market work (8.99 hours) than factory worker (8.73 hours). Even though the difference in time spent on market work is not significant, during the survey we found ever-married workers spend nearly 12 to 16 hours per day.[8]

Likewise an unmarried worker spends more time on market work (9.68 hours) than the ever-married factory worker and subcontract worker. The difference in time allocation to market work by factory worker and subcontract worker could be due to the nature of employment (formal and informal).[9]

8. Refer to the case studies in section 'Pattern of Work Organisation'.
9. We categorise the factory workers as formal sector workers because the factory is registered under Indian factories act 1948 and labour legislations are applicable to factory workers. Subcontract workers were categorised as informal workers because their jobs are not registered and they are unprotected by labour legislations.

Factory workers have fixed working hours and are assured of a fixed monthly salary. In contrast, for the subcontract worker, the mode of payment is piece rate and the monthly earnings depend on the number of pairs she does in a day. This may put pressure on her to devote as much time as possible to market related production in order to raise her earnings. Moreover there is no stability of employment, which makes the ever-married subcontract worker to spend nearly 37 per cent of her time to market activity. The unmarried worker is able to spend more time on market activity at least partly because, in the case of 90 per cent of the unmarried workers' household, other female members contribute to reproductive activities. The income pooling strategy of the household dictates that each able bodied member participate in market work to meet their own expenses and family expenditure. It could be because of this reason that, unmarried girls are 'freed' relatively from domestic chores to attend to market work at home.

In the present study the time spent for travelling is included in non-market activities. The data suggests that the factory women worker and unmarried subcontract workers spend considerable time in travelling to the work place. The majority of married subcontract workers do not spend time for travelling because they either go to a workplace (subcontractor's house) close to their homes or work in own household. The shoe upper making factory (linked to firm A) is located in Mettupalayam industrial estate, which is situated outside of Pondicherry city. Hence the factory workers spend time to commute to the work place. Likewise some of the unmarried workers in the saddle making unit are residing in villages in the city's hinterland, hence they spend considerable time to commute to work place.

7. Time Spent on Non-Market Work

The time allocation to non-market work by women workers reveals the significant difference based on work status and marital status. The table 2 gives the comparative picture of time spent by three categories of workers on non-market work.

Table 2 : Average Time Allocation (in hours) to Non-Market Work by Work Status and Marital Status

Sl. No.	*Non-market Work*	*Factory Workers*	*Subcontract workers*	
			Married	*Unmarried*
	Average time spent on Non-Market Work	3.85	**4.46**	**2.21**
	Percentage of time spent on Non-Market Work	16.06	18.60	9.20
	Cooking	1.52	1.38	0.28
	Cleaning vessels	0.41	0.52	0.38
	Washing clothes	0.42	0.83	0.23
	Purchase vegetables	0.02	0.16	0.01
	Purchase provisions	-	0.02	-
	Buying milk	0.01	0.04	0.01
	Household poultry	-	-	-
	Kitchen garden	-	-	-
	Collection of firewood	-	0.025	-
	Collection of drinking water	-	0.12	0.32
	Preparation of snacks, pickles	0.023	-	-
	Grinding of food grains)	-	-	-
	Community services and help to other households	-	-	-
	Child care activities			
	Preparing them for school	0.47	0.86	-
	Taking care of children below school going age	0.1	0.1	-
	Travel time			
	Going to workplace	0.35	0.20	0.48
	Travelling back to home	0.35	0.20	0.48

Source : Field Survey 2002.

The average time spent in non-market work by ever-married factory worker (3.85 hours) and subcontract worker (4.46 hours) suggests marginal difference between the two categories of workers. When we look into the time spent in individual activities, it reveals that there is difference in activities like cooking, cleaning, and washing clothes. It could be because, majority of the factory workers have at least one or two labour saving machines which reduces the time spent in domestic work. As we mentioned earlier, factory workers have relatively larger families than ever-married subcontract workers. Domestic work is shared among the female family members, which reduces the time spent on domestic work by the factory workers. However the case of unmarried subcontract workers was quite distinct from ever-married subcontract workers in this respect. The table reveals that subcontract workers spend sometime on collection of firewood and collection of drinking water. Whereas majority of factory workers use LPG gas as fuel and have water connections in the house.

Factory workers spend less time for childcare activities than subcontract workers do because factory workers are distributed in the age group of above 30 years. Their children are older on an average than children of subcontract workers. It is also clear for reasons already gone into that unmarried workers spend less time on non-market work.

8. Time Spent on Leisure, Personal Care and Self-Maintenance Activities

Table 4 explains the time allocation to leisure, personal care and self-maintenance activities by women workers. The table indicates that the unmarried workers (9.91 hours) spend more time on leisure activities than any other group of women. They are followed by ever-married factory workers (9.05 hours) and ever-married subcontract workers (8.55 hours) who spend the least time on leisure activities.

Noticeably, watching TV accounts for the single largest block of leisure time spent by factory and subcontract workers, though this is considerably higher among factory workers. However unmarried women workers among subcontract workers watch TV for number of hours close to that of factory workers. Fixed working hours in the factory allows factory workers to allocate the remaining day to non-market and leisure activities. The list of time spent on individual activities

Table 3 : Average Time Allocation (in hours) to Leisure, Personal Care and Self-Maintenance by Work Status and Marital Status

Leisure, Personal Care and Self-Maintenance	*Factory Workers*	*Subcontract Workers*	
		Married	*Unmarried*
Average time spent on Leisure, Personal Care and Self-Maintenance	9.05	8.55	9.91
Percentage of time spent on Leisure, Personal Care and Self-Maintenance	37.73	35.65	41.29
1. Watching TV	1.43	0.9	1.31
2. Music	—	—	0.03
3. Personal care			
a. Personal hygiene	0.2	0.18	0.18
b. Eating/drinking	0.2	0.17	0.17
c. Dressing	0.2	0.17	0.17
4. Reading	—	—	0.01
5. Games	—	—	—
6. Hobby	—	—	—
7. Time with friends	—	0.01	0.09
8. Prayer	—	—	—
9. Sleep	7.12	7.125	7.93

Source : Field Survey 2002.

makes clear that factory workers have considerably more leisure time. An important reason for this is the help they get at home and the labour saving devices used. Notably unmarried workers spend more hours than both ever-married factory and subcontract workers in market work and more than ever-married subcontract workers on leisure. As we will discuss in a later section, ever-married subcontract workers do not observe fixed working hours for market work and for them there is no clear separation of spheres between market work, domestic work and personal care or leisure. Ever-married subcontract workers in organising their time resort to a wider range of overlapping activities than factory or unmarried workers, less burdened by a combination of all three sets of activities.

Thus it can be said that for ever-married subcontract workers there is lengthening of working hours in terms of market work and domestic work, whereas for factory workers there is lengthening of working hours in terms of domestic work but they have enough leisure time to relax themselves from the burden of work. In the case of unmarried workers, there is lengthening of working hours in terms of market work.

9. Determinants of Time Allocation to Market Work

This section analyzes the determinants of time allocation to market work. The study calculated the time ratio by taking the ratio of time spent for market work to time spent for domestic work.[10]

$$\text{Time ratio} = \frac{\text{Time spent for market work}}{\text{Time spent for domestic work}}$$

It was found that average time ratio is 3.62 which shows that women workers are allocating more time for market work than domestic work. The study also found that women workers (ever-married, unmarried) are spending maximum time for market work than domestic work and leisure activities. There is difference within the groups of workers. So an attempt is made to find the factors which account for women workers to allocate more time for market work than domestic work. The study estimated two models. The variables included in the model are described in Table 4.

In the first model the study includes all the variables mentioned in the table 4. The results of the estimated model show that the work status dummy, category of workers dummy and mode of payment dummy are highly correlated and statistically insignificant.

---

10. If this ratio is 'equal to 1' then women workers are allocating equal time for market work and domestic work If it is less than 1 then women workers are allocating more time for domestic work than for market work. If it is greater than 1 then women workers are allocating more time for market work than for domestic work.

Table 4 : Description of Variables

Dependent variable	Time ratio
Independent variables	
Age of the respondent	In number of years
Respondent's earnings	In rupees
Work status	$D_1 = 1$ for factory workers
	$D_1 = 0$ for others
Category of workers (dummy)	$D_2 = 1$ for saddle makers
	$D_2 = 0$ for others
Mode of payment	$D_3 = 1$ for time rate workers
	$D_3 = 0$ for others
Presence of labour saving machine	
Number of children in the age group 1-5	In absolute number
Number of children in the age group 6-10	In absolute number
Number of children in the age group 11-14	In absolute number
Family size	In absolute number

The presence of labour saving machine has positive association with time ratio. It shows that higher the presence of labour saving machine higher will be the time spent for market work since it reduces the time spent for domestic work. But it is statistically insignificant. The possible explanation for the insignificance may be 34 per cent of the subcontract workers do not have any labour saving devices and others have one or two machines. So the study excluded the variables, the work status dummy, category of workers dummy, and presence of labour saving machines and estimated another model.

The new model is represented as;

Time ratio = constant + a_1 respondent age + a_2 family size + D_3 mode of payment + a_4 respondents earnings + a_5 spouse's number of days worked in a year + a_6 child 1-5 + a_7 child 6-10 + a_8 child 11-14 + v_i

Where a's are the parameters to be estimated

D_3 represents dummy variable for mode of payment.

v_i represents the error term.

Table 5 : Regression Results

Variables	*Coefficients* β	*Standard*	*t-value*	*Significant*
Constant	5.761*	1.368	4.213	.000
Respondent age	–.133*	.043	–3.087	.003
Family size	.619*	.187	3.303	.001
Mode of payment	–1.149**	.568	–2.023	.046
Respondent's earnings	.0009688**	.000414	2.338	.021
Husbands number of days worked in a year	–.004709**	.002	–2.066	.041
Child 1-5	–1.276*	.395	–3.226	.002
Child 6-10	–.829**	.420	–1.974	.051
Child 11-14	–.927**	.423	–2.193	.030
R^2	.427			
Adjusted R square	.383			
Durbin-Watson Statistic	2.028			
F-value	9.863**			

*–Significant at 1 per cent level.

** –Significant at 5 per cent level.

The regression results are presented in Table 5. The age of the respondent has negative relation with the time ratio and is statistically significant. It shows that lower the age higher the time spent on market work and lower time for domestic work and *vice versa*. The survey result shows that 90 per cent of the unmarried workers are in the age group of 15 to 25. Since they are unmarried they have less responsibility over domestic work enabling them to spend more time on market activities. The results also show that 67 per cent of the married workers in the higher group of above 25 do not receive any help from other family members which reduces the time spent in market work and increase their time spent in domestic work.

The family size has significant and positive association with the time ratio. It represents that higher the family size higher will be the time spent on market work and less time on domestic work. It is true in the case of unmarried workers. The study found that unmarried workers' family size (4.80) is higher than that of the ever-married workers (4.38). From the above discussion it appears that unmarried workers spend maximum time for market work (9.68 hours) and less time for (2.21 hours). As we saw earlier, the larger family size among these workers includes female members who can take care of domestic work freeing the unmarried workers for market work.

The mode of payment shows that there is significant difference in time spent for market work. It shows that piece rate workers are spending more time for market work than the time rate workers. To some extent this result is biased.[11]

Respondent's earnings have positive and significant relation with the time ratio. It shows that higher the earnings of the respondents higher will be the time spent by respondents for market work. But the magnitude of the coefficient is very small, which implies that a one unit increase in respondent's earnings increases the time spent in market work by .096 per cent. The empirical evidence from various studies based on new household economics, reveals that women's labour force participation responds positively to increases in women's wages and reduces her time in non-market work. In informal (subcontract) nature of work where women's wages are low, there is high participation of women in market work given the

11. In our model there are two groups of workers, firstly piece rate workers (shoe bottom, shoe upper workers), secondly time rate workers (factory workers, saddle makers). However, as we have emphasized earlier, although saddle makers are paid time rate, they are made to do work like piece rate workers. Hence we cannot treat them entirely as time rated workers since theirs is a combination wage resulting in the saddle makers spending maximum time (9.94 hours) for market work. To bring this out, the study used category of workers dummy (D_2) to represent the saddle making workers. But this variable was highly correlated with work status and mode of payment dummy, so it had to be excluded from the model.

need to enhance household incomes even while they contribute to reproductive activities. So the wage need not be the prime factor which increases the women's labour force participation. This could possibly be the reason why the magnitude of the coefficient of respondent's earnings is small.

The husband's number of days worked in a year shows that it has a significant negative relation with time ratio. It shows that lower the number of days worked by the husband in a year, higher will be the time spent by wife to market work and less time for domestic work and vice versa. It represents that when husbands are in irregular or seasonal jobs, monthly earnings could be low to compensate which women workers have to spend more time for market work. It is true with the subcontract workers because 46 per cent of the subcontract workers' husbands are working less than 270 days in a year. The number of children in the age group of 1-5, 6-10 and 11-14 has negative and significant relation with time ratio. It shows that the presence of children in these three age groups reduces the women workers' time spent on market work and increases their time spent on domestic work.

10. Pattern of Work Organisation

We have seen the lengthening of women's working time on account of a combination of productive and reproductive activities and in this context the importance of distinctions between categories of workers according to work status and marital status. We turn now to understanding the way women workers organise their working time and cope with their responsibility for multiple activities; where the strategies used suggest the intensification of work performed per unit time.

11. Overlapping Activities

From the pattern of work organisation, we found that women tend to overlap activities in order to save time or speed up their tasks. Overlapping activity refers to simultaneous performance of more than one activity at a time. Floro (1995) refers to three different categories of overlapping activities. First, category involves overlapping between two domestic activities. The second form of overlapping activity involves the simultaneous performance of market work and non-market activities. The third form of overlapping activity applies to leisure and domestic activity or leisure and market work activities. We have used this categorisation of overlapping work to understand women's allocation of time.

Floro (1995) points out that whenever an activity requiring some level of physical or mental energy or continuous attention is performed in combination with some other activity, then the overlap of activities indicates intensification of working time. Overlapping activities actually involves frequent switching from one activity to another and work intensity in this sense means heightened fragmentation of work. Thus combinations of activities, which may not strictly overlap, in the sense of both requiring attention at the same time, can suggest work intensification when they are done at a rapid pace and in a fragmented manner. On the one hand, overlapping activities could raise the level of efficiency by increasing the level of output and breaking the monotony of the job, on the other it

Table 6 : Number of Workers Performing Overlapping Activities, Based on Work and Marital Status

Overlapping activity	*Factory*	*Subcontract Workers*	
		EM	*UM*
Number of workers	15	70	30
Category : 1 Two domestic activities	10 (66.7)	61 (87.4)	1 (3.3)
Category : 2 Domestic activity and market work	—	43 (61.4)	2 (6.7)
Category : 3 Domestic activity and leisure or Market work and leisure	1 (33.3)	50 (71.5)	7 (90.0)

Source : Field Survey 2002.

EM- ever-married workers, UM-unmarried workers.

Figure in parentheses show percentage values to number of workers in each category.

could lead to increase in stress and deterioration in the quality of output, with adverse effects on worker and household. Another element of work intensity pertains to the nature of the combined activities and the motivation behind the combinations of tasks.

The table 6 indicates the number of women workers by work and marital status who reported performing different categories of overlapping activities. The numbers in the cells indicate those reporting overlapping activities. The first category of overlapping activity *i.e.* overlapping two domestic activities is performed by an overwhelming number of factory workers and married subcontract workers. According to the respondents these included cooking rice and cutting vegetables, cleaning vessels and preparing breakfast. These activities are done over the same stretch of time, the woman's attention being on one or the other at each point of time. In case of factory workers, the motivation to overlap two domestic activities is to finish the work within a short period of time (before they leave for the factory). Due to time constraint in the morning hours, when they have to attend to several domestic tasks, despite the help of labour saving devices and other female members, these workers reported having to switch frequently from one activity to another.

In case of ever-married subcontract workers, a 'normal' working day comprised 'fixed' and fewer hours of domestic work and 'flexible' and longer hours of work related to market production. On an average they spent about 4 hours on domestic tasks but interspersed with market work. To compress and reduce time spent on domestic work and extend time spent on market work, they resort to overlapping activities. More than half the married subcontract women workers overlap two or more domestic activities.

The second category *i.e.* overlapping domestic activity and market work is performed by 61 per cent of ever-married subcontract workers. However, it was clear from our interviews with the workers that there were considerable variations. During certain periods of time there is pressure to finish the subcontract work, which leads them to resort more to overlapping work.

Seventy two per cent of the ever-married subcontract workers reported that they used to overlap market work and watching television. These workers pointed out that it breaks the monotony of the job. On the one hand it serves as a coping mechanism which reduces the burden of work but it also means a severe constraint on leisure time. Only one factory worker reported that she listens to music when she does the domestic work. The performance of overlapping activities based on marital status shows a lower tendency to overlap activities among unmarried workers. Almost 90 per cent of the unmarried workers reported that they used to overlap job work with watching television.

It would seem that work intensity is greater for ever-married subcontract workers than other categories of women workers. Needless to say factory workers even though they overlap activities due to time constraints during the morning hours before they go to work, they are able to get some leisure time in the evening. Whereas for unmarried workers there seems to be less compulsion to perform domestic activities because it is shared by other family members. Whereas ever-married subcontract workers combine domestic and market work. They seem to have no time separately for leisure. Notably then they pointed out that they preferred to go to the subcontractor's house for market related work also to mingle with other women. In the following sub sections we attempt to substantiate the mode of women's work organisation and the resort to overlapping work through case studies.

12. Ever-married Subcontract Workers

Broadly speaking most married subcontract workers organized their work in such a way as to compress time spent on domestic work in order to be able to allocate more time to market related productive work. Married subcontract workers spend close to 4 hours for reproductive work like cooking, cleaning, washing clothes or purchasing vegetables and milk, each day. The workers' domestic activities are interspersed with their market work such that women workers take time off from market work when necessary for domestic work. They also have the flexibility to take breaks during the day and go home from the subcontractor's house if they have to attend to childcare or other domestic responsibilities. Nevertheless overall the women workers' strategy is to compress the domestic work within a short period of time and extend their time for market work.

Case Study : 1 (Amudha is a home-based worker)

> Amudha is 40 years old and works for a shoe upper stitching in Shanmugapuram, the locality she lives in. She is a home based worker. Her husband is working as an attender in Jawaharlal Institute of Postgraduate Medical Education and Research (JIPMER). He earns Rs. 7000 per month. She has two daughters and two sons. Her youngest son and daughter are in school while other two children are in college. From 1994 onwards Amudha has been working for this shoe upper unit, which according to her provides work for almost 8 months in year. She pointed out that she needed to work, despite her husband earning a good salary, as they would need resources to educate the children and get their daughters married.
>
> A typical day for Amudha is hectic. When she has a considerable amount of work from subcontract, she gets up at four in the morning and does the job work. From six in the morning she attends to domestic work. She finishes cooking, cleaning vessels, washing clothes, and prepares the children for school before starting shoe upper stitching work again. To finish the domestic work by 9 in the morning she overlaps activities. She spends about three hours on domestic work in the morning and an hour interspersed over the rest of the day. While cooking she cleans vessels, washes clothes and prepares children for school. She cooks lunch too at this time. She then attends to subcontract work upto 1O' clock in the afternoon. While doing the work she watches television also. At 1 in the afternoon her husband comes home for lunch and she takes a break to serve his

food and have hers. She cleans up after that and by 2 in the afternoon is back to subcontract work, which she continues to do till five in the evening. Again at 5.30 p.m. she takes a break to prepare coffee or tea for the children. At 6 O' clock she and her daughter start the work and continue till 8 p.m. in the night. Then at 8.30 p.m. she serves dinner for the family, does some preparatory work for the next day, cleans up and attends to the children. At night too she works for an hour or two, between 9 and 11 p.m., depending upon availability of orders from the subcontractor. Amudha spends between 12 to 16 hours on market-related work, when work is available.

Factory Workers

Factory workers organise their work responsibilities in a manner quite different from subcontract workers. However factory workers too prefer to finish the major part of their domestic work in the morning before leaving to factory which takes them about three and half hours in a day. In the factory, workers have fixed hours to spend for market work and if they are willing to work overtime, they can extend their working hours. On return from the factory, women workers spend their time on domestic work and leisure activities.

Case Study : 2

Malathy aged 32 is working in factory (linked to firm A), which is located in Mettupalayam Industrial estate. Her husband is working as an office assistant. He is earning monthly salary of Rs. 2500. She has one child and lives in a joint family, which includes her mother in law. She has been employed in the factory for the past 13 years and currently earns a monthly income of Rs. 3000. Malathy wakes up at 6 in the morning. She has to report at the factory at 8.30 in the morning and tries to finish all her domestic chores before leaving for work. It takes her about 15 minutes to reach her work place. Her mother in law helps her with some tasks. However she overlaps cooking with cleaning vessels and washing clothes in order to speed up her tasks. Her mother in law helps her in preparing the child for school. Malathy is in the factory till 5 in the evening. She takes 15 minutes to reach back home. At home she does the domestic work for 1 hour and spends her time with her child. She spends evening hours in watching TV. She goes to bed at 11 in the night.

Unmarried Workers

An important feature influencing the time allocation of young unmarried women in our sample is that they are less bound by reproductive responsibilities than their mothers or other older ever-married women. However these women too do assist in domestic chores like collecting water and helping in the kitchen. Ninety per cent of the unmarried workers spend 1 to 2 hours to help their mothers or other family members in domestic chores like cleaning house, cleaning vessels and washing clothes. Nevertheless there does seem to be a greater emphasis on their contribution to market related work. As we mentioned in the previous chapter a section of unmarried workers (from the saddle making units) are residing in the surrounding villages and commuting to the work place takes more than an hour of their time.

Case Study : 3

Jayamalani aged 24 years is an unmarried girl. She has been working as subcontract worker for seven years in a saddle-making unit. She receives a monthly income of R.s.1050. She is residing in a place called Thirubhuvanai and from there she goes to the subcontractor' house which is nearly 20 kilometers away. She travels one and half-hours in the bus to and fro. She has to reach the unit at 8.30 in the morning and works until 5.30 in the evening. In the evening she reaches the house by 7 and carries some saddles home to complete there. Again in the house she does this work for 2 hours while watching TV. She goes to sleep by 10 p.m.

13. Implications on Health

A high work burden leading to lengthening of working time and work intensity has been associated with negative implications for well being of the worker. We documented the perceptions of women workers in our sample of their health.

Table 7 : Perception of Health Problem and Nature of Work

Health Problems	*Subcontracted Workers*			
	Factory Worker	*Shoe Bottom*	*Shoe Upper*	*Saddle Making*
Number of workers	15	47	34	19
Digestive problems	—	—	—	—
Acidity	—	—	—	—
Ulcers	—	1	2 (6)	—
Back pain (low back pain)	9 (60)	42 (89.3)	31(91.1)	14 (74)
Pain in shoulders	5 (33.3)	42 (89.3)	31 (91.1)	13 (68.4)
Pain in neck	5 (33.3)	42 (89.3)	31 (91.1)	13 (68.4)
Pain in limbs	8 (53.3)	42 (89.3)	31 (91.1)	13 (68.4)
Body aches	9 (60)	42 (89.3)	32 (94.1)	14(74)
Headache	1 (6.7)	13 (28)	7 (21)	11 (58)
Scratches & injuries in hands	1 (6.7)	20 (43)	27 (79.4)	4 (21)
Strain in eyes	—	3 (6.4)	1 (2.9)	—
Dizziness	—	—	—	1 (5.3)
Respiratory problems	1 (6.7)	1 (2.1)	—	—
Skin problems	1 (6.7)	—	8 (24)	2 (11)
Tension and stress	11 (73.3)	28 (60)	24 (71)	12 (63)
Tiredness	5 (53.3)	25 (53.2)	21 (62)	3 (16)
Others	6 (40)	17 (36.1)	13 (38.2)	7 (37)

Source : Field Survey 2002.

Figures in parentheses shows percentage values to number of workers in each category.

Table 7 shows the number of workers who reported different kinds of ailments, many of them reporting multiple ailments. Distinctly, factory workers reported less physical ailments when compared to subcontract workers but a higher proportion of them reported tension and stress as well as tiredness. The better working conditions in the factory, fixed working hours, greater leisure and higher standard of living (as also the division of work at home) could be contributing to relatively better physical dimensions of health. Despite this however they report greater stress levels. Lower reportage of stress among subcontract women workers could have to do with one aspect of 'flexibility', for instance the reported preference of several subcontract women to work in the subcontractor's house, which provided an opportunity to be with other women.

The high reportage of body ache and pain in the back, neck, shoulder and limbs are striking. While about one third of factory workers reported these ailments, among subcontract workers 90 per cent of married workers and nearly 80 per cent of unmarried workers reported the above ailments. Occupational health is a consideration here and the association between these ailments and the requirements of work *i.e.*, the posture of the worker, the need to sit or stand long hours and do a repetitive task need to be explored. This is true of such ailments as scratches and injuries, skin problems and headaches. A consideration of reported ailments and nature of work throws more light on occupational health.

Among subcontract workers, skin problem is prominent among the shoe upper workers and saddle makers. More than half of the saddle making workers reported headaches, while nearly 80 per cent of shoe upper workers reported scratches and injuries. Significant proportion of shoe bottom workers reported headaches, scratches and injuries. Some workers mentioned other problems like irregular menstrual cycles, white discharge, chest pain, stomachache, swelling in wrist, cold, fever, water from eyes, dark rounds under eyes, hair loss, dandruff.

14. Conclusion

Nature of employment seems to play a decisive role in the way women allocate their time between their productive work, reproductive tasks and other more personalised and leisure activities. It is also significant in the way women organise their 'working' time, whether in productive, reproductive, leisure or in a combination of tasks. A strategy that all categories of women reported using to cope with their heightened work load was overlapping activities. The resort to overlapping activities by factory workers, ever-married subcontract workers stemmed from different constraints. Factory workers perform overlapping activities due to time constraints very specific to their work requirements. They feel the need to finish as much domestic chores as possible before leaving for work in the morning. Hence for them there is less overlapping of leisure activities with domestic work in the evening hours and they are able to spend time separately on leisure. The presence of older women or older daughters among this group of women was important in lowering the burden of reproductive responsibility.

In contrast to factory workers, ever-married subcontract workers perform overlapping activities to compress domestic work in a short time period and extend the time for market work. It is performed out of perceived need rather than self-fulfillment. There is no line of demarcation between leisure and market or domestic work because they overlap the activities. They could not afford to spend separate time for leisure activities, if they engage in leisure they tend to overlap it with other activities.

There is less resort to overlapping activities among unmarried workers because other family members in the household share the reproductive work. Some unmarried workers reported that they overlap leisure activities with market work to break the monotonous of the work, which relieves the burden of work.

The performance of overlapping activities which is done of out of necessity serves as an indicator of intensification of working time. The intensification of working time is more pronounced among the ever-married subcontract workers than other category of workers. The lengthening of working hours shows that ever-married subcontract workers spend more time than factory workers on market related productive and reproductive work. The unmarried workers allocate maximum time to market and leisure activities than other group of workers. The study provides empirical evidence that age of the respondent, family size, mode of payment, husband's number of days worked in a year, and presence of children play a major role in determining women's time allocation to market work.

REFERENCES

Becker, G. (1965) : 'A Theory of the Allocation of Time', *Economic Journal*, 75 : 493-517.

Beneria, L. (2001) : 'Changing Employment Patterns and the Informalisation of Jobs : General Trends and Gender Dimensions', International Labour Office, Geneva.

Benton, L.A. (1989) : 'Homework and Industrial Development : Gender Roles and Restructuring in the Spanish Shoe Industry', *World Development*, 17(2) : 255-266.

Bhatia, R. (2002) : 'Measuring Gender Disparity Using Time Use Statistics', *Economic and Political Weekly*, 37(33) : pp. 3464-3469.

Cagatay, N., D. Elson and C. Grown (1995) : 'Introduction', *World Development*, 23(11) : pp. 1827-1836.

Carr, M., Martha A. Chen, and J. Tate (2000) : 'Globalisation and Home-Based Workers', *Feminist Economics*, 6(3), pp. 123-142.

Chen, M., J. Sebstad, and L. O'Connell (1999) : 'Counting the Invisible Workforce : The Case of Home-based workers', *World Development*, 27(3) : pp. 603-610.

Floro, M.S. (1995) : 'Economic Restructuring, Gender and the Allocation of Time', *World Development*, 23(11), pp. 1913-1929.

Government of Pondicherry (1997) : 'Industrial Policy 1997', Industries Department, Government of Pondicherry.

Hirway, I. (2002) : 'Employment and Unemployment Situation in 1990's—How Good are NSS Data?', *Economic and Political Weekly*, 37(21), pp. 2027-2036.

Khattak, S.G. (2002) : 'Subcontracted Work and Gender Relations : The Case of Pakistan' in R. Balakrishnan, (ed.) *The Hidden Assembly Line, Gender Dynamics of Subcontracted Work in a Global Economy*, USA, Kumarian Press : 35-61.

Mehra, R. and S. Gammage (1999) : 'Trends, Counter Trends, and Gaps in Women's Employment', *World Development*, 27(3) : 533-550.

Unni, J. and Bali, N. (2002) : 'Subcontracted Women Workers in the Garment Industry in India' in R. Balakrishnan, (ed.) *The Hidden Assembly line, Gender Dynamics of subcontracted work in a global economy*, (USA : Kumarian Press).

24

OBA Voucher Approach in Health : Promoting Safe Motherhood Through Participation of Private Medical Practitioners in West Bengal

—Biswajit Panda[1], *David Griffith*[2], *Hengjin Dong*[3], *Abdul Rahim*[4]

1. Introduction

Providing adequate health care for the poor is an essential input into economic development and poverty reduction (Sachs 2001). It is no surprise that five of eight Millennium Development Goals (MDGs), agreed at the UN General Assembly 2000, are related with the improvement of health in developing countries. One target mentioned in goal five focuses on (MGDs 5) maternal health, (UN, 2004). International

1. M.Sc. I.H., Dept. of Tropical Hygiene and Public Health, Heidelberg University, Correspondence should be address to this author: *biswajit71@gmail.com* (Biswajit Panda).

2. Consultant (Kfw-German Development Bank).

3. Senior Lecturer in Health Financing and Health Economics, Dept. of Tropical Hygiene and Public Health, Heidelberg University.

4. Deputy Team Leader, TAST managed by Option & IPE, Kolkata.

developments targets that seek to reduce maternal deaths have yet to be reached. It is estimated that each year, some 8 million women suffer pregnancy-related complications and over 500,000 women die, with 99 per cent of these maternal deaths taking place in developing nations, mainly in sub-Saharan Africa and South Asia (WHO, 2004; Abou Zahr and Wardlaw, 2003). Thus, most maternal deaths result not from 'disease' per se, but from pregnancy-related complications, which are now widely recognized as a leading cause of death and disability among women of reproductive age in developing countries. The five direct obstetric complications that cause the majority of maternal deaths throughout the developing world are haemorrhage, sepsis, unsafe induced abortion, hypertensive disorders of pregnancy, and obstructed labour (WHO, 1996). What is especially tragic is the fact that most of these maternal deaths could be averted with very cost-effective interventions, even where resources are limited (Koblinsky, 1995; WHO, 2004).

Traditional public health policies of local governments and international donor agencies are input oriented. They provide investments in form of infrastructure, financial and human resources and technical assistance. The funding focuses mainly on the public sector. Private health care providers mostly play a minor role. Despite some achievements in the public health situation these activities often fail to reach the poor in most developing countries. Some of the reasons for this failure are : *(a)* public services often work inefficiently, *(b)* the rich is favoured over the poor; *(c)* only little incentives are provided for service providers to perform well and *(d)* the poor often do not demand the services (World Bank, 2004).

These inadequacies have made many patients, especially the poor, turn to private service providers. Experiences show that in most poor countries the majority of health care is provided by the private sector and funded by out-of-pocket payments. For example in India, 80 % of doctors are in private practice (Yamamoto, 2004).

The private sector is believed to be a more efficient provider of health services, more flexible and innovative and more responsive to patient expectations (Gorter *et al.*, 2003). However private provision presents two mayor concerns: One is the unreliable quality of care in the absence of effective regulation; the other is that because of limited financial resources the poor often cannot afford essential services (Yamamoto, 2004).

Output Based Aid (OBA) is a way of allocating public resources, which could eliminate some of the constraints for achieving Millennium Development Goals (MGDs). With OBA approaches, government delegate's responsibility to deliver basic services to a third-party under contracts and ties disbursement of the public funding to the services or outputs actually delivered (Yamamoto, 2004). OBA voucher schemes clearly aim at using the potential of the private sector and integrating private practitioners in the health care system in order to improve the access to care for the poor and ensure a better service quality.

Typical OBA concepts are voucher schemes. Vouchers schemes usually function in the way that vouchers will be provided to a specific target group which entitle them to receive a pre-defined package of best practice service in certificate health facilities. The cost of treatment will then be reimbursed by a voucher agency (Sandifort *et al.*, 2003).

OBA voucher schemes clearly aim at using the potential of the private sector and integrating private providers in the health care system in order to improve the access to care for the poor and ensure a better service quality. To private health care providers, participation in voucher schemes can mean both market potentials and risks. On the one hand vouchers may increase the market share and provide incentives to upgrade services and on the other hand providers have to fulfil high requirements that relate to accreditation, delivered output, monitoring and evaluation.

OBA approaches to generate demand have been used in several Asian countries under the World Bank pro-poor project to increase the access by the poor women to maternal and neonatal health care. The Voucher schemes provide a way to target specific groups and overcome the barrier of access to cash because they don't require advance payment for care. A small number of successful examples of running voucher schemes (*e.g.* Reproductive Health / Family Planning including maternal health: in Bangladesh, China, Kenya, Nicaragua, Uganda and insecticide-treated bed nets for pregnant women and children in Tanzania) and their impact on certain health issues have been documented (Gorter *et al.* 2003; Ensor 2004).

2. Public Health Importance to Maternal Health in West Bengal, India

The life expectancy of the population in India has shown remarkable improvement from 41 at birth in 1961 to the present day of 65 years. Yet, over 100,000 women in India continue to die of pregnancy-related causes every year. The maternal mortality ratio in India is high and is estimated to be 407/ 100,000 (SRS, RGI 1998) with wide regional disparities. However, reliable estimates of maternal mortality are not available. Maternal mortality is a cause of great concern. The major causes of these deaths have been identified as haemorrhage (both ante and post partum), toxaemia (hypertension during pregnancy), anaemia, obstructed labour, puerperal sepsis (infection after delivery) and unsafe abortion. Delay in accessing specialized maternal care happens at all levels, starting with delayed family decisions in seeking care to delay in reaching health facilities, and delay in getting quality emergency obstetrics care could be provided. The "Three – Delays Model" analysing the barriers to utilization finds the reasons to be as follows :

- Delay in deciding to seek care;
- Delay in reaching health facility;
- Delay in getting treatment at the health facility.

The Population Policy 2000, Tenth Five Year Plan, and Millennium Development Goals provide impetus to the ongoing efforts for reducing maternal mortality. Although the link between pregnancy-related care and maternal mortality are well recognised and, over the last decade, national programmes have stressed the need for universal screening of pregnant women and operationalising essential and emergency obstetric care, little has been done. Therefore, it is essential to build a continuum of care that increases access to and use of skilled care during pregnancy, birth and post partum period.

Within the overall framework of Millennium Development Goals and the National Health Policy prescriptions, West Bengal, contributing 7.4% to total maternal deaths, has set reduction of MMR as one of its priority health objectives. Despite being an average state in terms economic development, West Bengal has a better maternal health figure, with MMR declining from 266/100000 to 194/100000 live births over the past few years, with the pregnant women in this state having a life risk of 0.5% compared to 1% at National level but these figures do not emerge favourably when in comparison with other States like Karala (110), Maharastra (149) and Timal Nadu (134).

According to National Family Health Survey (NHFS 2, 1998-99) only 40% of births in West Bengal took place in a health facility. 46% of births took place in the woman's home and 13% in her parent's home. Trained health personnel conducted 44% of deliveries, whilst 30% were helped by traditional birth attendants (TBAs) and 26% were helped by family and friends. Just 7% of births taking place outside a health facility were conducted by a trained health professional. Only 32% of women having a non-institutional delivery received one postnatal check. Anaemia is a serious problem among women in all population groups with prevalence rates ranging from 55-74%.

West Bengal certainly does not have the worst maternal health statistics in India–that spot is taken by Rajasthan and Uttar Pradesh–but as a modern and progressive state West Bengal has realised the importance of prioritising maternal health for both health and socioeconomic reasons and has set serious goals towards achieving what is known to be possible in India.

The Department of Health & Family Welfare (DHFW) of the Government of West Bengal (GoWB) has developed its Health Sector Strategy for 2004-13. The strategy is a significant step towards alignment of resources in the sector to address major shortcomings in provision, accessibility and quality of health services in the state. The Health Sector Development Initiative (HSDI) is a programme of the GoWB to address the concerns in the strategy with support from Department for International Development (DFID, UK). Health System Development Initiative (HDSI) recognises Maternal and Reproductive Health as being the State's highest priority with targets in maternal and child health, including :

- MMR (Maternal Mortality Ratio) reduced from baseline of 250 in 2004 to 150 by end of 2013
- Achieve a 50 per cent increase in institutional deliveries in poorer districts (baseline < 35%) by 2013.

Initiatives in both the public and private sectors are being explored to address the Millennium Development Goals. A range of activities to Public Private Partnership (PPP) in health care are being piloted by DHFW, GoWB.

The decision to focus on Reproductive and Child Health and work with private sector provides in certain areas of health care provision in West Bengal is supported by both national policies and local strategies thinking.

Key policies and initiatives include :

- The 10th Plan which indicates that government should *"find ways to optimally utilise the immense potential (of the private sector) for improving RCH services"*.
- The 2000 National Population Policy which identified opportunities to collaborate with the private sector to *"Create a national network consisting of public, private and NGO centres, identified by a common logo, for delivering reproductive and child health services free to any client"; and*
- The 2001 National Health Policy which recognises the importance of the private health sector in India and deals with the issues around minimum quality standards and statutory clinical guidelines.

More recently two important national initiatives have focussed on Maternal Health, the second phase Reproductive and Child Health Programme (RCH II) and the National Rural Health Mission (NRHM).

The RCH 2 programme, which is still in the pipeline, focuses *inter-alia*, on the Population and Reproductive Health of the people of India. The main focus of the programme is to reduce Maternal & Child Mortality & Morbidity. Building on lessons learnt from RCH 1 more flexibility has been given to the States to set their own goals and plan locally appropriate interventions to achieve specified milestones.

The MDG 5, target 3 (to reduce by three quarters, the Maternal Mortality Ratio between 1990 and 2015), is very much on the agenda. The RCH programme has placed a high premium on institutional deliveries conducted by Skilled Birth Attendants, to ensure reduction of MMR. Several infrastructure, staffing and governance issues are to be addressed under RCH 2 in order to achieve this goal. For example, it is aimed to operationalise about 2,000 First Referral Units (FRUs) to provide Emergency Obstetric Care. All CHCs & 50% of PHCs are also to be made functional to provide 24 hour delivery services.

The National Rural Health Mission, 2005-2012, launched in April 2005, is an umbrella programme that integrates all vertical health and family welfare programmes (including RCH 2). Since NRHM looks for optimal utilisation of resources and strengthening delivery mechanisms, convergence of related departments is deemed to be one of the key strategies in NRHM.

Locally, West Bengal has developed a ten year Health Sector Strategy, 2004-2013, and the HSDI, supported by the World Bank and DFID, operationalises this Strategy. West Bengal has created the Strategic Planning and Sector Reform Cell (SPSRC), headed by the Special Secretary of Health, to initiate and lead the change and development required in the health sector. The cell is supported by a group of national and international consultants and local specialists, the Technical Assistance Support Team (TAST).

The HDSI also sets out the following targets to be achieved by West Bengal by 2010 :

Table 1 : Reproductive Health Targets–2010

	Current	*Target*
Total Fertility Rate	2.4	2.1
Couple protection Rate	NA	90%
Maternal Mortality Ratio	266	70
Deliveries conducted by a Skilled Attendant	44%	100%
Institutional deliveries	40%	80%
Neonatal Mortality Rate	29	15
Infant Mortality Rate	46	21
Children fully immunised	44%	100%

Source : Census 2001, SRS 2003, NFHS 2 1998-1999, Health on March & HSDI, 2003.

The National Policy on Public Private Partnership and State strategic thinking explicitly mentioned the need for partnership with private-not for profit providers and private–for profit health practitioners. This clearly proves that partnership with the private sector in West Bengal to achieve health sector objectives has become an important issue on the agenda.

3. Working with Private Sector Providers

Health care in India is predominantly financed by out of pocket spending. This is generally recognized as an inequitable and inefficient way of funding health care as it requires people to find funds when they are least able to (*i.e.* when they are sick) and ensures that health care is provided according to ability to pay and not according to need. Nearly all the private spending in India is out-of-pocket at the point of service, an inefficient way to finance health care that leaves people highly vulnerable (Kanjilal *et al.*, 2002).

In India when people seek treatment for an illness they often visit a private sector provider first (PSP). PSPs are active and successful competitors in most health care markets, often more popular than the public sector services (Aljunid, 1995; Swan and Zwi, 1997) because of :

- Ease of geographic access, shorter waiting times, longer and more flexible opening times, with more flexible payment options.
- Greater availability of staff and supplies.
- More confidentiality in dealing with disorders that carry a social stigma.
- Perceptions that PSPs are more caring, considerate and sensitive to patients concerns.
- Continuity of care and – in the case of doctors – a belief in the value of the 'family-doctor' relationship.
- User charges levied in the public sector may make public sector services equally or more expensive than those in the private sector .

In countries such as India where the poor predominate and most people visit PSPs, the poor who are often more in need of health care, form the greatest proportion of the private sector's workload. The poor also spend a larger proportion of their income on private (and public) care. Studies from a number of countries indicate that the poor have less access than the wealthy to more sophisticated tertiary level public sector facilities. When the poor use the private sector they often use less qualified or traditional practitioners, where care is often of poorer quality. The wealthy are more likely to have health insurance, to use the formal rather than the informal private sector, to have greater access to information and to make better-informed health care choices (Smith *et al.*, 2001).

There is evidence, which suggests that bearing the burden of health care costs among the poor can lead to greater poverty, especially when this care is for 'catastrophic illnesses' and those requiring surgical intervention. Although public sector provision is intended to be free in practice patients have to pay, particularly for diagnostic tests and medicines. Since these payments have arisen in an adhoc manner there is really no effective system of exemptions for those below the poverty line (BPL) that make up nearly 30% of the population in West Bengal. Health care expenditure can add significantly to the financial burden of poor households. The GoWB introduced "user fees" in March 2002. So far this has yielded only very low levels of cost recovery, at around 3% of the DoHFW budget, and probably acts as another disincentive for the poor and very poor to access public services.

Like other states in India, West Bengal's health sector is also dominated by the private sector and the State is exploring a variety of ways of working this sector including the implementation of Public Private Partnership schemes in areas such as :

- Providing diagnostic interventions at PHC level by leasing space to private service providers;
- Establishing affordable drug supplies;
- Working with NGOs to run community ambulances.

This represents a radical departure for a state like West Bengal and if pursued seriously has the potential to significantly improve the effectiveness of the predominant private sector, which has until recently been largely neglected by the state. In keeping with the times, Public Private Partnership has been clearly woven into many current programs and projects.

4. Output Based Aid (OBA)

Input Versus Output Based Approaches

Traditional approaches of health financing base on financing inputs such as the construction of a hospital, equipment of the facility with beds and biomedical technology, training of personal or allocation of resources for entire health programmes by governmental programmes or NGOs. The main argument for the provision of public health resources is that private markets fail to provide sufficient supply and can not ensure universal access, especially for the poor population (KFW 2004). However, experience shows that the public provision of services is often inefficient and often does not succeed reaching the poor (World Bank, 2004).

Output based approach focuses on the financial support

of performance whereas input oriented approaches ask how results were produced. The output based voucher approach explicitly appreciates the growing importance of the private sector in the national public health system. The basic idea of OBA in health is to delegate specific services to certified private or public providers under contracts that link payments or donation on certain outputs and results for a specific target group. The State is responsible for establishing adequate legal and regulatory frameworks in order to control the delivered service quality and the performance based reimbursement system (Brook & Smith 2001). The OBA concept focuses on improvements in three intervention levels (KFW, 2004) :

- Improving the access to social services for the poor through provision of subsidized delivery services by public or private providers.
- Strengthening the efficiency of allocated public resources by providing performance based incentives.
- Ensuring provision of adequate services through establishing quality standards and performance monitoring.

Output Based Voucher Schemes

Typical OBA concepts are voucher schemes. Voucher schemes belong to demand side financing mechanism. Vouchers can be defined as *"a token that can be used in exchange for a restricted range of goods or services, either partially (e.g. as a discount) or in total"* (Sandifort *et al.*, 2003, 19).

Voucher schemes are instruments to subsidize health delivery. They can be used to entitle a specific target group to access a defined package of services. The service provider will then be reimbursed for delivering the desired output (IHSD 2004).

The most important part of OBA approach is that giving clients the chance to choose their providers on the basis of the performance can be a way to efficiently and effectively use the limited resources to help marginalized groups and target important medical condition (Griffith, 2007).

Voucher programmes, if well designed and administered can help to achieve a broad range of common policy goals : improving equity, efficiency, quality and access to services.

The aims of the voucher schemes are to :

- Target available subsidy to low income group or other vulnerable people, thereby increasing the benefit incidence of public subsidy to poorer households and improving equity;
- Influence the behaviour of the beneficiaries, and encourage the consumption of specified services which have a health benefit;
- Provide an incentive to providers to offer value for money and better quality service, and improve their accountability, by increasing competition among providers and consumer choice.

Voucher schemes take many different forms. Four issues are important in defining the nature of a voucher system (IHSD 2004). These are :

- To whom vouchers are to be distributed (Recipients/ beneficiaries)
- Who will be eligible to offer the services (Health Care Providers)
- What services will the voucher holder receive (Benefits/ service package)
- What proportion of the price of services will be covered by the voucher (Value)

Voucher schemes can be divided into two main types.

- *Incentive based voucher schemes*, where the beneficiary directly receives a subsidy to encourage a specific behaviour or to reduce the costs of using a service (Ensor 2004). Examples include cash incentive payments to offset the costs of services conditional on service use (*e.g.* PROGRESA, Mexico; education for girls, Bangladesh); cash or in kind incentives such as food and clothes on condition of socially desirable behaviour (such as breastfeeding and drug rehabilitation in the USA, institutional delivery in Andhra Pradesh, India); and grants made to a representative community body that are earmarked for a specified service (*e.g.* a private school for girls in northern Pakistan managed by a village education committee, where the funding is conditional on a minimum number of students).

- *Competitive voucher schemes*, where the provider only receives the payment after the beneficiaries have used the service. They introduce some sort of competition among providers because the voucher bearer has the purchasing power and the choice of selecting the appropriate service deliverer. These types of voucher scheme link the subsidies with the patient flow, thus producing incentives for the providers to increase their quality of health care (Sandifort *et al.* 2003). Examples include STI treatment for sex workers in Nicaragua, and mother and child health (LIP-CINI) in Kolkata, India. This paper discusses mainly the competitive voucher schemes.

5. Basic Steps of Voucher Scheme

The Diagram1 shows simplified model of OBA voucher programme, which illustrates the basic steps with the numbered arrows corresponding to the steps enumerated in the side text boxes.

While individual voucher flows in the sequence, all the steps are occurring simultaneously once the voucher programme is operating. The government or donor agency that funds the OBA voucher programme transfers funds to a neutral voucher management agency (VMA) to implement the programme (Step 1); the VMA administers the rest of the process. The VMA produces the vouchers and distributes them directly to recipients (Step 2a), or hire third-party distributor agency for distribution and marketing of vouchers (Step 2b) that then distributes them (Step 2c). The voucher recipient selects health care provider (participating in voucher

Diagram 1: Steps in a Typical Voucher Programme

1. Government or Donor Agency establishes a voucher Management Agency (VMA) and transfers funds to the VMA
2. VMA produces vouchers and distributes them to the target population, either :

2a : directly by itself, or

2b : through a third-party voucher distributor, who

2c : offers them to the target clients.

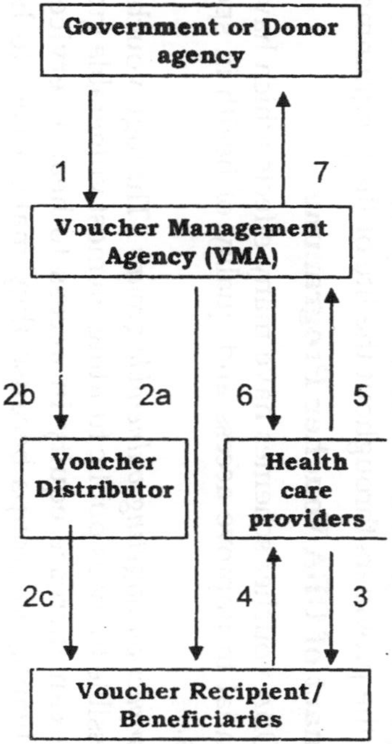

3. Voucher recipient selects a provider and takes the voucher to the provider of choice redeems the voucher for a pre-specified service or product)
4. Provider accepts voucher and delivers service or product.
5. Provider returns vouchers receiver to VMA with any necessary documentation
6. VMA pays the service provider a contracted amount for each returned voucher.
7. VMA monitors programme and report outcomes to the Government/Donor Agency

Source : Adapted from World Bank, 2005.

programme) and redeems the voucher by handing over it to the provider, in exchange for receiving the service covered by the voucher programme (Step 3); simultaneously, the provider accepts the voucher and delivers the covered service (Step 4). The provider then submits redeemed vouchers to the VMA for reimbursement, along with other documentation of services rendered as stipulated in the provider's service contract (Step 5). The VMA reimburses the provider the contracted amount for each returned voucher on certain interval mutually agreed by VMA and Health care providers (Step 6). The VMA does monitoring and evaluation (M&E) of the programme and reports outcomes to the government or donor agency (Step 7). The VMA may contract monitoring & evaluation aspect to independent agency but will generally have to work closely with the providers throughout the life of the programme.

6. Imact of OBA Voucher Programme

OBA voucher schemes have many effects which have the potential to improve access and quality of health in specific areas.

Impact on targeting vulnerable groups : Through vouchers it is possible to focus public funding on most vulnerable groups. They can increase equity in access to health services for disadvantaged groups because they make access to health services more affordable. This can positively influence their health seeking behaviour and utilization of services (Gorter *et al*. 2003).

Impact on cost-effectiveness and productivity : Targeting on the vulnerable can also improve allocation efficiency of public funds to the extent that many health problems are concentrated in this group. Governments don't pay for assumed output but reward performance. Payment for low performing providers will be lower than for well performing clinics. This means that funds are automatically channelled to those who perform best. The way of rewarding outputs provide stronger incentives for innovations and gives certain autonomy to service providers. In order to increase the utilization of services and therefore their revenues, providers may extend their opening hours, their services; they may start outreach programmes or patient information and education campaigns. Such innovations could reduce the level of governmental support, scale up productivity of services and improve cost-effectiveness of service delivery (Yamamoto, 2004). Monitoring and evaluation of the voucher scheme is relatively straight forward because it is based on measurable outcomes (Gorter *et al.* 2003).

Impact on quality of care : Vouchers can provide instruments for quality control and assurance. By contracting only the qualified providers which are eligible to receive public funds, the government has an effective mechanism to regulate and control medical practices. An OBA voucher scheme foresees that those providers have to go through an accreditation process. Accreditation set benchmarks for quality standards, and assess whether the providers meets the requirements. Payments are restricted only for those interventions that are known to be evidence based. Ongoing monitoring and evaluation allows controlling delivered quality of health care (Gorter *et al.*, 2003).

Impact on patient satisfaction : OBA voucher scheme promote competition among service providers and strengthen patients choice. Patients will automatically seek treatment by those providers who have a good reputation and perform well (Campell *et al.*, 2004). This will encourage providers to provide qualitative, comfortable and convenient care to their patients.

Impact on public Private Partnership : The difficulty for policy makers is to find practical ways to introduce PPP. OBA voucher schemes offer such mechanism because they clearly aim at using the potential of the private sector and integrating them in the health care system.

Impact on sustainability : Voucher schemes which may involve copayments have potential for move towards sustainability. When societies get richer, the willingness and ability to pay for health services increase. Voucher schemes with small copayments could be used as a first small step to national or private health insurance schemes (Campell *et al.*, 2004).

7. Cross Cutting Experience of Voucher Schemes in Health

One of the earliest suggestions for the use of voucher schemes was put forward by M. Friedman in 1962. Friedman introduces voucher schemes as an instrument of funding education (*Gorter et al.* 2003). The aim is to empower households to choose the school (public or private) which suits best to the preferences of the parents and their children and to improve the access of low-income families to private school. In the USA a large number of voucher schemes have been initiated (Ensor, 2004). The experiences in many US cities have indeed demonstrated that vouchers have a positive impact on service quality and better access for the poor to education (Gorter *et al.*, 2003). Outside the USA similar experiences have been made in Chile and Argentina (McEwan, 2000).

OBA approaches in health were first introduced in the Taiwan in the 1960s (Gorter *et al.* 2003). Vouchers were distributed on large scale for family planning services. OBA made a significant contribution to the cost-effectiveness and the success of the programme (Campell *et al.*, 2004). Now-a-days demand-side financing have been used in a number of contexts in low and middle income countries with good evidence of impact.

In Tanzania a discount coupon for insecticide treated bed-nets (ITNs) was launched aimed at poor, pregnant women. A recent evaluation of this programme has shown that the scheme had sold 65.000 bed nets in 4 years (Ensor, 2004). A similar approach was piloted two districts in Uganda, 2004.

In a slum area of Nairobi, Kenya the centre of disease control has supported a local NGO that is implementing voucher scheme for voluntary counselling and testing service (Campell *et al.*, 2004).

Possibly the largest scale voucher scheme in health outside the USA is the PROGRESA project in Mexico. In the 1990s PROGRESA, the government's education, health and nutrition programme introduced a set of conditional cash transfer to encourage the use of health and education services by poor families. More than 80% of transfer reached the target group. A significant impact on school enrolment has been found accompanied by a decreasing number of child labour. There was an increased use of health services and improvements in the height and weight of young children. Illnesses dropped by 20% in children under five (World Bank, 2004). The successful programme has been replicated in a number of other countries including Honduras, Nicaragua and Colombia (Ensor, 2004).

Since 1995 Nicaragua has used voucher scheme for STI treatment for female sex workers and their partners. The target group have received subsidized vouchers entitling them to a specified set of diagnose and counselling service from their choice in pre-identified health facilities, in both private for profit and non profit organisations (Sandifort *et al.* 2002). The programme has been well monitored and evaluated. Although evidence is still weakened by lack of control of confounding of any confounding factors (IHSD 2004). However the experiences have shown that the voucher scheme has improved the quality and access of STD services and efficiently reached the target group (Sandifort *et al.* 2002). There has been a high take up and use of the coupons accompanied by a remarkable decline of syphilis (9%) and gonorrhoea (5%) per year amongst poor sex workers. The creation of competition amongst the health care providers has shown a positive impact on quality of care, technical efficiency and client-friendliness (IHSD, 2004).

Bangladesh : In Bangladesh, BRAC introduced an OBA approach in its health education programme which aimed at teaching mothers how to prepare and use oral re-hydration solution to treat diarrhoea. Health workers' salaries were linked to results of the training they provided to mothers, namely knowledge of the causes and effects of diarrhoea and their ability to prepare solutions properly. A monitor visited about 10 per cent of the mothers who were trained over the past month and asked them to answer questions about the "10-point message" and had they prepare the solution. To determine a health workers' payment, a mothers' responses were graded from A to D. For each A, the health worker received Tk 4 and for each D, nothing. The result was quite positive and 90% of the mothers scored in the A and B categories. The monitoring also required an analysis of the solutions prepared by the mothers. For this purpose, an international agency helped BRAC set up field laboratories where 10 % of the samples were reanalyzed. BRAC has recently begun to use the technique again in a community based education programme with four clearly defined HIV/AIDS messages.

Even though there is still limited evaluated experience with voucher schemes in health the few examples show that OBA approaches can provide incentives to health care providers to improve their quality and thus improving the health of the poor. In future more evidence can be expected from the upcoming programmes in Uganda, Kenya and India. Based on the Nicaragua experience in *Uganda* a pilot for an OBA voucher scheme for STD treatment is launched in 2005. To date the programme has started in small scale and it's too early for evaluation. *Kenya* has also introduced voucher programme aiming on reproductive health, safe delivery and family planning.

In *India* several initiative are on and some are in the pipeline small or large scale across the country. In early 2007 State Innovation in Family Planning Services (SIPSA) initiated Voucher Programme in 7 blocks of Agra targeting BPL families for pre-determined RCH services.

Department of Health and Family Welfare, Government of Gujarat launched Chiranjivi Scheme in 5 pilot districts for maternal health care with a voucher approach targeting BPL segment of society. Voucher method has instilled a sense of competition amongst the Obstetricians and made them more accountable (IIM, Ahmedabad). It is beyond doubt that the pilot in 5 districts has showed significant improvement in increase of institutional deliveries among the BPL population with high levels of clients' satisfaction (UNFPA, India).

In early 2007, Department of Health and Family Welfare, Govt. of West Bengal has also designed a scheme with similar OBA voucher concept called Ayushmati Scheme which is being introduced to engage private sector in providing quality essential and emergency obstetric care to pregnant women belonging to Bellow Poverty Line category (BPL) and all Scheduled Caste/Scheduled Tribe (SC/ST) families. Initially the scheme is proposed to be launched in 10 districts of West Bengal and two private providers will be selected from each district in the pilot phase of the programme. In this scheme the DHFW, GoWB would enter into service contract with the empanelled private health care providers to provide service regarding institutional delivery, inclusive of both normal and complicated deliveries.

8. Lessons Learnt for from Voucher Programme Across the Countries

There have been a small number of voucher programmes in health to date, they provide useful lessons for designing voucher programs for reproductive health and family planning services and engaging the private sector and some of these lessons from different country programmes are presented below.

Target vouchers to population groups that are identifiable and reachable : To ensure that the target population will increase its use of the desired health service and to reduce misuse, the criteria and process for identifying voucher recipients should be clear. It is best to target groups that share a characteristic or have an identifiable illness, for example Pregnant women, Infants and young children (below a specified age), High-risk groups (such as sex workers) for STIs, Priority diseases that take time to treat such as malaria and tuberculosis etc.

Define service packages that are easily identifiable : Vouchers programs yield best results when benefits are clearly defined and standardized package of services that they will cover under the voucher programme. This makes it easier to explain and market the programme to the target population like Specified antenatal care such as four antenatal visits and two doses of tetanus toxoid immunization, Delivery assisted by a skilled health personnel etc.

Price the voucher according to target population's ability and willingness to pay : One reason for low use of vouchers in some programmes has been the inability of the target population to pay for the unsubsidized portion of the price of the service. If the voucher is not a full subsidy, *i.e.*, the user must make a co-payment, then it is important to understand the users' ability to pay. A willingness-to-pay study may have to be conducted; this can be costly and time consuming but the information garnered is critical in determining the appropriate subsidy – and ensuring uptake of the vouchers by the target population.

Building awareness about the voucher programme among community members : Low use of vouchers in some programmes was attributed to the targeted population's lack of knowledge and understanding of the programme. Substantial time and effort may have to be expended to make the target population aware of the specifics of the programme through formal information, education, communication (IEC) campaigns. This may take several months and use multiple communication channels.

Communicate benefits of the voucher programme both to clients and service providers : Along with awareness about the existence of the programme, the benefits of the subsidized services need to be explained to the target population. This often requires intensive behaviour change communication (BCC) programme. Programme benefits and procedures also should be communicated to participating providers, so that they know how to work with voucher holders.

Monitoring the programme : Any voucher programme should be monitored from the start in order to understand how the target population perceives the programme; the extent to which, and why, they are using the programme; how providers perceive the programme; the overall impact of the programme; and what adjustments modification are needed based on the local setting.

9. Conclusion

Voucher scheme has been praised of late as a valuable alternative to finance in health which is an output-based use of finance. This is driven by the limited success of supply side financing and health reforms in improving service delivery as well as increased role of private sector in delivering health care even to the poorer segments of the population. OBA is a form of demand side financing which places purchasing power in the hands of the customers to spend on specific services. Experience has shown that financing inputs do not necessarily result in the improvement of health outcomes. The output based voucher concept envisages financing agreed outputs, rather than pre-defined inputs, by selling vouchers to the beneficiaries at subsidized price. Voucher approach have the full potential to increase use of services by target populations, engage the private medical practitioners, increase competition, and improve quality of service of the providers. However, there are some areas of concern in private health facilities to improve particularly in quality of health service delivery which need to strengthen the control and regulations mechanism for better health management. OBA Voucher system could be a good entry point for mainstreaming private providers, integrating private medical practitioners into the health care system and use their potential for improved health care.

BIBLIOGRAPHY

AbouZahr, C. and Wardlaw, T. (2003) : Antenatal Care in Developing Countries : Promises, achievements and missed opportunities, World Health Organization, Geneva.

Aljunid, S. (1995) : The role of private medical practitioners and their interactions with public health services in Asian countries, Health Policy and Planning, 10 : 33349.

Brook, J. and Smith, M. (2001) : Contracting for Public Services. Output-Based Aid and its Applications, World Bank, Washington.

Brugha, R. and Zwi, A. (1998) : Improving the quality of private sector delivery of public health services : challenges and strategies. Health Policy and Planning, Vol. 13, No. 2, pp. 107-120.

Campell, M., Janisch, C. and Potts, M. (2004) : The Need and Potential for Output-Based Assistance in Health and Family Planning, KFW, 2004, Bankengruppe.

Ensor, T. (2004) : Consumer-led demand side financing in health and education and its relevance for low and middle income countries, International Journal of Health Planning and Management, Vol. 19, pp. 267-285.

Gorter, A.; Sandifort, P.; Rojas and Z.; Salvetto, M. (2003) : Competitive Voucher Schemes for Health, Background Paper, ICAS.

Griffith, D. (2005) OBA : Programme in Uganda, Kampala (unpublished).

Griffith, D. (2007) : Output-based Aid : Financing Specific Intervention in Health, PPP, M. Sc. IH.

Health Management Information System, (2004-05) : Data, DHFW, GoWB.

Health on the March (2005) : DHFW, West Bengal.

Health Sector Strategy 2003-2012 (2003) : Department of Health and Family Welfare, Govt of West Bengal., India (Draft Copy).

Health System Development Initiative (2003) : Project Status Report, DHFW, GoWB.

IGES Institut für Gesundheits–und Sozialforschung GmbH (2005) : Baseline study report on OBA Programme in Kenya, (unpublished).

IHSD-Institute for Health Sector Development (2004) : Private Sector Participation in Health Sector Cooperation – Options and Experiences, Frankfurt am Main, KFW Bankengruppe.

Janisch, C., Pirie A., Varghese, B. (2006) : Financial Cooperation between India and Germany, Introducing a voucher scheme for safe delivery services in West Bengal : Initial scoping mission, Final Report (unpublished).

Kanjilal, B., Arya, J., Pearson, M. (2004) : Public Expenditure Review : Reproductive and Child Health Project –II, Draft Report, IIHMR, Jaipur, India (Unpublished).

Koblinsky, M.A. (1995) : Beyond maternal mortality – magnitude, interrelationship, and consequences of women's health, pregnancy–related complications and nutritional status on pregnancy outcomes, International Journal of Gynaecology and Obstetrics, Vol. 48.

Kreditanstalt für Wiederaufbau (KFW, 2004). Output Based Aid – Frankfurt Main, Germany.

National Family Health Survey (1998-99), India.

Raising the Sights: Better Health Systems for India's Poor (2001) : Health, Nutrition, Population Sector Unit, India, South Asia Region, The World Bank.

Reproductive and Child Health (2002) : District Level Household Survey, West Bengal.

Sachs, J.D. (2001) : Macroeconomics and Health: Investing in health for economic Development, World Health Organisation, Geneva.

Sandiford, P., Gorter, A., Rojas, Z., and Salvetto, M. (2003) : Voucher Schemes in Health. A Toolkit, Washington D. C., The World Bank.

Sandiford, P.; Gorter, A.; Salvetto, M. (2002) : Vouchers for Health : Using Schemes for Output-Based Aid. Public Policy for Private Sector, The World Bank Group, Note Number 243, Washington D. C.

Smith, E., Brugha, R., and Zwi, A. (2001) : Working with private sector providers for better health care, an introductory guide, Options and London School of Hygiene and Tropical Medicine, UK.

Swan, M. and Zwi, A. (1997) : Private practitioners and public health: close the gap or increase the distance, London: London School of Hygiene and Tropical Medicine.

The World Bank (2004) : World Development Report : Making Service Work for Poor People. Washington D. C.

UNICEF Statistics (2003) : Maternal Mortality.

United Nations (2004) : Implementation of the United Nations Millennium Declaration. Report of the Secretary-General, New York, United Nations General Assembly.

Voucher for Health : A Focus on Reproductive Health and Family Planning Services, (2006) PRIMER, USAID.

Wagstaff, A. and Claeson, M. (2004) : The Millennium Development Goals for Health : Rising to the Challenges, The World Bank, Washington.

World Health Organisation (2004) : Changing History, World Health Report, WHO, Geneva.

World Health Organisation (2005) : Make Every Mother and Children Count, World Health Organisation, Geneva.

World Health Organization (1996) : Mother-Baby Package : Implementing Safe Motherhood in Countries, Geneva.

Yamamoto, C. (2004) : Output-based aid in health: Reaching the poor through public-private partnership, WHO, Geneva.

Zwi, A., Burga, R., and Smith, E. (2001) : Private Health Care in Developing Countries, BMJ 2001; 323 : 463-4.

Index

F

N

O

P